J.G. Farrell in his Own Words

Selected Letters and Diaries

For my precious rollcall:
Poppy, Sophia, Joshy, Jay, Jack, Hadley,
Ela, Robyn, Joe and Callum.
Each unique, each loved.

J.G. Farrell in his Own Words

Selected Letters and Diaries

Edited by
Lavinia Greacen

CORK UNIVERSITY PRESS

First published in 2009 by
Cork University Press
Youngline Industrial Estate
Pouladuff Road
Togher
Cork
Ireland

British Library Cataloguing in Publication Data
A CIP catalogue record for this book is available from the British Library.

ISBN 978-185918-428-8
Printed in the UK by J.F. Print

Contents

Life is short. Life is very, very short. (Cliché of the week.)
JGF to Bridget O'Toole, 21 October 1969

Acknowledgements

M y greatest debt is to Richard Farrell, Jim's younger brother and literary executor (as well as sharing, to an uncanny degree, Jim's tone of voice). Richard Farrell and his wife Lindy welcomed this project at the start and have smoothed my path at every turn. My thanks, too, go to Jim's older brother, Robert Farrell, who lives in Canada. Deborah Rogers, Farrell's key agent for *Troubles* and *The Siege of Krishnapur*, has been unfailingly helpful and provided full access to her files.

Farrell's many friends responded promptly to my request to them to search attics, desks and drawers for any letters or cards from him. I know all too well the extra burden that entails. When Farrell died, in 1979, the fax was barely used and email was still shrouded in the future, but telephones, of course, were second nature. For that reason, those who lived nearest to Farrell found least; distance proved the greatest benefactor.

I would like to thank all the following for taking such trouble on his behalf: Gillon Aitkin, Brigid Allen, Ian Angus, Garry Arnott, Vincent Banville, Paul Barker, Franz Beer, Alan Bennett, Bernard Bergonzi, Pamela Bradley, Sue Bond, Kenneth H. Brown, Professor Peter Brown, Felicity Bryan, Susannah Clapp, Jill Cox, Bob Cumming, Patricia Cumming, Beryl Dawson, Malcolm and Clare Dean, Diana Ditchfield, Roger Donald, Margaret Drabble, Maureen Duffy, Roy Foster, Stephen Frears, Judy Friedlander, Sandy Fuller, Andrew Gemill, Sir Martin Gilbert, Martyn Goff, Tom Gover, James Hale, Francis King, Ann Kitz, Brian and Rose Knox Peebles, Rosemary Legge, Daniel Mankowitz, Oliver Marriott, Caroline Moorehead, Patricia Moynagh, Rosaleen Mulji, Edna O'Brien, Ruth Padel, Brian and Michelle Pearce, Catherine Peters, John Phillips, Neville Phillips, Piers Plowright, Piers Paul Read, Hilary Pratt, Ron Robertson-Swann, Michael Roemer, Sally Sampson, André Shiffrin, David Simpson, Hilary and John Spurling, Robin Stott, Alf Tansey, Bertrand Tavernier, Paul Theroux, Lavinia Trevor, Calvin Trillin, Carole Tucker, Stephen Wall, Marina Warner, Janet Watts, Margaret Windham Heffernan and Lacy Wright.

For everyone who came up trumps, I am grateful for their subsequent largesse in so unstintingly sharing their finds. The difference of light and shade between these letters and the diary excerpts, too, is poignant, pointing up the disparity between the public and the essentially private dialogue.

The most unguarded letters in this collection were written to the women who were closest to Farrell, and readers and scholars of his novels will continue to benefit from the generosity shown by Gabriele, Carol Drisko, Sarah Bond and Bridget O'Toole. There must be a sense of exposure in doing so, and yet they courageously took that risk. When researching my biography *J.G. Farrell, the Making of a Writer* (Bloomsbury 2000), I was given access to those belonging to Carol, Sarah and Bridget, and the newly-discovered letters to Gabriele, whose identity I know but who prefers anonymity in this collection, chart Farrell's earlier development. A completely different angle is revealed in his lengthy airmail correspondence with an Oxford contemporary, Russell McCormmach, which includes a cumulative reading list of the books which most influenced Farrell throughout his adult life.

He was a mutual letter-writer, just as he was a mutual conversationalist, and brief deletions have been made for comments about subjects that have nothing to do with Farrell himself or with current events; occasionally these include the need to avoid intruding on the privacy of living persons.

The detective work involved in trying to trace such letters or cards farther afield is bound to involve frustrating dead-ends and promising clues that prove misleading, as well as the exhilaration of unexpected discoveries. In the positive latter category, I would particularly like to salute Jeremy Brett of the University of Iowa Libraries, Robert Brown of the Faber Archives, Elaine Engst and Michael E. Luther of Cornell University, Chris Fowler of Oxford Brookes University Library, Dan Mitchell of University College Library Special Collections, Chris Shepherd of the Brotherton Library, University of Leeds. Professor Tom Staley and Richard Workman of the University of Texas at Austin, and Nathan Williams of the University of Reading Special Collections. I have had meticulous help throughout from Bernard Meehan, Keeper of Manuscripts, of Trinity College, Dublin, the custodian of Farrell's papers.

But my warm thanks go to the archivists and librarians on both sides of the Atlantic who enthusiastically (and, as it turned out, fruitlessly) joined in the search. These include Brenda Brown of McFarlin Library, University of Tulsa, Sarah Hutcheon of the Schlesinger Library, Harvard University, Patricia McGuire of King's College, Cambridge, Janet Moat of the British Film Institute Special Collections and Kristine Krueger of the National Film Information Service, Beverley Hills, California.

I am pleased to acknowledge the kind permission of the following for use of Farrell letters in their collections. The University of Iowa, Iowa City, (the papers of Angus Wilson), the University of Reading Special Collections and the Random House Group Ltd (the Jonathan Cape and Bodley Head archives), Cornell University Library, Ithaca, New York (the papers of Alison Lurie), The Harry Ransom Humanities Research Center, The University of Texas at Austin (the papers of Francis King and Knopf), University College London Library Services, Special Collections (the Orwell papers), The Lilly Library, Bloomington, University of Indiana (the Richard Hughes papers), The Brotherton Library, University of Leeds (the papers of Piers Paul Read), the Booker archive at Oxford Brookes University Library, and the Jonathan Clowes literary agency. For the use of excerpts from Farrell's Indian diary, which appears in full in *The Hill Station*, I am greatly indebted to Phoenix, an imprint of The Orion Publishing Group, London.

Friends of Farrell, and their families, have been generous from the start. I would like to thank Alison Lurie for permission to include the photograph and her letter to him, as well as to quote lines from *Foreign Affairs*, Mrs Betty Kirwan and Mrs Kathie Parrish for allowing the letters to their late husbands to be used, and Mrs Penny Minney, the daughter of Richard Hughes. Hilary Spurling kindly let me reproduce the final letter from Sonia Orwell, and my thanks also go to A.M. Heath & Co Ltd on behalf of the Late Sonia Brownell Orwell Estate. We are all indebted to Derek Mahon for his elegiac poem 'A Potting Shed in County Wexford', described by Seamus Heaney as 'beautifully orchestrated' and by John Banville as 'The best single poem written in Ireland since the death of Yeats', which is dedicated to Farrell in Mahon's book *The Snow Party*. I am also personally grateful for the alacrity with which Mahon agreed to its inclusion, and to his publishers Gallery Books for their permission.

For more general help or advice, I salute Julia Abel Smith of the Royal Society of Literature, Jean Briggs of Rossall School (where the Farrell Society now honours their literary Old Boy), Christopher Cox of the *Paris Review*, Professor Ralph J. Crane of the University of Tasmania, who has written knowledgeably about Farrell, Edwin Frank of the *New York Review of Books* who chose all three books of the Empire Trilogy for their Classic imprint, Trish Hayes of the BBC Written Archives Centre, Olivia Guest and Ann Evans of Jonathan Clowes Ltd, Bruce Hunter of David Higham and Associates, Dr Daniel Lea of Oxford Brookes University, John MacHale, John McBratney, Cathal McCabe of the Irish Writers' Centre in Dublin (who organised a celebration of Farrell's work in 2007), Dr John McLeod of the University of Leeds, (author of *J.G. Farrell* in the Northcote House 2008 'Writers and Their Work' series), Greg Neale of *Oxford Today*, Kate Pool of the Society of Authors, Michael Smith (late of Mexico), Peter Straus, Adam Thirlwell, Laura Wu of Brasenose College, Oxford (who placed an appeal for letters in *The Brazen Notes*), and Mary Yoe of All Souls, Oxford. Thanks, too, to Padraic Bohan, Susie Dockrell, Creeda Fitzgibbon, and Joseph Walsh for kindly waving a wand over certain translations.

Images of Farrell are precious, given his shyness and the brevity of his life, so how fortunate it is that he was photographed by the great Jane Bown for the *Observer* in 1978, whose task took patience: eventually she was able to persuade him to stop taking cover behind a bush near his flat in Egerton Gardens, and to face her camera indoors. Michael Leonard has uniquely captured the mischievous side of Farrell, and the comprehensive Faber Archive has reintroduced Mark Gerson's sensitive portrait of him on the cusp of literary acclaim.

To Jonathan Williams must go the credit for transforming a vague idea into a substantial tome, aided by the imagination of Professor Tom Dunne, and the creative team of Mike Collins, Maria O'Donovan and Sophie Watson of Cork University Press have indelibly linked these letters to the county where Farrell made his final home. My salaams, lastly, to my dear husband Walter, whose crucial support included the creation of delicious meals when I was otherwise absorbed.

Foreword

There are certain personalities which impress themselves indelibly on the memory, not by being large and gaudy but because of something essentially enigmatic in them. I met J.G. Farrell only once, many years ago, but I have remembered him with a vividness and clarity entirely disproportionate to the short time I spent in his company. It was an afternoon in the autumn of 1973, at the flat in London of Diana Saville, an old friend of Farrell's. My brother Vincent had gone over to collect the Robert Pitman fiction prize from the *Sunday Express* for his novel *An End to Flight*, and had asked my sister and me to go with him to celebrate the occasion. Diana was Vincent's literary agent in those days, and she invited the three of us to meet Jim Farrell over a sort of picnic lunch at her place.

It was a couple of days before the announcement of that year's Booker Prize winner; Farrell's novel *The Siege of Krishnapur* was on the shortlist, along with works by Beryl Bainbridge, Elizabeth Mavor and Iris Murdoch – Murdoch's *The Black Prince* was, I am sure, the favourite, but when I asked Farrell if he thought he had a chance he said yes, he did. What I did not know was that in those days winners of the prize were told of their good fortune a month before the announcement, a civilised practice which anyone will appreciate who in more recent times has been on the shortlist and has had to suffer through the ghastly suspense of the Booker-night dinner.

The jury in 1973 was a starry one, consisting of Karl Miller, Mary McCarthy and Edna O'Brien, and they had plumped unanimously for Farrell's novel. *The Siege of Krishnapur* is a fine book, but as he wrote in December that year to Catherine Barton, his editor at Cape, 'I still feel that if anything of mine survives it will be *Troubles* – though, being more readable, no doubt the *S of K* was a better book to win the Prize with,' [p. 282] a judgement the first half of which at least one would wish to endorse, for *Troubles*, a tragi-comedy set in a crumbling hotel in County Wicklow during the War of Independence, is surely Farrell's masterpiece, which does live on triumphantly, and will continue to do so.

Farrell the man was immensely attractive, tall and slender and possessed of a slightly jaded and even slightly sinister elegance. In the letters he frequently bemoans his prematurely grey hair – he knew how handsome he was, and so was free to make a comic turn of harping on the supposed shortcomings of his looks – but it was silver rather than grey; in fact, when I think of him I have an impression of a general sleek silveriness, of personality as well as looks. He had contracted polio when he was twenty-one and had spent some months in an 'iron lung', a ghastly contraption which must have seemed like a medieval torture machine but which supplied him with the inspiration and material for his second novel, *The Lung*, which he finished in 1964.

Perhaps the experience of polio, and the permanent muscular damage the disease had left him with, accounted for a faint remoteness in his manner; he was perfectly friendly, courteous, possessed of a sly and playful wit, yet one had the sense that behind the suave exterior there was a spirit withdrawn and self-absorbed. No wonder women were so drawn to him, as his biography, and his letters, attest they were. He had many lovers in his short life, but the thought of marriage seems never to have crossed his mind; as with Flaubert and Henry James, his work was to be his permanent companion and helpmeet. He was old-fashioned in that way, and in other ways, too – the letters breathe a courtly air that seems the air of another time.

Like all artists, he was aware of the personal cost of art, of the deprivations and interdictions it imposes on the emotional self. In a letter to 'Gabriele', the German girl he met in Ireland in 1960 whose youth and freshness captivated him, he identified the predicament of all writers, especially in their early years, as they struggle to strike a balance between the demands of art on one side and of feelings on the other:

> I wish I could decide what to do. At the moment I am just living from day to day, like a vegetable of some kind. Did I tell you that a French girl I used to go out with in Toulon last year used to call me a *'crustacée'* or a mollusc or something. She used to get very angry. At the time I thought this was unjust but now I am not so sure. [p. 54]

To live or to create? – this is the perennial question. For the genuine artist the answer is always inevitable. The passage quoted ends with this: 'However, I am still about to start writing again.'

In the four novels of his maturity – if such a word means anything when speaking of a novelist who died at the tragically early age of forty-four – *Troubles*, *The Siege of Krishnapur*, *The Singapore Grip* and the unfinished and posthumously published *The Hill Station*, J.G. Farrell left a unique achievement. Calmly indifferent to the depradations of Modernism and the avant garde, entirely immune to the stranglehold of Theory which in the decade or so before his death had begun to spread out of the *écoles* and colleges of France and America like bindweed, he stuck serenely to his own judgment and his own aesthetic. There was no one like him, nor will there be again. His loss was little short of a disaster for English fiction, but at least in this wonderful collection of his letters we are able to catch again the tone of his voice and the texture of his spirit; in these pages there speaks to us one who in his life was passionate, sceptical, wry, funny and, above all, wholly committed to the task of being an artist.

JOHN BANVILLE
May 2009

A Lost Autobiographical Voice

The novelist J.G. Farrell – known to his friends as Jim – was drowned on 11 August 1979, when he was swept into the sea by a sudden Atlantic storm while fishing off rocks in County Cork, in the south west of Ireland. He was in his early forties and at the crest of his career, having won the Booker Prize for *The Siege of Krishnapur* only five years earlier. As *The Times* would subsequently put it, a generation felt bereft.

It was not the last time Farrell's name was to be linked with the Booker Prize, however. In 2008 *The Siege of Krishnapur* was one of the six finalists chosen for the international 'Best of Booker' vote, to mark the fortieth anniversary. Salman Rushdie was the ultimate winner, and when asked afterwards which book should have taken the title, if his had not, he did not hesitate. 'Well, I have always enormously admired *The Siege of Krishnapur*,' he told *The Guardian*. 'Had Farrell not sadly died so young, there is no question that he would today be one of the really major novelists of the English language.' Referring to *Troubles* and *The Singapore Grip*, which complete Farrell's twentieth-century classic, the Empire Trilogy, he added, 'The three novels that he did leave are all in their different way extraordinary.'

J.G. Farrell, glimpsed as the author's name on the cover of a book, has an austerely confident ring to it. The man behind that name is revealed in these letters (spanning childhood to the day before his death) and diary fragments to be quite the opposite. Warm, and sometimes full of self-doubt, they trace his daily life and literary development throughout the 1960s and '70s, recreating a lost autobiographical voice. The more confessional letters are written to women whom Farrell loved and occasionally hurt, but his kindness, deft humour and gift for friendship reached across rejection, which is why so many were kept.

As the editor, and his biographer in *J.G. Farrell, the Making of a Writer* (Bloomsbury 1999), my priority is for Farrell himself to step forward here, to speak directly to the reader. Only a short introduction (and the occasional subsequent briefing) is needed before his educated drawl, described as having a tendency to trail away on the ends of words he emphasised, takes over. The childhood treble of the first three letters will not last long, nor the postgraduate introspection.

He was born in Liverpool on 23 January 1935, the second of two sons; a third brother, Richard, was to be born in 1943. After the outbreak of the Second World War, his parents moved the family to Southport, farther down the coast, to escape the heavy bombing of Liverpool docks. Boscobel, the large Victorian house owned by an elderly bachelor uncle whose housekeeper and gardener had been called-up, was auspiciously named after a Harrison Ainsworth novel, and Jim and his older brother Robert had full run. Bill Farrell, their English father, was an accountant excused active service because he suffered from the tinnitis – a form of deafness – that had cut short his managerial business career in India shortly before Jim's birth. War brought him a book-keeping role in a factory in Cumberland on twenty-four hour production, and Josephine, his capable Irish wife, took charge of everyone at home.

Family life in wartime was less disrupted for young Jim Farrell than for many of his age group. His father was allowed home briefly at six-weekly intervals when the factory closed for maintenance, and he introduced the two older boys to the cinema. In the evenings he read aloud to them in the black-out, sharing the wide-ranging books he loved himself. Meanwhile a stream of displaced evacuees began to be billeted on the family, to reappear many years later throughout the Empire Trilogy. Farrell's first letter is from this period, when he was attending a nearby kindergarten, Croxton School, run by wheelchair-bound Mary Roberts.

In 1944, at the age of eight, Jim was sent to board at Terra Nova, a prep school at Jodrell Bank in Cheshire. The school was run on military lines, and at first he developed alopecia, a nervous condition leading to hair loss. (This would recur later in his life at a time of stress, as these letters show.) Aptitude for work as well as sport eased the transition, and soon he adapted, to the extent that he became Head Boy and won a scholarship to Rossall, a public school in Lancashire. At Rossall he was soon a precocious talent on the Rugby First XV, and under the pen-name of 'Seamus' his essays dominated the school magazine.

In 1947 the Farrells moved to Ireland, to be nearer his mother's elderly parents. Jim loved his new home, The Gwanda, which was a comfortable family house on five acres in Shankill, to the south of Dublin. He returned to Ireland from school in England every holiday, as did his Irish friends on similar educational paths who lived within cycling distance of Shankill. In 1953, to Jim's resentment, his parents would sell The Gwanda and move to Balholm, a bungalow in Dalkey, overlooking Dublin Bay.

Starting with a glimpse back to his early childhood days, Jim Farrell's distinctive and increasingly companionable voice should now take up his own story.

Lavinia Greacen
SEPTEMBER 2009

Threshold
1943–60

To his father

1 Preston Road
Southport
[undated] 1942

Dear Daddy,

I'm sorry I could not get you a present as I am ~~h~~ hard up ~~aaa~~ and I had'ent [*sic*] time to earn any money.

I hope you get this letter in time to wish you many happy returns.

I wish you were home as I am saving up for a book and I might be able to wangle it out [of] you.

Love from
XXXX JIMMY
XXXXXX XXXX
XXXXXX

To his parents

Terra Nova School
Jodrell Bank
Holmes Chapel
Cheshire
15 October 1945

Dear Mum and Dad,

Please tell Miss Roberts I am in the 4th set for ~~Latin~~, Maths, French, Latin, English, and Modern. I am 9th in a class of about fifteen for Maths and I've beaten all the other new boys. It was the pictures last night, and there was a Laural [*sic*] and Hardy one which was quite good.

Love from
Jimmy

To his mother

Terra Nova School
Sunday [undated] 1947

Dear Mum,
It snowed on Saturday for about twenty minutes during French. If you can get the aeroplane I would like it for Christmas ... The S.E.5 is a last war plane and is rather hard to make so I'd better make it at home.

Love from
Jimmy

After Rossall, he had to fill in time before university owing to the backlog of undergraduates after the war. He spent a restless year as a junior master at Castlepark, an exclusive prep school in County Dublin, and a second year in Canada, where he earned good money labouring in arctic conditions at the Defense Early Warning System, known as the DEW Line, in Baffin Bay. In October 1956, feeling fit and optimistic, Jim went up to Brasenose College, Oxford; his aim was to read Law half-heartedly and to work extremely hard to gain a rugby blue.

Within six weeks of arrival, however, shortly before the end of the first term, that all changed. He was taken ill after rugby practice, polio was diagnosed in hospital, and he was put into an iron lung. 'The familiar road had ended', as he would mourn in The Lung, *his second novel, 'and the future was a jungle through which [I] would have to cut [my] way.' (A full account of his ordeal can be found in* J.G. Farrell, the Making of a Writer.) *In the spring of the following year, grey-haired and five stone lighter, with the muscles of his shoulders and arms and, especially, his breathing affected, he was allowed home. During the lengthy, inert months of convalescence in Dublin, he resolved to follow his instinct and become a novelist. In one useful way, hospital had equipped him. Typing had been encouraged as physiotherapy, to strengthen the muscles in his hands, and he practised diligently. Writing by hand would remain wearying, and it took years before the polio damage was erased from his previously meticulous classical script. Almost all the letters in this book were typed.*

His Oxford colleagues, like his old Dublin friends, found Farrell greatly changed, and the physical losses were accentuated by his new sense of purpose. He was advised to take up Modern Languages instead of Law because it was less physically demanding; the incentive for the switch, he liked to murmur, was to read Proust in the original. Privately he was beginning to write. These were sighting shots for a novel, and darkened by guilt, anguish and self-blame after 1959 when he eventually rejected his Irish girlfriend, who had aided his recovery, during her own protracted recovery from serious head injuries sustained in a car crash. She had been on the way to a party to which he, too, had been invited, and he had renegued on taking her there, preferring to write. On the surface, Farrell fitted back into student life. He made lasting friendships, wrote an occasional column for Oxford Opinion, *and in due course gained an undistinguished Third.*

To Sally Bentlif [1]

[Card postmarked Av. D'Italie, Paris]
8 April 1960

Dear Sally,
Wish you were here. Come to that, why aren't you here?

Saw *Les Liaisons Dangeureuses*. Fabulously sexy and immoral and great in every way.

Love
Jim

To The Irish Times

Balholm
Saval Park Road
Dalkey
Co. Dublin
28 July 1960

Letters to the Editor [2]
Westmoreland Street
Dublin 2

Sir,
Mr Monk Gibbon seems uncertain as to which position is best for attacking Sean O'Casey's determined support of Joyce. He adopts two positions: the denigration of Joyce as a writer on the one hand, and the claim that archbishops are entitled to freedom just as much as writers, on the other.

Mr Gibbon says that Joyce 'has been imposed on an unwilling world by his fanatical adherents, using all the formidable weapons of literary snobbery.' Now just as beauty is in the eye of the beholder, so snobbery is entirely the property of the person who is snobbish. One may not blame Joyce for the fact that a number of his partisans read him for the wrong reasons. And Joyce is not alone. Kafka and Proust have also been the password to literary circles and they remain great artists nonetheless. The tendency is for all great artists who are at all 'difficult', that is to say who require intellectual effort to be appreciated, to remain the property of the few rather than of the many.

Mr Gibbon may be nettled by the fact that these few are highbrow critics and intellectuals, rather than worthy peasants, but that is the way of the world. It is quite ludicrous to pretend that the majority of those who admire Joyce do not genuinely appreciate him ...

Now to consider the case for the 'freedom' of the archbishops – freedom being described by Mr Gibbon as a fashionable shibboleth ... Isaiah Berlin [made a] distinction between 'positive' and 'negative' freedom. [3] Should one person be allowed to exercise his freedom to the extent of depriving his neighbour of his? Should an archbishop be allowed to exercise his freedom to censor books if by so doing he deprives me of my freedom to read those books? It all boils down eventually to whether or not you believe the Church should be separated from the State. Most of the great European political theorists, from Grotius, [4] Pufendorf, [5] Montesquieu, [6] Hobbes, [7] Locke [8] and Rousseau, [9] believe that it should ...

Now as a citizen of a country of which the population is overwhelmingly Roman Catholic, Mr Gibbon may well feel that the good of the community requires the minority not to read books banned by the majority, but as an individual artist can he honestly agree that outside limitations should be imposed on his field of endeavour and experience? Only in an atmosphere of complete intellectual and spiritual liberty can great artists thrive, which no doubt accounts for the fact that the greatest of Irish artists, among them both Joyce and O'Casey, have felt it necessary to leave Ireland and seek elsewhere.

Yours etc

James Farrell

Plans were already made for a teaching job in France at the Lycée d'Etat Chaptal in Mende, high in the Lozère region of the Massif Central. Shortly before leaving he met a pretty seventeen-year-old German literature student, Gabriele, who was spending the summer as an au pair with friends of the Farrells who lived in County Wicklow.

A Man from Elsewhere

France

1961–62

To Gabriele [1]

Clair Logis
6 Boulevard Henri Bourri
Mende, Lozère
25 January 1961

Dear Gaby,

... I have almost written to you about thirty times in the last two or three weeks, mainly because I have been wanting to talk to some-one who would be likely to understand what I have to say – all the people here are real, genuine *swachsinnigen* [2] (however you spell – I have a German dictionary but it does not give the word). What happened was that I was reading Sartre one evening, chuckling happily to myself without a care in the world, when I suddenly stumbled on what seemed to me to be the fundamental idea of my book and which I had blithely imagined was original. You can imagine how I felt. I was faced with the prospect of tearing up the first half of the novel which I had completed.

Anyway, I stopped writing altogether for a week and read, or read again, everything I could find of Sartre. I more or less succeeded in convincing myself that my idea was as original as most ideas are (that is to say, not very original – Einstein once told Valéry, [3] I think, that he had only had two ideas in his life!). In reading Sartre, though, I found that I couldn't agree with the process by which he moves from his original position (which he borrowed from Husserl, [4] I believe) to establish man's responsibility for political action. I'm sure this has been pointed out before but I doubt whether it has ever been written into a novel. Camus, incidentally, did the same thing – that is, he squeezed his philosophy into a convenient shape to allow him to

9

join the Resistance during the war. So, I have thought it worth-while to try to reconstruct my novel to reject what seems to me, although I may be completely wrong, faulty reasoning. So anyway, that is what has had me in a frenzy and been keeping me awake at nights. I won't describe the book to you in case it bores you, but you can read it when it is finished if you want to. But I am going to have to work hard. I promised my literary agent [5] that I would have it finished early this year and the year has already begun!

Apart from that I have not been doing anything very interesting. I teach for a few hours a week in the school here. [6] Mostly girls: this is a very poor and isolated mountain district, the poorest in France it seems. So the pupils are all from farms or small bourgeois families; apart from that, very few of them are good-looking which is a pity (!) and have very few interests. In fact, the only subjects which interest them are a) boys b) dances and c) films, so that is what we talk about all the time. Some of them live in the school and some with their families in the town but they are all as strictly guarded as you were in Ireland! So, as I am tired of hearing about who danced with whom ... I don't spend much time with them ...

I will probably leave France at the end of July and go to Ireland for a while, but I have not really decided. Why don't you come to Ireland again ...? I thought of going skiing but I have seen so much snow here that I was tired of it. And going to bed at 3 o'clock every night (or morning)! Girls of your age should be in bed by 9 o'clock!

With love,
Jim

P.S. Send me a large photograph of yourself. I already have one of Brigitte Bardot.

To Gabriele

Mende, Lozère
21 March 1961

Dear Gaby,
Many thanks for ... the photograph. I agree that BB does not stand a chance in competition with those legs! I am returning it to you with regret: I imagine that it is a family heirloom and would not like to deprive you of it.

Have you been ill? You say you're looking like a (beautiful) ghost and that you are going to hospital soon. I hope this is nothing too serious. I hate to think about hospitals since I had polio [7] and hate to think that my friends may find themselves there. Do tell me about this. Strange to think that it is five years now since I was there myself: I only have to close my eyes to see it all again in such sharp detail that I feel that by stretching out my hand I could feel the iron frame of the bed, and sometimes at night I dream of a close friend [8] who was there at the same time, completely paralysed, and hear him talking very softly and forget that he is dead. If it were to happen again I don't think I could stand it – not so much a question of pain as that it is just so desperately tiring to struggle all the time and see nothing in the future. Oh well, I don't like to think about it very much either.

I have been working like a slave at my novel [9] and it is getting longer and longer but still does not look as if it is ever going to be finished ... I wish I knew how good it really is. Sometimes it seems to me to be really important, other times all my ideas seem to be second-hand and the characters and situations without life.

Spring is wonderful here; brilliant sunshine and excitement in the air; the girls in bright skirts with shining faces, which makes them look nicer but no more intelligent. I have not been painting very much because I have been working hard; I painted the most beautiful of my pupils who, incidentally, sleeps with everyone here (except me) and is very proud of her good looks. The picture was moderately successful ...

With love
Jim

To Gabriele

Mende, Lozère
7 June 1961

Dear Gaby,

... I'm sorry that I have taken such a time to reply but I was typing out my novel until last Saturday and since then I have been very tired and not very interested in doing anything at all. I am still waiting to hear from my agent what she thinks of it. I read it through again the other night and it did not seem as good as I had hoped and thought it was. Nevertheless it is very hard to judge impartially a book that one has written oneself – especially as I know most of it by heart now, or almost. However I believe it is a big improvement on anything else I have done up till now. I think that I will begin another very soon whether the one I have just finished finds a publisher or not ...

I won't be back in Ireland until the beginning of August and I will leave again at the end of September because I will be spending next year in Toulon. Next year should be very good because Toulon is nearer the sun and I will be able to lie on beaches all winter (I hope). Perhaps we will meet in France next year.

The children in the school are getting very hard to manage now that the end of term is approaching – especially the girls! Because I have not been severe during the year they now make as much noise as they like ... not that it make any difference to me ... I must stop now and post this before going to the school for another class.

> With love
> Jim

To Gabriele   Mende, Lozère
                                                                                21 June 1961

Dear Gaby,

... If, as you say, you can't come to Ireland we will have to put off see-ing each other until the end of this year or sometime next year. I will be back again (at Toulon this time) at the beginning of October. Anyway, perhaps by that time I will be rich and famous and will be able to manage the expense of travelling where I want to. Also, I may be able to understand German better by then. I have been studying hard.

I am still waiting to hear from my agent, although she promised me that she would let me know quickly, that's to say, a week ago. As you say, this is very nerve-racking because the novel may just be no good at all. However ...

It is terrifically hot here; the sun bakes down on us all day and the nights are so hot that I have to sleep naked. I was in Montpel-lier over the weekend at a meeting of the Communist party but I was not very impressed with the Communists. I was sleeping on the floor of the room of the President of the Communist students of Montpellier university (what a lot of 'ofs'!) but he didn't seem to have very much idea what Communism was about and I was disap-pointed to hear that he had not even read Marx's *Das Kapital*. Most of the Communist students I met seemed to be Communists simply in order to be different, to create a sensation. While I was there I bought a lot of books – Lenin and Marx mainly, although I could not afford to buy *Das Kapital*. If they were real Communists they would have given it to me! ...

Last weekend we also went to a little port near Montpellier called Sète where Charles Aznavour was singing in an open-air theatre – wonderful.

Have a good time and lots of love,

Jim

[*Handwritten*] P.S. ... I will be here till the end of the month and in Ireland from the beginning of August.

To Gabriele

Balholm
Saval Park Road
Dalkey
Co. Dublin
14 September 1961

Dear Gaby,

Many thanks for your card – I think you are too lazy to write me a letter but never mind, I am rather lazy myself and have not written to you all summer. I may as well start answering your questions:

i) I am in Ireland at the moment but I leave in two days' time to go to London where I will be for about ten days before going to Paris and then to Toulon. Thank heaven – I'm fed up with Ireland.

ii) My book – I've had a lot of trouble with my book. I've spent the summer exchanging irritated letters with my agent and a publisher [10] and it is not likely to come out in the near future, if at all. The publisher finds it too abstract, too introverted and too intellectual and I've been trying to point out that this is a new way to write a novel (the method I've used). But it seems pointless to try and re-write it to please him because the whole book was carefully designed a certain way and if I changed anything it would lose everything. He admitted, however, that I write 'extremely well' and is still thinking about it. I feel very depressed and find that this is very little reward for the amount of work I put into it (apart from anything else I am, as usual, short of money and have had to sell my car) ...

iii) I do sympathise in some things with the Communists but

less every day. The book I am writing now is about a young Communist who is sent to expose a writer (modelled on André Malraux) who used to be a Communist as a young man in the early days of the Revolution in China but stopped being a Communist during the war when he was famous. In the course of exposing him (he was suspected of collaborating with the Nazis during the war) the young man begins to have doubts himself ... etc. Have you read any books by your fellow-countryman: Robert Jungk? [11] I admire him a great deal ...

Now, I think I have the right to ask you some questions. What did you think of France? Did you like the weather? Drink? Men? How well do you speak French? ... Do you think there will be a war over Berlin? [12] Were you sorry about the death of Wolfgang von Trips? [13] ...

I leave Ireland tomorrow night, not with any great regret.

> With love,
> Jim

The Toulon appointment for the 1961–62 academic year was to the Interidant du Lycée (known to its inmates as La Rode). As a writing aid, Farrell soon began an occasional diary, in which his cold judgements of others were coloured by his polio ordeal.

Meanwhile, an Oxford contemporary, Bob Cumming, one of the three Americans who had been Farrell's favourite companions there, prescribed a visit to Paris, where his young and recently widowed sister-in-law had moved.

To Patsy Cumming [14]

> 35 Avenue Vert Coteau
> Toulon
> (Var).
> 6 October 1961

Dear Patsy,
I just had a letter from Bob ... giving me your address and suggesting I establish contact with you. I should tremendously like to see you. Bob didn't seem to know too clearly what your plans were, whether and for how long you intended to stay in Paris etc.

For the moment, and possibly for some time to come, I am immobilised here by my job and (more seriously) by lack of money. The grey dogs of bankruptcy are already snapping at my heels and I have only 4000 francs between me and the end of the month when, God willing, I'll be paid. However, at some future date

I should be able to travel to where you are.

I live here in a strange little house with an old lady whose husband was a *cheminot* and who recites to me poetically the names of the trains that thunder past the house all the time (*Celui-la vient de* Strasbourg, Vintimille, Béziers, Marseille, Bordeaux etc.). She even tells the time by them. I have a kitchen and a bedroom with a giant bed, as vast as Asia, from which I find it virtually impossible to rise in the mornings. Outside my window there's a palm-tree and a capricious tortoise wanders about the garden. The other day I went to my lavatory in the yard and found it staring guiltily up at me from behind the bowl. Another thing it does is to capsize and wait lying on its back till someone comes along and turns it the right way up again. Towards the end of the month it will be hard to resist the temptation of whipping it into a saucepan and making some mock-turtle soup.

The people I've met here so far haven't been too interesting and, generally speaking, it's a long time since I've been with the kind of people I like to be with. Or maybe this is just what it means to grow old ...

I'm looking forward very much to seeing you.

> Yours
> Jim Farrell

To Gabriele

> Avenue Vert Coteau,
> Toulon
> 21 October 1961

Dear Gaby,

... The above address will get to me. That is I where I live (with my huge bed). Did you know that Gérard de Nerval [15] used to own a beautiful Renaissance bed but, out of respect for it, used to sleep on the floor beside it? Personally, I find the floor too hard ...

I was glad to hear you had such a good time in France (although envious of the French boy with whom you fell in love). As for me, both my life and myself seem to have remained curiously empty. Pessimism seems to have become installed as a permanent part of my character. I was talking to a young mathematics teacher I know here this afternoon and in the course of the conversation I remarked gloomily (we were talking about the weather) '*Le mistral, le cafard,*

et les pauvres, nous avons toujours avec nous – comme dit la Bible.' [16]
And he laughed, thinking I was joking.

Since I've been here I have only written 3 pages and even those I had to tear up the next day. When I got up this morning I counted my money and found that I had 8.70 N.F. [17] left so I went out and bought as much coffee, cigarettes, spaghetti, tomatoes, butter and bread as I could and I'm determined not to leave the house again until I've written something good (except to post this letter). With luck we should be paid next week. When I've finished this letter I'll try making spaghetti for the first time.

It would take ages to explain why I thought *La Notte* [18] was so good, but briefly: I identified myself very much with the young man and everything Antonioni had to say about him seemed to be true about me. That in some way one chooses without knowing it ... that, as a result of choosing to be one type of person rather than another, one can wake up one morning and realise that something important has been destroyed. Antonioni made this concrete with a love-affair between two people; with me it has been much more intangible. From a bright boy with (people said) a future as a writer just three years ago, I now find myself to be something different and much less hopeful without having noticed any change or transition. Even two years ago I felt that I had something of value, a precious bird imprisoned in my hands ... but somehow I've lost the bird or it has flown away without me noticing it. But there I go! Describing feelings and not facts which, you say, interest me more.

If you are still in love with your French boy I think I will wait another year before coming to see you. Lovers are always so single-minded and the only topic of conversation that interests them is the person they are in love with. Besides, all my friends seem to be in love and it is very disturbing as I feel I have become what Tennessee Williams calls 'The Fugitive Kind' and, of course, I hate being jealous ...

With love,
Jim

Diary

1 November 1961
Reading for the first time a copy of *l'Humanité*, [19] I was struck by two things: one – the willingness with which the paper goes

along respecting institutions which one might believe contrary to communist doctrine: e.g. respect for the dear departed and visits to their graves at Toussaint [20] (on the front page there was a photograph of a girl collecting flowers). Only in an article on the sports page was there a hint (and a very vague one at that) of doctrinal influence. A large part of the paper was gossipy, light reading ...

We had lunch at La Rode,[21] and afterwards walked slowly out in the sun to my place [22] where we had tea, bread and honey in the kitchen, bathed in blue, orange or plain sunlight from the extraordinary window-wall: 'baroque lavatory' style of architecture, I explained. M., who since her drab arrival has been progressively opening out like a flower under W.'s soft touch, lit up a little more and showed herself to be a competent mimic of the British lower classes. She still does not seem to have any ideal point of view, though, except that she is permanently dissatisfied, doesn't want to teach but does not want to do anything else either. She told us earlier about how, until the ages of respectively 12 and 13 (and yet later for special occasions such as Xmas) she and her brother had been made to sleep in the same bed, and that her brother still wanders about naked in front of her, dressing in front of the fire in winter, without any qualms. She claims that, as a result, her brother does not have anything to do with girls and that she is often physically repelled by men she likes. She also says that at certain times of the month she is practically overwhelmed by physical desire for a man ...

P. talked all afternoon about her dissatisfaction with life in Toulon – she gradually developed the feeling that La Rode is a concentration camp and developed further her growing irritation with the teachers and the pious – accusing them all, and especially the latter, of being uninteresting (which they certainly are) and talking nothing but light and tedious banter, mostly sex-orientated (which they certainly do). The trouble is that it's hard to know what else she wants. She talks vaguely and naively about stopping and talking to the man in the street, though what exactly she would find in common with him was not immediately clear ...

P. is at the awkward stage of being bright enough to be dissatisfied but not bright enough to let things pass over her head and look for some kind of resource within herself. I had said enough earlier to her about the *ennui* suffered by spoilt little *petit bourgeoise* girls to make it pointless entering the conversation again ... On this subject she made a very interesting comment: she said, with obvious pleasure, that she could twist O. about her little finger, that he was crazy about her (and yesterday she referred proudly for the second time to the fact that he had gone on the bottle for 3 days when he thought she was being unfaithful). Well, that's fine and normal for a 19-year-old girl but not for the mature creature she pretends to be. I pointed out (of course!) that most girls would prefer a man they could not twist around their little fingers and she backpedalled lightly, but the damage was done.

Taken together with her readiness to explain herself right from the beginning ... that all adds up to a trace of exhibitionism perhaps. Another interesting thing: when reproached with lack of interest in the gypsy colony over the road, she replied: 'Well, did you bother about things like that when you were only 19?' My reply: 'Age is no excuse. Also you have somebody telling you that it's wrong – I didn't.'

She is, perhaps, more shy and self-conscious than she seems – one thing is that she falls very readily into a little-girl act and voice the minute you start caressing her – the other is that she virtually extinguishes her character when meeting new people – she speaks in a very soft, dead voice and only hazards the most acceptable re-marks. It is virtually impossible to imagine what she will be like at the age of forty.

2 November

A journey to Montpellier. R. arrived promptly ... to take me to see his baby daughter, now 6 weeks old. Extraordinarily small, fragile and quite attractive, with great eyes of a darkish blue staring vacantly about once she was (reluctantly) awake. Her right ear seemed slightly crumpled like a boxer's and on both of them there was a fine down, due, it was said, to her premature birth. R., as might have been ex-pected, treated her with rough heartiness, pinching her nose and ex-hibiting for our benefit what he presumably takes to be a virile approach to the whole business, though for most of the time he sat in a corner and read *Le Canard Enchaîné,* [23] as he read the *Express* the following morning while we were having breakfast together in the café on the ground floor of the hotel where he lives opposite the Jardin des Plantes. I got the impression that he was gleaning oddments with which to keep up in his circle of friends (the young communist gods of the faculty). Coming back ... with the record he

18

bought (an old 1st World War song his mother used to sing) at the *foire aux puces* [24] under the arches, he dashed to the car to get it when he saw them, in order to get their approval, it seemed to me, although this may be unjust.

J. (pipe-smoking, eyes close together in a large, pear-shaped face and not nearly as bright as R. seems to think although certainly pleasant) and a swarthy young man with rimless glasses who holds some other position, appear to set the tone for the group and the others crowd around offering comments and jokes to show they are pointing in the right direction, really quite depressing – it made me think, though God knows I had a low opinion of the place, how much more mature their counterparts in Oxford seemed ...

Walking back from the hospital after saying goodbye ... and glad to be on my independent own again and going back to my 'home' in Toulon, I had one or two random thoughts – one was that I must stop wasting my time with 'friends' with whom I have so little, temperamentally, in common – another was that I must face the fact that I no longer have any claims on the sort of girls one sees in Montpellier. Beautiful, shapely brown legs and chic hair-styles and smartly dressed, often in suits (the fashion of half-pleated skirts I like very much) but now too young for me. As I said to Frièdel Ott [25] the other day when we were joking about our age, I may not have had my share of that age-group but I just have to pass on. This is a pity – I like them so much, these young *étudiantes*. Something happens to a girl from the age of 19–25 which, while not changing her appearance, drains her of charm.

On the debit side of the visit: a great deal of boredom, a mercifully brief interview with R.'s fat peasant mother, childishly stupid and smelling of urine – a struggle for the baby between her and [her daughter-in-law] is just starting. On the credit side: J.'s girlfriend, skinny and attractive with big sensitive eyes; the film of Roger Vailland's novel *Les Mauvais Coups* [26] with Simone Signoret and a big raw-boned, grey-haired Englishman with whom I promptly identified myself. A slow atmospheric film with some good grey landscapes when they are out hunting in the early morning and some good muddy country lanes with their connotations in atmosphere. The man's silence, strength and sensibility were very eloquent. A meeting in the street with A., whom I like a lot for his friendliness and pleasantness. Above all, the relief of getting back to Toulon.

Saturday, 4 November
Keeping a diary, even the kind of diary which seems to be necessary for a writer, is really only another way of magnifying one's personality in one's own eyes. Perhaps, after all, the kind of diary we used to keep at prep school: 'It rained today' or 'Match v Sandbach – we won 15.0' was a healthier proposition. Well, today it did not rain in Toulon but the big winds arrived and drove the people inside from the *terrasses* of the cafés. A man next to me in the café to which I repaired on the Boulevard de Strasbourg told his neighbour that some masonry had fallen off a house near the Poste and made a hole in the roof of a car and in general there was briskness and excitement in the air with a number of ballooning skirts in the cross-wind by Le Claridge – I suppose I still have a perverted interest in windblown skirts (and women undressing unobserved) but in general the keynote of the afternoon was one of health and vitality.

Finally got around to reading Huxley's [27] article in the *Observer* of Oct 22 discussing parapsychology, acupuncture etc. Weird and fascinating – especially the latter ... But much more interesting (and disturbing) was what Huxley says about the necessity of formulating psychology for the handful of politicians [and] generals at whose mercy the remaining 290,000 million of the human race now find themselves. '[They] are themselves the hypnotised prisoners of political and philosophical traditions which have in the past invariably led to war ...' A.J.P. Taylor reviewing *What is History?* by E.H. Carr: 'All history tells us is that something will happen, though probably what we do not expect.' Very good! ... Huxley's ideas could generate a doubt in Sayer's [28] mind.

5 November
Sometime in the early hours of this morning I woke up and told myself that I must get out of the habit of thinking of myself as 'becoming' and think of myself instead as 'being'. It is so hard to drop the idea that a big future is in store when life will begin beginning and that the present is, so to speak, all the future we can expect – with variations, of course. One of the more tempting things about Christianity is that it keeps the future always ahead, like a carrot.

In any case, between then (this morning) and now I have developed a feverish cold (and the shops are closed as it is Sunday) and am more inclined to think of myself as 'having been' ...

5 November

P. read us part of a very frightening letter from her father – 'I think we can safely say that French life is sub-standard in comparison with our own' – and [remarking] about her Italian boyfriend that he was a 'peasant', stated in a very insidious way with a large number of concessive clauses. His whole letter was redolent of Jesuitical bourgeois reactionary thinking (if you can call it that). It gave me an urgent desire to take him by the shoulders and shake him and tell him, 'You know nothing, but nothing!'

7 November

Cocktails on the *Centaur* aircraft-carriers [29] seem to be exactly what one would imagine – and the officers on board. Talked with a lot of young, polite, earnest young men. Talked with the attractive woman I had seen before at the Association for G.B.[30] Very nervous and electric – her hands tremble badly when she lights a cigarette. Once again she was beautifully dressed, this time in yellow. She was born in Algiers and finds it hard to have to leave her home, understandably.

When the *Centaur* party was over a couple of young officers took me down to their cabin, where they changed, and then over to another smaller party on the *Tidesurge*. This was paradise – lots of lovely French girls (I had a head start here because apart from a French officer called Claude none of the males spoke French) and buckets of whiskey. So I set about bombarding my cold with whiskies. Another young *pied noir*, wife without her husband, *une grace* by the name of Danielle ... and an English girl. When I was already well lit-up I had two long and over-earnest conversations with a couple of mildly misfitting officers who had been seduced by the fact that I said I was a writer. This party was such a pleasant surprise that I fell asleep chuckling drunkenly.

8 November

I told W. that I had drunk seventeen whiskies the night before and this may even have been true. But the dates must have got out of hand because on a subsequent day De Gaulle came asking the *jeunes gens* in the crowd to remember that on the 8th November

21

they listened to and saw De Gaulle in Toulon. He looked older and greyer than his pictures and on tv, and although the Place de la Liberté and the Blvd de Strasbourg were thronged there was very little applause. In his speech he said nothing new, insisted on the unity of France and the *ambitions malsaines* [31] of the colons. [32] To get a spark of enthusiasm from the crowd he began singing *La Marseillaise* but ended up singing largely by himself. It was rather pathetic. For those who like, as I do, big men trying to roll boulders up mountain slopes, the whole event was full of sadness ...

9 November

Nobody new in my life. The old people have entrenched themselves and as usual I am fighting the *cafard* and general inertia – but with no success. Nothing is going really right. Endless futile (pleasant) conversations but, as I remarked, all this does not add up to a life.

11 November

Le onze Novembre, in fact. Processions took place *en ville sous une pluie battante et sans moi.* [33] I was sleeping unhealthily in the clammy wreckage of my bed. As for the rest – still gathering speed – *Qu'on n'en parle plus.*

But I have forgotten A. [34] In a lot of ways his ideas lack astringency and have vaguely emotional and naive overtones that ring false but he really seems to be a dedicated writer (he has rather romantic notions about this too – talking of it as a *maladie*) and what the hell, he has published. He's on the other side of the indifference barrier. Even if there is no direct intellectual benefit, at least his company may get me back to my typewriter and stop me wasting time with the La Rode crowd.

P.'s hair – long and fine and very, very beautiful. Yesterday's argument with O. is still hanging in the air, although this evening it seems a bit ridiculous. A question of pride, really. He certainly isn't worth taking seriously as a fascist – nor me as a sincere left-wing intellectual, if it comes to that. Yesterday, though, I was genuinely annoyed by his allegation that Servan-Schrieber and Beuve-Méry [35] were financed and influenced by the Swiss-Jewish banks. I still believe that the only way to handle that kind of situation is to do what I did – that is, flatly contradict the truth of the so-called evidence. A'.s remonstrances afterwards were quite futile however – the sort of double-dealing with one's beliefs which mark the *non-engagé* writer. Does he really believe (a) that it is dangerous, and (b) that it is not worthwhile to profess any kind of leftish sympathies in France? Also, it seemed to be taking a little *gamin* like O. far too seriously. His best justification, though, as I had to point out to him, was that he has a wife and child and cannot afford to take risks with them – whereas, of course, I am only responsible to myself.

But where (or when!) will I finally be able to take myself seriously as a liberal intellectual and not feel myself to be a miserable faker when I get annoyed the way I did yesterday? What do I have to do? Perhaps one must first experiment to see how far one is willing to go – whether for example one could allow oneself to be put in prison without feeling simply a bloody fool.

No ideas today. Toulon is muddy, wet and oppressive. I ask myself whether I will ever be able to write anything worthwhile in that damp greenish glow of filtered light which is my *vert-coteau* kitchen. Really my situation is basically the same as Luc's [36] – I have become hypnotised by the externals to such an extent that I have become completely impotent ...

26 November

... I'm no longer able to do more than sympathise with uncomplicated people. I think that any relationship with me would be something of a disaster for M. in much the same way as it was for Judy [37] (whom she resembles quite a lot in some respects). Perhaps she is simply a Judy returned to health for me? But I hardly feel that the rivalry that poisoned my relations with her would occur in the same way. Perhaps I'm simply too cunning now to make the same kind of frontal attack on her way of life, involving everything that she most loves and respects. M, thanks to the failure of her parents, is trying to find her own way. But at what age can a leopard still change its spots?

In the last couple of days [the manuscript of] *A Man From Elsewhere*, now struggling along at page 56, has come to a head. I can no longer go along in the same mechanical manner ...

To Gabriele

Avenue Vert Coteau, Toulon
30 November/1 December 1961

Dear Gaby,

I really regretted afterwards having written that last letter [21 October] because it seemed so childish: I have decided to be less depressed in future and more virile. The main trouble over the last few months has been that I have been wondering whether, in fact, I have any talent as a novelist or whether it might not be better to go and grow tomatoes in County Dublin. Now I've decided that the problem isn't as important as I thought it was and – I still get slightly depressed from time to time but that isn't very important either.

The other day I got a letter from an American girl who used to be engaged to a close friend of mine ... She married an Italian who had already been married [and] says that her husband can no longer live with her and she has to go away [but has] no money, no friends and nowhere to go ... and so she wants me to go to Florence at Christmas to try and sort things out for her ... I think I will buy a suit of armour, climb on to a white horse and go over to see what is going on. Although I must say I don't relish the thought of spending Christmas arguing with some sinister Italian and comforting this poor girl. However, that's why I won't be able to come to Munich.

But let us definitely arrange to meet in Paris at Easter. I will absolutely guarantee to be there, unless I am on my death-bed and if you have already decided to go there then, if you decide you do not like me then it will not be such a great disappointment as you will have other things to do. Why am I so particular? Yes, there are certainly many attractive girls here and I enjoy their company very much. However, once in a while (very seldom) one meets someone who seems to understand always what is going on in your mind *on se comprend à demi-mot* as they say in French, without having to go into long explanations which never succeed; it is more that one feels things the same way. I may be wrong but I believe that this was the impression I had when I was with you – that is why I have been trying not to lose track of you over these two years. So many people drift in and out of one's life but so few that one really feels are important. But of course we have probably both changed quite a lot since we last saw each other.

With love,
Jim

Diary

Christmas Eve, Florence

But to take up the story. P. left – a *coup le cafard*. Her boyfriend wept rather touchingly at the station, and this brought about a temporary thaw in our relations. I offered him a drink as we were walking back to the car; he refused.

Subsequently she writes to say she is coming back 'for his sake and for my own'. Perhaps she will prove me wrong after all, but by this time – by now – anything she might do is a matter of indifference to me.

One week of an intensely virulent *cafard* – perhaps the lack of interest in me shown by M. was the real reason – combined of course with general boredom and lack of future. I had been determined to sulk through Madame B.'s *soirée*, not to go, in fact, as a protest and illustration of how I had 'really the blues'. In the end, of course, I did go; it was as expected, although Mme B. descended much lower in my esteem, ordering M. about as if she were the maid, displaying much stupidity.

To Gabriele

Avenue Vert Coteau, Toulon
6 January 1962

Dear Gabriele,

... A very strange thing has happened to me. I forget whether I told you that just before Christmas I had a bad attack of the 'blues' – really the 'blues', in fact (i.e. *le cafard*). I used to drag about the town all day from one café to the next until they closed at night, and then not be able to sleep. And of course I couldn't write either. In fact I don't think I did tell you because I decided a long time ago that I had better stop complaining in every letter I wrote you or else you would stop reading them. Well, just before I left for Florence I was combing my hair and a handful of it came away in my fingers from the side of my head! I was astonished, and alarmed, as you can imagine ... (Don't laugh! You must find this very funny, but it wasn't for me). I then found that there was another bad patch at the back of my head. I thought I must have caught some infection at the barber's ... Well, I hate doctors but I finally decided I'd better go and see one ...

So I went the other day and he told me that I had 'alopecia'. This is a derangement or illness of the nervous system which has the effect of making all your hair fall out and you go as bald as an egg! ... [*He*] told me that I would have to eat properly (no more home-made spaghetti!) and take pills to make me sleep and spend as much time re-laxing and thinking of nothing as possible. So now I eat tablets and drink tonics and sit in the sun doing nothing all afternoon, repeating to myself that '*tout est pour le meilleur dans le meilleur des mondes*' [38] and other optimistic thoughts. I must say that I feel better and, of course, I daren't consider having the blues in case all my hair falls out ...

My visit to Florence was very bizarre. The girl was much more beautiful than I had remembered from six years ago but her character had changed a lot – I remembered her as being warm-hearted and dreamy and rather defenceless. Now she is much more hard ... This made me very sad as I believe her present cynicism to be more the fault of the people she has known than her own. However. It rained all the time and I did not enjoy my visit very much. I stayed in a *pensione* (the only guest so I lived with the family) run by a woman who had been the mistress of Carlo Levi [39] (who wrote *Christ Stopped at Eboli*); she still has the manuscript and some of his paintings – opposite the Palazzo Pitti – I'll tell you about it sometime when I see you. There isn't space here.

Love,
Jim

Diary
January 1962
This was *le mois de Françoise* – almost to the day ... She poured out all her troubles – I converted mine into a mild egomania and suc-ceeded in divesting myself in all interest for her. The vapidity with which her parents procreated themselves after the war ... ruined her adolescence, leaving her with a permanent chip on her shoulder ... I asked her whether she had ever wanted to have children, even when she had been in love with someone. '*Non*', she replied. '*La maternité ne me tente pas.*'

She said she was used to being alone – and I believe her. She was very wilful and self-sufficient ... Often ill-informed, she liked to contradict. The real key to her character, it seemed to me, was that she was unable to 'share herself', unable to take a sympathetic interest in others ... More than once she said that she would have preferred to be a boy. Certainly her attitude to men was ambivalent. The last time I saw her she described me as a *larve*, herself as a *chrysalide, oui devient papillon.*

On the other hand, it would be hard to deny that I put a big strain on her. She believed that I had a fixation about myself and needed only a passive admiring audience to reflect myself back. This may have been disturbingly near the truth. But from the way she talked with contempt about other people of all kinds I could not help thinking that she shared my egomania with me.

The end, by letter, was depressingly banal – although I did my best to retrieve some dignity by my closing epistle. Moral: stop writing any but purely factual letters.

To Gabriele

Lycée de Blvd. de Strasbourg,
Toulon (Var)
[undated] 1962

My dear Gaby,

... This is mainly to tell you that I've decided to move out of my room here at the end of the month – I finally decided that my old widow and her nasty little dog were getting on my nerves and stopping me from being creative. I don't yet know where I'll be living ...

Not much news. The days have been swimming past me like swollen, pink fish. A love-affair I was having with a girl here has come to an end because I ran out of money and conversation at the same time. (French girls like money.) I hoped it would all end peacefully but she got very angry with me (for some reason which I don't understand) and told me I was selfish and conceited. This worried me quite a lot as a suspicion crossed my mind that she was right. However, it is all forgotten and buried now. *Requiescat in pacem. Amen.*

Politically this country is in turmoil. There have been a number of manifestations and plastic *attentats*. [40] But I expect you already know about that from the newspapers. For a foreigner it is exciting. A Communist friend in Montpellier has written to say that he has just bought a second-hand *mitraillette* [41] with 3,000 rounds of ammunition in order to be ready for the civil war! ...

With love,
Jim

To Patsy Cumming

Blvd. de Strasbourg,
Toulon
21 February 1962

Dear Patsy,

Many apologies for not having written back sooner. The fact is that I've been ill. I had a mild *crise de dépression nerveuse* around Christmas, followed by, of all things, alopecia ... So I've been lurking in a darkened room talking to phantoms and juggling with imaginary thunderbolts for the last few weeks – or is it months? ...

What I really wanted to say is that I will probably be coming to Paris at Easter and if I do will look you up if you are still there ... I wish I could say definitely when I am coming but physically I have been feeling quite rickety, a new and disagreeable sensation for me. I'm sorry to harp on it like this. The temptation to crawl away into a hole and wait for eternity is very strong.

I hope the girls are in good form and beginning to pick up the language. Children learn so quickly. The very thought of it makes me green with envy ...

All the best to you,
Jim

To Patsy Cumming

Hôtel Sainte Hélène,
Blvd Sainte Hélène,
Le Mourillon
Toulon (Var)
6 March 1962

Dear Patsy,

Many thanks for your letter and excuses for mine. There's a point where sensitivity about one's *vie intérieure* becomes feeble childishness and, in my last letter, I feel that I reached it. However.

... It was very kind of you to offer a roof. In fact, I've already seen George [Whitman] [42] once or twice (I can't claim to know him). I imagine he knew me although, for reasons of his own, never gave any hint of it – feeling, I expect, that I was a fake or a hanger-on. Although if it became a question of separating the fakes and the hangers-on from the others in the Mistral I imagine Saint Peter himself would find himself in difficulties. Still, I can't see George being thrilled at having me there unless he is eager to do you favours ...

Talking of mistrals, one has been whistling through the streets of Toulon for the past few days. I don't think I know anything more chilling or more demoralising. Curiously enough, whichever direction I walk in I always seem to have it full in my face. But this may be sheer imagination – a definition of myself, so to speak.

Cheers,

Jim

[*Handwritten*] P.S. Do let me know if you are short of anything (i.e. money). I'm paid considerably more than I need here and with 2 small children I'm sure you must have trouble managing. Or, let's say that I'd like to give presents to the girls. What do they need?

To Gabriele

Hôtel Sainte Hélène,

Toulon

10 March 1962

Dear Gaby,

... I will probably be in Paris from the 13th or 14th onwards because there are a couple of people I have to see ... maybe more if the bohemian regiment is in town. Among them is the widow of an American writer of my age who died of food poisoning almost two years ago now, leaving his wife with two little girls to bring up. He had written eighty pages of a satire on the American-way-of-life which was published after his death in the *Atlantic Monthly*. His brother[43] was a close friend of mine at Oxford and it happened that I was with him at the time the tragedy occurred. It was one of the most harrowing experiences of my life. Anyway, I would like you to meet her, and also Nelson Aldrich, [44] the editor of the *Paris Review*, [45] if he is still in Paris at Easter. You must promise not fall in love with him though – he is incredibly handsome and dynamic! I hope that some of the beatnik poets will be there too ... I will almost certainly be staying in the Latin Quarter, either in a hotel or in a small bookshop opposite Nôtre Dame where penniless writers and artists are given beds by the American who owns it ...

My health (and hair) is much better. I have changed my room and am now beside the sea which I can see from my window. Palm-trees too. I hope that makes you jealous!

I am working very hard to have the first draft of my novel finished before going to Paris. I can't decide whether it's any good or not. I wish you were here. I have the feeling that with you *je ferais des merveilles*. [46] I am like a clock-work toy which has run down. I need someone to wind me up again.

That's all for the moment.

Love to you,
Jim

To Gabriele

Hôtel Sainte Hélène,
Toulon
16 March 1962

My dear Gaby,

There's no particular reason for this letter, except that I feel like writing to you. About an hour ago I received a letter from home telling me that my Siamese cat [47] died last Monday, and this news has given me the blues again. I was very much attached to this cat and the news of her death is quite a shock. Nobody knows quite why she died, although my mother thinks she may have eaten some poisoned food which had been left for rats in one of the neighbouring gardens. Anyway, she was very beautiful and young and it seems such a waste that she should die so young. I know it's ridiculous to be upset about the death of a cat when people are dying in Algeria by the hundreds, [48] and not only in Algeria. But knowing that it's ridiculous doesn't re-ally make it any better. When you find it hard, as I do, to love peo-ple, it is not surprising that one gives one's affection to an animal.

In particular, this news has come at a bad time for me. For the last few days I have been besieged with thoughts of death and illness, and nightmares about an incident that occurred three or four years ago – when a girl I knew was in a very bad car-crash in Ireland. [49] Also I have been thinking a lot about the ageing of my parents, their life and my own. I have not been able to write or concentrate on anything and just at the moment life seems a very black affair. You must forgive me for boring you with all this. I'd much prefer to write you a cheerful letter.

I'm doing my best to look forward (according to your instruction) to Paris and I really am looking forward to seeing you again. I hope I won't be in one of my black moods. In some ways it's much easier to be friends with someone by letter, it is so much easier to be natural and to be oneself.

Do write!

With love,
Jim

To Patsy Cumming

Hôtel Sainte Hélène,
Toulon
28 March 1962

Dear Patsy,

It was extremely boorish of me to offer you cash and I really did it without thinking at all about the personal feelings you might have on the subject. I was thinking merely of the cost of living and that perhaps you were living without any visible means of support; very sorry. I'll be happy to take you out to dinner ...

What kind of people are there in George Whitman's place now? Do Burroughs and Sinclair Beiles [50] still patronise the place from time to time? I saw an article on the bookshop in one of the literary papers not so long ago which was unbelievably silly: i.e. about George they said: *La tête de Lawrence et le sang de Walt Whitman dans les veines* ... [51] I imagine that as a result of that article it will have had something of a vogue among the *derrière-garde*.

One of my reasons for coming to Paris is to show the sights to a German girl with whom I have been corresponding for the last two years and whom I haven't seen in this time ... I have a sordid desire to spring Napoleon's tomb on her and see what she makes of it.

Looking forward to seeing you,
Jim

To Gabriele

Hôtel Sainte Hélène,
Toulon
2 April 1962

My dear Gaby,

... Paris would be a wonderful place to meet you because there is so much to do there – theatre, dancing in cellars, sightseeing, the markets, museums etc. (I remember how difficult it was to find something to show you in Dublin! Apart from James Joyce's house!)

Dear Gabriele, do come!! I am most curious to see what you look like after two years. The first time I saw you I thought you were a beautiful little girl of fourteen or fifteen; you were dressed (*circa* 1900) in long, frilly petticoats and a straw hat with ribbons hanging down over the nape of your neck – only when I saw what vast quantities of gin you were drinking did I wonder if you were older!! You looked very like a pastel by Renoir entitled *Jeune Fille au Chapeau* of which I have a copy at home.

In any case, I hope you can get well soon. Write as quickly as you can.

With love,
Jim

[*Handwritten*] Perhaps this illness is a divine punishment for all the heart-breaking you have been doing recently?

To Gabriele

Hôtel Sainte Hélène,
Toulon
7 April 1962

My dear Gabriele,

Tant pis! Ce sont les choses qui arrivent, as the fatalistic French would say. *Les mauvais coupes, quoi!*

Perhaps we shall meet somewhere in the summer. My plans are very vague but I don't think I want to go back to Ireland. When I was there last summer I felt very much like Thomas Mann's character Tonio Kroger [52] (although when I read this story it rather irritated me). I found that I no longer had anything in common with the friends I grew up amongst there. I still found them 'nice' but we no longer understood each other, or had anything to say to each other, and so I felt very solitary.

Depending on the state of my morale I will either stay on a beach on the Côte d'Azur for the month of July (school finishes here at the end of June) or go straight back to England to stay in a cottage with a friend and his wife. [53] I forget whether I have already told you about this couple – the boy (he is younger than me) was at Oxford with me and is very intelligent and good-natured. His wife is a real 18th Century English rose, blonde and fair-skinned and who is actually called Rose by some happy chance. They live in a cottage in a picturesque little village in Sussex, about an hour on the train from London. Brian [Knox Peebles] works on the local newspaper as a journalist (reporting on such momentous events as village concerts and garden-parties!)

Well I shall probably go and stay there for the summer and write another novel which I already have planned in my head. If I have no money I shall also work as a journalist but the work is amusing and not very hard. He has often pressed me to bring girls down to stay at the cottage (he and his wife are very anxious to see me married!) and I know that you would be more than welcome to stay there as long as you wanted (he speaks German fluently by the way) and, of course, you would be entirely free to do as you please. We would spend our time reading, listening to records, or walking in the fields – but if you found that dull London is near to hand and some other friends of mine who live in the city would give you a bed. And if you felt uneasy about not doing any work you could give me German lessons or help Rose with the housework to earn your living! ...

In about ten days I expect to have finished the first draft of my novel. Sometimes I think it is very good and certain to be a success and other times I think that it is rotten. I shall be glad when I have finished it because I'm very tired and nervous at the moment. I've been sleeping badly and having bad dreams again. I keep dreaming that I'm in hospital again and death seems very close. Also, the mistral has been whistling through the streets of Toulon and that, too, sets my nerves on edge. Yesterday as I was leaving the hotel an elderly woman was knocked down by a motor-cycle just in front of me and I had to pick her up and help her into a *pharmacie* near at hand with blood streaming down her face ... and all the time with the wind tugging at our clothes. It was horrible. To cheer myself up (I found that I couldn't go on writing after that) I went to the cinema to see a film directed by Elia Kazan, called *Splendour in the Grass* (the French title was *La Fièvre dans le Sang*!!) and I found it crude but powerful. It caused me some depressing thoughts about my own life and didn't cheer me up very much.

With love,
Jim

To Patsy Cumming

Hôtel Sainte Hélène,
Toulon
7 April 1962

Dear Patsy,

Many thanks for your letter and the instructions on how to get to B-L. [54] I'll come about one o'clock then – but don't bother to get anything in, or in anyway change your daily routine. And if you should want to go out don't worry about missing me because I'll either wait in the nearest bar or come back another time. The one thing is, though, that I think I will delay my arrival until Tuesday 17th ... The reason for this is that if I leave earlier I won't have time to finish the first draft of my novel, as I have been hoping to do. The extra four or five days should give me the time I need – and the short holiday a breathing space to look at it with fresher eyes when I come back, before re-writing. This isn't important so do tell me if it doesn't suit you ...

There has been a terrible, unceasing wind here which has reduced my nerves to shreds again ...

I must stop now.

All the best to you,
Jim

P.S. There's a chance that if I have the *cafard* I may come on Friday anyway.

PPS. Two or three days later: I wrote this letter but didn't send it as I felt I couldn't stand staying in Toulon any longer – novel or no novel. Since then the wind I mentioned has gone and my determination to finish my book before Easter has come back, so I think I'll make it the Tuesday after all. Excuse these hesitations. I only wish my book was worth them ... it isn't.

To Patsy Cumming

Hôtel Sainte Hélène,
Toulon
[undated] 1962

Dear Patsy,

I was just thinking how like Bob[55] you are (or how Bob is like you) and how I have the impression that I've known you for ages. It's strange to think that I was only a week in Paris, it seemed more like a month (and not because of boredom, on the contrary).

Anyway, thanks a lot for putting up with me and I'm sorry I became so peculiar in the last couple of days. These periods of 'feeling strange' are a fairly frequent occurrence with me and can make me hard to get along with – they may even be a bit *voulu* (as you would say) now I come to think of it, although why I should *vouloir* I have no clear idea. In any case, it all makes for a better display of a cross-section of my character if that (my character) should interest you at all Racine-wise or Alexander Korda-wise – god forbid ...

The only point was to thank you – and also to tell you that I've decided against asking you to be my broker for Joyce's letters; [56] after an agonising reappraisal I have decided that I must be out of my mind. If I start lusting for them again I'll let you know and send you the cash. But please don't consider sending me them as a present (or anything else); I should feel terrible. Besides, I enjoy stalking the odd material possession through the dripping, autumnal woods of my salary and would feel cheated if Joyce were suddenly delivered to me bound hand and foot and swinging from a pole.

Nothing new in my life except the nice weather.

All the best to you and the girls,

Jim

To Gabriele

Hôtel Sainte Hélène,
Toulon
24 Mai 1962

Dear Gabriele,

... My friends say that they will be delighted to have you stay with them and that you can stay for as long as you like. I forget whether I told you that Rose, the girl, is expecting a baby around the end of

October and, I believe, likes the idea of having another girl around the house for part of the summer for moral support. They say that they want me to be godfather to the child when it arrives. I find this rather a peculiar choice don't you? ...

I finished my novel [57] last week and sent it away to the publisher. [58] This is the one I told you about last year which I was determined was going to be a commercial success. Now that it's finished I don't really know what to think of it. As far as I can judge, it's a fairly competent, easy-to-read, rather unoriginal novel, illuminated (perhaps) by one or two of my own strange ideas. But I've been very careful this time to give the pill a sugary coating. But, as I say, I have no real idea whether it's any good as, up to the time of writing, nobody has yet read it and given me an opinion of it ...

Soon after finishing it I went to see a film which has come out here recently called: *Cléo de 5 à 7*,[59] directed by a woman, Agnès Varda,[60] rather in the style of an Antonioni film. I found it really wonderful and at the same time very discouraging for a novelist. The only conclusion I could draw from it was that it is far more effective to write novels with a camera than with a typewriter.

With this in mind I have been thinking of applying for entry to the Institut des Hautes Etudes Cinématographiques in Paris (a school for cinema directors to learn the *métier*) but for one thing the age limit is 27 (my age) and for another I simply have no money ... So for the moment I've shelved the idea with regret (another reason is that foreigners have to sign a contract not to make a film in the French cinema for a period of 12 years, and France is really the only country that interests me from the point of view of actors and public). At any rate, I have the firm intention of breaking into the cinema sooner or later. Do you still act? My one (slender) hope is that someone will like my novel well enough to want to film it ... and in this case I would refuse to part with the film rights unless I could participate in some small way on the film in order to get some of the necessary experience. However, all that is simply castles in the air.

At the moment I'm doing nothing. I lie on the beach all day trying to avoid the disagreeable thought that I'm going to have to get a job soon, and in the evening I go to the cinema or watch television in a small café I frequent here. Life is very pleasant. I'm also planning another novel ... this time a novel which is entirely personal and original and which could not have been written by anyone else. [61] The main thing is to find a style which can express the density of life as Joyce did (where the characters don't simply perform a sequence of actions like laughing, speaking, stubbing out cigarettes, sleeping with each other etc.) but at the same time which can express coherent ideas and the pressure of circumstances. I think that I'm going to have another, and very different, attempt at using polio as a central device ...

> With love,
> Jim

To Franz Beer [62]

> Hôtel Sainte Hélène,
> Toulon
> [undated] 1962

Dear Franz,

Easter already seems a long time ago. In the words of Patsy's immortal poem (and mine): 'I clipped my nails in the Bois de Meudon, *c'était bon!*' You will be happy to hear that I have clipped my nails once or twice since then. I have also finished my book and sent it away to a publisher in London. It seems to be fairly competent but at the same time a book which could have been written by a couple of hundred other writers. At the moment I'm hopefully making notes for a book which can only be written by me. Patsy has just written me a moralizing letter with the idea, I think, of improving my character. I'm on the point of writing back to tell her I like myself fine the way I am ... This morning I passed in the street a bald little man in overalls carrying a sign saying: *LA BONNE VIE* – No comment. Hope to see you at the end of June.

> Jim Farrell

To Patsy Cumming

> Hôtel Sainte Hélène,
> Toulon
> 28 May 1962

Dear Patsy,

It was nice to hear from you, especially as I was thinking in my usual neurotic way that I'd said something to offend you in my letter ... It's quite hopeless arguing with women and I'm now officially giving it up ...

I'm sure I could defend myself adequately if I were sure exactly what you meant [*sic*]. You have a very gripping and arresting prose style but it sometimes seems rather as if you were on a desert island writing hasty messages for bottles during a world paper shortage. You go very abruptly from one idea to the next. And another thing is that the argument could go on indefi-nitely – and my starting point for the way I live or try to live my life, which I take it you're attacking, isn't logical but emotional anyway. I went to see the film of *Le Rouge et Le Noir*, [63] in the course of one scene somebody says: '*En France on fait les plus grandes cruauté – mais sans crautés*. [64] (Damn! Your inscrutable style is catching). And a little later Gérard Philippe, who plays Julien Sorel, [65] says that he wants to pass through life *comme une tempête*. Both these remarks seemed to me to be significant. I'm prepared to admit, though, that at the moment I'm a poor apology for a *tempête*. And who's racked? I find myself very balanced and normal. And was there something I should have apologised to Franz and Claire for? How alarming. That's not all – your letter was full of dark innuendoes, totally unconnected it seems to me with anything I know about. E.g. 'Never visit people who have fifth thoughts.' 'I think you probably have more courage than I, in spite of England.' In spite of England? What cowardice did I perpetrate in England? Well, many thanks for the compliment (although personally I doubt if I have more courage than you) but it was rather an alarming one.

And many thanks for Joyce's Letters which I'm sure I will enjoy very much in spite of the fact that I was sincere in what I said before ...

This is a silly and futile letter but I may as well send it just the same as in my present state of *désoeuvrement* [66] I don't feel I can do any better. I'm beginning to plot another novel.

Love

Jim

[*Handwritten postscript*] I decided to immortalise the Rue B-Lafont in the opening of my novel – but it's not very good and I expect it will have to be changed.

To Patsy Cumming

> Hôtel Sainte Hélène,
> Toulon
> 28 May 1962 [later that day]

Dear Patsy,

Just another word of many thanks for Joyce's letters which arrived this morning and which are really wonderful. I hope you read them before sending them off. And a word of apology for the silly letter I sent you. I'm sure you divined that it was more motivated by panic than by anything else, but I could have merely said that I didn't want to talk about Life as it pertained to myself without being so tortuously facetious about it. And also my comments about your style were quite unjust. The fact is that my mind goes blank when trying to recall conversations in which I have been put, however indirectly, on trial, and I really couldn't bring myself to remember what it was all about.

The weather here has stopped being so good and I'm rather bored at the moment as I don't seem to be able to sort out how I want to write my next book. I do know that I want it to be funny though and at the moment the author himself isn't feeling very funny. Perhaps as time goes on I'll feel funnier. As opposed to strange, which I feel more and more ...

I hope the girls are in good form.

> All the best,
> Jim

To Patsy Cumming

> Hôtel Sainte Hélène,
> Toulon
> 2 June 1962

Dear Patsy,

This is ridiculous. I never meaned [*sic*] to get mixed up in a wrangle with you over ... over what exactly? Or to hurt you in any way. I like you very much as I thought you realised. But, without wanting to, I'm always doing this kind of thing. The trouble, as I see it, is that I really have no fixed personality when I'm alone by myself (as opposed to when I'm talking to someone face to face ... then I can be the person that the other person expects me to be) and each letter is written by a different and experimental character. Somerset

Maugham says somewhere that he understands why the Church refused to bury actors in consecrated ground up to the 18th century: the actors he knew gave him the impression of having no soul off-stage. I think this is just as true of writers. And [Scott] Fitzgerald says too: 'A writer has got to be too many people if he's going to be any good.' I think I told you that one of the main characters in my book is a film-writer who has got so used to seeing everything in camera-shots that he has lost contact with reality. There's a lot of the Farrell syndrome in this character. But it makes it fantastically difficult to have a stable letter-relationship with somebody. In the last four or five years I've made constant resolutions to restrict myself to the weather in my letters ...

I think you're unfair about my English conditioning. After all I've lived the greater part of my life among non-English people (unless you count the Irish as English). And, as a matter of fact I think you're unjust to the English. I don't notice that the French, in general, give more credit to the emotional part of themselves. Nor the Americans either. I think you confuse emotional acceptance with a superficial bonhomie which I'm prepared to grant to both the French and the Americans ... However, I don't want to argue about it.

I meaned [*sic*] that B-L itself (not the ménage) was in my book. I take it that you have been picturing tabloid headlines: FARRELL REVEALS ALL ABOUT EXPATRIATE AMERICAN WIDOW IN NEST OF SIN.

I've decided that letters (the way I write them) are no good as a means of communication. It's significant that even before we knew each other our correspondence was riddled with misunderstandings. So I'll stop. Let's hope that we'll meet somewhere, some other time, as better, browner, people.

Love to you and the girls.

Jim

To Patsy Cumming

Hôtel Sainte Hélène,
Toulon
13 June 1962

Dear Patsy,
Many thanks for your missive and for the suggestion of the

chambre. In fact, I've decided not to stay in Paris. I'm feeling extremely nervous and restless and (yes) racked again. (But please don't sympathise with me!) I ... feel that a change of countries immediately is required to maintain my mental equilibrium. I can say with pride that I don't know anyone who shows more indulgence to his mental equilibrium than myself. That will have to stop too ...

Somewhere in my novel one of the more racked and sympathetic (to me) characters says that he would just like to crawl back into a nice warm womb somewhere, preferably with lots of tinsel and fairy lights. He adds that another dream he has is that one day a couple of big, burly good-natured men in white overalls are going to bundle him into a car and whisk him off to some mountain sanatorium where the air and the silence are like wine – without him having to make any decision about it ...

And my love to the girls

Jim

To Gabriele

Hôtel Sainte Hélène,
Toulon
Wed. 13 June 1962

Dear Gabriele,

By this time you will have got my card saying that I won't be staying in Paris so this letter is rather pointless. However, I have nothing to do at the moment and my morale is low so I may as well add a few lines. I have just spent a depressing time reading book reviews. I find that all the bad things they have to say about the novels being reviewed apply to mine as well and none of the good things – so I decided to stop reading them ...

This morning I had firmly decided to go back to England and take a job as a journalist [67] for two years. This afternoon I'm no longer sure that that is what I want to do. The thought of throwing away two years of my life (the contract would be for two years) in an English suburban town when there are so many other things I want to do and so many other countries I want to see is infinitely depressing. But my health has been bad this year and I'm so tired of living in sordid rooms and eating irregular meals. In a film of Dostoievski's [*sic*] *Crime and Punishment* [68] which I saw the other day somebody describes Raskolnikov as [taking] *un orgueil démésuré dans une chambre étroite.* [69] I feel that this applies to me and my dreams of becoming a great novelist also. So perhaps I will postpone my decision until I hear what the editor thinks of my latest book ...

I visited the Ile du Levant [70] the other day. Did you go there? This is an island off the coast where nudists congregate. Everywhere one looks there are beautiful girls sunning themselves naked on the rock like seals (well, not too like seals!). It was very interesting and amusing – although not at all exciting sexually as one might have expected ...

But that is the only amusing thing that I've done for a long time. I spend every day lying on the beach and becoming browner and browner and more and more stupid. Becoming sun-tanned is really the must futile occupation. It always amazes me that people take it so seriously. Every day you see people lying grimly on the beach waiting for their skins to change colour. Amazing.

Good luck for your exams. Don't work too hard.

Love,
Jim

To Patsy Cumming

Hôtel Sainte Hélène,
Toulon
Sunday [undated] 1962

Dear Patsy,

I don't suppose this will get to you before you leave but if it does it's to wish you all the best for the voyage and reintegration into the States. Ted, Bob, yourself and myself (and some of the minor characters writing pornographic novels or being towed about by big black dogs) form the kind of group that Durrell [71] might dash off a quartet of novels about (with names changed to something more exotic – Narouz, Nessim etc.). And as with Durrell's books I think there's something a bit *voulu* about all of us. We all take ourselves very seriously. That's all. I imagine that you and Bob think this is a good thing. I'm not sure that I do.

Thanks for the reviews – which I thought were bad reviews, especially the one on Camus which made me very angry. I happen to have read Philip Thody's book [72] and thought the man was very unjust to it, making points in order to squeeze in scraps of information he'd picked up at cocktail parties but having no central approach ... I note that he's an associate prof. at Columbia ...

For your sake I think you ought to go to Thailand, [73] for Bob's sake I'm not so sure ... What I do think is most important, though, is that you make an irrevocable decision immediately. I have no way of telling either just how important sexually Bob is to you. If it is merely the kind of 'melancholy lust' which I suffer from permanently then I think you should establish yourself definitively as 'not for him'. That is, establish yourself as a friend and sympathetic sister-in-law. I wouldn't say all this but you did ask me. As you can see, for Bob's sake I'm rather cool about it – but, on the other hand, people who understand each other don't grow on bushes and I think the girls should have some kind of father-figure and you some kind of husband-figure. I think this is more than I meant to say. But do do something. I find indecision rather unhealthy ...

Love to you all,

Jim

P.S. Toulon is unbearably hot and unpleasant now. Beastly town for weather.

In the autumn of 1962 Jim returned to England by ferry to seek publication of A Man from Elsewhere, *planning to stay first with Brian and Rose Knox Peebles in Kent. Gabriele had promised to visit him there. The light-hearted Channel crossing, spent chatting to a friendly Australian girl, Anne Hurst, boded well, and as the boat docked she gave him her American Express address in London.*

Life is Made Up of Separate Experiences
England and Ireland
1962–63

To Anne Hurst [1]

Spanish Court
Rotherfield
Sussex
[undated] 1962

Dear Ann [*sic*],

Let's hear from you! I have a nasty feeling that you've gone out of my life for ever. I still haven't heard anything about my book but I had lunch the other day with a girl who works for Putnam's who effectively shattered my hopes of getting a quick advance of £100 or £200 by telling me how exclusive Chatto & Windus were. I still feel that I'll get it published eventually but not quickly enough to prevent me having to get a job. So I've practically decided to work as a reporter in Tunbridge Wells for a year and save enough money to go to Greece, buy a hovel, and write more books. The thought of spending the coming winter in England appalls [*sic*] me but this time I'm afraid they really have me cornered ... If you still want to come here for the weekend let me know as soon as you can. My friends are going to the theatre festival at Chichester so I'll be alone here with their very tense and neurotic dog. If I don't hear from you I may leave here on Thursday or Friday and go to Dublin to see my parents. 'Oh bloody period!' as somebody [2] observed when Othello stabbed himself.

Jim

21st birthday card for Rose Knox Peebles.
[*Her dog was named 'Capone'.*]

Capone, the editor of the 'Hundeblatt'

Took his bath while wearing his hat,
Washed his fur with soap & water
Didn't notice it was getting shorter.
His fur got shrunk but he didn't care
His mind was on higher things than hair
For while he soaked, this dog most rare
Could think of nothing but Baudelaire.
With all the very, very best
From Jim and Gabriele

To Gabriele

c/o Brian Pearce [3]
17 Drake Court
Tylney Avenue
Farquhar Road
London SE 19
Monday 10 September 1962

My dear Gabriele,
It was wonderful to get your letter. I wish I could describe how happy
it made me feel, even though I think you only said you loved me to
make me more cheerful. Anyway, it did make me more cheerful!

I'm very tired now as I'm working all day[4] (teaching Germans
English!) and have slept badly for the last two nights, so I must go
to bed. But before I do that I must just tell you what little has
happened to me since you left.

I went back to Rotherfield for a few days feeling very 'blue'. I
spent a lot of time walking in the fields and everywhere I went there
were places where I remembered you – the haystacks where we went
for a walk on the very first morning and had a fight – the field with
the puff-balls full of yellow powder where you told me about your
childhood after the war – the hedge over which you threw your shoe
... I felt a dull ache the whole time (rather as I felt when my cat died
when I was in Toulon!) and loud noises and people talking to me
would hurt me physically, almost as if the skin had been taken off my
mind and it was very sensitive – *maladie de la jeunesse*, I thought.
Then, at the beginning of last week the field began to change. There
were no more mushrooms. A cold wind was blowing over the grass,
there was a smell of autumn in the air and grey, wintry clouds in the

sky. The summer was over ...

Lots of love and goodnight and sleep well, Gabriele dearest ...

Jim

To Gabriele

48 Redcliffe Square
Gloucester Road
London SW10
Sunday, 16 September 1962

Dearest Gabriele,

At last I have found a room of my own and can write you a long letter ... I spent most of last week in torment trying to decide whether I would accept a job teaching English in the Berlitz school in Regensburg but finally decided against it. I would have had to teach eight hours a day; in the morning and in the evening, and I know by the experience of this past week how tiring it is only teaching six hours a day – I wouldn't have been able to do any writing at all. But you can imagine how much I was tempted by the idea of being able to spend week-ends in Munich from time to time! ... Anyway, I'm very sad at the thought of missing a chance of seeing you before – who knows how long? This week I'm starting to learn German seriously ...

I am writing this letter with your smiling face looking at me from four photographs scattered about my desk. They are all very beautiful ... You say that I have given you a more positive attitude to people, mainly men (I hope it isn't too positive!) but I can't begin to describe what you have done for me. It makes so much difference to think that there is somebody else in the world I can care for besides myself.

I think the most important thing I want to say to you in this letter, Gabriele, is this: you will certainly have a lot of love-affairs between now and the next time we meet (and perhaps I will too) but if we really love each other that won't matter. One must have lots of affairs if one is to know what life is all about. Will you tell me all about them and what it is like to sleep with new people and so on? The only way that I won't feel hurt and jealous every time I think of you so far away with other people is if I know that you are telling me the whole truth about it and sharing it with me (although I might feel a bit jealous!). Will you promise? So you see, *petite* Gabriele, that I don't mind so much the idea of being put in the refrigerator if it means that we'll be able to live together again some day. Meanwhile I will become a famous novelist and you will be proud to have such a famous man as a lover!

Well, next week I will only be working in the mornings so I will have time to begin work on my novel. I meant to say before that another of the many things you have done for me is to give me the desire to write a novel which is not so hopeless and despairing – so perhaps you will like this one better than the last.

I have a huge basement room in Earls Court with two single beds. I wish you could come and use one of them (or both). I pay £3.10s a week for this and that leaves me 10s. a day for my food and other things I need. I have never tried to live on so little so I may have to ask you to bake me a cake and send it to me to relieve my starvation. Anyway I will feel very much like the genuine starving artist or writer ...

Earls Court is full of young people and one of the centres of artistic life, although I wouldn't like to say that many of the so-called artists one meets ever produce anything. Every day I hear new stories of seductions, pregnancies, abortions, perversions and drama of all kinds. The night before last, for example, I was present at a hashish-smoking party, although I didn't take part myself as I didn't have any money to buy the stuff, which is very expensive. However, I must try it some time when I get some cash ... Compared with the people here my friends in Paris are bourgeois. The difference is that I know some real artists in Paris whereas most of the people here are phonies.

I must stop now and eat something....

'Sweet, goodnight' (that's from *Romeo & Juliet*).

Love and kisses

Jim

[*Handwritten*] P.S. Do you still stand on your hands every night?

Another friend – in fact, JGF's closest friend – at Oxford had been Russell McCormmach, a Rhodes Scholar. whose deep interests spanned science, literature and painting. Russell had since returned to the US to pursue an academic career as a physicist.

To Russell McCormmach 5

Redcliffe Square

20 September 1962

Dear Russ,

I've spent the last two months looking for a reasonable job and without any fixed address, living with friends mainly. Now I have a job and an address but I haven't yet decided whether they are what I want. However, I got so tired of sleeping on couches and borrowing money that I succumbed – and here I am. The job is teaching English to foreign students in a Berlitz type school and ... the main trouble with it is that I'm so exhausted after doing a straight 3 hours in the morning and another 3 in the afternoon that I can't see myself being able to write a line. I'm just beginning to realise how ideal was the job in France as far as the work-money-time relationship goes ... I'm afraid I can see no alternative to spending the murderous English winter in bloody England ...

Chatto & Windus rejected my book but in what I interpret (once the entrails have been spread out) as an encouraging manner ... They paid me the dubious compliment of wishing me bad luck with other publishers so that they could see my next one – and also, paradoxically, they contacted Secker and Warburg where they have a friend and recommended me to him. So that's where the book has been now for about 5 weeks. I should be hearing soon. My feeling is that as Chatto are the best publishers, with Faber, in England, I should find some lesser publisher to take it. This may be a hallucination. I've long since given up placing any faith in this sort of deduction. I could certainly use a hundred quid though ...

I suppose that by now you will have started work on your new book. I should be interested to know how it's going. I can't think of anything else I should tell you. I had a brief affair with a German girl whom I like(d) a lot but she has now gone back to Germany. It was a little more successful than these things usually are with me but there's still room for improvement. Come to think of it, that may explain some of my enthusiasm for learning German ...

It's time for me to go and eat in Charlie's place. A workers' café where they serve chips and a hot, sweet cup of tea with every meal. Did you know that Arnold Wesker has just produced another play called *Chips with Everything*. Oh England! as D.H. Lawrence would have said, meaning something or other.

All the best to you, Russ,

Jim

To Gabriele

Redcliffe Square
Monday night. 1 October 1962

Dearest Gabs,

I got your letter this morning and carried it with me in my pocket all day because I didn't want to open it at the school, read a little, and then have to stop thinking about you when I started teaching again. Is this foolish?

Anyway, it was wonderful to get your letter and be able to read it in peace when I got home. And that's a beautiful photograph you sent me. The *avant-avant-garde* as far as I'm concerned. In fact you're the only *garde* I care about at all. Will you send me the photographs of yourself after making love for the first time? You know, although my reason tells me not to be, I can't help feeling jealous about that, about your virginity. But I think this is because I love you so much and want, even in retrospect, everything for myself. That is why I wanted you to tell me about it, so that I could share it a little with you. All of you, your whole body, is so precious to me, because one loves with all one's body and not just part of it or with one's mind. One loves with one's toes, and ears, and tongue and fingers and eyelashes and stomach and knees and hair and bottom and teeth and … well, everything. Does this sound crazy? I wish I had taken a photo of you with no clothes in Rotherfield so that I had something to remind me of all of you and not only of your sweet face, your lovely face. You don't know how much I wish this! I think I had better stop thinking about you lying in bed with bright eyes and shining hair or I will not be able to get to sleep tonight …

Don't worry. I don't intend to write my next book about 'social perversities', but God knows when I'll be able to start it. I know it will be good and I know that I will get better and better at writing if I can only get through these difficult few years without losing anything or sacrificing anything.

I am eating well. This evening I cooked myself two eggs and some radishes (uncooked!) and some bread and cheese. I bought a new frying-pan for which one does not need fat or grease. You must have them in Germany too. It is wonderful and much easier. No, dearest, I didn't stop smoking yet. Did you? …

All my love,
Jim

To Gabriele

Redcliffe Square
Sunday, 7 October 1962

Dearest Gabriele,

Yes, I am (faithful) as it happens, although I haven't been thinking about whether I was or not. It's nice to know that you are too
– although I hope you don't feel that you have to be. It is certain
that sooner or later (probably about Christmas when everyone drinks
too much and feels love for everyone else and it's cold and wintry in
the streets and it's warm and reassuring and eternal in bed) you will
meet someone attractive and interesting who will whisk you away to
his room and weave threads of silken magic about you – or perhaps
he will be whisked away by you. My study of sentimental reactions
tells me that it is better (for my interests, of course) that you don't
try to resist the temptation on account of being faithful to me. This
would just build up the pressure.

It seems to me that all the deepest attachments begin with some
such conflict, and, in spite of the fact that the future seems a long,
long way off, I haven't yet given up the idea of taking a string of
small Gabrieles by the hand for a walk in the park on Sunday mornings – and perhaps they would like ice-cream also. (I can't decide
whether the preceding sentence will sound horribly bourgeois to
you.) You may have guessed, anyway, that I have just come back
from a walk in the park where there were lots of children being led
along by their fathers or playing with model boats in the pond. The
fathers playing, the children watching. Anyway, I would like one too
(an excuse for playing with a boat).

I didn't do anything this week except sink a little further into
abrutissement. [6] In a wave of nostalgia for the vineyards and forests
of the Massif Central which must be all red and gold now, I bought
a packet of French cigarettes, some French newspapers, and wrote
long letters to all my friends there. D'you remember my record of
Jean Ferrat? [7] I had written to one of my friends asking her if she had
heard this record and saying how good I thought it was. She wrote
back sending me a photograph on which he had written me a
friendly note offering to sing for me next time I'm in Paris. It seems
that he is a relation of hers. If anything this increased my feeling of
dissatisfaction and *abrutissement* in London.

The one nice thing which has happened is that I met a Polish girl whom I haven't seen since Pamplona, four or five years ago.[8] She and some very attractive (but virginal!) Portuguese girls from Lisbon (where she lives) took me to the theatre to see a dreadful play of which I've forgotten the name. One of the Portuguese girls said she thought I looked like James Dean so I promptly invited her to come and eat with me sometime. This hasn't yet happened and I'm afraid there isn't much hope of me seducing her or of being unfaithful to you! I'd give all the girls in Portugal just to have you here with me for an evening ...

You know, I'm fascinated by the seduction of young girls, especially yours. What happens to a girl when she becomes a woman? Something happens, although nothing seems to. In some way this 'something' is as complete an event as a caterpillar becoming a butterfly – and yet, in other ways, it doesn't exist at all. It annoys me that there is this significant part of human experience which I'll never be able to understand. How can I be a complete writer without doing so? I've often asked girls about it but I've never had a satisfactory answer, either because they were too shy or because they made a romantic story out of it or simply because they could only remember one or two odd details when I wanted to hear all the details.

Some time you must write me a clinical account of it including everything from the first time that the thought or decision to make love with a certain man came into your mind. Did you walk to his house or go by bus? Were you with him or alone? What was going on in your mind? What were you wearing? The description of his room or rooms. Each thing you said to each other and each movement you made. Did you undress yourself or did he undress you? Each thought as it came into your mind, before, after, and during. Did you have irrelevant thoughts which had nothing to do with what you were doing? And so on, and so on.

It is the little details which can illuminate the whole scene which interest me. Perhaps you would find it too painful to re-create the scene in such detail so soon afterwards – or perhaps you have already forgotten? Have you noticed that seduction is invariably more succesful in films (in spite of the obvious censorship limitations) than in novels? In novels it is always given great structural importance but treated as a thing (never dissected or analysed), as if it were a loaf of bread or a chair or something everyone is supposed to know about. I find this very strange. Anyway, before you let yourself forget you must write down a methodical analysis of the event. If you are shy or have become virginal again you can call the girl Cinderella. I had better stop talking about this or you may think that I have a perverted obsession!

To get back to my other appetites (besides girls) I am about to cook my supper. Lamb chops and salad. What are you eating now? ...

All my love.

Think of me sometimes,

Jim

To Gabriele

Redcliffe Square

1 November 1962

Dearest Gabs,

I had just written you a long and very depressed letter saying that I thought it would be best if we didn't write to each other any more because waiting for the postman was too demoralising; then your letter came and I promptly forgot about being demoralised.

My job is coming to an end in a week or two so I'm very busy again looking for another job. I've decided that I want to go abroad again; I'm tired of living in England, especially now that the weather is getting bad. Perhaps I will come and live in Germany. If you know the names of any language schools in Munich you might send me their addresses. But perhaps you would prefer me not to come to Munich; in any case, I would be careful not to disturb you in your affairs (or '*affaires*'). Besides, now that *Der Spiegel* is in trouble [9] I think that Germany needs one or two more liberal writers to keep things going! Seriously though, everybody here was very alarmed by the *Der Spiegel* affair – more about the way it was done, than about the idea of censorship. It stirred too many memories.

D.H. Lawrence says somewhere that once you mention the word 'love' then all the feeling in it dies. Sometimes I feel that you are trying to love me because you feel you ought to for some reason, not because you really do. However, in spite of Lawrence, Jim can't resist saying that he loves you, and likes you too if it comes to that ...

And as for girls: two (out of six) girls in my class are in love with their teacher, and a third seems to be hesitating as to whether she should let herself go or not. One is Persian and the other is French but both are rather immature, virgins, religious ... and don't interest me at all, although I take a paternal interest in them during lessons. I think the reason for this success is that my lessons are so boring that my students have to find something else to think about ...

[My] book came back from the publishers with the news that they thought it was excellent but that they would have too much trouble selling it to be able to take the risk of publishing it; they added that they were 'immensely interested' in anything else I might write. Another publisher has it now ...

Lots of love,
Jim

To Gabriele

Redcliffe Square
15 November 1962

Dearest Gabs,

... You know, from what you say (and partly from what I've always thought myself) I think that we won't really be able to decide how we feel about each other until we've been together again for a while. Everything that happened in Rotherfield was condensed into such a short time and it was over so quickly (it seems so now, anyway!) that it somehow seems unreal. But while you were in England I certainly thought that you did not love me very much. D'you remember how I sulked on the day we went to the inquest together? The reason was that –

No. That is too much like dissecting a corpse and the summer is still very much alive for me, although now so distant. And if you think that, in some way or other, you are able to love me then I am the last person who is going to try to persuade you of the opposite. Let us simply wait patiently until we are able to see each other again and in the meantime try not to tell each other or ourselves any lie about the way we feel. Patiently! I don't think of you all the time or, indeed, very often but at least once a day in some moment of loneliness the thought of you comes into my mind for a few seconds and I long to see that magnificent smile of yours ... And remember that we are friends as well, and were friends for two years before we met this summer so we can talk and write to each other as friends; the wonderful thing about you is that not only do I need you and find you attractive as a woman but I also like to talk to you as I do to very few other people I've ever met ...

Perhaps I will go home for a few days at Christmas. I wish I could decide what to do. At the moment I am just living from day to day, like a vegetable of some kind. Did I tell you that a French girl I used to go out with in Toulon last year used to call me a '*crustacée*' or a mollusc or something. She used to get very angry. At the time I thought this was unjust but now I am not so sure. However, I am still about to start writing again.

My grandmother [10] died last week. I was very sorry about this because she was very kind and gentle, and loved myself and my brothers very much. And I always used to forget to send her postcards and so on. There are many times when I hate myself for being so selfish.

To go back to your letter and the problem of being connected to 'another man'. Really this is not so important for me. Life is made up of separate experiences and I do not see why all the old ones should be cancelled out in favour of the present one. For example, the fact that I now love you does not mean that I must forget that I was once in love with a Danish girl in Spain or that I should try to pretend to myself now that it was not important. On the contrary, these experiences have become as much part of ourselves as the scars on our knees where we fell and cut ourselves as children. And it is just the same whether the experiences are pleasant or unpleasant. Having polio was an unpleasant experience while it happened but I'm not sorry it happened now because it has allowed me to look into a whole new window of what it means to be alive and young at a certain time in a certain place. Anything is worthwhile which allows us a greater understanding. Don't you think so? Your [previous] affair is a part of your life and a part of you, just as you and I are now a part of each other's lives and of each other. You must accept this first affair* and as for me, we can only wait and see whether the Jim you gave some love to in Rotherfield was a ghost who only existed by reaction or a real Jim.

Anyway, now this Jim (or some other Jim) is tired and is going to go to bed, a narrow, virginal bed, because it is a quarter to two. Goodnight and sleep well. I wish I could tuck(le) [*sic*] you up!

All my love,

Jim

*[*handwritten*] And the best way to accept it is to re-create it, as a writer, without omitting the smallest thought, gesture or detail

– without either shyness or *pudeur*. [11]

To Patsy Cumming

Redcliffe Square
4 December 1962

My dear Patsy,

I bought this air-mail letter some time in August in order to reply to you and *me voilà*. Further comment is useless. Anyway, this is to wish you a Merry Christmas. As I write there is a thick fog outside the window but as I live underground this makes little difference ... I hope the only unpublished writers you know no longer include your-self, for, unfortunately, they still include me. My book has failed, is still failing as far as I know, in the most irritating manner. Every-body saying it is excellent but declining to publish it. That, the first part anyway, is a slight overstatement, of course, but you get the gen-eral idea. Chatto and Windus came within a whisker of publishing it as a matter of fact. Two of the directors out of three were in favour but they needed unanimity. Cecil Day Lewis was in favour. It's true of course that they must have been rather luke-warmly in favour or else they might have persuaded the third.

Anyway, they called me in for tea and gave me a nice paternal-maternal chat with the Christian names flowing like buttermilk. Then they called up a friend at Secker and Warburg and rec-ommended it to him to read (and he subsequently refused it with a few more woolly compliments). So, so far, all I have had in return for my years of anguish and effort is one cup of tea without sugar. In fair-ness I should add that I don't take sugar. I have sent it somewhere else now ... I have some more ideas for a novel but at the moment lack the energy and *le courage* to write it ... Last Easter with your friends, the children, and that big black dog (and *Don Giovanni*) now seems a most magical time to me ...

All the best to you; I'll write when I'm more decided about my future.

Love
Jim

[*handwritten postscript*] And happy Christmas and New Year. Next year, as I say every year, may be our year.

To Gabriele

Redcliffe Square
9 December 1962

Dearest Gabs,

I'm very sorry that I've taken such ages to reply to your last letter – but I've had a lot on my mind. Looking for another job, mainly. I had an interview a couple of days ago for a job in Sweden but the man who was interviewing me asked me questions in such an offensive manner that I walked out in the middle after telling him what I thought of him; I think that I was as surprised as he was, because usually somebody has to hit me on the head with a hammer before I get angry. Or perhaps I'm getting old. Anyway, this means that I will keep on doing the job that I have at the moment for some time. I'm quite happy with the idea, though, because I'm very excited about the book I'm beginning. I'll tell you more about it when the outlines have become more definite in my mind ...

Another reason why I've taken so long in writing to you is that I've been obsessed by the problem of deciding what shape my life should take ... I think that I would be miserable if I didn't try to keep on as a dedicated writer with the comparative freedom of part-time jobs – although I sometimes have doubts about how free one is!

Anyway, as we only have one life (as far as we know) it seems criminal to me not to do what one really wants to do rather than something else however 'interesting' and however nice it may seem (and continually does seem to me) to have a comfortable house, and a secretary, and a car, and unlimited square meals, and who knows? Perhaps a nice wife and family also. Even if I should be a failure as a writer it still seems wrong to me not to try ...

Apart from that I haven't done much. I've been to a few parties where I invariably get as tight (i.e. drunk) as an owl and then drift home without touching the ground. My friends see this as a sign of me going to the dogs, as we say (or going downhill). But I like the liberating effect that alcohol has on me.

Well, dear Gabriele, how does the summer seem to you now? Impossible that it could ever have happened? Or merely improbable? ... Gabriele, write to me and think of me once in a while....

All my love,
Jim

To Russell McCormmach

Balholm
Saval Park Road
Dalkey
Co. Dublin [12]
Christmas Day 1962

Dear Russ,

... I really think you should come to Europe again ... I think we both stand a better chance of getting a successful play through the indifference-barrier together than separately. I long to be working hard at something again with somebody. The thought of getting up early in the morning and working at something I like doing is just unbelievably good. At present, due to a sapping of my self-confidence and general isolation from people who look at things in the same way I do, my will to work is beginning to crumble at the knees. I should add, by the way, that, as any fool could have told me, my novel having nearly got over the first hurdle has taken a low dive under all subsequent ones: Secker and Warburg wrote me a letter saying in essence (and I don't think I'm being unjust to it) that they thought my book was good but wouldn't make them enough money. It's now with Hutchinson. Another reason is that there are all kinds of eccentrics and illuminati and fallen angels like ourselves in London so that it's just easier to live there. I have a spare bed for you in my room for as long as you want it and could keep you in food, if not always in cigarettes. Do think seriously about this. It might mean a measure of salvation for both of us if you can get together the fare.

One hopeful sign has, however, been emerging from the general degradations of the last months, and that is that I'm caring less and less about the commercial, and/or public success of what I write, and more and more about my own opinion of its quality. One day I may even give up sending things to publishers, or rather, not care whether I sent them or not. Like you I have also come to the conclusion that my personal hard times have exhausted their usefulness as literary material and have become very much more interested in the possibility of creating a (possibly fantastic) world of my own for my novels. Have you read *Henderson the Rain King* by Saul Bellow? I found this book very good and that it started a few interesting trains of thought for my own stuff ...

In London, I have been leading a rather strange life. Mixing on the one hand with assorted and less than more talented 'artistic' fauna who inhabit the district where I live and on the other, up to now anyway, with people I knew at Oxford or Cambridge who have moved, as if on strings, to influential jobs on the better papers, government depts etc. They have been inviting me (I suspect in order to add a little off-beat colour) to their dinner-parties where I sit, tieless, scruffy and speechless while the other guests take it in turns to relate with delicate wit and breeding their various machinations in the world of endeavour. One speaks, the others sit with interested smiles clipped to their lips and inwardly rehearse while waiting their turns. But perhaps I'm being unjust again. At one such party a couple of weeks ago I met a publisher called Graham Greene (a nephew) [13] who told me at great length and after many whiskies not to give up. (I'm always introduced as 'a writer' which causes me great embarrassment. You may recall Gatsby taking Tom Buchanan round his party and introducing him to everyone as 'the polo player'.) ...

All the best to you
Jim

[*Handwritten*] P.S. '62 wasn't our year, after all. Maybe '63?

To Gabriele

48 Redcliffe Square
London S.W.10
13 January 1963

My dearest Gabriele,

... I only spent five days in Ireland and felt very strange while I was there. There were moments, sitting round the dining-table, eating turkey and drinking my father's wine, when it seemed that I had never been away from home. When I had been drinking (I have been drinking a great deal recently) I had a lot of confused memories of Canada and France and Spain and America ... all mixed up together which served as a sort of background to what my mother, father and brother were saying – saying the same things, that is, as they have always said, or so it seemed to me. And these memories were really quite like an unreal dream that lingers on over breakfast and manages to resist reality for a while.

And then, on the day after Christmas, Jack Kirwan [14] and his girl-friend and I went for a long walk on Killiney beach [15] which is completely deserted and bleak at this time of year. We must have walked for about two miles along the beach when a heavy icy rain began to fall. There was no shelter so we decided to walk back by the quickest way along the railway line which runs beside the beach at that point. Returning it seemed to take us hours against the wind and rain, taking too-short steps from one railway sleeper to the next, following the shining curve of metal because we were unable to lift our heads and look where we were going on account of the rain blowing into our faces. At last we got home and changed our clothes and then got pleasantly drunk in front of a blazing wood fire in Jack's house. That's really all I remember of Christmas ...

The snow and ice have been so thick here that it has even become an ordeal to go to the shops two or three hundred yards away ... My life is generally a little empty at the moment, but I think this is mainly the fault of the winter. It is difficult to be passionate about anything when you are struggling to keep warm all the time. As far as heating is concerned English houses are positively medieval. Still, surprisingly enough, I seem to be keeping warmer than I did during last year's terrible winter in Toulon when I had to go down to the beach and collect driftwood for my fire. I'm beginning to think it is about time that Fate owed me a change of luck, certainly as regards my material existence. Will I see you this Spring or Summer? I hope so much that I will.

I would love to know what you are doing and thinking at the moment. I feel sure that you must have found a satisfactory boyfriend by now ... Are you happy? I hope that you are. Have you continued making plans for your trip round the world? Write me a long letter telling me anything and everything that comes into your mind.

Love to you,
Jim

To Gabriele

Redcliffe Square
21 January 1963

My dear Gabs,

... I am glad that you have found a reason to be happy again and hope that things will turn out the way you want – whichever way that may be. Your new boy-friend certainly sounds much more suitable for you than your old boy-friends – and that, I suppose, includes me. And what do I think about it? ('Everyone suspects himself of at least one of the cardinal virtues – honesty has always been mine. I'm the one completely honest person that I have ever met.' – Scott Fitzgerald: *The Great Gatsby*; I quote from memory.) Well, I wouldn't be entirely honest if I said that I didn't feel some twinge of jealousy – partly hurt pride, I guess, but then I only just received your letter this morning, read as far as the first mention of the boy-friend, went out to work, and finished it just now. It usually takes me a little time to get my feelings into perspective and so I may know better in a few days what they really are. And of course, any great concerto of emotion is muted by the fact that I have been expecting this for some time and so had, to some extent, got used to the idea already and had always known that you didn't love me in any particularly earth-moving way, as a woman ought to love a man ...

Incidentally, I detest the notion that the only way to write a contemporary novel is by using satire; the essence of literature, it seems to me, is beauty through compassion, whereas the basis of satire is standing aside and judging, however 'nicely' (i.e. patronizingly) this may be done. But perhaps we will be able to argue about this at some other time in some other place.

To return to our love-lives; I have been less fortunate than you (I can't imagine myself being able to shiver ever when somebody kisses my hands)*! but have had, for a reason which escapes me, some success with girls recently; ... Somehow I always seem to find girls (you excepted) who are down on their luck. Well, some affection and some sex but no love. [One] stayed with me for a while after Christmas but has now gone home again ... It was nice to have her here – she cooked meals and there was always someone to talk to – but I found it hard to write while she was here so in a way I was glad when she went home. I've been painting a lot recently to help me relax after writing and, thanks to some elementary instruction from my sculptor friend, [16] I believe I've made some progress. One thing I've found is that it's much easier to paint on canvas.

Perhaps this is a gloomy letter – but I think I was already gloomy before yours arrived. I suppose I'm depressed by the fact that I'll be 28 in a couple of days time. How did I get to be so old so soon? And anyway, to hell with it.

Listen, dearest Gab, don't write to me again until I next write to you. I think I'll let the sediment in the water settle for a few months and then we can begin to be real 'friend-friends' instead of 'lover-friends' ...

Love to you,

Jim

[*Handwritten*] *except when it's cold at the same time!

P.S. I was offered a full-time job but decided not to take it so that I could work on my book. Also I'm beginning to enjoy living from hand to mouth!

To Russell McCormmach

Redcliffe Square

23 January 1963

Dear Russ,

... I bought a new typewriter ribbon this morning with a view to creating something but having spent half an hour staring at the (miserable) gas fire without a single promising idea, I've now given it up and decided to write you a letter instead. At the moment I'm caught between the belief that novels aren't for giving information (whatever else they may be for) and the belief that the only way out of the problem is by artificial tinkerings with style. Perhaps the only way out of it is to abandon novel-writing and turn to poetry or stuff for tv that will make me money. And yet there are books I admire and wish I had written ... Perhaps you don't know what I'm talking about; the above lines, it's true, give off the musty odour of those dull ravings that a lot of minor writers are given to ...

On the personal front it's bleak winter here, the most debilitating I remember. Little birds are frozen upside down in ditches and the butter is hard to spread; I remember now that you don't like butter and had a sudden vision of you in Ireland. I wish you'd come back. Another sign of crack is that I've started reading newspapers again and mutter trivia to myself with scandalised incredulity. In this evening's paper, for instance, there's an item about a lady who was found dead of exposure in her living-room, aged 56. This is perfectly true.

I've been painting a lot myself recently but find some frustration there also; partly because I've never got further in painting than expressing (but not satiating) occasional lusts by painting nudes ... and I haven't the courage to let go of writing, as you seem to have done, and give myself over to painting. My talent, anyway, is small ...

I'm still teaching in the afternoons although this seems increasingly futile. I can't remember ever spending so long without attempting something positive. Do let me know how you are.

Yours
Jim

To Patsy Cumming

Redcliffe Square
18 February 1963

Dearest Patsy,

Many moons, *hélas*, since my last letter but here I am, anyway, on the keys again ... Thanks for the *New Yorker* article ... The Murphys [17] didn't impress me ... but then I've always been suspicious of sheer charm and good breeding ... and I suppose I was a bit irritated by the smug suggestion [it] conveyed of 'our boy' deliberately charming all those wild, iconoclastic Europeans into eating out of his hand. It did throw light on Fitzgerald though and on the thing which I've always found most difficult to understand about him: namely how such a good writer could have been so childish and immature a person for such a lot of the time ... My final, slightly defensive, feeling about it all is that, however patronising the Murphys were, and in spite of the giant painting of the inside of a watch [18] Murphy exhibited at the Salon (!), Fitzgerald was worth twice what they were because he had a real feeling for words and people ...

You'll be glad to hear that I've got through the publication barrier at last and am due to leap into print next September or October. Hutchinson finally accepted my book, but at a time when a lot of my enthusiasm for it, never enormous, had already evaporated. However, this does something for my morale as you can imagine and will give me more confidence for the next one. The money side is a little help (£50 now and £100 on publication, with possibly some more to follow if it's a success) and on the strength of it I have taken a rest from teaching. This is wonderful. I'm now laying plans for working during the summer, possibly as a courier, to save enough money to retire to write on a Greek island next winter. I couldn't stand another winter in England. This one has been unbelievably terrible for me and is still going on regardless. And the English I find increasingly hard to take.

That's about all I can rake out of my mind at the moment except that I keep wishing that I was back in Bouilloux-Lafont camping on the floor with the cat and the hot *croissants* for breakfast from round the corner, and you stopping your 2 chevaux[19] in the middle of streets to consult maps.

With love,
Jim

To Russell McCormmach

Redcliffe Square
6 March 1963

My dear Russ,

... About a month ago I got word from a publisher (Hutchinson) that they would take my novel and publish it in September. I spent about two weeks in steadily decreasing euphoria ... The evenings I find virtually impossible to get through without first anaesthetising myself with alcohol – and alcohol of any kind is too expensive in England to be able to do this effectively and repeatedly. I have definitely decided to get married now to the first reasonable person who comes along, though looking into my past ten years I can only think of about two girls whom I would have judged to be reasonable. All this is because I feel, banal though it may be, unwanted ... with the added factor that I can't think of anybody I want to feel wanted by. Enough of this nonsense.

I would feel better about my book if I thought it was really good but, as I think I said to you before, I don't. Besides it doesn't really seem to belong to me any more and my main interest in it is financial. I would die laughing if it made me some money. This is hardly likely however as it is sure to be massacred by the highbrow critics at the same time as being out of reach of the 'sheer escapism' readers. However, it does represent something to me, if only the fact that I've got through the publication sound barrier (as you once called it) and helps me to think of myself as 'a writer' rather than a naive idiot. I will, of course, send you a copy ... trusting that you won't regard it as my last word on the novel.

Did you go through with the karate idea? ... I have, in fact, often thought about it myself, my trouble being that I'm not strong enough, as a result of polio, to hurt anybody no matter how scientifically aimed my blows. It would be most refreshing to feel dangerous and arrogant for a change.

They gave me an advance ... and I hastened to leave my job at the language school. I just couldn't stand looking at the same faces anymore and walking through the same streets to get to the place. I have now spent most of this but I am doing a couple of evening classes per week for the London County Council and this will help me to get by until I think of something ...

All the best to you,
Jim

P.T.O. Now I come to think of it Céline's *Voyage au Bout de la Nuit*[20] is very similar to *The Tin Drum*, [21] and rather better except for the passages on America. I've just got hold of Malcolm Lowry's *Hear Us O Lord from Heaven Thy Dwelling Place*. [22] I thought *Under the Volcano* was wonderful ...

To Gabriele

Redcliffe Square
9 March 1963

Dearest Gabs,

Friend or ex-lover, I can't help wondering how you are. The days are still frighteningly long though, even if I have got used to the idea that – etc.

The nervous illness I had in Toulon last year came back a few days ago, and with it the mental darkness which used to make me feel so tense and wretched without any reason. I used to think it was because I wasn't having any success as a writer but since I found a publisher for my book that reason doesn't work any more. I saw *The Eclipse* by Antonioni [23] last week and realised that he knows exactly what is happening to me. At one place Monica Vitti says: 'There are days when a chair, a man, and a book are all the same thing.' Anyway, I feel a bit better ... *A Man from 'Elsewhere'* [24] comes out on the 9th of Sept. price 18 shillings (rather more than it's worth, I'm afraid) and I've decided to leave England by the beginning of October; I just couldn't stand another winter like the one I've been through, and by this time I thoroughly detest England. I have been considering spending the winter on a Greek island, possibly Hydra or Corfu, but I'm afraid of what such complete isolation might do to my already rickety nervous system since this psychological trouble came back, and I don't suppose I will go there unless I can find someone to go with me. Otherwise I've thought of Munchen. I still want to learn German and there seems to be a lively intellectual life there. If I don't like it I'll go back to France ... By the way, if I do come to Munchen I will lead a peaceful life of my own and won't bother you at all; I've quite accepted the fact that the '*C'était à Rotherfield – en Angleterre*' period of my (our) life is over and finished.

... I intend to go home at Easter and try to get this other book finished before going abroad in the Autumn. I will probably only keep this room in Redcliffe Square for another two weeks so if you write after that, write to Ireland ...

I thought I saw you in the street the other day!

With love,
Jim

To Russell McCormmach

Balholm
Saval Park Road
Dalkey
Co. Dublin
4 April 1963

My dear Russ,

... Earls Court and Redcliffe Square have finally got the better of me and have sneered at the vigorous resistance to their gloom that I've been offering all these months ... The one thing I have to report is that I have been adopted by a couple of pleasant and (relatively) sweet-natured call-girls whom I met by accident. At the beginning there was a vague idea that I should write their story but I never really took this seriously as it isn't my line. Anyway we are now good friends and they have provided me with something of an *entrée* into the underworld, not to mention first-hand accounts of some of the most unbelievable perversions. I'll give you a fuller run-down when I have assembled my ideas a bit better – I've only known [the girls] a couple of weeks.

I'm too weighed down spiritually by the thought of packing to write any more at the moment. I have a mental picture of you in your room at Oxford facing the same problem with no more resolution than I can muster at the moment. I swear every time I have to move that I will buy no more concrete objects and reduce my clothes to two of everything ... I read a couple of Graham Greene's recently with sympathy: *The Power and the Glory*, and *A Burnt-Out Case* ...

All the best to you,
Jim

To Gabriele

c/o G. Arnott [25]
23 Ridgmount Gardens
London W.C.1
[*handwritten and arrow*] Address for the next couple of weeks
15 May 1963

My dear Gabriele,

... I had almost given up hope of hearing from you again ... I have a cold at the moment and as I am feverish I take no responsibility for what I write. However, there is a great deal that I should tell you if I can think how and where to begin.

First, personal news: my 'literary success' as you call it has left me comparatively unmoved, as my idea of what a novel should be has changed drastically since I wrote *Elsewhere*. I'm not yet ashamed of it (perhaps I will be in a few years' time) but I'm no longer very excited by it: my idea of a novel now is something violent and wild, and poetic which all my enemies will tear to shreds in a frenzy of uncontrollable hate. Now I come to think of it, I don't have any enemies either. Well, perhaps you know what I mean. Strangely enough, the proof copy of my book arrived at the same time as your letter. I couldn't help being rather excited, though, to see it in print.

I've just finished writing the first draft of a television play (a really dreadful one) with which I hope to make some money and there also seems to be a good chance of working on a television adaptation of a play by Max Frisch for the BBC with a friend of mine called William Wordsworth (the great grandson of the celebrated but dreadful 19th century nature poet). From all this you may deduce that I've given up the idea of becoming a serious writer in favour of becoming a wealthy parasite. Well, you can rest assured. Come what may, I intend to leave England in October and write a great book before next March so that it can be published the following September ...

Rotherfield has now sunk peacefully into the past for me and is nothing more than a pleasant memory. I'm glad of this because I was very much disorientated at first and the whole thing became mixed up in my mind with more general feelings of pessimism and futility in my life. Can we be real friends now? I hope so ...

I've been living the most extraordinary life in the last few weeks since I met a call-girl (!!!) who decided she was in love with me and introduced me to all her prostitute friends, gangsters, pimps etc. I had no idea before just what the London underworld was like. I was astonished at the kind of life these girls lead and seem to have been living in a kind of dream ever since I have known them. All the values one has always accepted without question suddenly melt away and it gives you a sensation of vertigo. [The] girl who introduced me to it all seems to be genuinely a very nice person but completely amoral. This made it rather thrilling to be with her. We went to Paris together the weekend before last on an impulse and ... no, there is so much to describe it would be better if I could see your face to make sure that I don't shock you too much. I haven't seen her for about ten days now as some of my fascination wore off and she went to Milano with a rich businessman!! Needless to say I was careful not to become emotionally involved with her. That would have been a disaster big enough to form the story of an Italian opera! ...

I'm still looking for a nice girl to marry (as you can imagine my present girl-friend isn't exactly suitable!), partly because I have the feeling that a stable relationship with a girl would make it a lot easier for me to write a great novel – but this may be an illusion. There's a terrifying story by Albert Camus [26] about an artist who does some very good work when he's unhappy, then, as a result, becomes successful and well-adjusted and spends the rest of his life merely chatting pleasantly to his friends and enjoying himself! Perhaps, in any case, I'm too fundamentally neurotic ever to have a stable relationship for long. *Du bist am Ende – was du bis* [27] as Mephistopheles says to Faust. Though I'm not sure that I entirely agree ...

Your life now is beginning to open out like a flower.

With love,
Jim

To Gabriele

36 Pembridge Road [28]
Notting Hill Gate
London W.11
9 June 1963

My dear Gabriele,

[This] is mainly to wish you best of luck for your exam ... I feel sure that you will have your mind on Tacitus and Goethe and my friend Bill Wordworth's noble but boring ancestor. So, like any vain writer, I will write again later when I imagine that I am getting all your attention. Incidentally, I have only just moved into this new house in a rather lively part of London. I wish now that I had known London better when you were here last year, and known all the people I do now – you would have had a much more interesting holiday ...

You will have read of the Profumo scandal [29] that has broken out here. Wordsworth has been friendly with Stephen Ward (the 'doctor' and *eminence grise* behind the whole affair) for some years and my call-girl friends know Christine Keeler, the girl in the business, so I have been very well placed to hear what has been going on behind the scenes and have been watching the case unfolding with fascination. In fact, there are one or two other members of Parliament who have also misbehaved and who are trembling in case they suffer the same fate! There are some wonderful opportunities for blackmailers here!

I'd give a lot to be able to talk to you now – there are so many things to tell you. But for both talking and writing one needs leisure, the very thing that I seem to lack just now. My dream is that one day I will own a big house in Paris and be able to get all my friends together to talk and read and write and, above all, relax for a while. I'm determined to do this sometime. You know, I'm sure your studies and your love-affair will make a different person of you. I'm fascinated to see what she will be like; there are so many things I don't know about you already since last year.

Love to you and best of luck for those exams (which are, I firmly believe, an invention of the Devil to paralyse youth).

Jim

To Gabriele

Pembridge Road, Notting Hill
26 July 1963

My dear Gabriele,

... I have been working like a slave, drinking like a fish and arguing with everyone like – I don't know what – an Irishman, I suppose. All this is no excuse for not writing to you and I feel very angry with myself for not doing so. All I can say is that this is the first day that I have not felt so tired out that I could do anything else but sleep.

Conventional ideas of morality have been taking a terrific shaking here in London for the past few weeks and today is the day that Wordsworth's friend, Doctor Ward, the man who introduced Profumo, Lord Astor and others to the girl, is due to be sentenced. If he is sentenced, in my opinion, it will be a gross miscarriage of justice and he'll be the victim of bourgeois morality – so perhaps I'll be feeling angry again tonight ... [30]

Love to you,
Jim

To Russell McCormmach

Pembridge Road,
Notting Hill
23 August 1963

Dear Russ,

Many apologies for the long silence from me. This has, of course, been very much on my conscience but I haven't been writing any letters or, indeed, anything whatsoever. I don't intend this to be one of my usual peevish letters so I may as well just say that I haven't done anything or been anywhere since I last wrote, largely crippled by indecision and neurotic laziness, and leave it at that without making it into a tirade against the fates.

You should be receiving a copy of my book shortly as I posted one off to you last week. The only one I've sent apart from one to my parents. For years I've been gloating to myself about the thrill of sending copies to all my friends and enemies but now that I have some to send I can't be bothered. I don't think it's very good myself though I think there are some successful pages. I'd like very much to hear your opinion if you can find anything to say about it. I had a letter from Bob Cumming from Thailand not long ago in which he said that he didn't think it mattered that my book was no good. This hadn't occurred to me at the time but now that it does it makes me feel a lot better about it. In any case, I'm determined to have a better one finished by next Spring ... I'll be leaving here in about a month's time so if you write after that write to Dublin. I think that I'll go back to France but possibly to Germany or, failing all else, Ireland.

My book doesn't come out for another 3 weeks but I was interviewed [31] the other day by a girl with spots who asked me if I wrote with a typewriter or in longhand and said she knew that Sayer (the hero of my book) wasn't really a Communist.

'You mean that you knew he was one of us,' I said.

'That's right' she said.

> All the best to you,
> Jim

Farrell's first novel, A Man from Elsewhere, *was not 'massacred' by the critics, and in the summer of 1963 he returned to France, to take up a teaching job in Paris.*[32] *He had just begun his most autobiographical novel,* The Lung. *It is a sardonic twist on his own ordeal, in which the central character, Martin Sands, endures polio and its aftermath in a hospital setting.*

To Gabriele

> Fondation des Etats-Unis
> 15 Blvd Jourdan
> Cité Universitaire [*sic*]
> PARIS 14e
> le 5 octobre 1963

Dear Gabs,

... As you see I decided not to come to Germany after all and I have a job here in Paris. My main reason was that I wouldn't have had enough money to live in Germany without working for very long and it is so much easier for me to get the kind of job I want here: that is, a job where I don't have much work to do. Another thing is that I must write another book this winter, and a country which I know already is much less distracting. I don't have to worry about learning the language and being confused by new impressions etc ...

A lot has happened to me recently but I must leave that to another letter.

Love to you,
Jim

To Russell McCormmach

Fondation des Etats-Unis, Paris
Sunday 6 October 1963

Dear Russ,

Very many thanks for your letter which interested me a great deal, particularly what you had to say about the book. What you say about writing another book where *Elsewhere* left off and one that shows us 'how a man who has learned to doubt all final answers can nevertheless live a purposeful, value-centred life' ... is, of course, what makes the book finally a failure: that I merely described a situation that we all already knew existed without really having anything new to say about it. Sayer tried to give himself an artificial direction, as I think a lot of people do, but wasn't sufficiently good at self-deception to bring it off. He had kept the image alive by holding his emotional and sensual life at bay so naturally everything cracked at the same time. You're quite right to say that he had changed a great deal by the end of the book.

The reviews were pretty favourable on the whole, with the exception of the *New Statesman* 'unreal and cerebral' – 'dreamed up out of literature and the current French cinema' (this gave me one or two uneasy twinges) and the *Sunday Telegraph* which was rather patronising. *The Times* just described the theme and added 'Mr Farrell handles his material with an assurance uncommon in a first novel'. *The Observer* said a lot of kind things about it but thought there was too much evidence of manipulation and puppetry ... and so on. There are still a lot of reviews I haven't seen as I left England soon after it appeared.

I now have another job as assistant for a year ... here in Paris this time. I still hope to produce another book by next spring, but this will depend largely on whether I can get away with doing a minimum of work at the school (a girls' school this time). This place I am staying is a sort of international students' doss-house (I have to share a room with a Lebanese but my financial situation is such that I can't do anything about this for a while) largely full of young Americans talking too loudly in the lobby about their 'projects'. This freezes me to the marrow. The advantage is that it is very cheap and that I can get meals half the price I can anywhere else without having to make agonising decisions about what I want to eat. Generally speaking I find that I care less for Paris than I used to. I wish now that I'd asked for a job in the country. But who knows before evening what the day will bring? (Excuse the platitude but it has been pursuing me mercilessly for the last week as I felt exasperation rising). What I mean is: perhaps this is the year when a beautiful, intelligent, loving girl (maybe rich too) will come into my life. And other tattered fantasies ...

I'll write again about my new book. For the moment it's too nebulous for me to describe without talking it to pieces. But do write to me whenever you have time.

All the best to you,
Jim

To Patsy Cumming

Fondation des Etats-Unis, Paris
12 November 1963

Dear Patsy,

... I'm very glad indeed that you seem to like my book so much and your letter has done something towards restoring my own faith in it. Actually, I think there are good things in it too, but not really enough of them. My biggest cause for dissatisfaction is that I find something artificial about it and I don't think this is simply because I was present while it was being put together. Part of the trouble is stylistic, I think. Sometimes the cadence of sentences becomes sonorous to the point of meaninglessness. Strange, though, that you should select the phrase I liked best in the book ('the complicated flower'). This cheered me up no end ... The extraordinary thing was that the reactions as to its virtues and faults seemed to be entirely haphazard and changing from one review to the next. However, it is all over now and condemned to darkness. In a way it was something of an ordeal. I understand now why writers don't read reviews. I've begun another, very different, about which I won't talk for the moment as there are things that are still not clear to me.

As you see from the address I'm now back here, staying at the

Cité Université, and working as an 'assistant' again. This is really the only job I find I can write at – or maybe it's being in France. Anyway, this means that I have free time and eat more than in London. Looking back on last year in London it all seems to have been a grisly mistake – except for a few nice people I met.

I'm reading a biography of Tolstoy[33] and my amazement and admiration grow with every page ... He really had the talent I most admire – that of playing everything for keeps. I know you'll tell me this is sheer romanticism. I envy you your work with the theatre. I long also for a *travail d'équipe*. Camus, as you know, got a big kick out of this too.

Love to you,
Jim

To Gabriele

Fondation des Etats-Unis, Paris
19 November 1963

Dearest Gabs,

Very many thanks for your letter which I received ten minutes ago. I'm replying immediately as I'm bored stiff with the book I've been reading and bored stiff generally. And tired. I find I can only write in the mornings now ... and some mornings I must go and teach English at a girls' school (where I'm the only man-teacher, in fact, man of any kind, in the establishment). I should add that the head-mistress is delighted with me. She told a third person (who then told me) that she thought I was just like a big brother to her little girls! I'm not sure whether I should feel pleased or insulted that she regards me as being so harmless ...

You criticise me for the way I speak of girls. Unfortunately I can no longer remember what it was I said about them. Actually, as you know, I quite like girls but I don't find them very intelligent. In my whole life I have only met 3½ girls who [*sic*] I found as intelligent as a number of men I have met. I wonder what you will think of Heidi (the girl with whom I hope to walk in the Bavarian snow). In the winter (which was very cold in London last year) she was warm, in the summer she had an attractive sun-tan, and all the year round she had nice sharp, white teeth. Above all I like her name which has a certain *valeur touristique* for an Irishman ...

I hope you won't let university defeat you the way Oxford (I feel) defeated me. I spent my time there immobilized by my disgust for the other people. And yet I suppose it was an opportunity and not an attempt to destroy me ...

The rain falls on Paris, on the Seine, on De Gaulle, on Montparnasse, on the graves in the Père-Lachaise, on all the grey roof-tops and on the grey, deeply discouraged head of your friend:

Jim

To Gabriele

Fondation des Etats-Unis, Paris
[undated] 1963

Chère Gabs,

... I will almost certainly be spending Christmas in Munich as I have a rendezvous there with a German girl (one of my ex-students). [34] We have planned to meet there a couple of days after Christmas and then go and stay for a week in some little village in Southern Bavaria, stay in a Gasthof and go for long walks in the snow. This sounds idyllic. My nerves are in shreds with the noise and traffic in Paris ...

This morning while I was drinking my coffee I had a sudden inspiration to spend the summer on a Greek island, reading and writing. Life is incredibly cheap there, they say. Why don't you three [35] come too? Then we could rent a house ...

I'm very tense again and in my book I can only see the difficulties. Sometimes I feel that as a writer I'm already washed up. I'm reading a biography of Tolstoy at the moment and it's comforting to think that he felt the same and yet still went on to write *War and Peace* and *Anna Karenina*. What a man! I'm sure that genius is largely a question of energy.

I think that you'll find that I've changed a lot when we meet. The Rotherfield 'Jim' already seems a complete stranger to me ...

Enough of this nonsense.

Lots of love,
Jim

To Russell McCormmach

Fondation des Etats-Unis, Paris
21 December 1963

Dear Russ,

Many thanks for your letter. As regards what you say about long vacations and little money, I'd much rather have it that way around. I hate working at anything my heart isn't a hundred per cent in. And the longer the vacation the more sensation (anyway) of freedom one gets and of controlling however modestly one's own destiny. And lack of money becomes merely another element, like water or air, in which one learns to live naturally. This sounds remarkably optimistic but then for once I seem to have enough money ...

I'm glad you're thinking of attacking another novel this spring and hope it gives you some satisfaction. The one I'm working on now is still a shapeless salad of ideas and images and obstinately refuses all my attempts to explain to myself what it's all about ... As far as my job goes, I teach 11 hours a week and do no preparation or correcting (it's only conversation) but to get to school must travel for close on an hour in the *métro*. In all I must do about 9 hours in the métro per week. During this time, crushed and gasping like fish I saw in a Russian documentary about trawlers in the Sea of Azov, I try to learn German and have made a little progress.

I had a letter from the publisher the other day enclosing a panegyric from the *Pretoria News* of all things (I gather this must be a Sth African paper) and the news that sales were 'ticking' satisfactorily towards the 2,000 mark. The use of the word 'ticking' made it sound as if there was a certain inevitability about it, like a taxi meter. However, I doubt if there is the vaguest chance of them reprinting even if they sell all they have ...

I have a heavy cold which I'm sure has translated itself into the puddingy texture of this letter. In any case, I have been going through one of my customary periods of low vitality and have lacked the energy to do anything constructive except think of ways of dodging going to work ...

I've been reading a good short story by Malcolm Lowry in the latest issue of *The Paris Review*. [36] I must get this to the post office. The compliments of the season, by the way, (he added urbanely).

Your friend,
Jim

75

Farrell completed The Lung *in Paris, where his closest friend became a literary-minded Moroccan doctor, Claude Simha, whose medical training was a help in the accurate recall of the polio experience. Few letters exist from this period. Anxious to leave Paris once he had sent his manuscript to his agent Jonathan Clowes in London, and on edge about its fate, Farrell took up Claude Simha's suggestion to stay for a while with a colleague, Dr Elie Harar, who had a remote practice in Morocco at Ait Ouvrir, high in the Atlas Mountains.*

To Franz Beer [37]

Postcard from Marrakesh
[Postmark 7 November 1964]

... The weather is beautiful and I am working well, but am too isolated – I'm beginning to get bored! Most people speak only Arabic. So I am thinking of going away again in a few weeks, not sure where to – probably Paris, then London or Dublin. My contract is still dragging on. I'm beginning to wonder if they are not changing their mind!

Regards
Jim

While lingering in Morocco he attempted to write a money-making potboiler – 'a gangster book', as he called it – but anxiety over silence about the proposed contract for The Lung *drew him back to London later that month. Christmas, as usual, meant a few restless days at home in Dublin.*

Works in Progress
London
1965–66

To Russell McCormmach

Balholm
Saval Park Road
Dalkey
Co. Dublin
22 December 1964

Dear Russ,

Our correspondence seems to have taken another low dive again. This is something in the nature of a signal rocket to re-establish contact ... My life continues in the same vein. Getting older but not wiser. I planned to spend the winter in Marrakesh where I have a doctor friend but got bored after a couple of months when the scenery had worn off and so came home. I'll spare you my impressions of Morocco and Arabs. I had no money, of course, or I'd have stayed in Paris again.

I have another book [1] coming out sometime, probably next Fall, possibly in the summer. When he first read it the publisher was ultra-enthusiastic. He gave it to his readers who were infra-enthusiastic. There was some haggling about whether they were going to publish it. Finally they decided they would, largely I suppose because my other rotten book got good reviews. I should have been watching all this with the coldly sardonic smile of the Genius watching lesser mortals make fools of themselves but I had a sneaking feeling that so many readers (3) couldn't be wrong. Besides, I needed the money ... pitiful amount though it be. I'm still waiting for it, of course. Generally speaking, though, I think this book is better than the last. If only because it's more original. I'm now dashing off a sub-Chandler thriller [2] which I hope will make me some money ...

The other vague purpose behind this letter is to enquire whether [your] college is likely to need a French Assistant ... Last year I met some Americans who had enlisted as post-grad. students and had been given grants to teach Beginners' Courses although they could not speak French and only had the most elementary idea of the language ... If I'm ever to get back to the States this seems the most likely way to do it – until I become a seedy Grand Old Man of Letters that is. I don't think I can wait that long. I'm toying with the idea of doing a play about Gilles de Rais, [3] a very bizarre contemporary and friend of Joan of Arc ...

A merry Christmas uh huh. Let me hear from you.

> All the best,
> Jim

Diary fragment
[undated] 1965
Coming off the Irish boat early, an old man in the tube on the way to Marble Arch. He looked rather like an older and more unkempt Martin Gilbert, [4] something to do with the way he peered from behind his glasses, I think. 'I wish I was dead!' he kept saying. His wife had died three years previously; he'd spent the night sitting up. He, at first, refused a shilling I offered him for a sandwich. He had a good pair of boots, said he often spent the night in church.

To Russell McCormmach

> 170 Westbourne Park Road [5]
> London W.2.
> 15 February 1965

Dear Russ,

... I haven't much news and what I have isn't good. The first reactions to my thriller weren't good. The main trouble being, apparently, that I turned it into a satire on itself. This was a calculated risk. I got bored with it, you see, but thought that there was enough humour in it to make up for the decrease in horror. I could re-write it, I suppose, and maybe I will. For the moment I have a craving to write something good, however, and wouldn't mind letting it slither away down to the limbo to which all my attempts to make money appear to be doomed. I've been ruminating the idea of doing a love-story. To write a love-story that would be moving without being naive, simple-minded, sentimental, sordid, unreal or any of the other thousand and one ghastly things it might be – this seems a supreme challenge ...

[A] few days after I'd written to you I plunged into the American Embassy in Dublin ... and was given a list of colleges with French departments. The man I saw there told me the same as you – that it was pretty late to be applying but advised me to write to a large number. Well, partly because I was feverishly re-writing the thriller at this time (little knowing that it was all fruitless) and partly because I couldn't face the idea of actually writing the letters, I kept putting it off until I deemed it to be safely too late for this year. It is, however, my intention to try next year by which time I'll try to arm myself with an M.A. All this reads very much like a case-history from a psychiatrist's textbook I was reading not long ago.

The teaching assistantship was, in fact, all I had in mind. Brandishing my two published novels, my MA and my Third from Oxford, what college could possibly resist me? Let's not go into that. Another thing I might do is to look around for some kind of foundation or scholarship ... Incidentally, let me recommend to you a slim volume of Nabokov autobiography published here under the title *Speak Memory* ... Very good indeed. I'm looking forward to reading *Herzog* [6] which was recently published here and had excellent reviews ...

All best wishes,
Jim

To Russell McCormmach

c/o Arnott
23 Ridgmount Gardens
London WC 1
16 March 1965

Dear Russ,

[The] address I gave you collapsed into the rubble of all our poor aspirations. I never even got to spend a night there, as a matter of fact. The reasons why are too boring to go into but they included the owner going bankrupt with some of my money and a gaping hole in the floorboards ... After this fiasco I lived in a big old house by the river in Richmond. This would have been quite idyllic but the house was full of people. The landlady was an arty woman who locked her doors every afternoon and meditated for an hour before switching on her favourite tv serial (*The Saint Strikes Back*). She meditated quietly, of course, but the thought of her sitting there on the other side of the wall became very discouraging ... There were also some Paris friends of mine, an unmarried Scandinavian couple, who ceaselessly dismantled each others' egos in interminable Bergmanesque, *Huis Clos* [7] arguments about nothing – at least I imagine they were about nothing – most of the time they were conducted in Swedish which has an agreeable sound at first. Anyway, I moved off after a while. When I left the girl was easily ahead on points. The boy is very charming but weak whereas she has a dash of the old praying mantis in her. Or maybe he loves her more than she loves him.

I haven't made much progress with anything since I last wrote to you. I'll let you know when I do. I think I'll go and live in a greenhouse in Notting Hill Gate next – for £2 a week.

Yours,
Jim

Jim's greenhouse was, in fact, less stark. It was a conservatory annexe at the rear of 35 Palace Gardens Terrace in Kensington, between the ground level and first floor. Overlooking the garden, it was entered from inside the house, via double doors which opened off the return of the main staircase.

To Russell McCormmach

35 Palace Gardens Terrace
London W.8.
Easter Monday 1965

Dear Russ,

Many thanks for your letter ... Odd that you should mention Antonioni as I had just seen, and disliked, his latest film: *Il Desierto Rosso*. [8] His other three major films I liked terrifically but this, apart from some stunning colour photography of industrial areas, seemed to be very much a parody of himself ... It rather reminded me of Jacques Tati's satire on modern living: *Mon Oncle*, but without the satirical intent ...

As far as my own humble opera are concerned this latest idea of the love-story [9] has made considerable progress in my head, if little on paper. Briefly, the idea is now to present a man's love-affair with his wife and an idealised, poetic love-affair he is living through in his imagination, concurrently. I think I may finally have hit on a satisfactory way to do this – a problem that has been dogging me for the last few weeks. I'll spare you details, however, from a superstitious feeling that if I tell anyone about it the idea will turn sour on me.

Some good novels seem to have been written in England recently though I'm afraid I haven't got round to reading them ... I find I'm already surfeited with fiction with the dreary, self-therapeutic monsters I have to report on for the publisher. [10] The only thing I've read recently that has inflamed me with enthusiasm is V. Woolf's *To the Lighthouse.*

All the best to you, Russ. Let me know how things turn out.

Jim

To Franz Beer

Palace Gardens Terrace
[undated] May 1965

Dear Franz,

So far I have no great news for you. At the Drian Gallery [11] a rather disagreeable woman (the director) told me she liked your style and would like to see your paintings – but she said this in a very blasé tone, barely looking at what I was showing her. At the New Vision Gallery [12] the director also liked your style but the gallery is very small and he is already full up for quite some time. He gave me the address of two other galleries where, from the 'style' point of view, you would have a chance. I went there, but there was a television crew there so that it was impossible to meet the director. I intend to go back.

However, I think I can't do much without your paintings, apart from bothering people a bit! A good friend of mine, Ron Robertson-Swann, who is a sculptor and works as an assistant to Henry Moore, has told me he will accompany me to two or three other galleries where he knows people. He gave me the impression that everything is already booked up long in advance and he also thinks that New York is where everything is happening now.

I don't know if I should advise you to come here to try your luck or not ... I think you need to know people before they will even look at what you are doing.

I am glad I am not a painter!!!!

And you? It's going better, I hope.

Best regards
Jim

To Franz Beer

Palace Gardens Terrace
[undated] May 1965

Dear Franz,

I'll do my best to go to Dover ... Bring me a packet of 'Meccarillos' – I must warn you that cigarettes are very expensive here.

So, see you soon. I await the telegram,

Jim

To Russell McCormmach

Palace Gardens Terrace
30 May 1965

Dear Russ,

... I must read *Mrs Dalloway*. [13] From your description of the plot I've already decided what the theme is but being an Oxford-trained intellectual I feel I must withhold my ideas on it until I've read the book. I've been reading Cesare Pavese's Diary, called over here *This Business of Living*. As you may know, Pavese committed suicide at the height of his literary fame at the age of 42, having just been awarded the Strega Prize. And this, of course, colours a lot of the things he has to say, particularly about his relations with women.

All the best to you
Jim

Diary

21 August 1965

What I thought of this afternoon in the cinema & then forgot, & then thought of again at the Swanns [Ron & Anne Swann] and then forgot again and now, at the very end of this rainy & depressing Saturday is (end of preamble) simply this: how thin the shell of civilisation that holds anarchy out. During the Los Angeles negro riots [14] I was horrified by the sight of civilisation breaking down, people at last saying 'This isn't good enough. There is nothing in this way of life for us'. And then every little crime is a crack that lets anarchy seep through the shell ... The LA riots have happened now & will have to be lived with (but perhaps it was only us whites who even thought a fellowship across the race barrier was possible, because we had the patronising position.) ... Being 'good' & 'human' seems to have lost a lot of its currency since I was a child; or is it simply that I have changed myself. And yet it's a challenge of self-discipline to be tolerant & sympathetic, the kind of challenge that in almost any other field would interest me. Materialism, rocketing crime, pop-singers & the worship of youth, it seems too easy to let oneself slide into the sort of arrogant fascism that Montherlant [15] offers; a rejection of life because you feel that it hasn't gone your way ... Rather as Russell was saying that it seemed to him that Einstein felt that physics had gone Bohr's way & not his. The idea being that I should really have liked to be a pop-singer, & had all the girls. How appealing Montherlant seems!

22 August

Reading in *Elements of Biology* about the beginnings of life on earth – well, where does this leave us egocentric novelists? On the other hand, why should I care about my origins (in reacting chemicals)? I exist, if only temporarily, & in my imagination I can make things as I want them. No need to feel guilty if there's only the blind cosmos to (fail to) take account of my ducking of reality. Those chemicals should have thought twice about creating something that became Shakespeare who was a lot more real than they are themselves.

24 August

Increasing isolation. Twice this week I've been woken up after nightmarish dreams about being isolated & unloved, in one of which my mother was indifferent to me. But this must be inevitable when I'm writing full steam. I still believe myself incapable of writing when living in close contact with someone, at least having the sort of unstable relationships that I normally seem to have with girls. All the same this can't go on ... & what terrifies me is that it will. On the other hand I'm now fully conscious of this curious anarchy inside me that requires me to smash to pieces any promising relationship so perhaps with care & self-control. The trouble is to meet people. I must give this serious thought. There's no reason why it shouldn't be solved like everything else by exercising the mind ... Another 2 or 3 months, though, & I'll be out of this particular wood, at least (& no doubt into another). Thank heaven for Russell's visit, for the fact that the Swanns are always at home, for the K-P's [Knox Peebles] & for the swimming-bath that soaks up some of my physical energy, possibly too much. [16]

25 September

An invitation from the Pearce's to a birthday party on condition that I agree to play some boardgame. This reminded me of an appalling & humiliating Christmas party given by Mlle Dessus of Mende at which games were played. The only thing that remains firmly fixed in my mind is that one of the games involved sitting on something sharp, a bottle perhaps.

Undated

Sitting in the Duke of York surrounded by the most depressing collection of beatniks I have ever seen, I glimpse through the bar the photograph of a boxer on his knees in the ring. The white-shirted, black-trousered referee is inclined towards him, counting. Beyond him one can glimpse the vertical torso of his aggresssor. For an instant I am inside the photograph looking in the direction of the bar, feeling dazed. Williamson, his name was. No pain that I can recall. But what was I trying to prove anyway? What a depressing day this has been.

Undated

Would I have felt like this in a comfortable flat, travelling in taxis and with a healthy bank account? Even then there still must be the moment when you turn the key in the lock, switch on the lights in the dark rooms, look around at the empty furniture standing exactly where you left it ... Really one must live an idea if one is not to be wounded by the moment that lies bertween opening the door and taking off your raincoat.

With his six-month lease on the conservatory about to expire, Farrell had to move again. He found cheap accommodation not far away in Notting Hill, in the misleadingly named Stanley House Hotel, a rambling block of bedsits. The tall, seedy building had an air of anonymity which he liked, and his room was on the ground floor at the back. He had by now heard about Harkness Fellowships, which generously funded two postgraduate years of study in America. Their aim was to promote a favourable view of the country among those with the potential for public influence, so applicants had to demonstrate promising experience in the arts, politics, journalism or academia.

To Russell McCormmach

Room 17
Stanley House Hotel [17]
13/14 Stanley Crescent
London W.2.
13 October 1965

Dear Russ,

I only just got your letter as had to move out of the greenhouse; the landlady suggested I go because, she said, she would like to find 'a student' who would be prepared to live there [when] the weather got bad. As she was so dilatory about forwarding my mail (I suspect a plot of her husband's – and imagine him striding up and down the now empty greenhouse carving at the air with his scimitar, mouthing oaths against the spectre of Jim) I called round this morning. I noted with satisfaction that they have still not found a tenant ... I'm now living in this hotel in reduced circumstances, as they say. Since I've been here I've been sleeping an alarming amount. Yesterday, however, I discovered a gas leak from the stove. The idea being that it was easy to fall asleep but waking up again presented problems. With the gas turned off I find I hardly sleep at all! ...

I still make trips to the baths and smoke Dutch cigars (Schimmelpenninck). My book is still going forward though the move from the greenhouse has disturbed me somewhat. As for the US, I hope to apply for a Harkness if I can find any referees to back me up. I also dropped in at the USIS [18] and dutifully copied down the names of all US colleges with creative writing courses ...

As for THE LUNG, the good news is that the paperback rights have been sold to Corgi (who also publish the Marquis de Sade,

Brendan Behan and some lesser pornographers) ... The bad news is that the French publisher of whom I had been nourishing vague hopes has turned it down. No news of any American interest yet either which is a pity ...

I'm reading *A* [*sic*] *MAN WITHOUT QUALITIES* with great pleasure. I can see why you liked it so much. Musil[19] has a lot to say about science and mathematics in a rather ironic way which harmonises perfectly with your own attitude as I remember it ...

All the best to you,

Jim

[*Handwritten*] P.S. When I finish this book I'm planning to make some investigations of Pétain [20] and also examine some successful plays to see if I can discover their secrets. I'll let you know how I get on.

To Dr Lansing V. Hammond[21]

Balholm

Saval Park Road,

Dalkey

County Dublin

November 1965

Dear Sir,

I enclose completed application forms for the Harkness Fellowships. [22] As my submission is not on academic grounds I have not included evidence of my degree which is, in any case, an undistinguished one. Should you feel this is necessary, however, I shall be glad to send it.

I can also supply reviews and/or copies of my work.

Yours sincerely

James Farrell

APPLICATION: ... I very much want to live for a time in the US. It is a commonplace (and possibly not true) to say that everything that happens in America happens five or ten years later in Europe. Nevertheless, it would seem that for a novelist interested in the way that individuals manage their lives in the middle of the twentieth century, some experience of the US would provide valuable, if not essential, insights. I am deeply interested in trying to write universal, as opposed to regional, novels; the sort of books in which people trying to adjust themselves to abrupt changes in their civilization, whether it be Ireland or in Japan, may be able to recognise themselves ... Faulkner was reported to have said that nobody on a Fellowship ever wrote anything good. I should like to prove him wrong on this score ...

To Russell McCormmach

Saval Park Road, County Dublin
19 November 1965

My dear Russ,

... I duly filed, without hope, my Harkness application, a most unconvincing one, I'm afraid. I found it hard to disguise the fact that my main purpose in going to the States was that I wanted to continue our conversations of this summer. I said, however, that I wanted to join the Yale Drama School to learn enough about the theatre to be able to write for it. Oh yeah? they'll say.

I came home here last week. The hotel got to be too awful and I hadn't any money. Besides, I remembered how successfully I had worked on the last occasion I was at home. So far, though, things are not working out. I re-read the two-thirds of my novel I have written and it didn't seem to be working at all. The thing is badly out of focus. The tone is wrong. It is unreal without creating a reality of its own. I haven't yet abandoned hopes of succeeding with it, though. I'm merely disappointed that it wasn't as good as I thought it was.

I forget whether I told you that there were two excellent reviews of THE LUNG in the *Daily Telegraph* (your favourite paper) and *The Guardian*, a favourable short notice in both the *Observer* and the *TLS* and vague hostility from *Punch*. And that's all (apart from being elected as a favourite son by *The Irish Times*). [23] The book has now vanished into the sea of indifference that captures all our best efforts ...

All the best to you,
Jim

To Russell McCormmach

Saval Park Road, County Dublin
12 December 1965

Dear Russ,

Many thanks for your ... reaction to my book which, needless to say, made me very happy. With the largely favourable press reaction I rather lost sight of my own feelings about it, which I now remember to have stopped somewhere short of euphoric satisfaction. Actually, thanks to my terrible memory the book has become mercifully something of a blur to me (which is a help when it comes to allowing myself to believe the nice things people say about it). Out of this blur, however, looms the sinister impression that the book lacks a strong enough main thread to bind it all together; something I often detect in mss. I read by other authors, the feeling that the thing has been made up as the author went along and that the various events don't have a powerful enough inter-relation between each other and the theme as a whole.

Since I last wrote the *Guardian* selected the book for their Fiction of the Month slot (a smaller deal than it sounds) but with a re-appraisal of it curiously more hesitant about its virtues than their original review. In this they suggest that there are passages written with maximum ability but that the book is uneven ... which is entirely my own view. They end by saying: 'Certainly in the first quarter of this novel, and in flashes thereafter, one sees sure signs of the developing powers of a considerable talent.' I should add that the idea that my powers should be developing covers me with alarm and despair as I fancy they are diminishing ...

I can't help feeling that my new book will mark a recession unless I get more ideas and more inspiration than I feel myself to be commanding at the moment. I'm now nearing the 300 ms. page mark which should make it 20 or 30 pages longer than *The Lung* in print and I still have a couple of major events to record ... This is good really because it gives me plenty of material to work with when I set about cutting away the dead wood ... which, I fear, is in large proportion. Part of the trouble is trying to work at home and at the same time prevent myself from being strangled by the invisible tendrils of electricity constantly wavering about and preparing to snatch me back into adolescence.

I've been reading with great interest ... Eisenstein's notes on his work. [24] I see why he appeals to you; the enormous care he took with the construction and meaning of his works which I believe would be your own method of making a film or writing a novel. I don't think this is the only way to do it (*vide* Godard [25] etc.) but it is certainly one which would appeal to me. I have the impression that the more consciously one creates something the more satisfaction you get from it (the author I mean) ...

In bed last night as I was crawling painfully towards unconsciousness I was thinking how petty and sordid it was. However, before finally going under a slightly reassuring thought occurred to me: namely, that my own life was sunshine and clear skies compared with that of some people (Tolstoy, for example) who found themselves forced to conduct their business from the most appalling psychological infernos.

I have the optimistic idea that if we can last out just a while longer things will change drastically for the better ...

All the best to you,
Jim

To Dr Lansing V. Hammond

Stanley House Hotel
10 February 1966

Dear Dr. Hammond,

Very many thanks for your reassuring note that arrived this morning. I append a letter of acceptance as requested.

I'm sorry to keep bombarding you with queries ... but the implications of the fact that I shall be going to the US are only slowly dawning on me. I've been wondering whether it would be possible to fly to New York by Icelandic Airlines rather than go by ship. I understand that the fares are roughly equivalent or, if anything, cheaper. The reason is that this would permit me to stop off in Iceland for a few days to confer with a young Icelandic film director, Reynir Oddsson, [26] who for some time has been trying to persuade me to assist him in writing a film treatment of one of the old Icelandic Sagas. I understand he is offering me an additional carrot in the form of a possible interview with Laxness, [27] the Nobel prize-winning novelist. If there is anything heretical about this suggestion or if it would involve the Harkness organisation in any difficulties then please don't give it a thought. Any additional expense I would expect, of course, to pay myself.

Yours sincerely,
James Farrell

To Russell McCormmach

Stanley House Hotel
[undated] February 1966

Dear Russ,

Things are looking up at last. I learned the other day that I have hit the jackpot with my application for a Harkness Commonwealth Fellowship, so if all goes according to plan I should be in the US come next Fall.

I should be getting $300 a month, a block of $400 for book and equipment allowance (I suppose equipment means French letters), car rental for not less than 6 months, $300 bonus for Christmas travel and $500 for some other time of the year, return ship passage, any tuition fees – and one or two other fringe benefits. The idea is that I shall be loosely (very loosely, I hope) attached to Yale Drama School but allowed, and expected, to travel round seeing the sights as I like. It really couldn't be better as far as I'm concerned. So it really seems as if we shall be able to get together towards the end of the year ...

I see I forgot to mention that this Fellowship is for two years. I can't believe my luck.

All the best,
Jim

To S. Gorley Putt [28]

Stanley House Hotel
16 February 1966

Dear Mr Putt,

Thank you for your letter of the 14th of February. Yes, of course you may assume that the original plan stands. It was only an idea, partly generated by the thought of playing Bingo for five days (but perhaps they only do that on British boats). In any case, I'm sure it will be good for my soul.

I can quite understand the difficulties that an exception to the rule might cause.

Yours sincerely,
James Farrell

To Mrs Widra [29]

Stanley House Hotel
3 March 1966

Dear Mrs Widra,

Thank you for your letter of the 2nd March. The booking on the *Nieuw Amsterdam* [30] on the 24th August is fine by me.

I think the Mount Street office of the American Express would suit me best geographically.

I shall hope to startle the American Express with the enormous efficiency with which I shall try to handle their correspondence!

Yours sincerely,
James Farrell

To Rose Knox Peebles

Stanley House Hotel
3 April 1966

My dear Rose,

I have just finished your book [31] and I must say that I consider it to be quite an advance on your last one (which, admittedly, I read many years ago – or so it seems). As I know you, it's not easy to be detached about it but here, anyway, are one or two random thoughts for what they are worth (and please don't feel obliged to believe them).

On the credit side, I liked very much your spare and detached style. Your writing is a great deal less self-indulgent (in fact, not self-indulgent at all) than is customary in the steady blizzard of manuscripts that snows down on Hutchinson. I was impressed by the kaleidoscopic effect evoked during the drinks as the couples assemble for the weekend. Also the reverberations passing between the doll's house and the real house ... this is just the sort of thing I personally eat up in novels. There were lots of other good things too – the sense of loss in Mary – the somewhat sour amusement as they listen to Stewart and Virginia on the job in the next room – and so on. The main thing that disturbed me about the book is something that a lot of serious writers would find a distinct virtue: viz. the uncompromising way in which you display what is, after all, a large cast of characters. I think most readers (and publishers) would resent the effort demanded of them in sorting out who is who ...

particularly in the beginning. I found that I couldn't read the book with any fluency (because I had to stop and think who was who) until about page 100, by which time the book was almost over. Added to the shifting time scale a lot is demanded of the reader. To get away with this I think the plot would have to be as ambitious as the structure, which it really isn't. What publishers are dying for (pathetic creatures that they are) is nothing more ambitious than an unusual story ...

I think it's unlikely that any book publisher would be interested in taking it on. A book of this length would really have to be nothing less than THE OLD MAN AND THE SEA [32] before they could be persuaded, I should think. However, it might be worth trying out on one of the more reputable magazines. If you like I'll deliver it to Hutch and see what they make of it ... or possibly one of the big novel publishing houses like Heinemann or Michael Joseph would be a better bet.

Tuesday and Thursday mornings, at least until 11.30 approx. I'm usually in my lair here if you want to interrogate me more deeply and snatch back the ms ... but in any case I shall be giving you a ring later in the week, I hope, and dropping in on you.

Love,
Jim

To Russell McCormmach

Stanley House Hotel
6 April 1966

Dear Russ,

I was just on the point of writing to you when your letter dropped on to the mat of this seedy hotel. Good news that you'll definitely be at Princeton next year and that we'll be able to get together (always providing I can get a visa). I still haven't heard for sure that I have a place at the Yale Drama School but I'm still hoping that this is a formality. At the end of my new book 'The Succubus' [33] the main character, Boris, becomes convinced as the beautiful feathers slowly moult away from his dreams that the postman is withholding his letters. Now this may seem an odd coincidence but it so happens – well, never mind. It may be the landlord who is jealous of my fame, wealth, and success with women.

I've finished the book incidentally and delivered it to my agent who read it with rather muted enthusiasm; his eyes narrowed to inscrutable, oriental slits when I asked him for an opinion. At present he is dangling it seductively in front of various publishers here. I'm still not happy with it, I'm afraid, and feel that I shall have to perform some surgery on the beginning. In the meantime I sit in the British Museum documenting myself on Gilles de Rais and casting around for a gripping idea that will bind him into a play. This I still haven't found though there are a lot of possibilities. I'm also still interested in your idea of writing a play on Pétain ... One interesting fact I discovered about him – Louis-Ferdinand Céline, [34] the strange man who wrote *Voyage au Bout de la Nuit* was his doctor and confidant at Vichy. He might make a useful character to act as ringmaster to the Marshal's glories and reverses ...

Nothing much new here. I read a good novel the other day, *The Ice Saints* by Frank Tuohy, [35] set in Poland. I had the impression that it made my own work look desperately over-expansive, garrulous and anxious to please.

All the best to you,
[unsigned]

To Russell McCormmach

Stanley House Hotel
10 July 1966

Dear Russ,

... Last Sunday, the day you were writing your letter to me, I was reminded of our discussions on anarchy by a couple of young men on a bus who started baiting a tired old peroxide blonde sitting not far from me. In these situations I always get a creepy feeling that polite society can dissolve into a bloodbath at the drop of a hat. I think it's the apparent lack of motivation that worries me ... Incidentally, I didn't know that Johnson [36] had taken to scowling and shaking his fist. Vietnam is becoming more nightmarish every day.

I've been going through a bad patch, sleeping badly and so on. This is partly due to lack of success with a girl I didn't even like much (I chuckled the other day when it occurred to me that I had gone through a reduced version of what Proust's character Swann went through with Odette) but largely due to general apathy and dissatisfaction with the

revisions I'm making to 'The Succubus' (which I've contracted to deliver by the end of this month to Jonathan Cape who were enthusiastic when they read the first draft). Perhaps America will revitalise
me. Both the Gilles de Rais and Pétain plays have vanished into my
general inertia ... Novels are somehow much more tempting though
no-one ever reads them.

For some time now I've been casting around for a way of doing
justice to a mammoth theme of life in all kinds of modern aspects,
as Musil did with his Viennese Society for the Promotion of whatever it was in *The Man Without Qualities.** I'm tired of isolated skir-
mishes on the sex and politics front. The only idea I've had to date
is to set it in a town under siege where the different strata of society continue to function more or less normally in spite of the odd
shell landing in the market place. It occurs to me that Camus did
something like this in *La Peste* ... [37]

My interim address in the US will be c/o Harkness House, 1
East 75th. St. NYC but as soon as I've found somewhere to live in
New Haven I'll let you know ...

All the best to you,
Jim

*You see, Johnson isn't the only one visited by megalomania! When
with my publisher I've taken to scowling and shaking my fist.

*The publisher who had shown enthusiasm was Tom Maschler, the ebul-
lient head of Jonathan Cape. Only two years older than Farrell, he had
joined the company as editorial director in 1960, and his buccaneering
style had re-established its reputation for being a major literary imprint.
As the writer Francis Wyndham would say of Maschler one day, [38] 'Tom
had an extraordinary knack, without apparently being all that literary
himself, of being aware of what was happening and seeing what was good.'*

To Tom Maschler [39]

Stanley House Hotel
PARK 8296
25 July 1966

Dear Mr Maschler,
I've now virtually finished revising 'The Succubus' except for a
couple of reads-through from different angles. Unless they reveal

something glaringly awful I should like to deliver the ms. to you on, say, Thursday or Friday if you have a moment to spare. I shall then return to Ireland for a week from the 4th to the 10th August. If you or someone else could read it during this time we could then settle any further queries before I leave for the US on the 24th August.

I should also like to discuss the jacket with you, having been deeply traumatized over the jacket for my last book. My feeling is that unless there is the possibility of some exceptional artist doing it (Charles Raymond [40] is the only name I know but I suppose there are others) I'd like a plain lettering jacket. Cream and scarlet *à la* Gallimard would be the colours expressing the content, I think. Does all this fill you with dismay?

I think there are other things I want to discuss as well but my thought is opaque this morning, with holes in it. Perhaps you could give me a ring some morning this week between 10 and 11 a.m.?

Yours sincerely,
James Farrell

To Tom Maschler

Saval Park Road,
County Dublin
5 August 1966

Dear Mr Maschler,

If, as you said the other day, a pictorial jacket automatically sells 500 more copies than a plain lettered one then a pictorial jacket is obviously what is needed. In any case, rather than risk irritating you further with my somewhat querulous demands, it seems best to withdraw them and leave the matter entirely to you. However, I may as well set out the ideas I have had, for what they are worth, in case any of them should appeal to you. They are:

a) A detail from Botticelli's 'Birth of Venus' to recap pp. 159–160 of the novel. I'm afraid that to show the whole thing might be insulting to Botticelli.

b) A girl photographed in the same Venus position. If in black and white and under-exposed in the printing so that only the outlines and the strongest shadows appeared this would help suggest Inez' unreality. I think this is a better idea but possibly too difficult or expensive to do.

c) A medieval woodcut or drawing of a witch. I enclose an amusing example of love-magic but I'm sure there are any number of striking possibilities in this line.

However, as I say, I leave it entirely up to you. [41]

You will have noticed that in the revised mss. I delivered to you no chapter divisions are marked. If you feel the book would be improved by being divided into chapters (rather than mere spaces and asterisks) then the new chapters should begin on pages: 16, 31, 47, 65 (line 4), 77, 97, 107, 120 (line 14) 133, 155, 171, 182 (line 4), 196, 206, 224, 243, 263, 280 and 295.

I don't feel strongly either way but perhaps these divisions would help improve readability ...

[unsigned]

To Tom Maschler

Stanley House Hotel
[undated] 1966

Dear Tom,

Re the title, I consider myself to have been delivered a low blow. In the early stages of writing the book I tortured myself with a number of different titles. Of these THE BONFIRE ON THE ICE seems the most promising though this would probably mean restoring the passage where Boris remembers the corresponding incident in his youth. Other possibilities include THE WHITE BIRD IN MY HEAD or, more simply, *A Girl in the Head*. 'Head' I seem to remember is American slang for 'loo'. If you have strong feelings about any of these you might let me know.

As for the italics, do as you think best.

Sincerely,
James

To Tom Maschler

Stanley House Hotel
22 August 1966

Dear Tom

After many drastic *volte-faces* and agonizing reappraisals about the title of the erstwhile 'Succubus' I have now finally decided that it shall be called:

A GIRL IN THE HEAD

If you have any queries about this or about anything else you could contact me next Wednesday or Thursday *chez* Garry Arnott, 321 East 14th St.. His telephone number is 982.5585.

Sincerely,
Jim Farrell

A Craving to Write Something Good
America
1966–68

To Russell McCormmach

173 Park Street
New Haven, Connecticut
22 September 1966

Dear Russ,

Sorry I've taken so long to write but I've been going through the usual excruciating boredom of getting myself established, finding an apartment and starting classes at the Drama School. The apartment I found is somewhat shabby but has the advantage of being just round the corner from the school. A bigger disadvantage is the fact that it is somewhat spartanly furnished which means that I've had to buy a lot of stuff to fill in the spaces: nevertheless the main room still looks like a railway platform. I've also found myself buying sheets and a blanket for the first time in my life: I feel sure that this is in some way symbolic of my decline. So much for these base material matters. (I also got a telephone in the hope that some day a beautiful girl will ring me up ... so far the machine has remained obstinately mute, however).

The Drama School looks as if it is going to be not only valueless for me but also positively obnoxious, thanks to the garrulity of the students who are a rare collection of imbeciles. Brustein[1] who is giving a course on modern drama seems a nice man but ... is either so vague as to be meaningless or simply wrong. Playwriting courses are given by an avant-garde playwright called Arnold Weinstein [2] (the entire faculty incidentally are straining their guts out to be dynamic and hip) who has an aggressive nature but few ideas. In fact, the only course that I've been attending of any interest is given by a pair of blokes called Rohmer [3] [*sic*] and Young on writing for the screen.

They made a film I haven't seen called *Nothing But a Man* and are currently working on another. They show good films (Fellini, Bresson etc.) and then comment on the various techniques employed. This would be splendid if it wasn't for the above-mentioned garrulity of the students who get them involved in long and dreary arguments about their own views. In general, everyone around here seems to be equipped with a king-size ego that renders an exchange of ideas impossible. Well, there it is. I expect I shall gradually phase myself out of it all and take to sitting in my apartment and scratching my scalp while waiting for something to happen ...

The desire to withdraw into the private world of another novel becomes more overpowering every day. However, enough of this dyspepsia. How are things with you? I picture you in your new quarters battling away at your thesis while cockroaches as big as cats snap at your ankles. I hope it's going well ... For the moment I feel that to preserve my sanity I must get myself involved in some work which in turn partly involves staying here and getting used to living in this apartment. I'm not actually sorry to have left London but it's brought a lot of problems: the main one being life in a town where you don't know anyone you care to talk to ...

> All the best to you,
> Jim

To Russell McCormmach

> New Haven, Connecticut
> 29 September 1966

Dear Russ:

Here's another note from me, no particular reason except that you're the nearest person I feel I can communicate with. Yesterday I took a deep breath and paid out ten dollars for Lowry's correspondence [4] with the result that today I'm identifying madly with him ...

I'm finding it hard to adapt to America though quite what it was that I found so wonderful about London I can't remember. Last weekend I went to Boston to see Patsy Cumming and, on the way back, Franz Beer ... Well, all through the weekend I felt ill at ease somehow: rather the feeling one gets on seeing a good film for the third or fourth time. It's wonderful but I've ceased to react ... That's not to say I didn't enjoy seeing them again. Simply that it's hard to recover intimacy with someone whom one hasn't seen for a long time. Actually, it's probably nothing more than a symptom of my bewilderment at America and general *dépaysement*.

I've virtually stopped going to classes here as I felt that [they] were merely escalating my feeling of demoralisation. Instead I sit at home and toy with ideas for a new novel, none of which seem satisfactory. This is really the root of my problem: I haven't yet found an idea I can absorb myself in. So far the only moment when I've felt at all glad to be here (apart from frequent expeditions to the local liquor store for gallon jars of Californian burgundy) came when I went to the Yale Gymnasium to register as a user of the pool and a rugged, paternal old man (no doubt a football hero of the '20s) enclosed my hand in his massive fist and told me that he'd been to England and that after Italy and France it had seemed like home. He positively radiated goodwill and all the other old-fashioned virtues ...

All the best,
Jim

To Jonathan Clowes [5]

New Haven, Connecticut
30 October 1966

Dear Jonathan,

A matter of some importance that has been plaguing me for some time. I'd like to know what you think about it. It's this: I feel that I should reduce my name from James Farrell to simple initials 'J.G. Farrell' – and that if I'm ever to do it now is the time.

The point is that I'm sick to death of being confused with the famous, or notorious, James T. Farrell. Every time he brings out a new book, which he does with monotonous regularity, I get commiserating letters about the awful reviews (sample quote from his book before last: 'This book is so boring as to be almost against nature' – the *Observer*. Some paper said about his last opus: 'What's so nice about Farrell is that he's so consistently bloody awful.' And it's not just a matter of my personal feelings – countless people I've met (well, they could be counted rather easily as a matter of fact) have assumed that my books were by him. It seems to me that the whole job of imposing oneself as a distinctive figure on the highly distracted mind of the reading public is hampered by this sort of similarity of names.

I agree that I should have thought of all this before but it seems to me that it could be done now with minimal confusion since hardly anyone knows me anyway and, presumably, the Corgi edition of *The Lung* due out this time next year could bear my amended name.

If you agree with this could you pass this letter on to Tom Maschler and see what he thinks. It seems to me that having shuffled off my original publisher there's no reason why I shouldn't shuffle off my original skin altogether ...

All the best,
Jim Farrell

To Brian and Rose Knox Peebles

New Haven, Connecticut
5 November 1966

My dear Brian and Rose,

... Yale turns out to be very like Oxford in a lot of ways, though less interesting. This may be because of a crushing impression of *déjà vu*. In particular the Drama School seems to have attracted every phoney and *poseur* on the continent: the place is crammed to the rafters with pretentious and acneous youths with shades on ... The one course that I am attending with passion and enthusiasm is on writing for the screen and given by two young blokes called Roemer and Young who ... are both highly intelligent and *sympathique*. The methodical and ruthless way they work is just the example needed, I think, for someone like me who is always ready to grow flabby and self-satisfied on a few crumbs of journalistic praise. Also in this class as a student is a bloke called Kenneth Brown [6] who wrote a play and film called *The Brig*. He's a pleasant chap ... rather given to adenoidal pronouncements about his art. It, the class, mainly consists of showing films (why didn't they have something like this at Oxford?) and talking about them in detail. With Bob Young, the cameraman, we wander about the streets of New Haven trying to aim our movie cameras at girls' legs. All very stimulating ... One nice thing is that I have a reasonable apartment here and no shortage of money for once. With a woman things would improve vastly, however ...

Love
Jim

New Haven, Connecticut
16 November 1966

Dear Russ,

Many thanks for your letter. Sure, I can be in New Haven or in New York whichever suits you best [7] ... No, I've been getting progressively more bushed here, progressively more tantalised with dreams of returning to Europe ... though of course I could never allow myself to admit defeat in this way. However, I'm confidently expecting things to get better and getting nearer and nearer to starting some work (I think) ...

Looking forward to seeing you,

Jim

Diary

22 December 1966

This is addressed to an absent third party ... in all respects like me, but not me. Alright then, the idea of this diary is to help me to get control of my talent for writing. I hope that it will help me in the following ways:

1) That I shall bring myself face to face with things that I normally discard through sheer mental laziness.

2) That I shall be able to remember things people say that make an impression on me as well as things I read.

3) Get in the habit of discussing problems with myself.

4) Catch some of my life before I forget it. I'm appalled to think how little I can remember of my first trip to America, even though it was only ten years ago. However, avoid being garrulous or it will become a chore. Avoid self-pity and sentimentality. Avoid haranguing myself uselessly like this.

On Monday I had lunch with Mike Roemer. He was busy and somewhat harassed; I noticed for the first time how he tends to talk too loud, as if afraid that he won't be able to assert himself if he doesn't. He had been to see Polanski's *Cul de Sac* [8] and hadn't liked it. I was unable to understand his reasons for not liking it. He said he thought it was badly written; that it hadn't gone far enough if it was supposed to be black humour etc. Well, perhaps I do partly see what he means. For all that, he couldn't convince me (he didn't try) that it was a bad film. I still find parts of it sublime: the kitchen scene at the beginning and the visit of the friends, in particular ... Roemer told me that he had once dined with E.M. Forster and been very impressed with his modesty and simplicity. F. had only wanted to talk about films. In the course of lunch R. repeated his theory that writers use up their experience when young, then go through a middle period of hard work before they can learn to invent their own material. In return I talked to him of intuitive writers, citing Edna O'Brien[9] as one who had gone off the rails once she had begun to think about it ... I don't think either of us were particularly convinced by this. Nothing, anyway, will convince R. that writing is not a field in which one only succeeds by hard and ruthless work. With deep misgivings I gave him a copy of *The Lung*.

Reading Virginia Woolf's diary in the train to N. Carolina to spend Christmas with Bob.[10] Odd and curious flashes of contempt for the lower classes appear every now and then that seem sadly out of date (these are the only things that seem unusual for a person like V.W. by today's standards) ...

26 December

Only when I discuss my work with someone else do I begin to see its glaring deficiencies. It's inevitable that it will be deficient in some respect ... the disturbing thing is that I'm inclined to forget this except when seeing it through my interlocutor's eyes as I try to explain it to him. This happened with Dr Cumming last night when I was trying to tell him about my books. The truth seems to be that what Claude [11] called my *coquetterie* is solidly based on a fear of discovering defects in my work myself.

Christmas in North Carolina. The people round here (and, I suspect, in the US generally) are real hard-core Christmas celebrators. Hardly a house without a holly wreath nailed to the door and festooned with red ribbons; coloured lights on the trees and around windows; red plastic illuminated candles; Santa Clauses plastered everywhere; Christmas songs and carols issuing from public address systems and revolving on turn-tables. If my intention was to circumnavigate Christmas by coming to N. Carolina then I made an enormous miscalculation.[12] To Bob I said something about the atmosphere of severity I find in Davidson. The extreme coldness of the architecture, both of the church (Presbyterian) and of the college; brick and cement without flourishes or follies or romantic illusions, nothing in which I can recognise myself.

I've had some surprises ... Carols sung or grace said before meals (*chez* Cumming also). No negroes in the Presbyterian church on Christmas morning (Bob says they've tried to get them to integrate with the negro church but the negroes weren't interested in the dull – dull as all hell – middle class service) ... My final impression is of cruising in a car by night through endless ranks of neon-flashing motels, garages, supermarkets and Christmas trees and other decorations. The streets are almost deserted. Occasionally other cars slide past, glinting like fish in the reflected lights ...

To Tom Maschler

c/o Garry Arnott
321 East 14th Street, NYC
5 Jan 1967

Dear Tom,

In a week's time I plan to leave New Haven and set up house in New York. I'll be staying at the above address until I find a more permanent place.

I'm curious to know if you have a publication date fixed for *A Girl in the Head*.

Happy New Year to you,

Sincerely,
Jim Farrell

Diary

6 January 1967

I received shortly before Christmas a letter from my mother in which she described a visit from [a neighbour].

'... She will only let [her husband] smoke in the dining-room and she won't go in it to clean it. She said she can't ask us as he would smoke in the sitting-room and she can't have that; they never use the sitting-room at all as she won't let him smoke there ... Daddy[13] says he thinks he just lets it all ride over him but it must be terrible for them both.'

[He] was, I think, head of the Assam-Bengal railway during the war and, if not knighted, given some sort of royal recognition. And now he isn't allowed to smoke in the sitting-room ... In the evening I went to see Gielgud and Irene Worth doing bits from Shakespeare. Good in parts but really – how unreal, for the most part, how declamatory, actorish. Strange to see Irene Worth who at the Spurlings' [14] dinner parties I always thought dull put on that perfectly fitting cloak of gestures, tone and attitudes. But how unreal all the same!

A quotation (from *A Midsummer N's D*?) that got through to me: about someone sleeping 'in a bank of thyme'. What freshness that conveyed!

14 January

I was intrigued by *Memento Mori* and impressed to begin with; it really seemed to me that Muriel Spark had got hold of a way of penetrating deeply – but in the end I was disappointed. The novel seemed to degenerate too much into the story of the relationships and although parts of this were marvellous ... I felt that she hadn't fully exploited her brilliant idea of looking at life from the angle of her old people. It's the idea of seeing familiar things from different angles that is so valuable ... This book and this thought also give me an idea of what I failed to seize in *A Girl*. Also of what I failed to seize in *The Lung* – how the world is different for a cripple, how ordinary actions (such as the one I included, breathing) are made new and interesting when they are no longer taken for granted. An old lady in *Memento Mori* getting out of a car and cautiously feeling for the ground with her foot. It's all in Ecclesiastes, of course. Things that we don't think about now we'll think about later. The trick (for a novelist) is to think about them now. Think about all the possible angles. A novel, perhaps, where the characters all see things from different angles. This is what almost everyone tries to do – but it's hard to make it really meaningful.

To Mrs Masters, Jonathan Cape

Room 1204
Hotel Belvedere
319 West 48th. St.
New York, N.Y. 10036
30 Jan 1967

Dear Mrs Masters,

I return herewith the proofs of 'Girl' to you. My memory of proof-correcting signs is unreliable so it might be a good idea if you were to go through it again before returning it to the printer. I'm sure you do this anyway. There are one or two things I should mention.

1) On p. 21 a whole line has been omitted. I don't have a copy of the ms. But have supplied the line from memory. If it should be different from that in the ms. choose whichever you like.

2) on p.136 I came across some defective grammar, 6 lines from the bottom of the page: 'Once somebody has gone they have gone for ever.' This should, of course, read 'he has gone for ever.' I haven't marked this but if it's possible to change it without resetting half the book I'd like this to be done.

3) p. 201 I should very much like 'Treat them rough. That's my advice' to be raised to stand by itself on the line above ... I think it's a lot more effective this way and feel sure that it was like this in the ms. (but possibly not.)

4) There are a number of places where the print seems defective. I've ringed these lightly in pencil and put a question mark in the margin as I imagine it isn't my province to legislate about such matters. However, I get the impression that it was proof-read somewhat cursorily at the printers.

5) My congratulations to your blurb writer for his performance in a difficult art! However, if it's not too late I'd rather like the word 'Russian' to be removed from the description of my prose! Incidentally, I hope that a copy of the jacket design will be shown to my agent, Jonathan Clowes, before it is minted – but perhaps the jacket has already been printed? ... I think that covers everything. At least, I hope it does.

Yours sincerely,
Jim Farrell

Diary
1 February

Picking up the pieces. A week ago I moved into the Belvedere Hotel [15] on West 48th Street. A sunny 'room with a view' from the 12th floor. I can see the Hudson River (just), the Empire State Building and other assorted skyscrapers to my left. I have a splendid feeling of living up in the sky. If it wasn't for the cockroaches everything would be nearly perfect. Against them I am having the same somewhat obsessive war as against their comrades in New Haven. Wall to wall carpeting, what luxury! And a telephone that rings, if it rings (which, to be sure, it doesn't often) for me alone.

I had lunch with Roemer again the other day; while waiting in his office I saw from the window ant-like human beings picking at débris in a collapsed building; ambulances arriving, crowds gathering ... I suggested, only half believing it, that they might be watching sympathetically. On the tv in the evening they said, I think, 5 people had died when the building collapsed on them. One man, being carried away in [*sic*] a stretcher, said to a photographer, 'Be sure and take a good picture of me,' and died shortly afterwards.

I finally got around to correcting the proofs of *A Girl in the Head*. My verdict: there's lots of good writing in it, particularly towards the end – and I don't think that there are any parts that are actually badly written or conceived. Simply, it lacks momentum. It takes ages to begin and never picks up speed. It's like a Christmas cake, solid with fruit and nuts and sugar decoration like cast-iron – but leaden to the palate. I hope to God someone will disagree with this verdict.

18 February

... A thin, freezing snow is falling on Fun City. I woke sometime in the middle of last night and the elderly couple next door were having another fight. 'I'll kill you', the lady kept saying. 'I'll kill you', shouted the man. As for me, I went to sleep again. These threats and arguments coming through the wall have become as much part of the furniture of this apartment as the bed, as the scarred cream-painted table on which I write, as the indefatigable cockroaches that patrol the bathroom and kitchen. And now, this morning, these two old people are quarrelling again – or perhaps they never stopped ...

20 February

The fact is that I keep remembering isolated passages of *A Girl in the Head* with pleasure. Parts of it are, I'm sure, funny and touching, especially towards the second half of the book. It remains to be seen whether anyone else finds it so. What I need to do now is to think more deeply about plots, about events, about binding books together with some sort of homogeneity ...

Saturday, 11 March

Roemer didn't like *Girl in the Head* – He said that he thought there was something tired about it – that I was projecting a character I wasn't – falsifying something – I'm not sure I understood what he was trying to say and, if I understood, that I agree. Boris, fantastic though he may be, still seems more real to me than Sands. [16] I like to think that there's music in the book that R. can't hear. The snag is: can anyone? ...

Meanwhile I plough resolutely on through books about the Irish rebellion, gathering more and more information but scarcely adding to my feeble conception of how the thing should be. [17] The one consolation: Iris Murdoch's book on the same subject [18] seems to be a dull and crude effort to judge by what I've read of it so far.

Meanwhile, I'm lonely and find it hard to work. I need people like a flower needs water. Self-confidence too.

18 March

The way to approach the writing of a novel is obviously through the form it is to take – once one has that then things can begin to fall into place, having a place to fall into. With *Girl in the Head* I accidentally stumbled on this (*pourtant*) idea after reflections on the way Bellow and Nabokov set things up for themselves, finding a form (letters and pseudo-footnotes respectively) which allows them great freedom and flexibility. This is the first problem I have to solve if I'm ever to get beyond the stage of wild and fruitless speculation that never gets anywhere ...

[A friend] just rang to say Bernie, a dark, frizzy-haired, blue-jowelled semitic-looking chap who used to be in the Cité [19] in Paris and whom I've met once or twice here, has polio and is in an iron lung – poor devil, even in good health he never looked cheerful. I'm suspicious of the alacrity with which I agreed to go and see him (if his wife thinks it a good idea). Was it sympathy or merely the desire to expose my superiority of already having been through it? Sympathy, I think, but only just.

Saw Strick's film of *Ulysses* with Russell and the Fleissners. [20] The Fleissners were enthusiastic. Russell and I both thought the film didn't add anything to the book, even diminished it in places. The best part, I thought, was Molly's reflections at the end since this was more suited to cinema than the rest – flashes of youth and Gibraltar and so on, very moving.

A coincidence: I wrote the first page of 'It'[21] on St Patrick's day with Irish pipers tuning up down in the street 12 floors beneath. In the parade along 5th Avenue they carried banner portraits of Sean McDermott, Kevin Barry and, no doubt, other martyrs. I didn't stay since the wind was bitter, the pavement covered in slush and my bones frozen to the marrow. These parades make the Americans look like imbeciles. But, the first page: I wrote it twice, satisfactory neither time.

23 March

A couple of tense days partly because of yet another snowstorm that has kept me immured in this sad eyrie, partly because of another attempt to limit my smoking – mainly, no doubt, because I'm still groping around in the maze looking not even for the way out but merely for a likely direction in which to start going ...

26 March

Erwin [Fleissner] was talking the other day of how the brain appears to prefer using the same circuits of cells time and again. I remember Margaret Mead's assertion in the lecture she gave at Yale that we only use less than $1/9$ of our brain potential. Certainly, all the brilliant ideas I've been having recently seem to melt rapidly into reminiscences of other people's books. Perhaps simply because, like ants marching, the track has already been laid out for them. No doubt this is nonsense scientifically. Nevertheless, getting drunk more often might help me to make new connections ...

Another thought: could it be that my ambition has outrun my talent? Certainly the thought of writing an 'ordinary' novel has no attractions whatsoever. If it doesn't have some sort of personal impression on it, it's not worth doing ...

29 March

A cold has been gaining on me remorselessly all day; in fact since yesterday evening when I went to see two monumental '*navets*'[22] with Greta Garbo – *Ninotchka* and *Queen Christina*. It was hard to say which was worse ... A hostage to my cold-blurred wits, I went to a small barber's shop on 8th Ave to have my hair cut by a tiny wizened Italian with bad breath who had been in the US about a week less than I had. As he clipped away he chattered incomprehensibly about himself ... I grinned goodnaturedly all the time and made one or two elementary remarks which he failed to understand. Cost: $1.25, the cheapest haircut so far.

Russell spent a couple of days here over the weekend and we talked a great deal. He seems lonely and more oppressed than I am by his bachelorhood. He seemed to think that the only possibility was an Oriental girl, his own countrywomen being so brash and assertive as to paralyse him completely. Riding up in the loft to my room a couple were necking passionately, oblivious of us.

How to make a large novel centripetal instead of centrifugal? Musil does it with the character of Ulrich who, by being uncommitted to anything, acts as the touchstone to all the committed characters around him – yet Ulrich isn't a cipher as Hans Casdorp [23] tends to be. This is a very subtle piece of organisation. Another way, of course, is by using a very tightly organised plot that draws all the disparate elements together. Perhaps it should have both these things – but whatever it is at the centre must be substantial like the stone in a peach and it must exist before one can ever begin to start thinking constructively. A myth might provide the stone? Somehow I have the feeling that the answer must lie in the character of Spencer, [24] the protagonist; perhaps his very passivity would act as a foil to the other characters.

John Guare [25] called on me yesterday afternoon and we took a walk together as far as the A.B.C. building on 6th Avenue. He said he thought *Girl* was 'wonderful' but then he has a habit of speaking hyperbolically – much better than *The Lung* – but then he had told me earlier that *The Lung* was 'wonderful' too. Well, even if my confidence in his judgement (or what he reveals of it to me) is not quite complete (unfortunately) I must say I like him – big, dishevelled, bespectacled, breezy in manner, and with a quick wit, there is something very genuine about him ...

The man next door must have had a stroke sometime, I think. He looks very ill, poor devil, walks in a stiff marionette fashion and his face is gaunt and yellowish, wearing a constant expression of petulance and weakness. 'Be sure to have your pyjamas on by the time I get back at 11 p.m.' his wife was saying the other evening. As if he were a child. I thought of Gide's *Immoraliste*: '*Tu lèveras la main*'.

7 April

Three or four relatively optimistic and energetic days (energy mainly spent in trotting down 7th Avenue to Macy's at 34th St. and looking for Arrow shirts at reduced prices) followed by an equal complement of black days. Last Friday Anita[26] rang up to say that an editor at Pantheon had written an enthusiastic report on *Girl* and that Shiffrin [27] was going to read it over the weekend. Hopes dashed the following Wednesday when he turned it down – though he told Anita to say that he 'liked it'. All I can say is that he can't have liked it too terribly much if instead of it he prefers to publish the ephemeral bilge which I expect he will be publishing instead. Harsh words. But I'm convinced it's good and that Shiffrin is an imbecile.

Yesterday I had lunch with Anita who somehow turned out to be younger ... than I remembered from my one brief encounter with her on a sunlit afternoon in Lynn Nesbitt's office [28] of the 40th floor of the Time-Life building – with skyscrapers poking around outside the window in the upper atmosphere ... I'm afraid I had to abandon my plans to marry her – formed rapidly in the above-mentioned sunlit, sky-scrapered office some days ago – and leave the position open, as they say in newspaper advertisements. No they don't ... I invited her to the circus but probably inertia and despair will prevent me from executing the project. Depressing, all the same, how in spite of the Arrow shirts women seem to find me so consistently resistible. Women and publishers, I should say.

The Barnum and Ringling circus, performing at Madison Sq. Garden in the next block, has descended on the Belvedere, adding a welcome touch of surrealism to the already motley crowd of guests. I now ride up and down in the lift with dwarfs, giants and clowns in full regalia. One giant of almost, I think, 9 feet tall and a lady, perfectly formed and mature, who reached only up to my knee. This reminds me of the armless, legless prostitute Russell and I saw a photo of in the newspaper some days ago who had been arrested by the police – a policeman had been offered her favours – in Mexico. The sole support of the family, all damaged in some way. Roemer is right. Reality throws up things far more powerful than our imaginations can devise ...

The gloom at the moment appears impenetrable. Damp, foggy weather. My hair falling out. Knowing nobody here I want to talk to. The heels falling off my Japanese shoes and refusing to remain stuck on in spite of a lavish investment in glue. Only minor progress in work. I've also been reading Léautaud's [29] diary which has added to the cheerlessness of the scene ... In the public library on 53rd St. opposite the Museum of Modern Art this afternoon I stood and looked at the vast shelves of novels travelling at a brisk pace into limbo and savoured my own anonymity, even compared with them. The difficulties both of living and working satisfactorily seem, at this moment, to be quite insuperable. I remember thinking last night almost with a feeling of congratulation how my father's quiet and un-egotistic method of living has got him satisfactorily through a lot of years – or seems to have. Contrapuntally, the old couple next door were threatening to 'dig each others' eyes out' the other night. I wonder how long I shall be able to last out in New York after the summer? Even after eight months the streets of Manhattan still seem intolerably dirty and hostile ... Sipping Bénedictine just now I suddenly remembered – the sweetness and sharpness, perhaps – how I used to sip port in my dormitory box at Rossall, having brought back a bottle, I suppose, after a holiday.

To Franz Beer

Hotel Belvedere
26 April 1967

Dear old Franz, [30]
How are you? I wonder whether life is still good to you and if you are working well. For me, it is no better than it was this winter.

This is why I am writing to you: From Friday 5 May I am thinking of going to spend a few days in the only hotel on Block Island. [31] For Block Island I must take the boat from Narrangansett, which is not very far from Providence, I think. I wonder if I could come to your house on Thursday evening? The problem is that the boat leaves at eleven a.m. Could you put me up and bring me to Narrangansett on Friday morning? If it is any trouble, don't hesitate to say no – but in any case write to give me your news.

Best regards,
Jim

To Franz Beer

Hotel Belvedere
Postcard of Block Island – 'Gracie Point in the distance']
May 1967

Dear Franz,

Sorry I haven't phoned you. I found I had lost your number. The island isn't quite as uncivilized as I thought and well worth a visit! But
the weather has been pretty bad. I think I will leave this weekend ...

Amitiés,
Jim

Diary

11 May

Over a month since the last entry – an interval during which things
went downhill at a fairly brisk pace, with the roaches multiplying in my
room at the Belvedere faster than I could control them ... In this time
I took out Anita Gross a couple of times. She's attractive, sure. But
there's something slightly wrong somewhere, something that reminds
me a bit of *La petite poupée* (I've forgotten her name! though I was once
mad about her) in Toulon – an over-self-sufficiency. She doesn't need
me, I guess, that's what's wrong with her. I find myself saying things I
know she wants to hear, which disgusts me with myself. I may be
wrong about this but that's my impression at the moment ...

A week ago I came to Block Island to stay at the Surf Hotel
under the aegis of Mr and Mrs Sear. He is a fat, genial chap and she
is somewhat severe with elegantly rolled white hair that makes her
look like an immigrant from Versailles. They also have a young
daughter, Lorraine, who waits on table. The food is copious but un-
appetising. The rooms very clean but with thin walls so that one is
likely to hear one's neighbour hawking and spluttering. No girls on
the island, and not much of anything except rocks, birds, beaches
and empty shuttered houses belonging to summer residents – there
are said to be about 300 permanent residents – only one or two
shops. There is 'Ernie's' restaurant [and] also a local tycoon who waits
at the ferry to nab any unsuspecting tourists and talk them into renting one of his apartments or cottages. 'Take it or leave it,' he is reputed to say ... He sits slumped in his huge car for most of the day
driving aimlessly around. A pastime much favoured by the islanders.

At first I found myself eating with an English couple called Porter: she is a psychiatrist, he described himself as a 'poet' but I didn't question him about this and he didn't volunteer any further information. He was much older than his wife and, in general, sensitive about himself, I thought. His wife was more amusing and I felt she would have been even friendlier towards me had it not been for a slight strain emanating from him. As a young man he had his first Pimms at the bar in Shepheard's hotel in Cairo. 'I suppose I was a bit of a blimp in those days. A young blimp, mind you'...

I've covered most of the island on foot in the past week and feel much healthier for it. The weather has been a mixture of terrible storms and sunny, windy days. Last weekend the ferry was unable to make the return trip because of a storm. Now the rain has returned I think I shall return to NY tomorrow.

While here I have made yet another 'fresh start' on my book – partly inspired by the charred remains of the Ocean View Hotel which stands, or stood, on a cliff overlooking the old harbour where the ferry comes in. It burned down a year or so ago. 'A place with a thousand rooms,' Mr Porter (the poet) said. '200 to 300' said his wife.

This morning I went up to look at the remains while the sun was still shining. Old bedsprings twisted with heat; puddles of molten glass; washbowls that had fallen through to the foundations; a flight of stone steps leading up to thin air; twisted pipes; lots of nails lying everywhere and a few charred beams. I think the way the glass had collected like candlegrease under the windows impressed me most. When you picked it up it was inclined to flake away into smaller pieces in your hand. I must remember to ask someone how many storeys it had. Anyway this gave me an idea, which seems to me a good one, for the dwelling place of the family. [32]

A letter from Maschler saying he'd 'love to hear' about my new book. I started by writing an effusive, friendly letter but tore it up the next day, remembering his airs of pique at being disturbed and his being too busy to see me in NY when I needed to talk to him about the title. The hell with him.

The first day I got here I read Bassani's *The Garden of the Finzi-Continis* [33] and was very struck by it – by the great air of sincerity he manages to convey. I suppose, too, I kept recognising myself in the narrator – vis à vis the Kirwans in Dalkey.

On return from Block Island, Farrell got in touch with Carol Drisko, a senior editor with the educational publishers Scholastic. They became lovers, although she was about to leave for a holiday in Europe almost at once. To be nearer her 3rd Avenue apartment he swiftly found rent-controlled but cramped 4th floor accommodation at 203 East 27th Street.

To Carol Drisko

c/o Garry Arnott
321 East 14th. St.
15 May 1967

Dear Carol,
My name is Jim Farrell and I'm an old friend of Franz Beer from his Rue Juanès days. When I was staying with Franz in Providence a couple of weeks ago he gave me your address and suggested I call you. I'd very much like to invite you to lunch one day. If you're not too busy maybe you could call me at 982.5585 so that we could fix it up. Virtually any day would suit me. I tried calling you once or twice without success – so maybe you're away at the moment?
Sincerely,
Jim Farrell

To Carol Drisko

Apt. 14
203 East 27th Street
New York 10016
Monday morning
[undated] May 1967

Dear Carol,
I picture you this morning staggering through the snow-drifts of South Kensington in that coat of yours (which seems to be made out of an eiderdown) bristling with anti-nuclear buttons, with your library of reference books and instructions to yourself. However, I expect that (apart from the eiderdown) all the seduction-defying clothes you wear will keep you warm even in the English Spring ...

I'm afraid I've given you the wrong impression of myself. I'm not normally so affectionate (partly because being affectionate always seems to lead to complications and threats to my independence).

But I think you took me so much by surprise ... and then disappeared before I had time to take a grip of myself. Actually, even now I'm still not able to accuse myself of being an idiot with any conviction. By the time you get back, however, I should have recovered my refrigerated poise.

So, baby, there it is. I wish you were still here but it's probably a good thing that you aren't. The expression 'baby' is intended to sound hard-bitten and Anthony-Quinnlike so that you'll expect the worst ... I'm no good for a nice girl like you. I do like you, though (there I go, spoiling it all again). Anyway, love to you from a somewhat tormented,

Jim

To Tom Maschler

203 East 27th Street
18 May 1967

Dear Tom,

Thanks for your note and the ad from the *Bookseller* which I did rather like. I look forward to seeing a copy of the book itself when you have one to spare. I think I already mentioned how impressed I was by the skill of your blurb-writer on the evidence of the proof copy.

I'm sure you'll understand that I prefer not to talk about the book I'm working on at the moment.

Kind regards,

Jim Farrell

To Carol Drisko

203 East 27th Street
27 May 1967

Dear Carol,

... You claim that you haven't yet begun to tour London and then proceed to describe visits to Chelsea, the Horse Guards, Number Ten Downing St. and so on. *Nom de Dieu!* What'll happen when you finally do begin? The mind boggles.

I haven't been doing anything so exciting (tsk, tsk, there I go being ironic again) in New York. I've spent the last two days in an advanced state of exhaustion, attempting to clean my new apartment (see above) ... Anyway, after two days with mop and broom I did something awful to my back and now spend most of my time reclining indolently on an ottoman fanning myself wearily. From time to time I stagger out into 3rd Avenue and stare soulfully up at your curtained windows (discreetly, though, so as not to embarrass the burglars flitting in and out with grand pianos, diaphragms, and *New York Times*es).

Carol dear, I wish you hadn't gone away. For the first time in the awful nine months I've spent in this country things seemed to be going better. My God, I even began to get some ideas for this novel I've been failing miserably to get off the ground for so long. But I suppose I can't grumble since I shall be gone three times as long as you at the end of June with my cargo of boring slave-girls. [34]

Last night I had dinner with a fantastically rich young American who had his house decked out with large original Constables side by side with his own (really terrible) paintings. The effect was quite appalling. Nevertheless, in spite of all the luxury ... I couldn't help feeling there was something sad about the bloke. Tsk! (my favourite new ejaculation) I shouldn't waste my pity on such imbeciles.

When you do come back my phone number is 684.7963. I expect you to go straight to Soho and have it tattooed indelibly on your left breast ...

Love to you,
Jim

He had already decided to use the travel grant and car provided by Harkness House to make a detour to Lowry's Mexican setting for Under the Volcano *during the compulsory trip around America that summer. In good time, a few months beforehand, he had invited Sandy Ellis,* [35] *his girlfriend in London, to fly over to join him for the trip at the end of June. Meanwhile, the prospect of driving the Chevrolet for such a vast mileage with his weakened arm muscles was disturbing.*

To Carol Drisko

203 East 27th Street
3 June 1967

Carol dear,

... I'm delighted to hear that you are apparently liking your stay – even though the machines refuse to vend cigarettes to you. You needn't think that this is because they have you spotted for an American though. They normally take my half-crowns too, this being one of the principles of British democracy. Or maybe, I wonder, it is simply that they have detected my Irish blood ...

Memorial Day I spent on Jones Beach with the Other Carol (as opposed to Carol the Magnificent) ... Part of the idea was that I should have a go at driving her car, never having driven one with an automatic shift. I was somewhat apprehensive about this. It soon turned out, however, that she herself was so unbelievably reckless and had such primitive notions of traffic lore that it was with a great feeling of relief that I finally managed to grab the wheel, leaving her to powder her nose and chatter on without having to interrupt herself by saying 'Woops!' every now and again as we shaved some other vehicle. I finally staggered home about 7pm, a wiser and redder man (having got myself sunburned).

Oh well, it is now only two weeks until you'll be back by my calculations.

Love to you,
Jim

[*Handwritten postscript*] It's getting very warm here. You are lucky to be in a country where even the out-of-doors is air-conditioned.

To Tom Maschler

203 East 27th Street
13 June 1967

Dear Tom,

Many thanks for the copy of *A Girl* and your good wishes.

I must say that if the contents of the book are judged to be half as attractive as the book's appearance then there will be no problem (which is a somewhat tortuous way of saying how much I like the jacket).

Sincerely,
Jim

To Carol Drisko

804 Woodland Avenue
Chapel Hill
North Carolina
[undated] late June – early July, 1967

Dear Carol,

Things are a lot better here than in NYC, partly, if not exclusively, because of the lush vegetation, tall trees, blue skies, and clear country air. So impressed have I been by the latter that I have almost given up smoking. Bob being a great outdoor fiend we spend a lot of time picnicking idyllically among the cowpats. We've also had a bash at playing tennis. I used to consider myself a rather impressive performer at this game but was sadly disillusioned by my inability to hit the ball where I wanted to. The fault, however, almost certainly lay in the defective tennis racket that Bob lent me, don't you agree? I hope you do. In any case, the life of the mind is the only one of any interest to an adult human being. There, I'm sure you'll agree, being no good at tennis either, I suspect.

Bob has a number of agreeable friends around here ... [and] the impression one gets is that all America isn't represented by LBJ. In Chapel Hill yesterday morning we witnessed the weekly silent vigil against Vietnam (the war, that is). The people demonstrating were impressive because they were of all ages and included a number of distinctly bourgeois looking people and an elderly clergyman holding an American flag.

Of personal news there is very little except that for some reason the glands under my arms have started to swell up. For that I blame the great dinosaur of a Chevrolet that I am still trying to pilot. The cause, however, may be something even more sinister than General Motors, if this is possible. I hope not ...

Love,

Jim

PTO. In the meantime your letter arrived ... Your question [36] filled me with exasperation: I haven't the slightest intention of getting married or engaged to 'her', you, or anybody else. If I could get rid of her without hurting her feelings, disappointing her and reneguing on my idiotic invitation, I'd do so instantly. I find I have nothing whatever to say to her and vice versa. It also irritates me (and this is the main cause of my irritation) to be spending money on such a futile enterprise. I'm sick and tired of feeling no other emotion but exasperation. My former womanless state now seems like a time of bliss. Of course, you have a perfect right to ask such questions. My exasperation is with letting myself get in a position where this is so. ... I'm an idiot. I'm sick of the whole mess.

To Carol Drisko

[Postcard of El Volcan Popocatepetl' Mèxico]
15 July 1967

Dear Carol,

Here's a portrait of the Consul's Volcano. I hope to nip over to Cuernavaca to make a pilgrimage ... maybe this weekend. I got your letter at the Post Office. Many thanks for all your labours on my be-half. I still haven't seen *The Times* and *Observer* reviews. Were they very bad? Or merely indifferent? I shall be calling at Laredo General Delivery on 27th. I am being consumed by retrospective anguish about these reviews. I'm bored.

Love, Jim

To Claude and Anna Simha [37]

[Postcard of Cuernavaca]
15 July 1967

My dear Friends,

... The town where I am now reminds me of Morocco and especially of Casa[blanca] with its mixture of great beauty and deprivation.

Best wishes,
Jim

To Brian and Rose Knox Peebles

[Postcard of 'Diego Rivera Mural in the Hotel del Prado, Mèxico]
15 July 1967

Dear Brian and Rose,

How is my god-daughter? [38] How are you? ... I hear that my book got massacred by the critics ... Mexico is delightful after the US.

Love,
Jim

To Carol Drisko

                    [Postcard of Jardines del Hotel Borda, en Cuernavaca]
                                                            25 July 1967

Dear Carol,

Every word is torture as I partly dislocated my right arm in the surf
at Acapulco. Cuernavaca is the only place I like. Life no fun with
arm in sling. Saw doctor, cost $20 (American).

                                            Love,
                                            Jim

To Carol Drisko

                          Camp at Lake Wohlfort near San Diego
                                                1 August 1967

Dear Carol,

... *Nom de Dieu*, those reviews were pretty awful, weren't they? I
really can't believe that the book is that uninteresting. In fact, I still
think it's the best thing I've done and it perplexes me that no-one else
thinks so. However, luckily the paperback edition is already sched-
uled [39] so the thing may have a chance of survival (if it is any good).
Camping turns out to be more amusing than I expected but as my
shoulder is still very painful I find sleeping (on the ground in a sleeping bag) pretty arduous. However, apart from that I feel very healthy,
have given up smoking and so on. I find it almost impossible to read
(let alone write) anything and in general my mind seems to be going
soft(er) than usual. Odd snatches of appalling news filter into my apathy: the negro riots [40] and so on – but in a camp in the mountains it
doesn't seem very real ...

                                            Love,
                                            Jim

To Carol Drisko

        [Postcard of the [Provincial] Parliament Buildings, Victoria, B.C.,
                                                            Canada]
                                                    15 August 1967

Dear Carol,

Getting more and more feeble-minded as exposed to more and more
mountains and fresh air. Saw my brother for first time in years. Very

agreeable. At last a fairly good review of my book in *Times Literary Supplement*. Start back East soon.

Love,
Jim

To Russell McCormmach

203 East 27th Street
New York
29 August 1967

Dear Russ,

... Got back here a couple of days ago – alone as the girl is visiting her sister in Toronto. The best part of the trip, as it turned out, was spent camping in your home state and vicinity. The fact that I should enjoy camping took me by surprise (it was an economy measure) since I have always considered myself to be something of a lounge lizard ...

My book got nothing but abuse from the critics (with the exception of the *TLS* who thought it my best so far). This sticks in my gullet as I'd much rather be an instant ephemeral success than have to seek election as one of the great misunderstoods. One is more likely to end up as an ephemeral misunderstood, now I come to think of it.

If you get to NY give me a ring.

Cheers,
Jim

To G.M Arthursen [41]

203 East 27th Street
30 August 1967

Dear G.M.A.,

... Actually, the reviews were so awful, with only one or two exceptions (fortunately you saw one of them!) that I feel maybe I should be pretending that the author was James T. Farrell 'the Small Bore from the Mid-West' as Cyril Connolly once described him (or was it someone else?) rather than trying to press copies on people. As it happens, since I've been away all summer in Mexico, California and the North West ... I've only seen the Sunday reviews (abusive without exception) and the *TLS*. However, I understand the rest were not much better. This perplexes me, really, as I consider this book as by far my best. Hardly anyone, even the people who liked the book, had any sympathy for Boris and his predicament. Well, apart from all his appalling defects of character, pride, dishonesty, self-centredness and so on, I couldn't help thinking that Boris was significant in some way. Anyway, authors have been right and critics wrong about their books before now (though not often) ... so I refuse to allow it to be counted out so soon.

You didn't say where you were going for your holiday. Am I right in picturing you astride an enormous motorbike of some kind making the windows of sleepy French towns tremble as you roar by? I find I miss France dreadfully. Mexico, though interesting and attractive, is no substitute. I forget whether I told you that my dream is to buy an abandoned farmhouse in Lozère some day and live there half the year ...

I have another nine months to serve here before my Harkness Fellowship expires and leaves me to earn my own living once again. By that time I hope to have completed another book but I find that there is something about the American ambiance that makes it hard for me to settle down here.

A good deal of this summer I spent camping in the huge forests and mountains of the West coast – in particular around Oregon and Washington State ... A lot of the time we didn't bother with tents and just slept under the stars as in most places it is sufficiently dry to do this. Are you an efficient camper? I have the feeling that you probably are ...

Amitiés,
James F.

To Tom Maschler

203 East 27th Street
22 November 1967

Dear Tom,
Thanks for your note and the clippings for A GIRL IN THE HEAD. I hadn't seen them, actually, and though disappointing on the whole they were a shade less terrible than I had been led to expect. I was sorry that so many people called it Nabokovian as I feel that I had got there independently, via my other books, though of course I can't

deny the superficial similarities.

Within the next six months or so I hope to finish another book, one with a stronger story line, something I haven't tried before. At the moment, though, I'm inclined to feel pessimistic about it being a success. In any case, I shall look forward to having your professional judgment on it in due course.

Sincerely
Jim Farrell

To Russell McCormmach

203 East 27th Street
27 February 1968

Dear Russ,
I just got back from Puerto Rico whither, on an impulse, Carol Drisko and I fled for a week to escape the mounting garbage, both moral and physical. [42] It's an agreeable place, though heavily Americanised, as you can imagine. However, it was nice to walk around in shirt sleeves for a change ...

Looking forward to seeing you soon.

Jim

But Farrell's dependence on Carol was about to end. In mid-April 1968 he answered a note in the post from an English newcomer, twenty-four-year-old Sarah Bond. She had been given his address by Robin Cook, a fellow-writer whom he had got to know in London at impromptu get-togethers in the Jonathan Clowes Agency. Glamorous, sexually independent and strong-willed, Sarah's impact would influence the development of Troubles, *from the character of her namesake, to the Major's still indistinct and powerful emotions.*

To Sarah Bond

203 East 27th Street Saturday
[undated] April 1968

Dear Sarah
How's this for service! ... The reason for the speed is that I happened to acquire some fresh mackerel this morning and plan to cook them with an English friend this evening. If you happen to be free give me a ring between 4 p.m. and 6 p.m. at 684.7963.

In any event, give me a ring. I'm in most days most of the time.

Yours,

Jim Farrell

His Fellowship was almost up, however, and on 28 May he had to leave Sarah behind, after four short weeks of an intense affair. His old Oxford friend Bob Cumming escorted him to the ship at 52nd Street Pier and waved him off. Among Farrell's few possessions was the partially completed manuscript of Troubles, *minus the most recent pages which Sarah had promised to duplicate and send on.*

Beginning to Ship Water
London
1968

To Carol Drisko

c/o Knox Peebles
34 Gunter Grove
London S.W.10
6 June 1968

Dear Carol,

Just a rapid missive to let you know I arrived after a calm, uneventful (if not to say dead boring) voyage. I shared a cabin with an 80 yr old bloke, half senile, who spent the entire voyage stretched on his bed groaning for a doctor. I was afraid he'd croak there and then but he survived as far as Southampton, his life hanging by a thread. In one of his rare lucid moments he informed me that he had spent most of life managing stores in Nicaragua; the climate, he said, was very debilitating and, indeed, he looked debilitated. Also in the cabin were two weathered old bogtrotters from Kerry, one of them with an accordion, the other claiming to be (I see no reason to disbelieve him actually) the progenitor of 14 children ... well, we each have to do our own thing!

I shared a table with a young couple, the bloke Irish, the girl a New Yorker, just married, both pleasant and entertaining. He supports himself by gambling with greyhounds and his father was an I.R.A. hero who shot an informing postman (and killed him) during the Troubles. We became friendly and he offered to introduce me, both to the doggy world and to his Da' if I ever appear in Dundalk. Also at the table were two loud girls from California, neither of whom, unfortunately, were too quick with the wits. One of them warned me solemnly that if I went to France I shouldn't drink the water. I could think of no reply to this except to stare gloomily at my plate ...

> Love to you,
> Jim

[*Added in pen*] I just heard on the radio about Kennedy. [1]

To Carol Drisko

> 34 Gunter Grove
> 14 June 1968

Dear Carol,

Guess what ... I just returned from the dentist after having all my sins and decay and corruption x-rayed and repaired ... After all the fuss (I made in New York) none of the sins were mortal: I just needed to have a couple of venials filled and my upper and lower virtues polished. Not bad for two years of neglect ...

The flat sharing thing fell through: at the moment I'm inhabiting the basement of the parents of my god-daughter. There are children crawling all over the place ... and they are inclined to chant things over and over driving your poor friend out of his wits.

For a while I thought about hopping straight over to Ireland, but then thinking about it discouraged me ... At the end of this month I intend to move into the room I used to live in in my pre-America days at the Stanley House Hotel. This will come as a considerable shock to you who have known Jim in his palmy days since it is a some-what seedy establishment and the place is merely a bedsitting room *sans* bathroom and *sans* kitchen: it's only redeemed by a balcony over a private garden: a wash-basin it has also, and a gas ring on which one may warm up one's humble meal of boiled groats. However, I was content there before ...

I had supper the other night at Lif and Oliver's. [2] The Swedish theatre directed by Ingmar Bergman are in town at the moment and also at table was an oldish rather gaunt actor and his wife. I'd seen him in a number of Bergman's films (though I don't know his name) and he lent a rather weird quality to the evening ...

> Love to you,
> Jim

To Russell McCormmach

34 Gunter Grove
15 June 1968

Dear Russell,

... [At] the end of the month I shall move back into the room I occupied before in the Stanley House Hotel ... I remember being content there because the place has a balcony that looks over a garden on which I could sit and type on sunny days. On the other hand it will be hard to do without a kitchen. Garry [Arnott] once remarked that one's standard of living had a ratchet effect that prevented one from slipping back to a situation less comfortable than the previous one. However, it's easier to do without a kitchen in England than in the US since there are good cheap meals available in restaurants. Anyway, one reason why I decided to go back there was that it's easy to leave. Perhaps next spring I shall decide to settle here for good and look around for a more permanent place ...

Bob saw me off on the boat and before leaving handed me a Holt, Rinehart and Winston paperback of two short Dostoievsky [*sic*] novels called *The Friend of the Family* (the Russian title is 'The Village of Stepanchikovo and its Inhabitants') and *The Eternal Husband*, both of which are marvellous. Have you read them? *The Eternal Husband* starts with some splendid things rather like *Notes from Underground* ... I read some of my book yesterday and on the whole it seemed better than I had supposed (but then I hadn't supposed it to be very good.) I really must push on with it.

The worst thing about being back is that my best friends live in America. I wish you would all come and live here. London, I'm convinced, is a far more agreeable place than New York or Philadelphia.

Cheers,
Jim

To Sarah Bond

34 Gunter Grove
16 June 1968

Sarah dear,

Your letter has just been poked under my bedroom door (with great difficulty because it was so fat) ... I was delighted to have such an enormous epistle: it was carried from the Post Office by two sweating postmen, one on each end, and then winched up to the letter-box. Needless to say, it stimulated fresh pangs of Sarahlessness. However, although the gloom is still thick I'm becoming faintly more resigned to these withdrawal symptoms. As a doctor once said to me while in the iron lung, 'You can get used to anything' ('thanks a lot' I replied).

Sorry to hear about your troubles with the pill; for a moment I thought you were going to tell me that the doctor had diagnosed the problem as the imminent arrival of a small grey-haired infant. Ouf! After all the bathing in gin and so on [3] that would have been too much ...

I forget whether I told you that I'm staying in a house where there are children crawling all over the place like cockroaches. One of them is my six year old god-daughter who is a pretty little girl and seems to like me. I think I shall dandle her on my knee when she's eighteen or nineteen.

I'm glad you like the bits of my book [4] you read (though I hope it wasn't just because it was by me): I looked at it myself the other day for the first time in a couple of weeks and I was really quite pleased with it on the whole. I find it almost impossible to work here with all the kids yelling and dashing around ... One reason I didn't keep looking for a better place was that I expect to be travelling around this winter, spending Christmas with my parents in Malta [5] and then maybe going to North Africa to see some French friends [6] in Sidi bel Abbes in Algeria. Paris, too, of course, and maybe Italy. Anyway, I feel so unsettled (without you) that I couldn't bear to take a permanent place and sign a lease and so on. With a gas oven I'd be content: I don't mean to put my head in, I mean to cook the odd duck stuffed with sausage and apple. That was a nice evening, wasn't it?

... By the way, the only picture I have is the one you don't like. I want one of you preferably with no clothes on.

Love to you, Jim

XXXXXX

XXXXXX

To Sarah Bond

34 Gunter Grove
21 June 1968

Sarah dear,

Many thanks for *The Itch* which arrived yesterday under plain cover, as they say. Well, well! You are becoming interested in the subject! I wish now that I'd either given you *The Story of O* sooner or hung around longer to reap the rewards.

You say that 'Mr Hammer' took a week to write this book. Well, I haven't finished it yet but on the evidence of the first sixty pages I'm surprised that he took so long. But perhaps it improves as it goes along. I don't mean to sound ungrateful but I have strong views on how pornography should be written and intend to write just one superb pornographic book myself one of these days ... maybe when I finish this thing I'm doing now. That sounds dreadfully arrogant now I come to think about it; however, I do believe I understand what works and what doesn't in pornography.[7] We'll see, anyway.

Incidentally, how d'you know he only took a week to write it? ... Is he a friend of yours? If so, I suspect him of being the rather haggard, saturnine individual I glimpsed in a taxi the day after, drunk with generosity, I bought you the dress and we met by accident on your doorstep (Proust would have squeezed three volumes out of that). But enough of this nonsense.

I feel full of ideas, but as far as morale goes I'm beginning to ship water once again.

Love to you, babe,
Jim

To Sarah Bond

Room 17
Stanley House Hotel
13/14 Stanley Crescent
London W.11
25 June 1968

Sarah dear,

I've been suffering from mild despair in the past few days and gloomily deciding that we should abandon writing to each other: the trouble is that I decided that there was nothing to look forward to: I wouldn't mind if there was and could get happily down to work. 'What a weedy way to begin a letter!' I can see you exclaiming ... I'd seriously consider coming over [but] ... two or three weeks really wouldn't change the basic problem, would it? In fact it would just take us back to square one ... (walking around the Kings Rd. I've been feeling that I am Square One – excuse the weedy joke). Misery. The only other thing I can suggest (apart from suggesting that you should chuck in America and come and live with me indefinitely – I could give you a voucher good for one year and a day but you could apply for an extension by submitting an application in triplicate with nude passport photographs) is that you wheedle some extra vacation out of your boss, spend Christmas with your parents and then join me on my Continental Drift this winter. That might not be any more satisfactory than me coming over for a couple of weeks. Maybe the best thing is to meet, have a terrible row and then part again, feeling relieved. Otherwise I genuinely think the best thing is to drop the correspondence until one fine day you appear back in Blighty (we'll probably find that our wheelchairs are parked next to each other on the seafront at Brighton) because my letters are inclined to get morose and aggressive (cf. my last one, a mixture of professional arrogance and personal misery that must have amazed you) and we'd merely end up having our row by post (which is highly unsatisfactory since one can't throw things). However, we could exchange Christmas cards and changes of address at intervals. Failing either of the above solutions (impractical, no doubt) I think this is really what I want to do ...

There are some difficulties about sending you the next instalment of my novel – the main one being that I haven't written it yet. I'll seriously think about sending a clump of pages if/when I'm satisfied. Another thing is that soon I shall have to go back to the beginning to introduce a completely new and vital character who doesn't exist yet. Vital to the plot, I mean. Not vital to civilisation.

Please don't show what you have to anyone. You're the only person I've ever allowed (actually I couldn't really stop you) to see my scribblings before completion (big deal) ...

Lots and lots of love,
Jim

To Sarah Bond

Stanley House Hotel
27 June 1968

Dear Sarah (I agree with you about the difficulty of finding some other formula), dear Sarahkins, then.

... I really can't write letters and remain detached. I started off just now planning to soothe you with honeyed words and instead of honey there is nothing but acid bubbling out of my typewriter. Have you ever had a subconscious drive to start a row which will wreck everything so that one's emotional landscape in turn becomes barren and tidy once more? I have it all the time.

That's one reason why I think we should stop writing while we're still friends. The other is that I hate to see a fine love affair gradually wilting over the months as always happens with postal relationships until they reach a stage of vaguely benevolent indifference ...

What else have I got to say? Nothing much. Vaginas appear to be 'in' this year. Reading a copy of *Honey* I found in someone's flat I counted no less than four advertisements for products that deodorise 'the most womanly part of a woman' (as they delicately put it) so that she can 'enjoy clinically clean confidence always, even in hot weather'. The weather, these last few days, has been freezing, as it happens, so perhaps there hasn't been too much lack of confidence among the birds.

I went to see '*2001*'[8] yesterday evening. I quite liked it on the whole but kept yawning for some reason. I then swayed home on top of a number 14 bus in the rain. Aren't you glad to be in the US?
Love to you with multiple xxxxxes

Jim

[*Handwritten*] I really am sorry about writing that miserable letter, I can assure you, and I thought yours was very restrained and reasonable in the circumstances. It made me feel like Othello being beastly to Desdemona!

To Lif and Oliver Marriott

Stanley House Hotel
27 June 1968

Dear Lif and Oliver,
After much heart-searching I've decided to move back here; the main

reason being that it's comparatively easy to move out of. Telephoning me, you may remember, requires tenacity of purpose ...

Oliver, your book [9] is marvellous.

Lif, the dinner you cooked the other night was marvellous.

The weather is awful, however.

> Love,
> Jim

To Carol Drisko

> Stanley House Hotel
> 3 July 1968

Dear Carol,

Many thanks for your letter. I note that you are arriving at Heath Row [*sic*] at 6.10 so I shall take up my station at Cromwell Rd. terminal at around 6.45 a.m. provided I have succeeded in waking myself up etc ...

The room problem looks as if it may solve itself marvellously. A very nice Scottish Italian lady cellist friend of mine [10] who was once my landlady, years ago, has agreed to let you use one of her rooms. She has a house on Pembridge Rd. hard by the tube and buses and not far from me. The room ... should be just what's needed for a few days. Norma is rather mad ... but terrific fun and someone you definitely should meet anyway ...

There are no decent mixing bowls to be had here. Would it be altogether out of the question, would you give vent to a strangled Arrrgh! if I were to suggest that you nip along to the Woolworths on 23rd Street and buy me that set of three Pyrex ones I used to have in me flat with the measure markings on the side??? If it's too heavy or too space-consuming then never mind (but what kind of friend are you? Eh?) No, seriously, I won't mind if you fail me in this respect. Only do it if it's possible without inconvenience.

Enough is enough. The weather here has been torrid for the last few days, in the 80s.

> Love
> Jim

To Sarah Bond

Stanley House Hotel
4 July 1968

Dear Sarah,

O.K. then. It's settled that we're going to stop writing to each other. The only problem is that I have a great urge to answer your letters so I don't find it very easy – like being on a difficult and dangerous bicycle [11] that one doesn't know how to get off. So I'm relying on you to stop first ...

To show you the sort of condition I'm in let me describe the following depressing, meaningless incident that occurred this morning. I was drifting along Kensington Church Street about noon, minding my own business and clutching a loaf of health food bread I'd just bought when an oldish fellow stuck some sort of printed matter in front of my nose. 'Are you giving me this or selling it to me?' I asked him. Selling it, he replied. I thanked him and wandered on a few yards and then he started shouting at me. 'Giving you it! I'll give you something!' For some reason I lost my temper at this, went back and asked him what about it in an ugly manner. To my amazement the fellow looked terrified and said sheepishly, pointing at his glasses, 'Oh anyone could beat me, I can't see.' I slunk off then, feeling bitterly ashamed of myself. Can you imagine? Me with my paralysed arm threatening an old man with glasses. If it had occurred it would have been The Fight of the Century. My only consolation is that he won anyway since I could hardly have felt worse if he'd laid me out with a right hook. This is just another matinée appearance of Nasty Jim Farrell whom I somehow managed to keep to myself while in your company in New York but who has been riding more and more frequently with the absence of the beneficial rays of your personality ...

I re-read the first part of my book and thought it was all terrible. It gets better though. Just one thing (which I'd completely forgotten) made me laugh. Edward feeding the dogs shows the Major a scar and one of the dogs leaps up and begins to lick the exposed skin. I have no idea why I should find that funny, incidentally ... If I said I'll come when I finish my book then that might make me get down to work. Oh bugger the whole business ...

I bought myself some corduroys so tight that I could fall asleep in them standing up. The other ones collapsed into a mass of rags fluttering feebly round my loins, held together only in one place (by your extraordinarily efficient stitching).

Love and xxxxxes to you too,

Jim

To Sarah Bond

Stanley House Hotel
5 July? [*sic*] 1968

Dear Sarah,

… I posted my letter just as midnight was being clanked out from the church tower down the road (it was a lovely, still, moony night such as we often have in W.11) then went to bed and woke again around four still thinking of you and your letters and me and the old man with glasses. I was really amazed at how absurdly I've taken to behaving recently and decided it was high time I called out the Red Guard for a cultural revolution on myself. For someone still reasonably young, in good health, eating when I feel like it, coming and going as I please, working at something I like, I have been doing an awful lot of moaning and groaning. Time for that when I'm old and sick, dependent, hungry and the work has gone down the drain. In particular, (final sentence of this harangue) I should be delighted that a nice girl like you should even want to write me letters – and I am! (Gulp!)

Oh well, that's about all I have to say at the moment. I dug up this absurd picture of myself (it's not posed although it looks like it) taken by Norma Fleissner in NY a couple of years ago when I was still smoking. Note grey hair …

Do wish you'd send details of your amorous exploits so that at least I could enjoy them vicariously if not actually. However, I suppose it might look a bit odd if in the middle of some passionate embraces you suddenly whipped out a tape-measure and started making notes in your diary. Has your reading of pornography enlarged your horizons at all? Well, I suppose it's none of my business.

Must get this to the post. In the meantime love to you,

Jim

Handwritten P.S.: I wish you were here right at this moment so that I could take off your clothes and get inside you.*

* This autograph postscript is supposed to make the letter invaluable

to collectors and is definitely not written while drunk!

To Carol Drisko

Stanley House Hotel
8 July 1968

Dear Carol,

... My conscience has been pricking me slightly about the rather onerous request I made in my last letter. That, however, isn't going to prevent me from making two more. One is: bring any spare matches you have lying around. The other is: could you bring me a Good Seasons salad shaker from d'Agostinos with half a dozen packets of Italian dressing mix. If you like you could substitute this last request for the mixing bowls one. However, please don't go to any trouble over any of them.

The weather has turned miserable again.

Love,
Jim

To Sarah Bond

Stanley House Hotel
12 July 1968

Sarah dear:

I realise it was my idea to stop writing, you don't have to keep telling me. Blimey – I can't help it if it didn't work, can I? Besides, that was before I'd decided I might come over when I finish my book (though I probably won't).

I had to reach hurriedly for my dark glasses when your letter arrived; though I rather liked the shocking pink, the landlady's dog's hair stood on end when he saw me reading it and he began barking at it, then fled to take refuge under the bed, refusing to come out for half an hour. In the end we had to lure him out with a packet of prime Wiltshire sausages ...

I don't believe a word about your 'vast, green jealous complex' re Carol since I remember distinctly you saying how you were never jealous even when your boy-friends slept with other women since you always knew they liked you best. You see, my memory for this sort of thing is prodigious. I wish I could also remember things that would help me to make money.

I was very encouraged that you liked so much of my book. It's awfully scrappy and inconsistent and inconclusive at the moment. It'll take me years to homogenise it. I've written a bit more but I can't possibly send it for a number of reasons which are too boring to go into. As for the reviews of my first book you can take my word that those idiots don't know what they're talking about. It's as dreary as anything and I don't intend to send it to you ...

I was in the public library the other day flicking through a dry and weighty volume of Victorian social history when I came on a love-letter addressed to 'Tony'. Naturally, I read it greedily. Actually, it was only half written ... the unnamed girl was begging forgiveness for some unspecified unfaithfulness which had merely been 'experimental' but that ever since 'the first time on the camp bed' (!!!) she had really known that he was the only one. This is the only amusing thing that's happened to me. You are wanted etc.

Love to you,
Jim

[*Handwritten*] P.S. My latest system to fortify myself against the acute attacks of Sarahlessness is to remind myself of how you bit my finger during the 93rd Street Gin and Bathing Festival entirely without provocation.

To Sarah Bond

Stanley House Hotel
15 July 1968

Sarah dear,

This time the landlady's dog, on seeing your pink notepaper, uttered a long drawn out howl and rolled over on its back, clutching its paws to its fat stomach. Needless to say it took another half pound of prime Wiltshire sausages to revive it.

I was delighted to get your offer of supporting me for life and I ACCEPT! (as I feel I owe you a favour or two). The only thing is that every time you say how well we get on together the example you choose is you eating my delicious meals. In other words should the sauce fail a couple of times I'm afraid I'd find myself standing beside a mountain of suitcases on Madison Avenue.

Actually, though, I'm amazed at the amount of things we think the same way about, from Richard Hughes [12] to sleeping in the same weird position, to being malicious about other people (though in the nicest possible way). Perhaps another thing we have in common is being impermeable to romance. I'm sure that if/when we see each other again we'll both have the feeling the Major has on p.18 when he sees Angela again. [13] One tends to stylise people in one's imagination, and the reality sometimes comes as a shock ... My latest brilliant idea is: let's meet for a winter holiday in the West Indies in January or February when it's bitterly cold both in N.Y. and W.11. By that time I may have got nearer finishing my book ... I'm somehow reluctant to go back to New York, having just spent almost two years there – most of which I didn't find all that marvellous. Also there are all sorts of people there that I'd have to see ...

I may be going in to read mss. for Cape in the afternoons to make myself some cash – that is, I've arranged to go in on Thursday but I feel so gloomy at the idea of working that I may actually fink out at the last moment. However, I suppose I should have a bash because my meagre savings are vanishing at an alarming rate. Also, I expect to be sacked for incompetence almost as soon as I sit down, scratch my armpits and yawn, waiting for the tea break. Reading for Hutchinson used to be much better since I could do it at home, horizontally. Oh well – I feel positively starved of gossip since you're no longer around.

Here's to you, babe! (as Humphrey Bogart keeps saying to Ingrid Bergman in *Casablanca*).

Love to you and multiple kisses,

Jim

To Sarah Bond

Stanley House Hotel
26 July 1968

Sarah dear,

Here's a rapid missive, beamed at you in the hope that it will arrive by/before the weekend, thereby reminding you of my presence on the planet just as you are preparing to relax in the company of your local floral-tied, long-side-boarded-up mashers. It would be absurd to think, things being what they are, that NY isn't full of men capable of being found irresistible by you – just as London me vice versa (you may judge from that last sentence that my impeccable prose style has finally taken its revenge). However, I've now prepared myself for the eventuality and have fixed my gaze on eternity, only sneaking an occasional glance at such temporal matters. Erm.

For the last few days I've been going off my rocker, working like a slave in the mornings (determined to keep my book on the boil) and dashing around with Carol in the afternoon and evening. Carol, as I already knew, is a relentless tourist. In her company I visited the House of Commons for the first time, visited it a second time to attend some committee meeting to hear Papandreou (Andreas) speaking about the iniquities of the colonels, [14] the British Museum, the London Museum, the British Museum again ...

When I would finally crawl home to my room the ticking of the clock in the silence was balm to my ears (or ear-balm). Also, I've been spending a dreadful amount of money in spite of the fact that Carol has been constantly thrusting money on me. Also my parents arrived back, passed through I mean, on their way from Malta to Dublin and I spent a day talking non-stop with them – and it has all been terribly exhausting. Well, Carol leaves for Paris tomorrow in a car with some friends of mine so I shall be able to recover my hermetic stride ...

I finked out on the Cape job. I decided that unlikely as I am to make it as a writer I'm even more unlikely to make it as a reader. Perhaps I said that to you before. Frankly, I've been so desperately busy that I simply couldn't have found the time ...

More things in common: we both possess rather weedy language degrees and like that Jeanne Moreau record. [15] It really is lucky that the Gin and Bathing Regatta was a success since the result would have been positively tone deaf, inclined to sleep in fantastically odd positions and given to exceedingly boring monologues on Lamartine and Verlaine. Not to mention having grey hair and bandy legs and a paralysed arm. And a double chin.

O.K., I won't be encouraged by your approval of my book then. I miss you.

Love to you,
Jim

To Sarah Bond

Stanley House Hotel
[undated] 1968

Dear Sarah,

Could you send the copy of my *Troubles* – in a few weeks I plan to start an alternative version and it would be a great help if I could use that as a matrix (if matrix means what I think it does – which it probably doesn't) without demolishing the original. If there's any change from postage use it to buy yourself an ice-cream.

Love,

Jim

P.S. Send it surface mail. IT'S URGENT THOUGH SO DON'T FORGET.

To Carol Drisko

Stanley House Hotel
5 August 1968

Dear Carol,

A rapid missive as I'm worn out, having spent a day doggedly creating away at my doggy work of art ... I'm trying to decide whether to go to the *Taming of the Shrew* [16] tonight. Don't think I will. I've been reading Olivia Manning's splendid *Balkan Trilogy* set in Bucharest and enjoying it guiltily when I should be writing me own novels.

Love and guilt from

Jim

To Sarah Bond

Stanley House Hotel
7 August 1968

Sarah dear,

I'm in bad form just at the moment as I went for a swim yesterday and since then my ears have gone peculiar; I'm alarmed that I may be going deaf like my father and elder brother, and spend a lot of time tapping things to see if I can hear. I was out on a houseboat at Kew last night and while being told by Bernard Braden's pop-singing daughter [17] about her latest disc I kept clapping a palm over one ear or the other. Needless to say, she thought I was quite deranged. The trouble is I keep forgetting. I hopped cheerfully out of bed this morning and it wasn't until I ran the tap that I remembered about it. Heavy gloom ...

I had a money-making brainwave the other day while walking over Greenwich Common with a Yale Chinese historian called Jonathan Spence:[18] namely, to write a book on 'De Gaulle in England'. This could hardly fail to be a huge financial success, particularly the sort of gossipy popularised history that I have in mind – it would explain why de Gaulle hates the anglo-saxons so much and be full of scurrilous anecdotes ...

I've been working at my book from dawn till dusk – and yes, I do have another chunk written but it's absolutely pointless sending it to you, even apart from the fact that I can't spare it. It's all so tentative and will have to be re-written and reorganised countless times before it makes sense, if ever.

I went to a dinner party the other night at the house of a lady I've known for years, a splendid character; the other guests included a wild-eyed nymphomaniac mother who gives her 15 yr. old daughter the pill every day in a marmite sandwich, a rather nice, soft-spoken, intelligent Hungarian doctor called Egon, and another positively appalling English *emigré* (to Kansas City) psychiatrist who is pro-Nixon and pro-Vietnam and who raised my hackles so much that I scarcely noticed how peculiar the food was (Liver Stroganoff if you can imagine). As usual, all the women were madly garrulous. From time to time Egon and myself would try to inject a little sense into the conversation but our feebly piping voices were completely drowned out by the crazy babbling of the ladies. Incidentally, that's probably what did for my ears.

The weather here is simply appalling. It's been raining or cloudy for every day since I can remember. Not that it makes much difference to me at the moment since I inhabit a fantasy world most of the time. Whenever I emerge, though, I feel very depressed. No, that's not true, come to think of it. If only my ears would pull themselves together I'd feel quite cheerful.

If, before *mon général* dies and all the people who knew him over here, you find yourself over for long enough (and are still friends) we must write a synopsis, get an advance and get down to work for 6 months. I'm at least half serious about this.

In the meantime, lots and lots of love,

Jim

P.S. Have you read Olivia Manning's Balkan Trilogy? [19] The first two volumes: *The Great Fortune* and *The Spoiled City* are marvellous – set in Bucharest in 1939-40. The third *Friends and Heroes* is less good.

To Carol Drisko

Stanley House Hotel
30 August 1968

Dear Carol,

... Russell arrived the other day during some good weather, part of which we spent on my balcony. We ate at the Standard [20] a couple of times, once with the Snellings [21] and the other time [with a] Pakistani girl. I was extremely gratified that Zaimé (the girl) approved of my command of the dishes when ordering, and she gave [us] some supplementary advice. She thought it was a wonderful restaurant too and held a brief conversation with one of the waiters in some 'savage lingo': the waiter in question who had always been extremely cool and reserved (a small chap) became positively roguish with the inclusion of Zaimé in the party ...

We [watched] a late night programme from the Demo convention in Chicago; with all that's been going on I should think that by now you've reached a state of near-satiation with all the nutritious beatings, riots, yippies, and so forth you must have been ingesting. The evening papers, this evening, offer a further serving of riots and clubbings as well as Hubert's [22] nomination: with luck this year's election may simply settle down into the sort of Conservative-Socialist polarisation that most other Western countries have; it seems to me (an untutored opinion) that a lot of the trouble stems from the fact that each party in the US includes such an impossible grab-bag of opinion that the actual party is meaningless. It may be a good thing if the Demos split into two groups though it would mean victory for the Repubs ...

I've been working well of late – though yesterday and today have not been good. Yesterday I appeared at the Chelsea Registry office to act as a witness at the wedding of the Snellings (they've been living together for 6 years). The service was remarkably swift and painless; it really is easy to get married ... Weather horrible again.

Love,
Jim

To Sarah Bond

Stanley House Hotel
31 August 1968

Dear Sarah,

Many many thanks for sending the photocopy of my opus whch arrived safe and sound this morning. I note that I owe you $0.90 and the only reason I'm not sending it to you is that you were insulted the last time. As I write there is an ominous creaking of bed-springs up above and a piece of white paint has flaked off the ceiling and fallen into my typewriter – I somehow feel this must be significant. England is impossibly dreary at the moment and you're better off in the US where at least you are making some money. I wouldn't stay here myself but for the fact that I write well here – probably because it's so boring there's nothing else to do. As soon as I finish this book I'll move off somewhere else, I expect. It's much better to be a foreigner in a country than a native, I find. One doesn't identify with the imbeciles one sees around ...

A couple of weeks ago I went up to Liverpool to spend a night with an old aunt and uncle, [23] he went through the First World War in the trenches and was at Verdun. I tried to get him to talk about it but he was reluctant to, for some reason, perhaps he had trouble remembering. He is extremely thin and not one of my aunt's comforts is too small for him to consider: he ... cossets her exceedingly. She is small and extremely fat and needs a great deal of looking after. Over the past few years she has had an unending series of illnesses and accidents, sprained ankles and the like. But lo and behold! One day the roles are reversed and he falls ill and has to have an operation. But hardly has he been out of hospital a day when she develops an eye infection (a serious one) which means she has to go into hospital and be looked after ... Uncle Arthur, a real hero, though still with stitches in him and weak as a kitten, travelled an hour into Liverpool and back to the hospital every day to visit her. Poor thing: she said to me: 'It's a mystery – I don't know why I got this eye infection.' I thought I knew why but of course I didn't say, I didn't say ...

The Humphrey nomination and Chicago riots combined with Czechoslovakia[24] have convinced me that living in an ivory tower is the only solution. Goddammit – another bit of paint has just come whizzing down on me as the people up above resume their gymnastics ...

I sometimes have trouble getting through the days and nights, particularly the nights, but I've decided to be stoical about it and my book is a great help, though the cause of much of my insomnia. My ears seem a bit better since I gave up swimming, though still peculiar. You mustn't take all this seriously. When writing I always feel starved of affection – which is one reason why I simply can't bear waiting for your letters and for the time being would prefer that you didn't write at all. So please don't answer this. I'll write again in a few weeks when the first draft of my book is finished and I can sink back into my normal state of apathy once again.

In the meantime, love to you

Jim XXXXXXX

To Carol Drisko

Stanley House Hotel
13 September 1968

Dear Carol,

You do write such long letters, even on air mail forms. My feelings of guilt at my own telegrammatic efforts are such that just this once I shall single-space you; this is particularly rash as I have almost nothing to say except that I think I'm developing stomach ache from having bolted an entire can of gastro-political lychees after my meal, about an hour ago. By the by, I've discovered that lychees and gin go together *à merveille* ...

It seems as if Hubert is doomed, doesn't it? In today's *Guardian* I note that he has made another bloomer about Vietnam, promptly and sharply corrected by Lyndon. But I find it hard to forgive him that tv wife-kissing you mention. Four years of that sort of thing would make a cornball like LBJ and family look like Talleyrand ...

I seem totally incapable of making any money ... Perhaps one of these days m'luck will turn. I've been writing fluently enough recently and my *Troubles* are already the length of a novel but I'm not the kind to weigh my genius out by the page, or even by the chapter. Indeed the thing is dragging on remorselessly and may never come to an end.

This letter will, though. I'm beginning seriously to miss our dual gluttonies on Third Avenue!*

Love,
Jim

[*Handwritten*] *Also have been thinking with pleasure of our winter visit to P.R. [*Puerto Rico*] disastrous though moments of it were. [25]

To Carol Drisko

[Postcard 'Toulouse-Lautrec' posted in Paris]
26 September 1968

Got seriously bushed in London (too much rain; working too hard) so I came here to recuperate. Here the weather is lovely. I'm on the 5th floor of the Beauvais and every time I climb the stairs I have to sleep for 8 hours ...

Love,
Jim

To Sarah Bond

[Postcard 'Chagall, Jeune fille au cheval 1929']
September 1968

Sarah dear: Lovely sunny autumn weather in Paris; leaves turning gold, hardly any mini-jupes to be seen; I'd forgotten what a marvellous place this is.

Do you realise that there is a plaque on one of the houses aux Gobelins which says DANS CETTE MAISON BOND A ÉTÉ DÉPPUCELÉE. [26] I saw it yesterday.

Came here to recuperate, incidentally, after it had rained in London solidly for 3 days and 3 nights.

Love to you,
Jim

To Tom Maschler

[ink stamp] J.G. Farrell
13/14 Stanley Cres.
London W.11
28 September 1968

Dear Tom,

Supposing that you should want to publish the book I'm now writing, when would you have to have it by in order to bring it out this time next year (late August, early Sept.)?*...

Regards
Jim

*latest possible [*handwritten*]
P.S. This is an entirely hypothetical enquiry but knowing the answer may help me choose between various alternatives.

To Carol Drisko

Stanley House Hotel
3 October 1968

Dear Carol,
Got back from Paris yesterday and I'm feeling a slight backlash from the holiday – in other words I need another holiday to recover from the holiday, long though it didn't last. It served to *me changer les idées*, however, and to remind me that France is really a nicer place to live than England – or perhaps I just mean that anywhere but one's homeland is a nice place to live. On the other hand, I feel that to take up the old Montparnasse life I was living four years ago once again might be more than I could endure; I recognised a good dozen of the *habitués* lounging in vague boredom around the Select. To start all that again might be depressing ... For the moment, though, I think I shall stick it out here; perhaps I shall pick a small town in Normandy or even go back to the Massif Central ...

Most restaurants in Paris you need someone to go with – one feels a bit of an idiot eating a massive meal by oneself, except in those with communal tables like Chez Wadja. [27]

Love,
Jim

To Russell McCormmach

Stanley House Hotel
5 October 1968

Dear Russell,
... Last week my empty sails filled out with great gusts of despair and I sailed over to Paris to see Claude and the Snellings. This did me some good for a while but I fear the effects are wearing off rapidly ... Incidentally, I'm sure I was in Paris. As I look up, I can see a half-eaten French sausage I brought back hanging from a nail (I

mean, it's hanging from a nail now) ...

All the best to you,
Jim

To Sarah Bond

Stanley House Hotel
5 October 1968

Dear old Sarah,

Something weird has just happened: my small brother [28] (actually he's bigger than me and looks like a gorilla) just phoned from Dublin to say that he has won a weekend-in-New York competition for two and do I want to go with him? So provided I don't run into visa problems I shall very likely be in New York the weekend 25th-28th October – to say Hello to old Broadwa-a-a-ay – tum-ti-tum – Farewell, Leicester Square! Or is that another song? You're the expert on these ancient, creaking ballads.

It's such a short time it's bound to be somewhat unsatisfactory and I shall have to dash around and see a few people and show New York to my bro ... but if you could keep an evening free, or failing that a lunchtime, I'd love to see you. I might park my bro on Carol or some other such good-hearted soul so that we could get drunk together or something.

I realise that you may be reading this with somewhat mixed feelings ... affections, like everything else in this vale of tears, being subject to the second law of thermodynamics, have a tendency to cool off, decay and get re-born. Well, what I'm trying to say is that I won't be too astonished if by now (without my magnetic presence) someone else is plucking your heartstrings (to put it at its most delicate). That would be only natural. But I would like to know if we're lovers now or old friends so that I can get acclimatised to the idea and digest it (to mix a metaphor) rather than spend the weekend with that awful skinned-alive feeling one gets when things come to an end. So, if you know yourself, could you write and tell me as honestly as you can. That's all I ask of you – naturally, when you see me I'll be the cheerful, phlegmatic Jim we all know so well, whatever your reply.

I'm writing a marvellous book but my nerves are in shreds, as always happens. I suppose I must enjoy it, though, in some odd way or else I'd give it up and become a market gardener. My doctor friend in Paris [29] gave me some amphetamine pills which keep me hopped up to the eyebrows and increase my productivity about 200 per cent. But at the end of the day I collapse like an empty suit of clothes ... which is alright too, of course.

Is it unfair of me to write you such a letter? Tell me if it is.

Love to you ... and reply soon,

Jim

To Sarah Bond

Stanley House Hotel
12 October 1968

Sarah dear,

... I've been buoyant and excited for the past week, by the thought that I was going to see you ... now all today I've been in the glooms because the conviction has been gaining on me that you aren't also enthusiastic – but I'm still hoping that it's just busyness which has kept you from replying ... I'm comforted by the thought that you once said in a letter that you didn't allow your friends to quarrel with you; I only hope I don't turn out to be the exception that proves the rule. The thought of going all the way to New York and then not seeing you is just too much, I think it would finish me off.

When we were together we never quarrelled, did we? I don't remember ever enjoying a girl's company as much as your's.

This may seem a feeble letter but I literally haven't spoken to anyone for days (except in shops where I buy my food). I'm beginning to feel like one of Dostoicvsky's mad students. Have you read *Notes from Underground?* The Spurlings across the way have invited me to lunch tomorrow. She's Arts Editor and Theatre Critic of the *Spectator*, he reviews for it under the unlikely pseudonym of Henry Tube (!). Thank heaven for lunch, anyway.

Another weird coincidence, Texaco are putting us up at the Abbey Victoria [30] which was where the Harkness people lodged us on arrival in NY three years ago.

My book doesn't seem as marvellous as it did last week but it's considerably longer ...

Love to you, then, in spite of/and/or/because of, everything, with dogged devotion,

Jim

Handwritten addition: It would be mean of you to give me the horrid job of NOT ringing you up while I'm in New York.

To Sarah Bond

Stanley House Hotel
14 October 1968

Dear Sarah

Your letter cheered me up immensely: I was seriously trying to reconcile myself to the idea that I wouldn't be seeing you – which shows you how paranoid I'm getting ... It's as if while writing my imagination dilates and begins to gorge itself not only on the characters in my book but on me and my private life: e.g. the Major, during the last few days, has had a bad cold and felt himself forsaken by his friends, Edward, Sarah and so on. [31] Yesterday, your friend Jim also got a bad cold and gloomily decided he had hardly a friend left in the world.

I got a letter from my friend Sandy, [32] the girl I travelled round the US with a year ago, saying some fellow wanted to marry her and she'd decided to accept and she hoped I wouldn't be too upset. I wrote back politely saying I was positively gnashing my teeth with despair – after all, it wouldn't have been very nice to say I didn't mind in the least – and though I didn't mind in the least this news did somehow seem to increase my already total feeling of isolation. Writing is simply too neurotic-making unless one has a woman one can get some psychological support from in the background, or at least some really close friends. Anyway, enough of this which is no doubt boring you to death.

Look, I would certainly bring some more of my book but really I should like you to wait until it's finished (no doubt years hence). One reason is that I've been vaguely thinking I might dedicate it to you (if you have no objection) and it would be nice if at least some of it came as a surprise. But by the time it's fit for the printers, of course, we may no longer be on speaking terms (and supposing it's NOT PUBLISHED AT ALL! I've been taking that for granted).

Yeah, Harper and Row are my publishers. I got a fat letter from them on Friday and thought to myself, well, at least Harper or Row loves me, but it turned out to be merely a publicity sheet asking unanswerable questions like: 'What additional comments have you to make about yourself or your work?' I toyed with 'It's all a big swindle', but in the end sent back nothing at all except the news that most of it had been written in a greenhouse. If you see great question marks looming out of windows around E.33rd. St. you'll know they're reading my publicity form.

My (first) letter about lovers or old friends was simply meant to make it easy for you to change our relationship if you wanted to. I have a horror (which I think you may have too) of intruding where I'm not wanted or being some sort of a burden on someone. This is a bad habit, really, just pride. Zorba [33] would have disapproved ...

Dear Sarah, I wish you didn't live in the only country in the world (except Iron Curtain countries and Guatemala) where I am actually not allowed to live, by order, as they say. I mention this to counter suggestions about 'leaving' you.

Love to you,
Jim

To Carol Drisko

Stanley House Hotel
16 October 1968

Dear Carol,

... I hope to be in New York for 2-3 days next weekend. My mother, when in Dublin, filled in some competition offering weekends in Paris and NY in the name of me and my bro., who won the latter – madness, *hein?* My mother is always doing this. To me it seems a miracle. The Almighty working through the Texaco Oil Co.

Mind you, it's an awfully long way to go just for three days, most of which one will presumably spend trying to adjust to the time shift. However, I don't have anything radically better to do with my weekends and it does give one a vaguely Jet Set air if one casually drops in from Europe for the weekend (particularly if one refrains from mentioning that the way it is done is by one's mother doing publicity competitions). Another slight problem is the fact that I'll be with my bro whom I obviously couldn't leave to dash around NY by himself – even I, hardened traveller that I am, felt somewhat fazed by New York when I first arrived: my brother has hardly been out of Dublin ... I shall probably wring [*sic*] you up on Friday evening and we might even eat etc. Also, you may have plans for the weekend already ...

Anyway, love to you,
Jim

To Sarah Bond

Stanley House Hotel
19 October 1968

My dear Sarah,

By this time you should have got another letter from me, disclaiming the first: I'm not surprised that it alarmed you, compounded as it was, mainly of amphetamine pills and loneliness. So this is just to say – RELAX – a wild-eyed Jim is unlikely to appear in your office mumbling sonnets.

Actually, things seem different now and I'm ashamed of myself – well, not really ashamed since there's nothing one can do about it ... Anyway, I've now given up the pills for a while and make some effort to get out in the evenings.

Although my intentions were originally honourable the 'friends and lovers' and 'skinned-alive' thing got hopelessly out of hand too. I swear to God I can't use my typewriter these days without turning everything into a drama. Anyone would think, from reading my letters, that we had had some dead torrid affair ... sadly or otherwise, this wasn't the case as we were both seeing other people etc. even when I was in New York. In other words 90% of this has been invented by me. Very sorry. It won't happen again.

And of course, we're just friends. It was idiotic of me to suppose anything else after all this time. Also, I'd completely forgotten what you are really like.

All the same, it will be marvellous to see you again and I'll endeavour to get the bra-slip for you from M and S. (A wild-eyed, bewhiskered Jim will be seen mumbling sonnets near the ladies' knickers counter and promptly arrested.)

The weather's getting chilly here. I'm thinking of following Jackie K.'s idea of going to a Greek island. [34]

Love to you,
Jim

The rendezvous with Sarah, however, was harrowing. Awkwardness and a fierce longing to escape replaced euphoria, and he left New York with a renewal of the raw 'skinned alive feeling' he had just described. This time it was made worse by knowing Sarah had felt the same. Troubles *was not dedicated to her (or to anyone else). The reunion with Carol Drisko, on the other hand, established her as an unpossessive and reassuring friend.*

To Carol Drisko

Stanley House Hotel
3 November 1968

Dear Carol

... We didn't actually take off until about 11 p.m. New York time ... in other words they conscripted us three hours or so earlier than necessary. The comments on the way back were quite funny, some of them, if you happened to be in the right mood, which I wasn't. The most amusing thing of all, though, was that as the plane's wheels touched down at Shannon there was a burst of spontaneous applause, no cheering, just dignified clapping! Richard suggested that perhaps our fellow travellers were connoissseurs of the three-point landing ... but I reckon that it was just relief.

We reached Dublin about noon, yours truly with a cast-iron attack of the blues. It was cold and there was a dull leaden sky, hardly a cat in the streets which, after New York, made the place look more like Ultima Thule [35] than ever. As you know, I'd been planning to take a trip down to Waterford to scan the area my novel is supposed to be taking place in. As things turned out I just couldn't do it. Went to bed for a couple of hours, but unable to sleep, got up again, rang the airport and got myself on a flight back to London. One really has to be used to living in a place like Ireland, it seems to me. My latest plan is to throw a party in New York for the publication of my book in the Spring ... but perhaps by that time I'll have had the sense to forget about such a foolish and expensive project.

It was nice to see you ...

Love
Jim

To Carol Drisko

Stanley House Hotel
17 November 1968

Dear Carol,

... I've now reached ms. page 425 of my book and somehow suspect that it's unlikely to go on much further than another hundred pp. or so (of the first draft) – my inspiration has somewhat deserted me in the last day or two; I've had one or two nagging suspicions that I no longer remember why I started writing the book or what it was all supposed to be about – rather like someone who starts telling a long joke and then, when he gets to the end, can't remember the punch line – well, I suppose I shall always be able to rig up a jury-mast to get it into some sort of harbour. After all 425 pp. must be about something! (Mustn't they?) Otherwise, I've been doing nothing, have hardly stirred from me miserable quarters except to see an occasional flick ...

Love from
Jim

P.S. I'm thinking of spending Christmas in Paris so I won't hear Bing Crosby singing *White Christmas.*

PPS. I can't think of anything to say about Nixon, [36] except I can't see why anyone should bother to assassinate him.

To Carol Drisko

Stanley House Hotel
2 December 1968

Dear Carol,

... No, typewriters are much cheaper in the US than in Europe, I think. My one is a Hermes 'Rocket' (known in Europe as the Hermes 'Baby' – which may tell you something about our different attitudes); there are one or two shops along the South side of West 42nd Street which claim to sell them at sternly reduced prices. I think I paid something like $50 in NY. Don't be talked into buying anything but an obviously brand new one – I strongly suspect that these shops are staffed by confidence men.

Promptly, as I begin to write, my mind empties of amusing incident ... I went to see *Hair* [37] and enjoyed it very much. If it's still playing in New York you should go and see it – it's very much your thing – all those students and hippies and things, you'd swallow them in one bite! ... The much publicised nude scene isn't very spectacular, though it is slightly surprising to see people standing on the stage with no clothes on at all – an attractive plumpish blonde girl plainly visible, pussy and all. The boys' genitalia were somewhat in shadow, I wonder why – perhaps because in the nature of the thing the male engine is too baroque and disturbing for West End audiences, the female being, after all, merely a rather whiskery absence.

My somewhat low writing metabolism continues. I may give it

up for a week and go and read newspapers in the British Museum until I get unstale again. I need a holiday. My friend John Spurling has just had a play accepted by the National Theatre [38] for their six performance experimental theatre season about – wait for it! Yes, Che Guevara! I haven't read it so don't know what it's like.… Had lunch with the Spurlings yesterday: there was a girl there with a pretty face and positively elephantinely enormous legs ... A weird effect, rather like looking at a Madonna with elongated canines ...

I've been reading my first Henry James novel for the past few days – *Portrait of a Lady*. It's taken me 400 pages of dogged effort to become faintly interested in the characters, none of whom seem even remotely human. When I'm presented with characters called Lord Warburton and Caspar Goodwood an inner voice keeps whispering 'Oh yeah?' in me ear ...

Love to you,
Jim

To Carol Drisko

Stanley House Hotel
17th December 1968

Dear Carol:

... My book is going a little better. I've been reading the Irish papers for fifty years ago [39] ... reading among other things about race riots in Chicago, circa 1919 – it reads exactly like today. I saw my young brother yesterday, on his way through London to Malta to spend Christmas with my parents. He was in splendid form and we got on much better than in New York – partly, I suppose, because we were only together for half a day. I had been quite depressed about our mutual uneasiness and inability to talk and so this came as a pleasant surprise.

The girl I travelled around the US with (to mention another person I had trouble talking to) is due to get married next month with the odd result that we've become quite open with each other (not that I see much of her). I've graciously agreed to appear at her wedding. She has no relations, her fiancé has many. I gather she intends to round up as many ex-boyfriends as she can find. Ah well.

Love,
Jim

[Handwritten] P.S. I go to Paris on Monday for a week – to avoid Christmas ...

To Brian and Rose Knox Peebles

[Postcard 'da Vinci: Portrait d'Isabella d'Este']
Posted in London
18 December 1968

Dear B & R,
Fleur's [40] card is lovely!
Merry Christmas to you all.

Love
Jim

To Carol Drisko

[Postcard 'Les Chimères de Nôtre-Dame']
Paris, Boxing day 1968

Dear Carol,
Thought I'd just send you this card to let you know that you aren't the only one with the gripeys. This gargoyle looks pretty depressed too! I ate Christmas dinner in the Coupole, [41] a big improvement on most Christmas dinners. However, Paris has somewhat lost its charm.

Love,
Jim

To Carol Drisko

Stanley House Hotel
6 January 1969

Dear Carol,
Here's a genuine orthographed letter in my fine Italian hand; the reason being that the hour is late and the walls thin. It might well be that the lady next door will lodge a complaint about the squeaking of my ball-point (or, for that matter, the scratching of my balls) so thin are they (the walls I mean). Well that's got us off to a good start, eh?

Glad to hear that your trip was a success, however comparative. My visit to Paris was O.K. too – the main thing being the avoidance of a merry Christmas in Blighty (did I mention that I discovered, in

Graves' *Goodbye to All That*, that Blighty is Hindustani for 'home'?)
I spent most of my time ... sitting around quasi-bored and quasi-en-
joying myself in the Select. [42] Went to see a few films, ate some good
meals, including a couscous at *chez* Aron, one of the two Tunisian
restaurants by that name – the other one, less gaudy, is also not
nearly as good. But I did slightly have the feeling while in Paris that
I was wasting my time; that I should really be beavering away at my
interminable opus, of which, incidentally, I soon hope to finish the
first draft.

Odd that you should have been reading *The Leopard*. I have just
been re-reading it myself. I remembered liking it, but this time it
came as a revelation. He does so well almost exactly what I've been
trying to do in the book I'm writing at present. Clear, very concrete
images; the characters beautifully portrayed. He never puts a foot
wrong! It's uncanny, I don't know how he manages. Does your
edition (I read it first in French years ago given me by a Dr in Toulon, [43]
then, recently, in Colquhoun's excellent translation, then bought the
Fr. again in Paris the other day) have Bassani's splendid introduction
describing his one meeting with Lampedusa? ...

Fingers exhausted. The G.P.O. [44] wins again!

Love from

Jim

To Carol Drisko

Stanley House Hotel

10 January 1969

Dear Carol,

A quickie ... just off to the National Film Theatre to see an early
Bogart *In a Lonely Place* [45] (viz. Hollywood). This is mainly to thank
you for the two books that arrived yesterday, having been 6 weeks en
route – both lovely! Norman Mailer must be a real hive of energy! [46]
How does he write these things so quickly? Or to put it another way:
how do I write my things so slowly! Now on p. 561 and determined
to finish the first draft in the next 4 weeks, but then my troubles are
only beginning (an unintentional pun since I plan to call the book
Troubles) ...

Love to you and, again, many thanks,

Jim

To Russell McCormmach

Stanley House Hotel
22 January 1969

Dear Russell,

... For the past few months I've been possessed by this vast and dreary novel ... a classic case of monomania, retarded development and god knows what else ... I hope to finish it by Feb. 10 when I'm going to Malta for a couple of weeks to see my parents. But the research and rewriting seems at present like an unscaleable mountain. The simple fact is that I don't work hard enough, or quickly enough. I've now given myself next November as the deadline for the finished version (the idea being that it would come out, if acceptable, in the summer of 1970, viz. 50 years after the events described) – once I was thinking of having it finished by this November. I wonder whether I'm going to have time between now and then to leave it aside. I guess I will. I've lots of other, much shorter, things to write ...

Norma [47] sent me three of her stories, all of which seemed very bad to me – I avoided the issue in my reply by saying that I liked one of them 'best'. However, I devoted a whole, somewhat feverish letter to taking her to task for the sloppiness of her writing – quoting passages from her stories and then saying how I would have written them. I fear that she may take this as an impertinence! All the same, she seems serious about writing and she's never going to get any better if one simply murmurs congratulations. Even if her writing were improved (dull, redundant adjectives and phrases roll over her pages like tear gas) I wonder whether it would help all that much. There's an anonymity about her writing that I find perfectly annihilating ...

I read *Voss* by Patrick White. I admired it very much, without enjoying it. I must try some of his other things.

Let me know about your summer visit. How are you? How is work?

All the best,
Jim

To Carol Drisko

> 4, Mariner's Court
> Bugibba,
> Malta G.C.
> February 1969

Dear Carol,

I'm off back to Blighty from here tomorrow – having spent a little over two weeks. The sun has been shining constantly but nevertheless it will be something of a relief to get back to London and my Notting Hill slum quarters; I've got a good suntan but idleness has been gnawing at my nerves; also, the fact is that this place has many of the aspects of an elephant's graveyard – all over the island one meets elderly English people who have come here to die in the sun. Well, good luck to them ...

On the whole they are likeable, kind, courteous and nice; there's a slight air of kibbutz about the place, people going to the village collect each other's newspapers and groceries and that sort of thing. All the same the absence of young people (I'm told that there are young people in the summer) is very noticeable and, in my eyes, a faint but pervasive air of gloom hangs over the sunshine ...

At a party given by my parents the other night (I just never stop swinging) I sat next to a wobbly eighty-two year old who had been production manager for the *News Chronicle* before it packed up some years ago. Sadly, this old boy was a bit of a bore – he would break into a conversation on any subject at all with some remark about how he used to do things when he was at the *News Chronicle*, dropping his few poor names as best he could. Out of my hearing he told my mother: 'I could tell that your boy was a writer – I've seen many of them come into the office of the *News Chronicle*.' My mother related this proudly to me ...

I finished my book before coming here, first draft ... More and more I fear that after all this roaring and bellowing I'm about to give birth to a mouse ...

Well, night is closing in on the island and the old-timers, your friend Jim amongst them, are wending their way with creaking bones to bed.

> Love
> Jim

To John and Hilary Spurling

[Postcard from Malta]
February 1969

Dear Spurlings,
I want you to know that a Maltese McRune [48] [*sic*] has just shuffled by wearing a green tartan bonnet. Hope your audiences have been behaving more suitably. Sitting in bathing trunks in hot sunshine, feeling like a vegetable. As a result I'm not having many constructive ideas about my TROUBLES. Got stoned on the local plonk last night.

Love,
Jim

To Carol Drisko

Stanley House Hotel
23 March 1969

Dear Carol,
... By now you may have seen a slender but favourable review of *A Girl in the Head* in the Sunday *New York Times*. [49] I'd long since given up hope of such an event so it came as a pleasant surprise. It would only take another two or three favourable ones like that to convince [me] to emigrate to the 'land of the Freeeeee/Where they understand meeeeee'. You may have gathered from this that I've been glugging Spanish wine with my 3/4d. tin of Polish sauerkraut. However, you probably did not see the report from the Virginia Kirkus circus [50] which was snide and awful and made me feel embarassed (for Virginia, not for myself). If you happen to see any ads for the book you might let me know. I have a strong suspicion, amounting almost to a certainty, that Harper and Row don't intend to do the decent thing by me. One nice thing, though, they do send me the reviews as soon as they get them. More than Cape did.

To compound my troubles I had a letter from Anita Gross, my US agent, this morning saying that it looked as if they and Jonathan Clowes, my English agent, were going to sever connections 'after a hassle'. Implicit was a query as to where I'd be standing when the division came, I think, in the nicest way. I have no doubts but that I'll choose Anita (she's young and pretty, whereas Jonathan has a beard and bags under his eyes – but also I feel that she exerted herself beyond the call of duty in selling my book). Really, I feel one might be spared this sort of thing. Agents acting like ballerinas ...

'*If*'[51] is terrifically good and although to you it will seem absurdly exaggerated I can assure you that the school I went to was hardly different. It seemed to me to have been influenced by *Zero de Conduite*[52] but none of the critics over here mentioned it, the idiots.

Oh well, that's it for the time being. I'll let you know when I think of moving.

Love
Jim

To Carol Drisko

Stanley House Hotel
14 April 1969

Dear Carol,

... I [may have] mentioned moving into a flat of Tom Wakefield's [53] [but] this possibility has now faded, as I went out to visit the place and it was just too far away for someone accustomed to NHG [Notting Hill Gate] like myself. One is obliged to cool one's heels on open tube stations whenever one goes anywhere, which offends my aristocratic notions about what is seemly (also one gets chilled heels) ...

I'm being steam-rollered by my re-writing of book still, though I'm enjoying it too. On the whole I think I'm making it better than I hoped I could make it (you may remember some earlier, gloomier prognoses), mainly because there are lots of good things to be found in the press of 1919, 1920. I'm even, homage to C. Drisko, [54] including a reference to the Chicago race riots of 1919. But whether it all blends as I want it to blend, I know not.

My captivity in this small, seedy cage of a room is irking me and I must definitely move out this summer. Over Easter we had some good weather, though, which meant I could sun myself on my balcon [*sic*]. I bought an impulse-chicken yesterday and plan to cook it *à l'ancienne* [55] today. First time since leaving the US that I've permitted myself such a luxury – mainly it was a rebellion against the fetters of my book and room. Ages since I read the papers (other than those of 1919) but I suppose the world can manage without me.

As far as I know my brother never got his raincoat back [56] ... But – he had it insured! I was astonished when he told me this – but he used to work for an insurance company so I guess the employees get brainwashed with their own sales-talk.

Incidentally, I've been meaning to tell you that I think you got the best kind of type-in-your-writer. My mother also got a Hermes recently with a much smaller type, which though neat, is much harder to read. I used it when in Malta and didn't care for it.

Love to you,
Jim

To Carol Drisko

Stanley House Hotel
23 April 1969

Dear Carol,
... Look, the reason I'm writing is to implore you to bring me some Escudo tobacco. I've finally run out of the stock I brought back from the US, supplemented by some from Malta, and received a nasty surprise when I found out how much it was here (like three times the price it is in NY, even though it's British tobacco). Bring me about six tins (they come in 50 gramme tins) if this doesn't provide you with a problem. It's available in several places, for example, Peterson's on 42nd. Street oppos. Grand Central, or at the Village Pipe Shop on is it 8th St. that has the Brentano's and the cinemas? Me memory is dreadful these days. My recollection is that it's almost opposite Brentano's. But any serious looking downtown tobacco shop would probably have it ... Times Square is full of them. I shall of course pay in full like an honest man. Don't bother if it's any trouble (though since you failed me last time, arrrrgh!) ...

Love
Jim

To Carol Drisko

Stanley House Hotel
9 May 1969

Dear Carol,
This will be a feeble letter as my energies are all being channelled into the typing of my enormous *chef d'oeuvre*. I reached page 400 of the re-type yesterday – another 400 odd to go. I feel I'm on a ghastly

161

treadmill. I now realise that my hopes to have finished by the time you arrive were illusory. However, I shall curtail my typing while you are here ...

Why not call me at PARK 8296 when you arrive at the airpot [*sic*] so I can head for the terminal arriving there at the same time as you. I'd meet you at the airpot [*sic*] itself only such a scheme would almost certainly be doomed to failure, you not arriving on time or me not finding the right terminal. I should bring one or two summerweight things, just in case. Easter was boiling here ...

Looking forward to seeing you.

Love,
Jim

To Sarah Bond

Stanley House Hotel
[undated] 1st week of June 1969

Dear Sarah,

It was very nice to get your letter. I had been wondering whether you might not already have become a Connecticut housewife with two cars and a color tv. It's awkward not knowing anyone who knows you because it makes it impossible to find out such things. I think you must have written that letter to me on a bad day: I find it impossible to picture you as being neurotic. You must be one of the most persistently cheerful people I've come across.

This letter reads as if I've had a lobotomy in the last few days, but I can't help it. For once the sun is pouring down on my balcony and baking my poor wits. However let me try and pull myself together. What's been going on here? I've still only seen two of the American reviews of *A Girl in the Head* – an appalling one from the dreaded Virginia Kirkus (Booksellers') *Review* and a favourable one from the NY *Sunday Times* Book Review, but they came out pre-publication. All I've had in the way of mail from the lamentable Harper and Row is an offer from some professional clipping agency of 8 specimen reviews for $12.50 (I suppose they try and dredge up eight good ones) or all the reviews for the year for $35. This provides me with a perfect excuse for not reading them. All the same, I think it's a bit mean of Harper not to send me them free. To make matters worse I got a bloody bill this morning for 4 copies of the book ordered (without my consent) by my agent in New York. However, I'm supposed to have lunch with David Segal [57] here on the 9th June so perhaps he'll let me know the worst. I met another American publisher at a party the other day and he told me Segal was splitting up with his wife, so perhaps the poor fellow has other things but me on his mind.

You're still the only person to have read any of my book but I've now practically finished the re-writing/typing so in the next three or four weeks I'm going to have to face the awful business of showing the finished product to someone. [It] will be about 500 printed pages long and if it's judged to be a load of crap I think I shall have to shoot myself. I'm desperately riffling through my address book in search of someone likely to be sympathetic to start off with. There's nothing for it but to swallow the toad and hope for the best.

Incidentally, when/if you get to read the published copy (I mean, if it is ever published) you may chuckle at some of the similarities between the Major's absurd behaviour with the Sarah of the book, and mine with you – but, for all that, I'm sorry to have been so nasty to you, since I really like you, even though the fact and fiction was all inextricably woven up together both in my mind and in the book. All of which goes to show that I'm an idiot. But in spite of all that I'm glad to have written it, since I think it's good, and has made me a different person and a better writer ...

Yes, I'm still thinking of India: overland trips in Land Rovers are constantly being announced in *The Times* for around £100 return trip, but my idea would be to settle there for the winter, find some agreeable place etc. The other place I'm thinking of for the winter is Trinidad ... The idea of living somewhere in the Caribbean appeals to me, I suppose through having read so many pirate stories as a child. Puerto Rico, though spoiled by the American influence, was incredibly beautiful. Six months in Trinidad and six months in England would be the ideal combination, I think. One thing is that I have so many things to write I feel I must settle in one place until I've done them – mostly short stories or short novels. I can't see myself ever embarking on something like *Troubles* again – or not for a long time. It's just too exhausting.

Provided that I can interest Harper in my *Troubles* I should be in NY in September. That is, I've already paid a twenty quid deposit on the ICA charter so I've been sticking my neck out a little. But don't be alarmed. I shall merely invite you to lunch, if you're there, in a friendly way to see how you're getting along.

In the meantime,

lots of love,
Jim

But at this low point Farrell was about to sign on with Deborah Rogers, the young literary agent who was to provide him with the impetus he sought. He had turned against Jonathan Clowes after the publication of A Girl in the Head, *and when he visited Deborah's top-floor office in a red-light district of London he found the contrast irresistible.*

Troubles (aptly named)

London

1969–70

To Deborah Rogers [1]

> J.G. Farrell
> PAR 8296 [handwritten]
> 23 June 1969

Dear Deborah,

I very much enjoyed your party a few days ago and, in particular, meeting you. I've now finished my book and given it to Tom Maschler to read. If he thinks it has any merit I'll seize it back from him and bring it along to you to read. I thought of giving it to you first but decided I'd feel foolish if it's no good: besides, it's extremely long and reading it will take you an age. Looking forward to seeing you again if all goes well.

> Sincerely,
> Jim Farrell

To Sarah Bond

> Stanley House Hotel
> [undated] summer 1969]

Dear Sarah,

... You'll hardly believe this but I still haven't heard the reaction of anyone who has read my book from beginning to end. People keep falling out on me. An American friend read the first four hundred pages, murmured 'Smashing' and rather shiftily went off to America before finishing it. Then Janet Dawson, [2] the film critic of *Sight and Sound*, who claimed that she had hypnotised some American film producer to the extent where she would have no trouble getting him to buy the film rights, took a week to read the first hundred pages assuring me that it was merely because she was frantically busy, her boss was going mad etc., but that it reminded her of Henry James, Scott Fitzgerald and Ford Madox Ford (all of them at once?). In a fit of impatience I have now seized it back from her temporarily to give it to my swinging new agent (she wears one of those fashionable chain belts and, no doubt, has dark glasses on top of her head like Rommel the Desert Fox), Deborah Rogers. Meanwhile, from the publishers, an ominous silence has been prevailing ...

For once we seem to be having a decent summer in England as I guess you'll have heard from your parents. All the same I feel very much at a loose end since finishing my book and find it hard to get going on my modern Robinson Crusoe [3] without knowing the fate of *Troubles*. I suppose I'll hear next week. What a life! Either one is agonised or bored stiff.

Love
Jim

To Deborah Rogers

Stanley House Hotel
July 1969

Dear Deborah,

Very glad to hear that you enjoyed *A Girl* on your weekend at home. My weekend was spent showing my parents round London ... it was nerve-racking. We kept passing notices which said things like 'Vagina Rex' ...

... In a way my feeling is that, though better than nothing, it isn't enough for [*Troubles*] to be saleable. It has to be seductive enough to publishers for them to agree to give it some promotion and put me on the map. *Girl* was given virtually no advertising at all, none that I saw or heard of beyond the *de rigueur* ad. in the *Bookseller*. My conclusion is that, marvellous publisher that Tom Maschler no doubt is provided he has decided to promote you, for people like me his virtues remain entirely of a mystical nature. In fact, though I like the Cape imprint, it wouldn't worry me to change if I could screw some modest advantage out of it. It seems to me that the question of the advance is trivial (though my financial situation is precarious, to put it mildly). The promotion is the important thing. Provided of course that Cape even want it at all, I thought that I might make some really excessive demands ... and perhaps allow you to compromise on my behalf later.* The other thing, if only the book turns out to be a desirable property, might be to hold a limited auction. Well, enough of these ravings. Obviously the sooner you read the book the better ...

Yours,

Jim

* It's obviously better for me to make excessive demands than you, since you have to live with these people.

To Carol Drisko

Stanley House Hotel

7 July 1969

Dear Drisk,

... I was delighted that both you and your *bagages* arrived safely ... I don't know what it is about you, but you always seem to be lurking near a metaphor for the human condition. I'm thinking of how lots of sad little old men got sloshed crossing the Atlantic (think of Lindberg or Alcock and Brown doing likewise); that reminds me of Roemer's image of a twentieth-century death, an old man dying in a taxi. Well, I guess it's just me that's hypersensitive to such things.

I still haven't heard what anyone thinks of *Troubles* and, in particular, the silence from Maschler is becoming distinctly alarming. Can it be that it's really no good? In spite of everything I find this hard to believe. I've never felt as confident about a book as about this one and if it should be judged to be mediocre then it means that my judgment has seized up. Jan Dawson ... observed that she thought it was 'a mistake' to kill Angela off so soon, 'the most interesting character'. You can imagine the state of alarm this threw me into. I hadn't the nerve to press her further and still don't know whether her apathy was her native Jewish melancholy (there's always a faint air of impending pogrom about her) or whether she thought the book had gone to pieces and couldn't quite bring herself to say so. Come to think of it, she's a little like Angela herself. Deborah Rogers is now reading the copy. At least I hope she is. It may be just propping up one leg of a rickety table. Anyway, I'll soon know.

By the way, while I think of it, could you write me a 'To Whom It May Concern' letter on office notepaper, saying that you C. Drisk, editor of *New Citizen*, an Amurican [*sic*] citizen, undertake to support J. Farrell financially during his trip to Amurica [*sic*]. That's all you need and it is (I hope) only a formality ...

Me days are appallingly empty ... I saw my parents for two days on the way back to Malta and all went well – the zoo and Kew Gdns. (childhood in reverse)....

[*Jotted across the top*] I at last got the jacket of my p'back, which they had forgotten to send me. It really is quite nice ...

Love to you,
Jim

To Tom Maschler

Stanley House Hotel
July 1969
Copy to Deborah Rogers

Dear Tom,

I was glad to hear that, with reservations, you took a favourable view of TROUBLES. Perhaps I should have stated earlier that what you have been reading was a tentative version. My own view is that it could probably be cut to about two-thirds its present size with profit. One thing that makes cutting difficult is the fact that the book is in some respects a grab-bag of three or four different novels written in somewhat varying manners that, even at present, only have a precarious homogeneity. One other difficulty at present is that I've hypnotized myself by working on it constantly for almost three years. It may be a little while before I'm sufficiently removed from it to perform surgery with confidence.

In principle, anyway, I agree with you and would very much like to hear what you have to say about it. I hope that you've made a note of the 'slow moments' you mention. On the other hand, I shall probably be reluctant to give the hotel-allegory side of it any more weight. It seems to me that a very little allegory goes a long way. Indeed, I was surprised you didn't think it had gone too far as it is.

A certain amount of the newspaper material could be cut without loss but I suppose that the most obviously superfluous parts of the book concern some of the minor characters – Padraig, the seduction of the twins, some of the stuff with the guests and so on. I haven't yet spoken to anyone who has read the whole thing from beginning to end and a number of incidents were included on an experimental basis. I must canvass some opinions and try to decide what I think about them myself. Perhaps if I consent not to take umbrage you'd let me see your reader's report at some stage.

Tom, there's another matter that I feel obliged to mention before involving you in any (more) work on this book. I've put a great deal of time, money, effort and anguish into it (and no doubt will have to put in more before it reaches the sort of perfection I'm hoping for) and will want it given some corresponding promotion. I realise of course that there are no prizes for Effort in this business (rather the reverse) and since you already have reservations, and perhaps more serious ones than you mention in your letter, you may well prefer to opt out. Naturally, I shall quite understand and bear you no ill-will since it's obvious that, from a business point of view, you can only afford to give solid backing to books you think will succeed.

On the other hand, I hope you'll see that, as I don't write for a hobby, I've got to shop around for the best sort of deal for my work that I can. For some time now I've felt that though my work is steadily improving (in my own opinion, anyway) its author is steadily getting nowhere. Perhaps it's optimistic of me to think I can find anyone to promote a slightly mannered book of this sort. Still, it does seem to me that TROUBLES is, potentially at least, something special – and yet might appeal to a lot of people – and even, who knows? Might survive a bit longer than most current fiction. And after all, in a country where Hutchinson can promote a dull and worthy book like *Strumpet City* [4] anything is clearly possible.

No doubt Deborah will tear her hair at this, like a mother whose homely daughter turns down an eligible suitor, but I really don't know that I have a great deal to lose, apart from your editorial recommendations which I greatly value. In any event, I mention it now simply because it would be dishonest of me to conscript your advice on the assumption that I'd be prepared to accept a £600 advance and an ad. in the *Bookseller*.

Anyway, whatever your reaction to this, I do hope that we can maintain our friendly relations ...

Sincerely,
Jim

To Tom Maschler

Stanley House Hotel
12 July 1969

Dear Tom,

Thank you for your letter and by all means let's wait for Deborah to mediate. It is, of course, more your intentions with regard to *Troubles* rather than the actual advance that concerns me, though I suppose the one might be an indication of the other. But I shall drop the subject now before I come to sound any more like a Victorian father. I do hope I haven't been over-optimistic in saying I might be able to cut the book by a third. The delight with which you pounced on this suggestion fills me with concern and I wonder whether I mightn't cause you a real paroxysm of joy by volunteering to cut it by three quarters. Well, not seriously.

There are, however, long stretches of the book to which I'm relatively indifferent and which I would willingly cut if it was generally felt they didn't add anything – exterior scenes for the most part: the great Victory parade of 1919, the business with the peasants and the corn, the miracle, the cutting of the twins' hair, the reprisals and so on. Most of these passages, however, were included for a specific purpose. Paradoxically, the passages that I simply couldn't bring myself to discard (because they are the best written) would very often be the easiest to cut ...

Sincerely,
Jim

In the summer of 1969 a felicitous meeting at a party enabled Farrell to exchange the distractions of the Stanley House Hotel for tranquillity in Knightsbridge at a nominal rent. Diana Saville and her flatmate, both ten years his junior, lived at 1 Pont Street Mews, had a spare bedroom, and thought he needed looking after. The arrangement suited him well. On weekdays, when they were at work, he could count on not being interrupted, and his lonely evenings and weekends were now transformed. As a bonus, Harrods Food Hall, his Mecca, was within a few hundred yards.

To Carol Drisko

as from 1, Pont Street Mews
London S.W.1
tel. 589.5932
14 July 1969

Dear Driskers,

... The above address may fill you with surprise. The fact is that I'm at long last planning to move out of here. I was offered a reasonable room in a flat in Knightsbridge, just behind Harrods. This coincided with an absence of hot water here (that has lasted two weeks so far and shows no sign of return) and a general feeling of surfeit with the whole scene here ... The flat is large, but with small rooms and somewhat dark and poky. I have engineered meself the best room. My flatmates are two girls. Unfortunately, or perhaps fortunately, the arrangements will be entirely platonic, since they both have faintly obnoxious boy-friends they are devoted to. One or two vague suggestions that we should all take our baths ensemble to economise on the hot water bills have so far failed to achieve a positive response. In fact, since they are out during the day and I'm usually out during the evening I shouldn't think we'll see much of each other. I may try to settle in a bit more comfortably this time, painting my room in a cheery and positive manner and so forth. On the other hand, there's always the possibility that I may be obliged to beetle off after a couple of weeks of nightmare. Once again, as with the finishing date of m'book, the timing of this is all wrong ...

You'll be glad to hear that since my last despairing note I've had a favourable reply from Maschler. His letter was a bit hard to fathom since it was a mixture of praise and suggestions that I should make substantial cuts. He didn't say what but I think he wants more of the hotel and less of the other. He may be right about this but I really haven't decided. But he said he was sure they would want to publish it. I'm still waiting for Deborah Rogers to read it; just at the wrong moment she went off to spend a week with Anthony Burgess in Malta (he's a client of her's). Having heard from Maschler I immediately dashed off a letter demanding lots of money and promotion, combined with threats to remove myself to another publisher if he didn't pay up. I received a temporising letter back saying why didn't we wait until Deborah got back but showing a very muted enthusiasm. To hell with the fellow anyway. He hardly misses an opportunity for heaping me with oily praises but does nothing for my books. It would be a relief to find someone, an editor, with whom I had a better relationship. But I guess all publishers' editors speak with forked tongues ...

Lots of love,
Jim

To John and Hilary Spurling

[undated, scrawled on a scrap of paper]

Dear John and Hilary,

At last moving out of the Stanley House ... Viva Che! etc.

Jim

To Tom Maschler

Pont Street Mews
[undated] 1969

Dear Tom,

I'll probably have finished revising and cutting *Troubles*, aptly named, within the next few days. I'll then try them out on a guinea pig or two and when I've got a definitive version will collect the original copy from you to transfer the corrections.

I hope you don't mind harbouring the original in the meantime. I'm superstitious about having both copies in the same place for longer than necessary.

Deborah tells me that you have now made it through to the end.

Yours,
Jim

To Carol Drisko

Pont Street Mews
[undated] summer 1969

Dear Driskers,

Many thanks for your very amusing letter. Let me reassure you on everything (as Nixon might say). I did receive your first moon letter, though I can no longer remember what was in it – not, I hasten to add, that it wasn't as gripping and memorable as all the others, but simply that, in me memory, it has metamorphosed into pure Delight, unflawed by base details. Er, did you ask me to do something in that letter?

As for the Naipaul ⁵ book, has Jim ever failed you? My eyebrows will remain quizzically raised until I receive your reply, which should be in the negative, in triplicate, the top copy signed ... Incidentally, I never managed to get going with Anthony Powell's series ⁶ – my pleasure centres turned out to be impermeable to his steady drizzle of incident. I'll be interested to hear your reactions. Most people I know, the Spurlings for example, are greatly enthused.

For London the weather has been extremely warm and agreeable. Yesterday was the only day so far when heat and humidity got beyond comfort level. Today it's grey and rainy, which is almost a relief.

At the moment I'm reading Lowry's *Dark as the Grave Wherein My Friend is Laid*, an unfinished work disinterrred by his wife and some professor of English at the Univ. of Virginia from his notebooks. It describes a visit the Lowrys paid to Mexico post *Under the Volcano* but, although there are flashes of interest for me because it summons up odd memories of the Lowry-oriented Mexico I was interested in, it really isn't any good; indeed, very self-indulgent and quite boring. I wonder whether Lowry would have countenanced its publication himself. The letters of the period where he tells it straight without fictionalising and romanticising himself are much more interesting. A big disappointment this. I'm also reading more stories by the simply wonderful, unself-indulgent Chekhov.

I'm in the middle of revising *Troubles*. I saw Deborah last week. She said she 'loved' it, but also advised me to cut it a bit. She talked to Maschler about it and he gave her to understand that he wouldn't offer more than the peanuts I hoped to discourage him from offering. Nothing definite has been settled but I think I shall probably look around for someone else. I'm finding it hard to decide on anything I want to discard from the book. I hate to think of some of those, admittedly scarcely relevant, goodies from *The Irish Times* resuming their sleep for eternity in the archives of the British Museum ...

Love
Jim

To Carol Drisko

Pont Street Mews
[undated] early August 1969

Dear Driskers,

... I was amused to read in yesterday's paper that the moon rocks [7] were covered with a blackish grit which is frustrating the scientists. To me this black grime comes as no surprise, since I have been predicting for many years that the moon was rendered extinct by automobile exhaust and improperly masked incinerators. [One] of the most splendid items was Nixon greeting the returned 'nauts through their little window. Perhaps you missed this, but it was exquisite. After some healthy joking and chaff (Nixon giving them the result of the 'All Star' baseball game, however in all sincerity, and the 'nauts saying, no less earnestly, that they were sorry to have missed it) Nixon invited the padre to say a prayer – whereupon the padre prayed the ears off everyone with a prayer of his own invention, full of telling cosmic references. Then followed the Stars of Stripes – I mean the Stars and Stripes, if not the Tars and Tripes (by courtesy of Liggett and Myers). During the singing or playing of this, Nixon stood with his hand on his heart, which is no doubt what the President always does. But at first it seemed to me that he was merely keeping his hand on his wallet, a wise precaution in my view, considering what a shifty-looking individual the astronaut was.

I haven't heard anything more about *Troubles*. I must call Deborah today and see what's happening. I'm in two minds about the cutting (and indeed I don't yet know what Maschler thinks ought to be cut): I do feel that there are certain quasi-action-political parts, perhaps unread by you, where the writing is weaker.

Living in a flat (indeed, a mews on a cobbled courtyard) is like a rest cure after the Stanley House Hotel. Among other things, it's a delight to have an adequate kitchen. I don't see a great deal of my two flatmates, since they are away during the day and usually out in the evening ... We don't have a lease here, however, and so this good fortune may possibly be temporary. With enormous energy I painted my room and made curtains – a job which has taken me an entire week.

I'm enclosing a $50 traveller's cheque for you to keep pending my arrival.

Love
Jim

To Russell McCormmach

Pont Street Mews
5 August 1969

Dear Russ

... It now seems very likely that I shall be appearing in New York sometime after the 12th. September so let's plan a reunion then. I'm eager
to hear more of your projected 'Death of Einstein'. [8] I fear that the historical side of my *Troubles* may seem pretty thin to you (and it's likely
to become thinner still because everyone agrees that I must make massive cuts to make the book palatable), one reason being that although
I may start out with the most serious and measured intentions, everything I touch has a habit of turning to the absurd. Also the things I like
best in the book (because I feel that they're the best written) are the
usual small change of farcical seductions etc., entirely without historical interest ... so it's certain that I'll keep them in reference to the cautiously written surgings of the Irish people. How daring Hughes is! He
manages to combine both in a way in which I feel I couldn't bring myself to attempt. Think, for example, of the splendidly done passages
where Hitler is hiding delirious with his dislocated shoulder. [9] One needs
more confidence than I have to be able to do that sort of thing ...

My personal life is as empty as usual these days. Funny to think
that over the past few years my only constant friend in London
has been a call-girl. [10] I feel it says a great deal for her warmth and
simplicity of nature that she has put up with me all this time. I
suppose experience at dealing with weird people helps too.

I'm surprised at the *NYT* book review criticising Lowry so
foolishly [11] ... It seems to me that the great thing about *Under the Volcano* was that he managed to distance himself from his own anguish by using the Consul as a lightning conductor – all the worst things
in Lowry's writing come from his not being sufficiently objective –
which isn't to say, however, that I wouldn't be glad to have some of these
worst things in my own humble efforts ... Thanks for the snippet about
the grants – I really must do something about that. Two or three years
ago I talked briefly to the man responsible for dishing out these
grants at a party and he was so pompous, avuncular and conde-
scending that he put me off the idea. But I guess I should apply.

All the best,
Jim

To Deborah Rogers

Pont Street Mews
Tues. 26 August 1969

Dear Deborah,

The reason that you haven't heard from me before now is that I've had the most horrible and undeserved attack of 'flu. I thought I was dying (but then I always think I'm dying) and kept crawling out of bed to make, as it were, posthumous corrections to *Troubles,* a book of which I'm now heartily sick. Though still wobbly I'm now back at my desk, beavering away ...

I've decided also that I've been tiresome as regards this publisher business and should leave it up to you to make the selection you think is best. As a last shot, however, I might say that Bob Lusty [12] of Hutchinson is rumoured to be unable to resist paying large sums of money for big books about Ireland – and mine is at least big and about Ireland ...

Yours,
Jim

To Deborah Rogers

Pont Street Mews
2 September 1969

Dear Deborah,

Here's a list of the principal cuts I've made. In addition I've done some streamlining here and there which isn't listed – for the most part flabby or redundant paragraphs or sentences. The total amount cut is unlikely to add up to the third I once rashly proposed, however ... I'm still open to persuasion if you, or a publisher's editor, feel strongly that certain of the remaining bits are dull or don't work.

p. 78-9.   Ripon and the Major discuss Connolly being shot in a chair – removed ...

p. 130.   Visit to sing *God Save the King* – shortened.

p. 167-8. Angela's funeral – shortened....

p. 269.   Tomato thrown at the Major – removed.

p. 274.   Climb up from the pigs – shortened.

p. 374.   Bolshevist menace – removed ...

p. 419.   Major's cold, twin's homework – shortened ...

p. 432.   The Major's reflections on law and justice – removed.

p. 451.   Edward's description of being attacked by 2 men –
           removed.
p. 466.   Sarah's cheating at cards – removed.
p. 485.   Edward's rescue of the piglets at night – removed.
p. 547-6. The shearing of the twins – removed.
p. 745.   The Major buried in the sand – shortened.
A number of the shorter news excerpts have also gone.

I wonder will these cuts make the book readable enough for you to start negotiating. If you don't think so, do tell me. I'm getting sick enough of the book to cut bigger and bigger chunks without a qualm.

Yours,
Jim

To Tom Maschler

Pont Street Mews
[undated] 1969

Dear Tom,

... I've now returned the ms. to Deborah so that she can consider the revisions I've made. These don't, I'm afraid, add up to a third or anything like it. Perhaps that was rash of me.

I'm still prepared to take out more of it if anyone feels that significant *longueurs* remain after my surgery. Dealing with such a large book is difficult in ms. form. There are so many pages and they just seem to go on and on. No doubt this is what the reader feels also. The best method I've found is simply to read it again and again, on the theory that one gets sickest quickest of the weakest bits ...

Yours,
Jim

To Carol Drisko

Pont Street Mews
3 September 1969

Carol dear,

You may have noticed a slight falling off in my letter-writing rate. Partly the result of a sudden attack of the 'flu which laid me low much to my disgust. Flu in August is really a bit thick. *D'ailleurs*, the weather has gone to pieces once more and there has hardly been a tickle of sunshine to warm your old friend's bones for the past weeks. Today, however, is better, as far as I can see from the window ...

My flight isn't on the 12th as I think I told you, but on the 14th. Thus we are deprived of a couple of extra days *sans* compensation ... I have a suspicion, however, that two weeks in New York will be enough for me. I'm not very good at being places without having a *raison d'être* there ...

Troubles has been revised and returned. I did cut out quite a bit of dead wood, I think, but I doubt whether I will have cut enough to satisfy Maschler. You know, reading it through again I feel I have to agree with him. Though naturally marvellous, it is rather on the interminable side and requires a certain amount of determination to read.

Well, we'll see.

Love
Jim

To Deborah Rogers

Pont Street Mews
8 September 1969

Dear Deborah,

... I'm trying to decide whether there is really any point in taking the copy of the book to America (there are only two of them altogether – the original and one copy). I'm only going to be there for 2 weeks which is unlikely to be enough time for either Anita[13] or David Segal to read it, let alone both of them. But if one is enough here then I could leave the copy with Anita. If only the wretched thing wasn't so heavy ...

Yours,
Jim

To Carol Drisko

Pont Street Mews
9 September 1969

Dear Carol,

I'm supposed to be arriving this Sunday around 2pm New York time ... I discovered to my dismay that it's a ten hour flight with a stop for re-fuelling, so now it seems that they're planning to cram us all into some obsolete flying machine, no doubt an extended Spitfire ...

Nothing new from here, except that Alex's book [14] is due to be published in a week or two and he has arranged some elaborate party in Hampstead where the guests are dressed up in costumes of the Peninsula War and he has had special tapes made for sound effects. He rang me up to tell me about it, but it all sounded completely incoherent ... He said that the guests (in uniform?) would be attacking his house and he would be defending it (!!!). Instead of wine I'm going to bring a bottle of paraldehyde, I think.

See you soon.

Love,
Jim

To Sarah Bond

Pont Street Mews
9 September 1969

Sarah dear,

Come off it, Sarah, you know very well you look lovely in that photograph you sent me. Enough of this false modesty. I showed it to my flatmates (2 girls) and they immediately turned green with envy and said that you probably had spots and, anyway, beautiful girls were always bitches, unlike themselves who were frightfully nice. I had 'flu at the time and protested feverishly that, on the contrary, etc. One of them said she thought you looked like Sarah Miles. I no longer seem able to find the picture so perhaps they have torn it up in a fit of pique.

You've obviously become fantastically successful to have an office to yourself. Good for you! Though I suppose this means there's less chance than ever of seeing you back here. Anyway, I hope to be seeing you next week if I can manage to locate you in the phone book. I'm flying over this weekend and will get in touch once I've got myself orientated ...

Don't talk to me of *Troubles* (aptly named), which I've just had to re-read three times. I'm now heartily sick of it and just want to forget about it (though naturally I'm still hoping it will make me a lot of money). Glad you liked the Olivia Manning. I'll try and get you the third volume.

Incidentally, I've now read *Cold Comfort Farm*[15] and everything is clear to me! You are exactly like Flora Poste. If I'd read the book I'd have recognised you instantly on the day we first met when you'd just been frightfully sensible with naked men dashing in and out of the flames, drugged up to the eyebrows. However, I was alarmed to recognise myself in the writer, Mr Mybug, who loves striding over the moors and saying how phallic everything is. An exchange I enjoyed was the following:

'We're friends, aren't we?' he (Mybug) asked.

'Certainly,' said Flora pleasantly.

'We might dine together in Town sometime?'

'That would be delightful,' agreed Flora, thinking how nasty and boring it would be.

'There's a quality in you ...' said Mr Mybug, staring at her and waving his fingers. 'Remote, somehow, and nymph-like ... oddly unawakened. I should like to write a novel about you and call it "Virginal".'

'Do, if it passes the time for you,' said Flora; 'and now I really must go and write some letters, I am afraid. Good-bye.'

I also liked the chap who keeps communing with the water-voles.

See you soon, I hope.

Love and xxxxxs,
Jim

To Russell McCormmach

Pont Street Mews
[undated] 1969

Dear Russ,

This is just to let you know that I'm coming to New York this coming Sunday, the 14th. So I suggest that if you're free we get to-gether, perhaps with Bob Cumming, on the weekend of the 20th or the 27th. I return to Blighty on Oct. 2nd.

Nothing much new here. My friend Hilary Spurling who is literary editor and drama critic of the *Spectator* offered me some reviewing but I doubt whether I shall do it,[16] although I need money, of course. I almost never read magazines and newspapers these days and I haven't read a review for ages. I think I'm happier that way though I'm sure I miss a great deal.

Somehow it seems so petty to be airing one's opinions once a week on other people's work that one probably hasn't even read properly. It seems to me that one must suffer an instant drop in one's already precarious self-respect – from Novelist to Man of Letters – like a Victorian boy's story by G.A. Henty I once read called *From Powder-Monkey to Admiral* (this book would have been more interesting if it had been the other way round) ...

All the best
Jim

Early in October 1969 Jim was invited by his flatmate Diana Saville, who worked in publishing, to go to the Chelsea launch of The Beatles' Illustrated Lyrics. *Her motive was to introduce him to her friend Bridget O'Toole, with whom she had shared a flat when both were students at Oxford. The meeting was a success.*

To Bridget O'Toole

Pont Street Mews
21 October 1969

Dear Bridget,

Whatever [they] say, let me make it quite clear that, in my view, the muses are already beckoning you into Literature's Hall of Fame – and most probably into the Inner Sanctum (where they keep the royalties). [17] Your letter was delightful, though in some ways not unalarming. It looks more and more as if we are the victims of a hostile congregation of planets. My agent's office was burgled three weeks ago. Two weeks ago the ceiling fell in. Last week she was in a car crash. I forget whether I told you that my new book, which has been lying in her office all this time like the giant emerald eyeball stolen from some sinister Oriental idol, is called *Troubles*. The poor girl is now flat on her back in hospital with suspected damage to her spine ...

Yesterday ... the phone remained mute, crouching there on its shelf like an evil black toad ... I tried to cheer Diana [18] by an extra-powerful demonstration of domesticity, cradling Mappin [19] in my arm and singing:

'Just Diana and me
And Baby makes three
My blue heaven ...'

For some reason this failed to revive her. When at length the phone did ring, it was the landlady inviting us to vacate the premises by December 31st ...

I suggest (and not only for therapeutic reasons) that you ditch your ... novel and instead write a long short-story about a lonely girl (not necessarily you) living in Leamington Spa in the grip of winter, melancholy teas in the pump room, still wanting to punish herself for an earlier tragic love affair by being rejected by other men, and her relationship with another man who likes flirting with her but intends to marry someone else, etc. The above isn't meant to define your relationship and attitudes, about which I know nothing. It's merely a suggestion for a story. I see it as a home-grown '*Hiroshima Mon Amour*'.[20]

My own life is totally shapeless at the moment. I'm taking out several girls, each more charming than the rest. But somehow they fail to impinge. I think it may be because I spend so much time talking. I'm perpetually drunk with talk these days.

When you want to see me, summon me to your side m'dear. Rub the magic bottle (preferably gin) and I will appear. Or even better, come to London again. If I leave it up to you it's because you have more problems to hedge you in. You could phone, reversing the charges, and have a chat, also.

Love to you,
Jim

P.S. Life is short. Life is very, very short. (Cliché of the week.)

To Carol Drisko

Pont Street Mews
27 October 1969

Dear Driskers,

What ho from here? Not very much. The winter is settling in on us, though we've been having more than our ration of autumnal sunshine. It now gets dark around six in the evening. One of my flatmates is off on a two-week tour of Russia and tells me that it's already snowing in Moscow. Russians, it seems to me, have a lot to put up with besides Nixon, China and capitalism.

There's still no news of my book, either from David 'the Brilliant one' Segal, or from anyone over here. Things have slowed to a point where only God and a trained observer could tell they were moving at all ... I'm still trying to get into my Robinson Crusoe with only moderate results. I've started it a number of times but am still not satisfied that it's off the ground. The irritating thing is that I'm sure Defoe just reeled his version off without a thought, the son of a bitch ...

Me and my flatties received a blow the other day: viz. we were given notice to quit by the end of the year. We could probably delay this considerably by going to a rent tribunal etc, but all that seems so much fuss. One of them, the General's daughter ... is leaving anyway, going to Hong Kong ... I've had one or two meetings with her parents since she invited me down one Sunday to where they live in and manage a beautiful 16th. century National Trust-owned house in Hampshire, built by one Challoner Chute (great name) and still belonging to the Chutes until recently. Her mother quite likes me, I think, (her maiden name was Wellesley, a direct descendant of Wellington) and I think the General does too, though more warily. I think he fears I mightn't make a good soldier. While there we had drinks with Lord Chandos' son and heir ... so you see your friend Jim is hobnobbing with the gentry these days, eh what? All a tiny bit dull, however.

What's new with you?

Lots of love,
Jim

To Deborah Rogers

Pont Street Mews
28 October 1969

Dear Deborah,
Hope you don't/didn't get coshed at the [Frankfurt] Book Fair.

As regards *Troubles*, why don't you just send it back to Maschler as it is, asking him to make an offer (and whether there would be any specific cuts on which the offer depended). I feel that you probably have your work cut out stemming the tide of natural disasters, burglaries, earthquakes etc. that are plaguing you and have no real time, at the moment, to give editorial advice. Besides, I feel that in the end I shall probably ignore all advice anyway and do as seems best to me ...

Love,
Jim

To Deborah Rogers

Pont Street Mews
10 November 1969

Dear Deborah,

The last thing I intended to do was harass you on your sick-bed about *Troubles* ... I'm glad you still like it ... Once you've had a chance to recover and free the log-jam of work caused by your misfortunes you must come over and eat here again, perhaps with the Reads,[21] who are now back in town. I saw them the other night.

In the meantime, all the best to you.

Yours,
Jim

To Bridget O'Toole

Pont Street Mews
23 November 1969

Dear Bridget,

... I was just thinking the other day how nice it must be to be sealed up in such good skin as yours – but what has been happening to the person inside, your letter scarcely mentions? What of the steaming passions of Leamington Spa?[22]

As it happens, without the assistance of any new information my view of what life is like in Leamington Spa has become much clearer. I now see that a grey fog hangs in the Pump Room. Faces are expressionless. People seldom speak, and never above a whisper. From time to time, however, one of these figures looming out of the fog will exchange a searing glance with another, a brief glint of passion or hatred, before their faces are rendered once more as impenetrable as masks. Sort of thing ...

I forget what I told you about *Troubles*. The affair has ended in a semi-capitulation by me (by who else?) to Cape. Having threatened them with leaving them for another publisher (my editor abruptly turned pale of course, and I had to find him a chair) in order to get more money and promotion out of them, I was dissuaded by my agent from this rash course ... and though I did get a little more than they originally offered I'm filled, nevertheless, with a vague dissatisfaction. Mainly, though, I simply got tired of the problem and couldn't face the thought of going through it all again with another publisher. Besides, my journalistic friends all assure me that Cape books get much better looked at by literary editors than other people's – novels anyway.

I'm also distressed by my inability to hit the right style and tone with the thing I'm doing now. Although I've written some forty pages to me they are difficult to distinguish from forty corpses stretched beside my typewriter. Life is not in them. I waste hours massaging their hearts and holding mirrors over their mouths. From time to time I become convinced that the mirror has clouded faintly. But the next time I look the thing is as dead as ever ...

Love to you,
Jim

To Carol Drisko

Pont Street Mews
24 November 1969

Dear Driskers,

... Did I tell you that I met an American at Malcolm's called Bill (?) Shannon [23] who wrote a book about Bobby K. called *The Heir Apparent* and who writes leaders for the *NYT*. I was making some of my usual discouraging remarks about my namesake James T. when this Shannon, who is otherwise a nice though rather prissy fellow, announced that he is a v. good friend of his. My mind boggled irretrievably.

My private life has been rendered even more chaotic than usual by the fact that our Dublin flat is being closed down and my younger brother is coming to live in London: I shall have to assist his *début* here to some extent, as he doesn't know anyone and hasn't anywhere to stay ... At the same time, my mother is hovering around in Dublin trying to arrange things, sell furniture etc. Both my brother and I will be going to Malta for Christmas. I should have had my fill of family by early in the New Year ...

I'm reading Peter Brown's biography of St Augustine. [24] I think it's marvellous. Anyone capable of interesting me in schisms in the Church in Late Roman times must be a genius.

Saw *Easy Rider*, which I quite enjoyed but didn't think was any great shakes: and *Midnight Cowboy* which I thought was a pretty rotten movie. Somehow the good acting by Dustin Hoffman and the other chap only increased my dissatisfaction with the crassness and superficiality of the writing and direction.

Let me hear from you.

Love,
Jim

To Bridget O'Toole

Pont Street Mews
3 December 1969

Dear Bridget,

I'm glad and surprised that you liked *The Lung*. I would no longer recommend anyone to read it since I find a lot of it distressing; in particular there's an off-key romanticism that grates on my nerves. I still think there are a few good pages in it, mind you (though not enough to redeem the rest). Incidentally, you are unjust to Ineige, [25] who is purely a girl in poor crazed Boris' head. I wonder what you'll think of *Troubles*, the book I'm now going through, the last of many editings (I hope), before it goes into the works. The first reactions were enthusiastic, but now more muted responses are coming in – my American editor has written that he is in a 'terrible dilemma' as to whether or not to take it. Scrutinising my resources this morning I discovered that I am almost completely broke. I really shall have to pull myself together and do something about earning some money again.

I wish you were here now instead of in two weeks time to advise me whether to keep or drop a couple of chapters (of *Troubles*). My own critical faculties have totally atrophied ... These days I'm seething with a grey dissatisfaction. When I look in the mirror I notice that I'm growing old and still I haven't done anything good. I remind myself of the main character [26] in Chekhov's masterly story: *A Dull Story*. You must read this instantly if you haven't already.

The cat Mappin is making repeated attacks on my manuscript. It's time to stop.

Love to you
Jim

To Sarah Bond

Pont Street Mews
[undated] November/December 1969

Dear Sarah,

... Although in some respects our relationship was the least satisfactory part of my successful visit to New York (apart from the
one evening when you told me about your lover I felt that we
weren't communicating at all) I was very glad to have seen you and
managed to remain on friendly terms – a triumph of British sensible-
ness, in my view. If I sounded critical about you (I don't remember
being critical) it was, of course, because I was peeved at you preferring
someone else to me – moreover, I was annoyed at myself for
behaving so predictably.

I can't imagine you (or any other girl) putting her hand through
a window-pane because of anything I might say to you (the fact that
I wouldn't want you to is another matter). What I mean is: it will
obviously take you years to work this person (I'm afraid I've forgotten his name) out of your system, whether you realise it or not. It's
a pity that you should have got so deeply involved with a neurotic
person but you obviously responded to him because he answered
some need in you – a symbiotic relationship, in fact. Such a deep
relationship isn't easy to find twice running since the first one is
liable to 'specialise' you. Anyway, as far as I'm concerned, I'm happy
to go on being a friend from your earlier days and no longer consider
you to be anything else for me. I hope we'll be able to be more
relaxed for this reason when we meet.

Love to you and merry Christmas!

Jim

[*Handwritten*] P.S. I see that *Cold Comfort Farm* is now in paperback!

To Deborah Rogers

Pont Street Mews
7 December 1969

Dear Deborah,

... For the past week I've been seething with impotent rage at the
non-appearance of £200 which, in my innocence, I imagined I had
coming to me from the p'back of *A Girl in the Head*.

You mustn't think I dislike Tom personally (I gather from your remarks on the phone the other day that you were apprehensive lest I commit a gaffe by saying something disagreeable about him in the presence of his girl-friend). I've only ever spoken to him twice and have no real opinion – though, since I know you like him, I feel he must be a nice person. I suppose I've tended to use him to personify Cape, which I see as a grudging and impersonal monster ...

Love
Jim

To Piers and Emily Read

1 Pont Street Mews
[undated] December 1969

Dear Piers and Emily,
Afraid I can't make it on the 19th because I'm going to Malta the day before. But many thanks all the same!

If I don't see you before Christmas, have a merry one.

Jim

To Deborah Rogers

Pont Street Mews
[undated] December 1969

Dear Deborah,
Some time ago you mentioned that you might like to have a bash at selling foreign rights in *A Girl in the Head*. I've now had a friendly letter from Jonathan [27] to say by all means go ahead.

... David still has not made up his mind about *Troubles* – he's in 'a terrible dilemma' about what to do (I can see the poor chap groping for the tranquillisers in the middle of the night). He feels apparently that not enough really happens in the book. I suppose I must have led him to expect that the British Empire would collapse on stage, rather than in the wings. But I suppose he still might come through ...

Love,
Jim

To Carol Drisko

Pont Street Mews
18 December 1969

Dear Driskers,
... I'm off to Malta this evening with my young brother, for two weeks. I plan to bring my bathing-trunks with me but doubt if the water will be warm enough to take the plunge. I hope also to get some thinking done, about my work in progress, which is sorely in need of a transfusion of ideas to get it off the ground. The bottom has recently dropped out of my coffers leaving nothing but thin air – notoriously poor for sustaining one. Pan Books owed me some money which Cape intercepted to pay off an unearned advance. The arrival of a cheque for £20 instead of £200 sent me into a fury from which I've only recently emerged. However, my fulminations over the 'phone may have done some good because I hear from Deborah that Tom Maschler is 'looking into the matter again'.

Apart from that I haven't a bean, as the dreaded Segal still hasn't made up his mind (I, however, have just sent Anita a letter directing her to get the ms. returned and tell him to piss off). Cape are definitely publishing it here, however, which I suppose, given the general collapse of everything, is something to be thankful for. So you see I must do some work, get something else finished. You can imagine the state of desperation I've been in from the fact that I accepted a hacking job, [28] writing a careers pamphlet for £50 from a number of leaflets. However, having wasted a week, hypnotised by boredom, unable even to bring myself to read the wretched leaflets, I gave it up. I simply couldn't do it ...

Well, a merry merry Christmas to you.

Love
Jim

To Claude and Anna Simha

Pont Street Mews
6 January 1970

My dear Friends, [29]
Thanks for your letter, Claude. I was going to reply from Malta (where I spent the rather grey end of year holidays) but fell ill with that 'flu which has gripped Europe. At my age, isn't it true,

one recovers only very slowly from these things? I came back to Pont St. Mews on the first of January to be welcomed with another phonecall from my landlord wanting to chuck us out of the house. We're staying, however, until at least the end of March (thanks to the Wilson government which has given tenants some rights), but we're going to have to find somewhere else soon. As usual, I can't decide whether I should stay on in London or leave, perhaps this time for Italy (I greatly admire contemporary Italian literature, especially Bassani). I shall certainly stay on here for some more months to establish myself a little better as far as my *metier* is concerned, before beginning to travel ...

You must come to London! I should really enjoy that. One of my co-tenants has left [and] my younger brother has taken her place for this month, until he finds a place of his own. I feel a little uneasy with him in the house, but what the hell! Apart from that things are going well; making love a bit, eating a bit too. However, if I were able to motivate myself a little for my new novel things would be going better ...

In anticipation, love and kisses from the old uncle,

Jim

And hello to Elie! [30] We are arriving on the evening of the 21st. [31]

To Carol Drisko

Pont Street Mews
[undated] 1970

Dear Carol,

Lovely to get your letter this morning ... Yesterday at long last *Troubles* went off to the printer, but not before a tedious battle through the copy-edited version, in the nick of time to save some gleaming pearls of style from the too-severely toilet-trained copy-editor's dreary insistence on the rules of grammar and syntax. I've been wondering whether I mightn't do a novel concerning the ill-fated Emperor Maximilian of Mexico, [32] I've been browsing through books about him at the British Museum. At present I haven't got enough of an idea to tell whether it will turn into anything or not ...

Love,
Jim

To Tom Maschler

Pont Street Mews
[undated] 1970

Dear Tom,

I gather that Deborah mentioned to you my astonishment and dismay on discovering that Cape intended to withhold the entire paperback advance from Pan on *A Girl in the Head* against the original Cape advance.[33] She said you were looking into it.

Jonathan Clowes seems unobtainable these days and since Deborah didn't agent the book I feel I can't keep asking her about it; besides, it was presumably Jonathan's job as my agent to protect me contract-wise against this eventuality. Could you let me know what conclusions you have come to?

I'm sorry that all my correspondence with you involves wrangling over money. Perhaps one of these days I'll hit on another topic.

Yours sincerely,
Jim

To Carol Drisko

Pont Street Mews
1 February 1970

Dear Driskers,

Many thanks for your letter which I just rediscovered among my effects. A terrible apathy has underwhelmed me recently in all departments ... the reasons for which you'll no doubt discover as this letter grumbles on. But somehow I'd got it into my head that you owed me a letter. Since this is clearly not the case, stand back! Here we go ...

My visit to Malta was v. boring, much more so than last time when I still had a faint interest in what the place was like. I feel that I now know. Things were complicated by the fact that I got 'flu the day after my arrival and spent half the time in bed. Things have been scarcely better in London, come to that ... I've decided to get a place on my own: although life is more pleasant living with other people I find that I spend too much time in idle conversation and not enough in 'creative' day-dreaming. It's sad that one has to be lonely in order to get up the steam to write fiction but this seems to be the case – as far as I'm concerned anyway.

I did a couple of reviews for the *Spectator*, a boring rightish magazine that's not worth reading normally. If you have it in your library, however, you might look up the issue of Jan. 31st and read a faintly amusing piece on a book about Scotland written by your friend. Also a hilarious review of a book about Firbank by a mad Australian comedian (who does the comic strip in *Private Eye*) called Barry Humphries ...

Apart from that, Anita is waiting for proof copies of *Troubles* before trying to sell it in New York. Segal hasn't yet definitely rejected it, however. Over here I'm pursuing an acrimonious correspondence with Cape over some money I mistakenly believed they were going to give me (actually I've pursued it and retired to sulk now). I still don't have a publication date ...

At a dinner party last week I met Anthony Powell and his wife (Lady Violet). He's very entertaining in a malicious, gossipy old Etonian sort of way. E.g. about Bernard Hollowood, [34] trying to explain how awful he is, he said: 'He's awful in ways which one would have thought were mutually exclusive.' He also had lots of harsh words about Malcolm Muggeridge, a former bosom friend, whom he declared to be completely mad, adding: 'Mind you, hardly anyone over forty is altogether sane.' And so forth. It appeared that Muggeridge had written a hostile review of one of his novels. 'One simply doesn't do that to one's friends. I mean, one can always find something good to say about a book, if only that it has a nice binding.'

Powell looks like a suburban bank-manager down on his luck (if s.b.m.'s are ever down on their luck): greasy tie, lumpy suit. He's much smaller than his wife, a cheerful, intellectual but inarticulate lady who searches interminably for words while one's forkful of food grows cold in front of one's nose and one's thoughts wander (I sat next to her). She's just written and published a book on Somerville and Ross, best known for a period funny book on Anglo Ireland *Some Experiences of an Irish R.M.* She's née Pakenham, i.e. Anglo Irish herself. We didn't really discuss Ireland ...

Love to you,
Jim

To Bridget O'Toole

Pont Street Mews
2 February 1970

Dear Bridget,
You'd better come at the weekend or, who knows? Your mustard may be flavouring the victuals of one of my other numerous women. From where I sit I can see them herded resentfully on the cobbles below, waiting for a glimpse.

Thanks v. much for *The Kindly Ones*. [35] ... I think I shall call him 'old boy', the way the garageman calls me ...

I tried writing again yesterday but only managed to reveal to myself once more the present barrenness of the land.

I'm finding the *Mayor of Casterbridge* almost as barmy as *The Return of the Native*. [36]

Love,
Jim

To Tom Maschler

Pont Street Mews
3 February 1970

Dear Tom,
The question of A GIRL IN THE HEAD's paperback advance is obviously now academic. The question arose in the first place because in a similar situation with a previous book of mine which also failed to cover the hardback advance, the publisher in question paid up without a murmur.

A conversation I had with Clarence Paget [37] last summer also supported me in the belief that it was not unusual for the author and publisher to split the paperback advance irrespective.

For the record, the discussion you had before on this subject wasn't with me. No doubt it was with some other bemused author.

As for *Troubles*, I discussed this question with Deborah and I had the impression that she supported my claim for half of any paperback sale irrespective of whether the original advance was covered or not. In fact, I thought that was the point of her amendment to the contract.

But perhaps either there won't be a paperback sale or else, as you hopefully suggest, TROUBLES will earn its full advance in your publication.

It's kind of you to try and get me an Arts Council Award. [38]

> Yours,
> Jim

To Bridget O'Toole

> Pont Street Mews
> 15 February 1970

Dear Brrrrrigid,

In the heavy mail that I customarily receive on St Valentine's Day there appeared, this year, a lovelorn missive from Leamington Spa, a town I have never visited. No doubt it was from some poor girl who on a visit to London glimpsed me from afar and was unable to resist the temptation (or, to put it another way, '*la tentation*') to advertise her hot feelings for me in this manner. If you come across some girl sighing in a bosky *pleasaunce* that'll probably be the one, the saucy little baggage, or, to put it another way, *la petite valise en sauce, n'est-ce pas*, Heinz?

Nothing much has changed here. Diana has gone home for her birthday taking the US Cavalry [39] with her (from which it's quite nice to have a rest) ... My efforts to find a flat are still proving fruitless. I invented a delicious dish yesterday *Le gratin aux cockles à la façon de* Pont Street Mews. Just as I was carrying the smoking *croûte* to the table, napkin tucked into my shirt and chuckling with anticipation, who should appear but Diana to eat half of it. Naturally, and with only the smallest amount of prompting, she voiced her appreciation – but then what girl could possibly resist ecstatic feelings at the taste of my cockles? Indeed, the merest sniff of them has been known to deprive some girls of their reason.

The hot water still hasn't been restored but ... I'm reading with enjoyment that novel by Pavese, *The Devil in the Hills*, having made it through to the tear-jerking climax of *The Mayor of* Casteroil.

I think fondly of you lapping up the Nescaff and puffing Woodbines with your working class friends, sitting around (I visualize) in their shaggy sweaters and college scarves.

> Love,
> Jim

To Juliet Page (Jonathan Cape) [40]

Pont Street Mews

13 March 1970

Dear Juliet Page,

I still don't care very much for the sentence beginning 'Prolific war-time correspondence'. That phrase itself suggests a 'war-correspondent' too much (or is that what it's meant to do? If so I still don't like it). Personally I think you've milked Angela [41] for whatever humour is available with your splendid 'rash afternoon's leave'. If you really want that sentence, however, I suggest you begin it: 'In spite of her many copious letters Angela proves, however, as inhospitable ...' though the 'however' should probably come after letters.

No, I think just 'a decaying mansion'. I don't think one could say it was Georgian. [42]

Nor do I care for 'its enduring enchantment' which is too travel-agenty. In general I think I can't allow myself quite so much praise and that we should condense the last two sentences into something like: 'he has perfectly captured the Ireland of fifty years ago in this compassionate and funny novel' or, if you don't think it's too much, 'in this distinguished, funny and compassionate novel'. The latter would certainly read better rhythm-wise.

If you still don't think it's right perhaps I could call in for five minutes to hammer it out *viva voce* with you next week. Otherwise this may go on for weeks.

Yours,

Jim Farrell

To Juliet Page

Pont Street Mews

13/14 March 1970

Dear Juliet Page,

A postscript to my previous letter to suggest that a rather clumsy sentence in my version of the blurb be split up.

For example, instead of 'Against a background etc.'

'This was a time of world upheaval (race riot in Chicago, disorders throughout the Empire, and the inexorable advance of the dreaded 'Bolshevists'). Against this background events at the Majestic move towards the inevitable conflagration, presenting us with the tragicomedy of a country's struggle for independence, miniaturized and set in amber in the world of 1920.' [43] Do please le me know if you don't like my version so that we can discuss it further.

Yours sincerely,
Jim Farrell

To Juliet Page

Pont Street Mews
[undated typed postcard 1970]

Dear Juliet Page:
I happened to re-read the biographical info. I sent you the other day and noticed that it gives the misleading impression that I review regularly for the *Spectator*. In fact I only review for them occasionally ... I hope it's not too late for you to amend it. Alternatively you could omit it entirely, not that there's much else I can say about myself. I hope you have recovered from your bout of blurb-writing.

Kind regards,
Jim Farrell

To Robina Masters (Jonathan Cape) [44]

Pont Street Mews
[undated] 1970

Dear Robina Masters,
I've now read through the copy-edited version and have replied to all the queries. Should I have missed any I leave the decision up to you. Although most of your green corrections are pertinent there were a number that either seemed unnecessary to me or that I feel I should query. I've listed them and perhaps you could look them up and unless you have a rooted objection restore the original ...
p. 24 Shouldn't 'rowing Blues' have at least one capital? In general I felt somewhat dubious about the way capitals were removed from the hotel rooms. While dining-room is O.K., shouldn't the more unusual rooms retain theirs – e.g. Gun Room rather than gun room? However, no doubt you know best ...
p. 69 I regard your additions as unnecessary and damaging to the style I was trying to achieve here.
p. 286 I should have liked italics for Angela's letter, the scraps of

which are supposed to stand out starkly in the Major's mind-wandering ...

p. 625 I object strongly to your smoothing over of what was a deliberate stylistic device ...

There were certain other cases where I couldn't see the advantage of your corrections but where your version seemed just as good; you'll be glad to hear that I've left these alone.

p. 685 I've added, somewhat clumsily in the margin, a sentence to explain the reappearance of Miss Devere which I hope you'll keep in brackets ...

p. 587 I prefer my spelling of meouwing.

p. 3 I've substituted 'died away' for eclipsed to avoid mixing a metaphor.

I hope this takes care of everything. In a number of places it says in pencil 'Rule?' I take this to be a communication to someone else. However, before realising what it was I foolishly ran a pencil through a couple of them.

Yours sincerely
Jim Farrell

To Russell McCormmach

Pont Street Mews
27 March 1970

Dear Russell,

What's new in Philadelphia? I don't think anything of interest has happened to me since I saw you last Fall. My new book *Troubles* went off to the printer a couple of weeks ago at long last – I was beginning to think it would never get there. I understand that they plan to publish it in September. However, to say that excitement is running high in the book world about its forthcoming appearance would be an exaggeration. Indeed, excitement appears to be running low here, and even lower in the US where, after months of study and a course of electric shock treatment the editor in chief of Harper and Row reached the conclusion that he didn't know whether he wanted it or not. He's waiting now until he sees a proof copy, hoping no doubt that this will inspire him to a decision – if not then it will be a question of calling in the seers to consult the tripes in the H and R boardroom ... However, I've resolutely decided to ignore these matters as best I can while I flirt with two other projects ... the newer of which concerns the innocent, doomed and fantasy-prone Emperor Maximilian of Mexico.

There are a number of contemporary accounts of his unfortunate Empire. The part that interests me most, I think, concerns a diabolical priest called Father Fischer (a former gold-miner and ranch-hand who fathered several illegitimate children while a priest). With Juarez' revolutionary army closing in on Mexico City Maximilian decided to abdicate and retired to hunt butterflies for 6 weeks. During this time it seems that Fischer made him change his mind, partly by organising counterfeit demonstrations of enthusiasm on behalf of the local peasants whenever Maximilian appeared. Actually, I still don't see a way to handle this. I don't think I know of any really successful historical novel that deals with a major figure, with the possible exception of Hitler in *The Fox in the Attic*. Anthony Burgess has also made a reasonable attempt at cornering Shakespeare in *Nothing Like the Sun*.

I move out of this flat at the end of the month. In the meantime I'll visit my folks in Malta. Let me hear from you ... According to the English papers it seems that the US is burning up in a frenzy of drugs and violence. Hope Rittenhouse Sq. is still standing. [45]

All the best,
Jim

Jim was determind to stay in the neighbourhood despite the average high Knightsbridge rents. He prowled the streets and almost at the last minute a 'To be Let' sign outside 16 Egerton Gardens led him to an unfurnished two-room ground-floor flat at a surprisingly affordable price. [46] He made a quick visit to his parents in Malta, and they contributed £750, ostensibly from a distant Farrell will.

To Bridget O'Toole

4, Mariner's Court
Bugibba
Malta G.C.
Thursday [undated] 1970

Dear Bridget baby, [47]
I fear that you are hard-lining me – though this is obviously no less than I deserve. Just before leaving PSM (of blessed memory) I spoke

to Tom Wakefield on the phone and, unprompted, he told me that I had behaved very badly to you on that evening – 'testily' was a word he used. So obviously it wasn't all in your imagination as I had automatically supposed. However, I fear that this crabbiness has now installed itself as part of my nature. It says a great deal for your tolerance that it has taken me so long to realise that I was behaving badly to you. I thought you were enjoying yourself.

I don't know what you want to do now since I'm afraid that a substantial change of spots isn't likely at my advanced age – however, I'm sure we can be friends and hope you'll want to go on being (them?). I'm assuming from your lack of enthusiasm about my coming to Leamington for Easter that the same applies to my projected visit around the middle of the month ... I'll write to you again when my movements are clearer so that we can arrange a meeting when you're up at the BM ...[48]

I had a fresh set of withdrawal symptoms for Baby Mappin combined this time with withdrawal symptoms for Baby Bridget, a gloomy Pascual season all round. An attack of the pasky glooms, so to speak, relieved by frequent visits to the cinema ... I also at last managed to do some writing and hope that the boredom of being here will help me get up some real steam ...

Love to you,
Jim

To Bridget O'Toole

[Airletter from Malta]
[undated] 1970

Dear Bridget,

Many thanks for your letter: very glad to hear that you aren't hard-lining me, as I thought (though of course I richly deserved it). I'll let you know when I'm coming a bit nearer my return.

Read the P. Larkin book [49] the other day and liked it very much. The last scene I thought was particularly good. I can see why you like it, since you must sympathise a lot with the main girl. I didn't get the impression she was very French somehow and felt I needed to know more than I was told about her background and so forth. Also, the bloke was somewhat nebulous, even at the end when the scales fell (clunk, clunk, clunk) from her eyes – no doubt this was partly intentional.

The weather has been not marvellous here either: though I'm sure superior to your snow. I took a dip in the swimming pool but it was icy and I had to hurriedly retrieve myself. The sun shines but there's a brisk wind in exposed places, such as my thinning scalp. I've been rising at half past six to combine writing with sun-bathing: but due to the reluctant zephyrs blowing up grey cloudies I've been doing more of the former, though with only marginal success.

I'm bored here, actually, and much too dissatisfied with myself at the moment to enjoy relaxing idly in the sun. Also, the people here, though friendly, are diabolically dull and materialistic to the last dog. However, I suppose I can't complain. I'll write to you again in due course.

Lots of love,
Jim

The Home Beautiful
Recognition – London
1970

To Tony Colwell (Jonathan Cape)

Apt. 2
16 Egerton Gardens
S.W.3.
[undated] 1970

Dear Mr Colwell,

I have now moved to the above address. My phone number is 584.5137. Perhaps you would give me a ring here when you have something on the jacket for *Troubles*.

Kind regards.
Yours sincerely
J.G. Farrell

To Carol Drisko

Egerton Gardens
28 May 1970

Dear Carol,

Many apologies for having taken so long to write but literally I have been submerged in a deluge of work, mainly manual, that has left me no time to do anything ...

After about six weeks of drifting around with no fixed address and living out of suitcases, I finally took up residence in this small (one room) but agreeable apt. just around the corner from the Aer Lingus terminal in Knightsbridge (handy for daring El Al flyers too, I should think). It had formerly belonged to an ageing faggot with a seigneurial taste in fake grandeur; old-fashioned, plastic-dripping electric candles on all four walls and hanging from the ceiling, enough Regency stripes to satisfy a colony of zebras and some luscious red and white brocade curtains that wouldn't have looked out of place in the *Field of the Cloth of Gold* (Hollywood version). Needless to say, all this has been a dreadful labour to strip down and renew or paint over. In addition I had to dye the carpet, which was an eyestinging shade of red and has now turned (after my ministrations) a patchy and weird, but to my mind agreeable, shade of mulberry ... I found that quite simple things such as putting up a shelf or painting a wall would take me literally hours and that I would collapse on my bed with exhaustion afterwards. Well, enough of this. I trust that I've finished with the Home Beautiful for a few more years. It'll certainly take me that long to recover ... The [second set of] proofs of *Troubles* are due on June 1st. also.

The news from America, at least as it filters through to the British Press, grows worse and worse. Beside Nixon, LBJ is even beginning to look desirable ... Nothing is new here except that all Britain is enraged because the captain of our football team has been arrested in Bogota charged with stealing a necklace. [1] People were discussing this indignantly in two shops I went into yesterday. These South Americans have no conception of how to behave ...

Love,
Jim

To Russell McCormmach

Egerton Gardens
29 May 1970

Dear Russ,

... I've been going on the assumption that this will be a semi-permanent dwelling. I have a lease here for the next five years at all events and my possessions (mainly cooking equipment I find it hard to do without) have long since swollen beyond the point where I could stagger around with them in a couple of suitcases ...

I haven't read or written a thing recently but now I'm furiously trying to make up by reading a re-issue of a somewhat tedious novel by Gissing [2] '*Born in Exile*' which I have to review for the *Spectator*. This involves also reading his more famous *New Grub Street* I'm afraid, so the £20 or so I get for the job will be hard-earned ... I'm somewhat blocked by the Mexican emperor and have shelved that project for the time being. How has your fiction-writing been coming along? ...

Now I must return to Gissing and his sonorous prose. Sample: 'He admired the physical vigour which enabled them to take delight in such a day as this, when girls of poorer blood and ignoble nurture would shrink from the sky's showery tumult ...'

All the best to you, Russ,

Jim

To Tom Maschler

Egerton Gardens
31 May 1970

Dear Tom,

I'm writing around to gather in the rights to various out-of-print works of mine that litter London. If, as I imagine, *A Girl in the Head* is now out of print and you have no further plans for it perhaps you would return rights in it to me.

Kind regards. Hope your Book Bang is going well.

Yours,
Jim

To Deborah Rogers

Egerton Gardens
Monday
[undated] early June 1970

Dear Deborah,

... You may have heard from Tom Maschler that the Arts Council are to give me £750. Needless to say, I'm delighted since the rising waters had just about reached my lower lip. I was going to ask you, in any case, if you could get Cape to hand over the second part of the advance now rather than at publication date. No doubt it will be some considerable time before I can actually get my hands on the Arts Council money and for the sake of peace of mind I'm planning to beard my local tax inspector (not having made a return for the last ten years) ...

When I've got myself together a bit more you must come to supper.

Love
Jim Farrell

To Deborah Rogers

Egerton Gardens
16 June 1970

Dear Deborah,

Many thanks for your nice letter. I may well ask you for the name of your accountant in a few days. It was kind of you to think of it. It may well be that my earnings are so microscopic that they won't drive the tax man into a state of unbearable excitement and cupidity ...

Love
Jim

To Robina Masters (Jonathan Cape)

Egerton Gardens
15 July 1970

Dear Mrs. Masters,

Here are the [second] corrected proofs of *Troubles*. I hope I'm right in assuming that damaged or defective type isn't my province and that someone will look through to review my corrections. When in doubt I've merely put a query.

I believe there are some words missing at the bottom of page 65. If the ms. is still at the printers and you can't find out what the exact words are, it would be sufficient to insert 'We'd be in danger'.

The only change I've made is the omission of 'of July 8th' on page 73, which I believe won't cause any difficulties in re-setting (if it does then it could be left in).

Let me say that I'm very pleased indeed with the appearance of the book. It looks splendid. None of my previous books has pleased me nearly as much in the print stage. Many thanks indeed.

Yours sincerely
Jim Farrell

To Deborah Rogers

Egerton Gardens
13 August 1970

Dear Deborah,

I talked on the phone yesterday with Tony Colwell about the

publication date of *Troubles*. He said it had been changed a couple of times because of various difficulties with Patrick White's novel. [3] Now they appear to have settled on October 8th. He said they have no novels on that date, though ... A. Burgess' book on Shakespeare and some other house is doing C.P. Snow's new novel. He said that the other possible date was Sept. 24th ...

Do you think Sept. 24th would be better? If I have to appear in the same week as a 'big' novelist I feel it might as well be boring old C.P. Snow as anyone (but maybe I don't). Tony also said that the later date would give the travellers longer to sell it ... but, strictly from my point of view, that sort of consideration is unlikely to make any difference [to] the chances of redeeming the advance ...

Sorry to land this problem in your lap but I'm lacking the relevant information to make the decision myself.

Nice to see you the other evening.

Love
Jim

To Carol Drisko

Egerton Gardens
27 August 1970

Dear Carol,

Many moons have elapsed (if a moon can be said to elapse) since your visit to the telephone exchanges of this country. I seem to have been in a welter of busyness ... but can't think of a single thing that I've actually accomplished in all that time, except that I've made some progress with the soufflés. I really must recommend the fish soufflé in the Julia Child book: [4] it's delicious and not hard to succeed with. The only thing I have against it is that it creates a large amount of washing-up. By now you may have had a chance to make that tandoori chicken recipe that you sent me. This now plays a substantial part in my life: many thanks for introducing me to it. I have also acquired a sort of 'ethnic' spice grinder of the kind available on Westbourne Grove here: viz. a great lump of rock hollowed out and a thing like a small baseball bat to clobber the herbs with. It makes short work of them, much more successful than my Moulinex which I've also tried using. I guess one could grind coffee with it too. I'm somewhat disappointed in the cookbook I got by Mrs. Balbir Singh. [5] I've tried a few of the dishes and they have all proved comparative failures ...

In another Indian cookbook, however, I've found an excellent recipe for 'nan' – d'you remember the ethnic bread they serve in the Standard? The recipe is as follows: 1 lb of flour, 1 egg, ¼ pint milk, 3 tbsp. butter, half tsp. yeast, clarified butter, salt.

Sieve flour and add salt (and a little aniseed if you want). Rub in 3 tbsp of butter till the mixture is crumbly. Then gradually add the lukewarm milk and beaten egg. Add yeast and knead thoroughly. Leave to double in size. Make balls of the dough and roll out to ¾ inch thickness. Leave to rise until double again. Deep fry in hot clarified butter. This is fattening but delicious. The balls of dough will keep some time in the warmer part of the fridge so you don't have to make it the same day.

Well, having got the question of food out of the way, I don't know that there's much else of interest going on here. I'm toying with the idea of visiting India this winter or next, if I can find some money. Things are very black in the book world at the moment. Neither the paperback or the American rights of my book have been bought. I just hope that it gets good enough reviews for someone to be interested. I still don't have the finished copies but as soon as I get hold of one I'll send it to you. After refusing a couple of ugly jackets I've at last got one that I like. So that's something. Did I tell you that I'm supposed to be getting an Arts Council grant of £750 with which to go on writing? I was told this some two or three months ago but have heard nothing since. I take it that it's definite, however[6] ...

It's been cold and rainy here for the last month. Now the weather is growing autumnal. Time passes so quickly.

All the best and love from

Jim

To Tom Maschler

Egerton Gardens
5 September 1970

Dear Tom,

Many thanks for the copy of *Troubles* which I do indeed like very much. I'm hoping that I may have rounded up one or two people to write about it when it comes out.

Still no word from the Arts Council. If you could pay the

remainder of what is due on *Troubles* to Deborah it would help me out.

> Kind regards,
> Yours,
> Jim

To Tom Maschler

> Egerton Gardens
> [undated] 1970

Dear Tom,

... You'll be glad to hear that I'm now solvent again thanks to you and the Arts Council.

> Kind regards
> Jim Farrell

To Deborah Rogers

> Egerton Gardens
> 11 September 1970

Dear Deborah,

Thanks so much for the salad serving equipment – what a kind thought! Now I can throw my plastic things away or use them for digging in the garden.

A *Times* extract would be too good to be true. However, I'm optimistic that a lucky break of some sort will occur. Perhaps Angus Wilson will like the book.

I'll let you know if anything else happens. Really, I'm delighted with your housewarming present and can hardly wait to use them.

> Love,
> Jim

To Tony Colwell (Jonathan Cape)

> Egerton Gardens
> 28 September 1970

Dear Tony,

I forgot to mention one piece of minor good news on the phone the other day. Hilary Spurling got Angus Wilson to read TROUBLES. He liked it and wrote to her to say he would try to help it along by choosing it for one of his three chosen books in the *Observer* at

Christmas 'with warm commendation'. I'm letting you know about this in case you should feel like advertising it in the same issue. Let us hope that he doesn't drop dead or change his mind in the interim.

Yours,
Jim

To Rose Knox Peebles
[Postcard 'Brennan's French restaurant in New Orleans']
[London, undated] 1970

Dear Rose,

Many thanks for your letter. I was very gratified to know that you liked it [*Troubles*] so much. There seems to be no more space on this half-baked p.c. to say any more.

See you soon.

Love
Jim

Since May, Emperor Maximilian's tragedy had been supplanted in Farrell's imagination by the Indian mutiny of 1857. India, unlike Mexico, evoked a possessive response after a childood of raptly listening to his father's memories, and as a historical turning point for the British Empire the shock of the mutiny matched the withdrawal from Ireland.

To Sarah Bond
Egerton Gardens
28 September 1970

Dear Sarah,

Many thanks for your letter. I'm very sorry to have taken such a time to reply but the last ten days or so have been hectic: mainly because my parents have been over here from Malta and I ceded them my flat. I find it much less exhausting to do this rather than have them stay in a hotel and eat in restaurants the whole time. At the same time I had to read and review 4 gigantic novels and cross London to feed an absent friend's Burmese kittens.

Really, it's high time we had an end to all the guilt and embarrassment in our relationship, most of it originally my fault, I agree. Actually, I had thought that during your last visit, after a somewhat tense start, we had got on so well and in such a friendly and relaxed fashion that a more normal sort of friendship had started. But it seems from your letter that you didn't think so. I should have sent you my new address and meant to but thought you'd be able to just look me up in the phone book when you next came to London, so let things slide in my usual fashion ...

I heard from Anita the other day to the effect that no less than 4 (four) publishing houses have so far turned down my book. No one has bought the paperback rights yet over here. As it is easily my best (I'm talking about TROUBLES incidentally) I can only conclude that publishing companies are staffed by idiots. It's due to be published here ten days hence and excitement is running low. We were going to get Elizabeth Bowen to review it for the *Spectator* (where they know me) and a copy was sent to her, but it seems she is away on holiday and nobody knows where she is. This coincides, to make things worse, with a complete change of editorial staff at the *Spectator*, the editor having resigned,[7] and so I probably won't be reviewing for them any more. Various other plans to get it before the eye of the public have failed so I feel the tide is running against me: this suspicion became a certainty when I learned that my book comes out the same day as new novels by C.P. Snow and Hemingway (Yes, Ernest is getting at me from Beyond The Tomb) ...

I forgot to say that I got a £750 grant from the Arts Council. I'm planning to use part of this for a trip overland to India this winter. I'm hoping to have started by Christmas in order to be there during the cool weather (and miss the British 'cool weather') but I still have a huge amount of reading and research to do before I go, so perhaps I'll still be here when you come for your annual visit. I'll drop you a line as soon as I know. There's a chance too that I'll put it off till next year.

Lots of love
Jim

To Carol Drisko

Egerton Gardens
28 September 1970

Dear Carol,

Thanks very much for the reviews. I enjoyed the Gore Vidal one about the sex book very much ... Have you read any of Vidal's novels? I keep meaning to but never have, for some reason. My own humble work is due to appear in 10 days or so ...

My latest craze is growing herbs: I have a minuscule patch of ground outside my windows which I'm gradually filling up with boxes of earth and rather sickly plants, including fennel, parsley, coriander, chervil, thyme, tarragon, and – the greatest success of all – basil. I recommend you to grow some basil on your window-ledge, it's delicious in salads. I'm currently in the process (I hope) of marjoram, rosemary, lemon thyme, and bergamot, plus numerous others in seed form for next spring ...

Love,
Jim

To John and Hilary Spurling

Egerton Gardens
30 September 1970

Dear John and Hilary,
Many thanks for the dinner party the other evening, not to mention all your other assistance for *Troubles*. Needless to say how amazed and gratified I was that E. Bowen should speak of it so warmly. I had been feeling v. despondent about its prospects.

Love
Jim

P.S. The pie was delicious!

To Bridget O'Toole

Egerton Gardens
5 October 1970

Dear Bridget,
I wonder how you are getting on now that you have been there a week. [8] Pretty exhausted, I should think. Here the weather has suddenly taken a turn for the worse: well, colder anyway and decidedly autumnal. I imagine that it must be correspondingly arctic in N. Ireland ...

E. Bowen having spoken to me so warmly about *Troubles* cheered me immensely. I had a longish personal chat with her while the conversation was general elsewhere and she really did seem to me (no doubt I'm prepared to like anyone who praises me) to be a tremendously good person because, in spite of her stammer and nervousness, she is v. open and direct, something most unusual in older people (such as myself) and is prepared to talk about herself without the usual caution and self-protection that most people go in for ... She mentioned that she was about contemporary with the twins 'though much less enterprising'. The paper strike here now seems to have ended so things look more promising in that respect. Deborah Rogers has invited me to supper to celebrate.

I had supper the other night with Malcolm 'It-don't-Make-No-Differentials-to-Me, Baby' Dean, father of six daughters. [9] He was interviewing me for the *Guardian*, [10] a circumstance that I have one or two faint misgivings about since he insisted on asking me some pretty peculiar questions of his own as well as taking away the thing I had prepared for him. I told him that if he stuck to what I had given him he would be alright. He went away chuckling at his own brilliance ...

When the book business has settled down I shall probably come over and pay you a visit to make sure you are behaving yourself. Has the parsley survived? I wrenched a small piece off a potted bay tree standing in front of a Bond street store the other day. I've given it the usual treatment and am now waiting to see if it grows. I think I may grab a couple more when the time seems ripe. Harrods are selling them for 15/- but it's a matter of pride ...

Lots of love,
Jim

To Catherine Barton (Jonathan Cape) [11]

Egerton Gardens
6 October 1970

Dear Miss Barton,

Many thanks for your kind letter about *Troubles*. However, you must let me return the compliment by saying that I feel – and have been telling anyone willing to listen – that I could not have been better advised on cutting and editing than I was by you.

Kind regards,
Yours
Jim Farrell

To Bridget O'Toole

A post office somewhere in London!
(where your friend has taken refuge)
9 October 1970

Dear B.

By now I expect you'll have seen the reviews in *The Times, Guardian* and *New Statesman*. [12] The two former could hardly have been better but I'm still smarting under the latter. I think it's bad luck that Campbell Black [13] didn't review it as he might have been more enthusiastic. In general, though, I think I prefer outright (or do I mean downright?) praise or abuse to vague suggestions that 'this novel isn't too unreadable if you tackle it with a bottle of whiskey and a box of Black Magic at your elbow' sort of thing. Everything now depends on the Sundays ... The strain of having my folks commenting on it all blow by blow is close to intolerable but I'm behaving with restraint and fortitude ...

Wish you were here.

Love,
Jim

To Sarah Bond

Egerton Gardens
19 October 1970

Dear Sarah,

I was about to write to you again to say that I am sending you a plump and sexy present in the shape (round) of Malcolm X. Dean, [14] cub reporter, who is supposed to be covering the American elections for the *Guardian*. Come to think of it, he should have called you by now if he is going to.

Meanness apart, the idea of not sending books to my friends is that it's such a job packing them up and sending them off. However, since I find it impossible to bring myself to return a sum as large as $5 I suppose I shall have to send you one.

I enclose a review and flattering picture of myself from *The Times*: my many female admirers claim that the picture approaches total irrestibility. This appeared shortly before a violent onslaught from the *New Statesman* which brought me down to earth somewhat ...

I hope to have set off before Christmas if I can find an overland expedition to join but failing that there's one leaving on 6 Jan. The idea is to get material for a novel set in Lucknow during the Indian Mutiny. I'll let you know whether or not we shall have to postpone our next meeting to Xmas 1971.

Glad to hear that you've cheered up. In haste –

Love

Jim

To Bridget O'Toole

Egerton Gardens
19 October 1970

Dear Bríd (sorry, got [the accent] wrong),

I've decided not to come tomorrow but at the beginning of November as this will split things up better. How does the night of Fri. 30 Oct. to that of Mon. 2nd. seem? ... I really mustn't stay too long. I feel that I have to read in the BM [British Museum] at a tremendous rate in order to get myself prepared for India this winter. It's extraordinary how *Troubles*, in the course of these manic few days of reviews, has classified itself and ceased to occupy my mind. I must confess that I feel somewhat encouraged on the whole by its reception.

Thanks v. much for sending *The Irish Times*. Don't worry about the *Irish Press*, it will eventually turn up by way of the clipping agency. I was somewhat amazed by the *I. Times* review and the lay-out ... This literary page has taken a steep dive since I last saw it, I think. I was delighted that B. Williamson [15] should have been so enthusiastic but like you I winced every now and again at his words ... 'Such a gilt-edged instrument in truth' (surely he means 'razor-edged' or something like that) is more extraordinary than being wrung by a piercing beauty. However, if the instrument means a bit of the old gilt-edged in the bank who am I to complain?

You may have seen a favourable but dim-witted review in the *Sunday Times*. [16] The incompetence of some of these reviewers is criminal ...

Lots of love,

Jim

To Bridget O'Toole

Egerton Gardens
27 October 1970

Dear B,

I think I'd better come on Friday night as planned. The thing is that I already have my ticket and have accepted an invitation to supper ... on the Thursday night. Moreover, or at least, moreunder, my plane [to Belfast] doesn't get in till the ungodly hour of 1.20 a.m. Flight no. BE 6572. Which seems pretty hard on you. However, I shall come laden with gifts to soften the blow ...

Some coke [17] has just been delivered at Egerton so things may be looking up. The humming upstairs has risen to a crescendo at the prospect.

My old school has written asking for a piece for their school magazine. Even the North of England appears to be electrified by my fame. They approached me via my cousin, John Russell, who is at present in the sixth form there, saying that they are planning to do an issue on the school's authors.

The only others I know of are a hack humourist called Patrick Campbell [18] (who is sometimes quite funny). Leslie Charteris, [19] and a recently deceased and rather good homosexual writer called J.Y. [*sic*] Ackerley. [20] Not wanting my cousin to lose face I have dashed off a subtly subversive piece suggesting how nice it is not to have to work for a living. Since parents inevitably read these things I imagine that some editorial minds have boggled. The Head is probably calling an emergency conference at this very moment ...

Love,
Jim

To Bridget O'Toole

Egerton Gardens
28 October 1970

Dear Bridget,

... I've decided that we must have a moratorium on all future discussion of *Troubles*. I'm sick to death of it now. Since neither *Listener* nor *D. Telegraph* has done it this week I think that there'll be no further reviews, except possibly E. Bowen.

I have a riddle for you. Do you know what kind of prose* I am writing with that pen you gave me?

> Lots of love,
> Jim

[*written in purple ink.*]

To Bridget O'Toole

> Egerton Gardens
> 10 November 1970

Dear Brid,

... Your account of the Labour meeting [21] struck a chill to my balls, er, heart. The sheer discomfort of standing in the open air arguing with idiots at this season (at any season) sounds to me to be beyond endurance ...

I'm now beginning to wonder whether I shouldn't defer my journey[21] until I've finished the book – or, at least a first draft of it. What distresses me is the thought of going away and having to come back to start at the beginning again. This is likely to land me into the hot weather when I do get there but *tant pis*, that's when the Mutiny happened mostly ...

Incidentally, I'm afraid 'fat' must be restored to the adjectives that describe me (if it had ever been removed). I weighed myself in Boots yesterday and to my horror and incredulity the treacherous needle climbed on past the 152 mark, on, on to 156!!! It's clearly time they had that machine fixed ...

Must stop now and get to the Museum.

> Lots of love
> Jim
> (Seamus O'Fearghail)

To Carol Drisko

> Egerton Gardens
> 20 November 1970

Dear Carol,

... No doubt you will have seen the worst review, in the *New Statesman* and a somewhat grudging one in the *Observer* by Stephen Wall. [22] There was a good one in *The Times* and the *Guardian* and a fairly good one in the *Sunday Times*. Elizabeth Bowen is said to have written a favourable one for a new mag. called *Europa*, the first edition of which has yet to appear. Apart from that the book seems destined to an early demise, neither paperback nor American rights having been sold but I suppose it can't be helped. I'm now digging through tomes of memoirs of people in India at the time of the Mutiny (or 'War of Independence' as it is now called) in dogged pursuit of another subject to get my teeth into ...

The news from the US gets worse and worse as the weeks go by. Who would have thought that the reign of LBJ would ever seem like a time of liberality? I'm glad that the electors had the sense not to surrender to the Nixon-Agnew witch-hunting campaign. [23] Too bad about Gore, though. Here things, in a lower key, have taken a sharp turn for the worse now that Heath's brand of conservatism [24] has manifested itself as the worker-bashing variety, not to mention his African blunders.

What news of your folks? What news of you? It seems ages since I heard from you. I'm planning a trip to India to snoop about Lucknow and Cawnpore early in the New Year if all goes according to plan. I'd like to spend four or five months there but am afraid that the money may run out before then ...

I wish some American house would take my book so that I could make a trip to America to see you all ...

Love to you,
Jim

To Sarah Bond

Egerton Gardens
30 November 1970

Dear Sarah,
I'm so glad you liked *Troubles*. I thought you probably would. Shortly before your letter arrived I got hold of a copy of Elizabeth Bowen's review of it at long last. Although I knew she liked it because I coincidentally met her at a dinner-party when she was in the middle of reading it, her review was far better than anything I had hoped for ('a major work' etc). So I'm feeling particularly cheerful today (the sun is shining for the first time in several days) and even feel prepared to lend a sympathetic ear to your financial groans. I can only assume that your standard of living has reached epic proportions if it mops up your massive salary. Bravo!

Malcolm said you were looking very pretty and that I would have 'licked my lips', or some such phrase, if I could have seen you; he also added his usual homily to the effect that, nevertheless, you were completely the wrong bird for me, a conclusion which, of course, I had long since accepted without him having to tell me.

I've postponed my departure to India for some weeks in the hope of getting some more of my book written before going there. I'll be in Malta from the 21st to about the 28th.

My girl-friend, Bríd Ná Thuille, [25] who is away most of the time teaching at the New University of Ulster, should be around after Christmas ... and I'm sure you'll like her. If you let me know a day or two in advance I'll invite the nicest people I know to supper and we'll have another binge.

A friend of mine, an oldish (50-60) one-eyed painter called Hyde Solomon, [26] has an exhibition on at the Poindexter Gallery, 24 East 84th St. until 10 Dec. His paintings, semi-abstract sea and sky-scapes in light colours always give me that sensation of freedom and elation that most people claim to get from 'pot'. If you're in the neighbourhood, drop in and have a look.

Merry Christmas,

Love
Jim

Diary fragment
1 December 1970

... A couple of days ago I at last had a look at Elizabeth Bowen's review of *Troubles* in *Europa* [27] and she quotes the description of the charred hotel. If I had bothered to look at [my] diary [28] I think I wd. also have used the 'flight of stone steps leading up into thin air', which I simply forgot. The above review pleased me very much because she was the only person who noticed, or bothered to say, that I was trying to write about now as well as then.

I now think about the time at the Belvedere as the lowest point of the last few years, although I had a regular supply of cash coming and no worries except complete inability to get a book started. I was evidently very lonely: it's hard to remember what loneliness actually feels like if you've stopped being it. My life has taken on a much more settled appearance since then; partly because of an increase in self-confidence, I suppose. Bríd has meant taking a more stable view of things too.

A letter from Sarah to say how she had laughed at *Troubles*, followed by a phrase like 'I do so love laughing' which somehow rang a little disagreeably in my ears ...

Last week Anthony Sampson [29] was brought to supper here by Sally ex-Bentlif. He turned out to be a nice, intelligent fellow, somewhat older and greyer looking than I had expected, with a small mouth. Paul Barker, [30] invited to entertain him, did so with a vengeance, never letting the poor chap open his mouth ... We drank 6 bottles of wine (one per person) but no one appeared particularly drunk. As the evening drew to an end Paul ... grew pale but no less voluble. And his nose began to bleed. After Sampson had left, he and Sally Barker decided it was time to go too. He took his leave, still trailing a vague aura of exasperation, though no one had said anything to cross him (or indeed anything).

To Bridget O'Toole

Egerton Gardens
[undated] 1970

Dear B [31]

Will you ... copy out the recipe for 'taramasalata' in the Habitat diary if there is one – I have a feeling there might be – and bring it with you.

I read with amazement in today's paper of the state of emergency in N. Ireland [32] in which people can be fined for using electricity when other kinds of fuel are available! (turf, for example).

Things are pretty dark and frosty in Knightsbridge.

Love
Jim

P.S. Don't leave your car in the sea breezes or it will rust by the time you get back.

To Catherine Barton

Egerton Gardens
3 December 1970

Dear Catherine,

Very many thanks for the dinner-party the other evening. I much enjoyed it and hope you didn't take my grumbles against Cape as being at all connected with you. As you know I very much valued your editorial advice and appreciate your sympathy and enthusiasm. I subjected poor D. Machin [33] to further grumbles on the way home, which he seemed to take in good part, however.

If there's still no review of *Troubles* in the *TLS* this week would there be any possibility of sounding out the dreaded Arthur Crook [34] to find out if this is intentional? I somehow can't believe, given the things they have reviewed, that they don't mean to review it at all. If so, then too bad. But I hate to think of missing out on so many potential library sales just because of an office muddle. Perhaps Deborah [Rogers] would do it if Cape's collective dignity would not permit an approach.

Love
Jim Farrell

To David Machin

Egerton Gardens
[undated] 1970

Dear David,
Thanks for putting in a good word for me with the Arts Council. I should certainly enjoy doing a tour sometime. From the end of January I hope to be in India doing some research but I should be back in circulation by early summer.

I too enjoyed that late-night session. Merry Christmas ...

Kind regards,
Jim

To Tom Maschler

Egerton Gardens
10 December 1970

Dear Tom,
Many thanks for *Europa* ... I was particularly glad that [Elizabeth Bowen] picked up the fact that I was trying to write a contemporary novel, which none of the other reviewers did. Too bad no one will see the magazine ... Angus Wilson said some weeks ago that he would choose *Troubles* as one of his Christmas books in the *Observer*.

Let's hope he remembers and delivers.

I suppose there's no chance of any of this making Penguin change their minds about taking it. I'm amazed that even in these hard times they should fail to see how well it suits their readership. I heard from Deborah that Knopf have made an offer for it in America, which is a great relief as I have been fearing that your's [*sic*] would be the only edition.

> Kind regards,
> Yours,
> Jim

To Angus Wilson [35]

> Egerton Gardens
> 20 December 1970

Dear Mr Wilson,

Very many thanks for mentioning *Troubles* in your Christmas books. I much appreciate the helping hand.

> Yours sincerely,
> J.G. Farrell

To Tom Maschler

> Egerton Gardens
> 29 December 1970

Dear Tom,

I do realise the unprofitability of publishing fiction of a serious kind. No doubt it is amazing that people continue to publish it at all. However, you mustn't be surprised if I struggle to get the best deal I can for my work: I'm sure you would do no different in my place. As a matter of interest could you let me know the sales figures to date?

Best wishes for the New Year,

> Yours,
> Jim

To Deborah Rogers

Egerton Gardens
[undated] 1970

Dear Deborah,

... To say that these are just about the best of the serious reviews may be some indication of how bad they were in general.

I shall now probably be leaving on 18 January. I'll contact you in a day or two to arrange a get-together.

I was v. disappointed to learn that *Troubles* has sold less than 2,000 copies.

Love,
Jim

Two Parts White Sahib
India and England
1971

To Carol Drisko

Egerton Gardens
London S.W.3
Friday 15 January 1971

Dear Carol,

... I forget whether I mentioned last time that I'm about to set off for India. I'm due to leave by United Arab Airlines on the 21st, in a week's time, flying to Bombay, armed with one or two addresses and a copy of *India on $5 a day* ... I'm preparing myself for something of a shock from the abrupt change from Blighty to Bombay – this is said, however, to be the most Western city of India. My movements after that are somewhat vague, but I plan to roam over N. India as best I can, perhaps getting as far as Calcutta, if I don't run out of steam and cash before then. I'll try to send you a progress report en route ...

In spite of good, on the whole, reviews, sales [of *Troubles*] have been very poor. I feel this may have something to do with the fact that Cape don't believe in advertising, though no doubt it also reflects a profound lack of interest in fiction ... I still haven't sold the paperback rights. I have faint hopes of a French sale, however. I'd love to have a book translated into French. One of the smaller houses has been showing interest. As you may have gathered, things are going from bad to worse under Heath ... It will be a real pleasure to get out of England for a while ...

Have you been cooking recently? Perhaps I shall collect some tips in India. I'll let you know.

Love,
Jim

To Bridget O'Toole

Egerton Gardens
16 January 1971

Dear B.,

... I received a letter from my Dad this morning exhorting me, when choosing a bearer, to elect a stalwart one capable of impressing his comrades. Since reading this a massive question mark has been hovering over 16 Egerton Gdns. I'm beginning to wonder whether my reading of guide books can have been quite deep enough. I've been reading Naipaul's *An Area of Darkness* which I'm finding very amusing, interesting and alarming.

Troubles – er – that is, the Unmentionable – has been availed of by Stock et Cie for the massive sum of M.F. 5,00 – almost £300 and rather more, Deborah says, than is usually paid. Some *pauvre diable* must now be faced with the job of translating it. I'm very gratified about this, needless to say.

I met Sonia Orwell chez the Tubes [1] last night, a splendidly bosomy, tarty, vivacious-type lady. George was on to a bit of alright there. She claimed to be lapping up a certain book ...

Lots of love
Jim

To David Machin

Egerton Gardens
18 January 1971

Dear David,

Sorry to trouble you again but I wonder could you arrange for any mail that comes to Cape for me in the next month (until the end of Feb. say) to be forwarded c/o Clients mail, American Express Int'l, Hamilton House, Block 'A', Connaught Place, New Delhi.

The thing is that Sonia Orwell, met at a party the other night, offered to send on via Cape the address of an Indian friend if she could lay hands on it.

The postal strike may well put an end to this, however. It doesn't matter particularly as, thanks to your help, I feel myself to be well supplied with addresses.

Sincerely,
Jim Farrell

Diary
23 January 1971

I must say that without [the air hostess] I should have been lost in the struggle of arrival; without her ordering me around as if I were a child, a sensation reinforced by her arriving promptly at twelve to shake hands formally and wish me happy birthday. (I had mentioned my birthday in one of the simple-minded conversations that we managed across the aisle.) ... Landing from the plane in Bombay I got a breath of that smoky, rubbishy smell that I remember from the poor parts of Morocco, Puerto Rico and Mexico, and from some of the French *bidonvilles* ... People everywhere, one has never seen anything like it; they crowd in the roads and in the streets, only wealth gives you a little peace: you can withdraw to the Taj Mahal [hotel] for tea or sit in the first class on the train. The streets are constantly crammed in Bombay: perhaps one's sense of security comes from the numbers as much as anything ... It's very easy to be a *sahib* in India, it seems. Servants are automatically deferential even to the most bizarre whims, which they seem to accept without surprise. Moreover, I wish my eye were better able to see the differences between them. I see things without understanding them. It took me ages to realize that what appeared to be splashes of blood all over the pavements of Bombay was merely people spitting betel juice.

To Bridget O'Toole

Bombay
25 January 1971

Dear Bríd,

... The trip over was somewhat exhausting but made very pleasant by the fact that I happened to find myself sitting beside a very nice fellow, a Norwegian journalist on his way to Vietnam. He had a good sense of humour, which was just what was required, United Arab Airlines being a very dodgy outfit altogether. To start with, when I reported as instructed at 2 p.m. to leave at 4 p.m. I was told that we wouldn't be leaving until 8. I nipped off to the flicks in Hounslow West. Then there were interminables in Paris, Rome and a late arrival in Cairo: of which we saw nothing except a few scroungers in Pharaoh outfits. From the air Egypt seems to be all desert. It looks like Bondi Beach without an Aussie in sight, nor even a camel come to that, nor even a Chesterfield. [2]

One feels v. secure here, in spite of the horrors one sees. There's a complete lack of hostility, as far as I can judge, which makes one feel much more at home than in New York, say. Beggars and street salesmen rarely insist. I don't think this would be a place for you, Bríd, all the same, with your sensibility. Even heartless old me finds it hard to get used to ... I'm ashamed to say that what shocked me as badly as anything was seeing a kitten lying on the pavement, so thin I thought it was merely a skin at first. I was horrified when I saw that it was still breathing. By the Church Gate station a girl in her twenties was stretched, one arm outstretched, naked to the waist. In the Sea Lounge of the poshest hotel, the Taj Mahal, a group of young Indians were talking very loudly, and possessively of England: showing off to each other ...

Towards five o'clock, however, a moment of peace. I had left the T.M. where I had had tea and gone to sit on a stone bench by an arch called the Gateway of India. There were a lot of people, rich and poor, some utterly in rags, sitting there enjoying the cool evening sunlight or strolling about. The girls look wonderfully feminine in saris, one has no idea from seeing the occasional frostbitten *begum* in Knightsbridge how good they can look. What was good was the harmony and tranquillity of everything. People really don't resent each other the way they do in the West in a curious way. A mild, bespectacled gentleman sat down next to me and began to read *Power* by Bertrand Russell ... Hope all is well with you.

Lots of love,
Jim

To Robert Gottlieb (Knopf) [3]

Bombay
25 January 1971

Dear Bob Gottlieb,
Thanks very much for your letter, which I got just before leaving, and the postal strike.

I am very glad that you enjoyed *Troubles*. By a strange coincidence, shortly before hearing that you were making an offer for it, I had sent Anita Elizabeth Bowen's review of it, suggesting that she try to stick the book on E. Bowen's American publisher.

Anent this review, [4] I would like to suggest that you try to find room for something of the first and last paras. which contain invaluable assistance to the reader on how to read it. E. Bowen was the only reviewer here who really picked up the fact that I was trying to write about now as well as then. The first paragraph might help to deflect the disappointment of readers ... who are waiting for Devalera [*sic*], Michael Collins *et alia* to start shooting it out with the Limeys. That said, I'll leave you in peace.

I wonder whether I'm risking amoebic dysentery by licking this air letter.

> All the best to you.
> Yours,
> Jim

Diary

Bombay 25 January 1971

A cloud of birds circles over the Towers of Silence where the Parsis expose their dead to be eaten by vultures. The birds circling are mainly kites, I think; the bigger vultures can be seen heaving themselves in and out of trees which hide the racks on which the bodies are stretched. In the park it is very pleasant; Indian families stroll in the evening sunshine. In England or America a huge crowd would have formed and someone would be selling tickets ...

Jaipur, 30 January 1971

What looks strangely like a vulture is perched in a tree about a hundred yards away, watching me as I write ... but no, it has left the tree and moved to another; it is only a kite ... It is very pleasant in the garden of the Jaimahal Palace Hotel: the weather is cold, crisp, sunny and perfect ... It very much resembles an English garden in summer except that there are not so many varieties of flowers. There are marigolds in beds, some red and white flowers that look rather like storks; also a little bed of pansies, not looking very content ... The lawn is very successful, a little coarser than an English one but green. A woman is working here, head and shoulders covered in a yellow shawl, ankles just visible and revealing thick silver anklets. She carries cut grass or weeds in a basket on her shoulders ...

On the train ... only a token attempt had been made to clean it. Going to the restaurant car I passed a sweeper brushing his way along with the ubiquitous handless broom of twigs. A job reminiscent of the walrus and the carpenter ... I shared the compartment with fat Mr Jain, a vegetarian with swollen lips of the kind known as 'sensual', mouth and teeth red-stained from betel juice, who punctuated the dark hours with snores and farts and hawkings ... Mr Jain was not a bad fellow, shared his bananas and biscuits with us. Gave his views on Mrs Gandhi (confused) and on other topics (also confused, or perhaps it was because his English, though fluent, was incomprehensible, a situation made worse by the fact that his mouth was often full). The other occupants of the train were Mrs Bhangabai, a very old, fat little lady being escorted to Delhi by her very nice and friendly son-in-law (I estimate). She sat dumpily cross legged (as did the others) for most of the journey. He was very gentle and loving with her. Indians, with whom I had become disaffected in Bombay, made a better impression in the train.

... A fortunate meeting with a Parsi girl, Roshan Lala, who took me to see the Amber Palace in the afternoon in her business rented car: here for a textiles firm. After that we went to see the cremation ground of the Maharajahs not far away, guided by a white-haired little old man who chattered enthusiastically to Roshan ... strange to think that she is likely to end as a meal for the vultures in the Towers of Silence ... She said that she thought I looked a sad and lonely person ...

To Sarah Bond

Jaipur
31 January 1971

Dear Sarah,

... I have a feeling that you must have been quite glad to get back to the US which henceforth you will no doubt regard as 'home'. I'm sorry that your visit [5] was a disappointment. However, you're bound to get out of touch with one crowd as you get back in touch with another. I can't think why I'm filling this valuable air letter with platitudinous comments.

I spent most of today drifting around the bazaar being nagged by a particularly sinister fortune-teller with one front tooth who kept telling me that he could tell me my mother's name. I had a feeling he probably could but it would have cost me a few rupees to find out – so I declined. He also offered me advice on my love life but I think that wd. have cost more and I didn't feel like any advice anyway.

The weather is perfect in Jaipur, crisp and sunny and there are green parrots with red beaks flying around the garden of the hotel where I'm staying. There are also vultures, but not in the garden. A few minutes ago a gnarled old Rajput gardener with a turban and white mustache [*sic*] shuffled up and offered me a rose. However, though picturesque, I have a feeling he has been programmed to do this by the management. Elephants and camels are to be seen in the streets of Jaipur. Peacocks drift about too. An encampment of untouchables lives in a dusty grove just outside the gates, however, to remind you that things are bad here, beneath the charm. Bombay seemed interesting but dreadful: people actually living their whole lives on a bit of pavement, sleeping, cooking and so on. And one is constantly seeing dreadful sights. I don't think the more prosperous Indians notice any more. And Calcutta is supposed to be twice as bad! I'm dreading going there, and may skip it, though I have an introduction to the great Satyajit Ray.[6] My tolerance for misery (other people's) is not all that high – I felt very depressed here at first. Things are better now ...

Love to you
Jim

To his parents

Jaipur
1 February 1971

Dear Mum and Dad,

... I was quite favourably surprised at the relative efficiency of the Indian railways: however, one is well advised to wear old clothes. I must have eaten about half a pound of dust in the course of this journey. I don't know what the *dhobi* made of the shirt I gave him to wash. He did it very well at all events ...

Jaipur, in spite of the famines that are supposed to hit Rajasthan, seems much less miserable than Bombay. Although there is no shortage of poor people here they don't look quite as desperate. The bazaar is very bright and colourful. I get myself ferried back and forth by cycle rickshaw, though I sometimes walk one way or the other to soak up local colour more effectively. I felt a bit sorry for the chap pedalling until I saw that on occasion they can cope with a brace of very fat gentlemen. The Indians are even more fanatical cinema-goers than the Irish. Yesterday, Sunday, there were immense queues in front of the local bughouse on a sunny and delightful afternoon. They seem to favour soppy Indian films. According to *The Times of India* the films showing in Delhi are a poor lot – ones that Richard and I saw years ago in Dun Laoghaire ...

Lots of love,
Jim

To Carol Drisko

Jaipur
1 February 1971

Dear Carol,
I thought I would send you a progress report on my travels ... Take a ten-minute walk through even the 'better' quarters of Bombay and you'll see enough dreadful sights to last you a lifetime. Oddly enough, or perhaps not, the worst thing I saw there was a hippy – English or American it was impossible to tell – wearing a *dhoti*, utterly on the skids, stoned out of his mind, his skin covered in dreadful scabs, staggering about in blinding sunlight, ignored by the Indians completely ... Prosperous Indians don't seem to notice this anymore and I find that I too am becoming inured: they get a bit peeved with Westerners emoting about the poverty: no doubt it is a nuisance for them ...

Bombay had an adverse effect on me [and] I found it hard to keep up my spirits. It is essential, if you come here, to come with someone else ... I'm afraid, like Naipaul, I am finding myself cut off by the hygiene barrier. I'm hoping to overcome this by degrees, however. Jaipur is lovely. Ruined maharajahs' palaces and whatnot [but] inclined to be chilly at night. Bombay was warm to hot. I'm heading for Agra and Delhi tomorrow and I should be there for a few days. So far I haven't had any Indian food as good as the Standard in London ...

Love from
Jim

To John and Hilary Spurling
[Postcard: 'A scene from the romance of Dhola Marm Marwah']
Jaipur
1 February 1971

Dear John & Hilary,
Heading North by degrees. I've been reading in the local papers about snowstorms in the hills so I think I might postpone my visit to Dehra Dun a little. I'll drop your uncle ⁷ a line in a day or two. For dessert at the hotel tonight we had Tipsy Cake – the last in a line of archaic English dishes, all served with thick yellow custard. I feel I should make some more profound statement about the country but will leave it for another time.

Love
Jim

Diary

Agra 4 February 1971
An encounter with a sinister fortune-teller with strangely piercing eyes, a turban with a jewel and a feather and only one front tooth. He kept whipping out soiled testimonials from Americans and asking me to read them – offering to tell me the name of my mother for ten rupees and suchlike. He said as a sort of trailer of the coming feature that three ladies were interested in me, one foreign – that there were some difficulties coming but they would be overcome. I told him I didn't want to know the future. When I finally escaped his clutches he was quite angry and spat – but perhaps purely for bronchial reasons ...

To Laurie's Hotel, the old-established place to stay in Agra, a room with an enormously high ceiling, the lavatory failed to flush hard enough but *hot* water poured in when one pulled the chain, steam rising around one's bottom. Pulled the chain again, more determinedly. No more water came, but a fat lizard crept out from behind the cistern ...

Yesterday at Fatehpur Sikri, the Red Fort, and the Taj Mahal ... While waiting for the tourists to arrive on the Taj Express from Delhi so that the bus would fill up and go, I sat in a little park. On a lawn a few feet away a figure wrapped in some canvas was lying, one bare brown foot protruded. It was early morning. He had evidently slept there (after dark in winter it must be cold). What I suddenly realised was that I hadn't noticed him. I'd seen him, been vaguely aware of the fact that there was someone there, and discarded the matter as not sufficiently interesting to think about consciously. It's amazing how quickly one shuts off areas of vision. Even the children now hardly engage my attention as they play in the dust. It's an acceptance that this is the way things are ...

The dogs are dreadfully thin and mangy [and] obviously just wander around living as best they can, like the people. They don't appear to belong to anyone: they appear to be tolerated in the same way as cows and tourists. With total equanimity. It occurred to me today that people here don't actually look unhappy. People in England, including Indians, look much more desperate ...

To Bridget O'Toole

Agra
5 February 1971

Dear Bríd,
This is to let you know that all is still going relatively smoothly; though I wish I'd brought you along as I think I wd be enjoying it more and possibly noting more things. I find that unless I actually acknowledge my thoughts by voicing them or writing them down they tend to melt in a vague blur. Also it's astonishing how quickly one takes things for granted. I find myself already beginning not to notice some of the more alarming sights that, if seen in London, you would dine out on for weeks.

I endured the train journey from Jaipur to Agra in Third Class ... I can't really afford anything better. This was something of a baptism of fire as I was in a compartment with a number of odious babies. The one nearest me was merely held away from the seat from time to time to piss on the floor. Well, so far so good. I pored studiously over my book. Presently, however, the child's wretched parents showed some more signs of animation and held the child out to CRAP on the floor. Fortunately it crapped a couple of fairly solid turds which the parents picked up and hurled out of the window. This sort of thing went on for about 12 hrs, during which we covered a miserable 240 odd kms. Most of the time was spent stationary in hot sun in barren plains.

It was a tremendous relief finally to get to Agra. We arrived at an inferior station somewhere and so self and luggage were pedalled on a bicycle rickshaw through miles of bazaar at night. I found this very exciting: every square yard in the bazaar has something going on in it – people cooking things mostly ... The relief of all this animation after being jammed in the train was wonderful.

Here I'm staying in another splendidly old British establishment [8] where the puddings particularly recall a bygone era. They aren't as ready to lash around the custard as they were in Jaipur but today we had something, I think it's called Queen's pudding, that my mother used to make in the old days. The Anglicised people here all go in for having tea on the lawn (roses in the flower beds), tea served with some biscuits and a slice of cake.

In the dining-room there's an air of faded decorum and a framed letter from the British High Commission, thanking them for putting up the Queen and Duke during their tour of India and enclosing a snap (of the regal pair). The Indian waiters, dressed in extravagant white uniforms with coloured cummerbunds and turbans, look magnificent and august but rather seedily try and cadge tips the whole time (good luck to them). The dogs in India are all dreadfully thin and mangy and don't appear to belong to anyone. All around the hotel, I should say, there is a wall separating the clipped lawns and rosebeds from the seething poverty of the bazaar. A little island of satisfaction. A fat and sleek dachshund belongs to someone at the hotel and sensibly doesn't venture out. I looked at its collar name-plate this afternoon when it came up to me greedily to try and get some of my cake while I was having tea. It said merely 'Dog'.

I hear the postal strike is still going on. I can imagine the lather the *Telegraph* must be working itself up into. I hope you've thought to smuggle a letter over the border to me.

Love from
Jim

Diary
New Delhi 7th February 1971
While waiting for the train in Agra I got into conversation with a little old man who said he used to work in the canteen for the British Army. He had been obliged as a Hindu to leave Lahore on partition.

He kept saying how happy he had been during the British time ... We were separated in the struggle for seats in the third class. All the way to Delhi I sat on a providentially disposed tin box of an official nature. A Sikh and numerous other people stood for the three-and-a-half-hour journey; towards the end of it a ragged and dirty boy of about fourteen sang a song (I believe about Kali) in a sweet and powerful voice, accompanying himself by clicking castanet-wise a couple of shells. I saw no sign of him trying to collect money. I enjoyed the song. For the greater part of the journey, in order to forget the physical hardships, I read, interested but dubious, Paul Scott's *Day of the Scorpion*.

This afternoon after my visit to the white tigers [*at Delhi Zoo*] I slept for a while and woke feeling bored and discouraged ... I feel a stranger everywhere in India but nowhere more so than in Delhi.

A dinner-party ... first of all Bhagat's car picks me up and whisks me to his house a few minutes' drive away: servants are bowing and holding open doors – that of the car, the front door, door to the sitting room; so that, without any of the customary pauses I find myself inside in a flash ... Bhagat [9] enters and sits on the couch beside me, perhaps so he won't have to look at me, which he doesn't appear to like doing, out of a sort of shyness ... A conversation limps, partly because he addresses the air in front of him in long conversational sorties, only at the end of which does he turn to me. I find this off-putting. The bearer hovering around is asked to furnish some gin and soda for me ... The party itself a very Western one, except for the ubiquitous servants; they are constantly at your elbow bowing over some dish they are offering you ... There is an air of decorous jollity; the hostess is fat and bouncy in a sort of sub-English way. I talk to an Indian Army officer who enlarges on the sins of Pakistan and doesn't care for me very much, I expect. Ditto another, more intelligent chap with an elaborately un-Indian English accent, who works for a British firm. Many educated Indians have chips on their shoulders about the British, I fear ... In my direction the hostess whipped out a book by some other visiting author and read a couple of lines referring to herself and husband. Chuckles all round. We faded into the night with my hypocritically good-natured grin chiselled on to my features. It would serve me right if the wind changed and it remained forever on my face ...

To Russell McCormmach

New Delhi
8 February 1971

Dear Russ,

... I was glad you liked *Troubles*. I hope you're right in suggesting that a personal view of the world is emerging – I don't think that any writer can be much good without one. I have the feeling, at any rate, that my various manners are homogenising.

I'm having very mixed feelings about India and found the rapid transplanting from Kensington to Bombay a considerable shock ... Outside the major cities people are more friendly than I found in Bombay: not that they are at all hostile there (to a Westerner the lack of aggression is astonishing), simply hard to engage on a personal level. The main trouble is that the colour of one's skin puts one constantly in a different category. Being treated constantly as three parts American tourist to two parts white *sahib* has a debilitating effect on you in the long run ... I'm thinking of going to live somewhere for a month or so and stop this insane viewing of historical monuments ...

I think Lucknow is where I'll make for. First I have to pay a visit to an eighty year old Englishman (Sir Edmund Gibson K.C.I.E.) a survivor of the Raj who lives in Dehra Dun, a hill station. He has invited me to lunch at the Dehra Dun Club! I hope to pump him for interesting sidelights on the British Civil Service here. I'm looking forward to this ...

I am vaguely thinking of a visit to New York in the fall where Knopf are due to publish *Troubles*. This will depend on having made some substantial progress on the book I'm supposed to be writing about India ...

All the best to you,
Jim

To his parents

New Delhi
11 February 1971

Dear Mum and Dad,

... I had a nice letter from Sir Edmund inviting me to lunch ... [so] I decided to take Daddy's advice ... to adopt a correct turn-out. As I had forgotten my black shoes I have bought a pair to go with my blue suit. A suit may be excessive for lunch but I estimate that it's probably better to err on the side of formality ... I shall probably stay 4 or 5 days in D.D. and then move on to Lucknow where I plan to make a longer stay, depending on how pleasant it is (the Victorians used to speak well of it) ...

I was very impressed with the Taj although I didn't expect to be, having seen so many pictures of it – quite astonished in fact. I also enjoyed visiting the Red Fort (did you go there?) particularly because I had read in the B.M. a gripping book by a certain Mark Thornhill called *Personal Adventures of a Magistrate during the Indian Mutiny*; the Europeans all piled into the Fort and lived there for some time ...

I've found Delhi less interesting ... Last night I went to a very Westernised dinner-party among the affluent D.D. set. It was quite jolly in a decorous sort of way and everyone was very friendly towards me and I received numerous other invitations. I was quite glad to be able to say I was regrettably moving on, however, as this really isn't germane to my purpose. Indians tend to be rather formal, I'm finding: also I find it hard to get used to the crowds of servants hanging around ...

Lots of love
Jim

Diary

Dehra Dun [undated]

In Dehra Dun it's a bit colder; it's pretty though; the air and the sunlight are very clear. A man with a spear sits beside the entrance to the Bank of Baroda. In the children's park, a fat boy with an air rifle keeps shooting squirrels and birds ...

While I sat in the children's park, from a nearby establishment I could hear the sounds of a school sports day. A master was conducting the show by means of a loudspeaker. I heard him asking 'house captains' to report at such and such a place. All this punctuated by boys' treble cheering. Another odd legacy of the British – like early morning tea, or was that an Indian invention copied by us?

Dehra Dun 15 February 1971

My sleeping self seems a lot less sanguine than my waking self; for the last few days I've been aware of waking out of feelings of sadness and loss or absence. This morning I was dreaming that we were giving a splendid party in a luxurious house; that Margaret [10] arrived feeling she hadn't been invited, she was dirty and wanted to take a bath. I handed her a towel and tried to tell her that she was wanted. Somehow the sadness persisted.

For the past few days I've been feeling that being a tourist in India one gets very little from the country – apart from the voyeuring of superficial curiosities and horrors. In Delhi an Austrian hippy came up to me with a story about having got there too late to cash travellers' cheques (it's never too late to cash travellers' cheques in Delhi), and said he was hungry, asking for a rupee. I gave it to him but afterwards was annoyed with myself, thinking that it would have been so much better to give it to one of the really destitute Indians – whose pleas I am constantly resisting. The fact was that I gave him the rupee (not a huge sum) because I recognised a fraternity with him as a fellow-European. The fact that it was unscrupulous of him to play at being an Indian and use his European-ness to scrounge money made it no better. The only morally satisfactory conclusion would have been for him then to turn the rupee over to an Indian beggar. I fear that this did not occur, however ...

Large, fat, red-faced, perspiring priests in white organizing the sports at St Joseph's Academy: one of them runs part of the race with his small brown charges and shouts, 'Take that tennis ball on out of that or you'll lose it!' in a rich Irish accent. Also, standing by, a youth (European) in his late teens, superbly togged out in athletic kit, spiked running shoes etc, but with no one his age to compete with. Recollections of my own mis-spent adolescence ...

To Bridget O'Toole

Dehra Dun
15 February 1971

Dear Brid,

D.D. is a nice place; there are views of a few not very impressive-looking baby Himalayas from along the main street, which has, among other quite presentable shops, what looks (I should say 'looked') suspiciously not unlike a CAKE SHOP. Some force greater than myself impelled me to purchase ½ doz tiny cakes yesterday: which unfortunately were not very good. I am sadly disillusioned. Perhaps it's just as well; already I think I hear whispers in the bazaar that the Fat Smoothy Sahib will soon be having to purchase new *churidars* (trousers to you) to enclose his ample proportions.

I think you wd. like it here: every morning at 7 a.m. the bearer thunders on my door with, you've guessed it, morning tea. The chap's English isn't good enough to explain that I don't want the fucking stuff. So I gulp it down not to hurt his feelings. This morning tea business is all over India, I gather. That's colonialism for you.

D.D. is where Henry Tube's uncle is: I haven't seen him yet but I had a letter while in Delhi beginning 'Dear Farrell' and inviting me to lunch at the Dehra Dun Club. I have a suspicion that the old codger is viewing this occasion with as much distress as I am. Perhaps if I garnish my conversation with 'Sir's things will be ok.

I see that the goddam postal strike is still going on so that you'll get these letters all in a lump, if at all. After D.D. I shall push on Eastwards. I might try to stay in Lucknow for a while and write and then have a quick look at Benares or Varanasi as it's now called ... After a while tourism becomes distressingly purposeless. However, I want to fly up to Nepal before leaving, if I can.

I didn't much care for Delhi. New Delhi is like a seedy European provincial town with Asian disadvantages. Old Delhi much more interesting, but distressing too ... the beggars slumped in the dusty sunlight on the wide stone steps that lead up to the main mosque, the Jama Masjid, have engraved themselves on my mind as an image of perfect despair. As for Old Delhi railway station late at night waiting for the Mussoorie express, it reminded me of pictures of Bedlam Jail. People slumped everywhere on the crowded platforms, great racket going on, lights so dim one could hardly see well enough to read. When the train finally drew into the platform a howling mob descended on it while it was still moving, wriggling through windows to bag seats. Meanwhile, Smoothy *Sahib* surveyed this leaning on his cane with a faint smile playing on his lips. Then, signing to the two dusky Malabars to pick up his steamer trunk and follow him, he picked his way through the malodorous natives to his first-class accommodation. I've forgotten to describe a pretty frightful 'Western' dinner-party I went to in New Delhi. Remind me

when I get back. I read in *Newsweek* about the bad riots in the North. [11]
Hope all is well with you.

Lots of love,
Jim

I feel I've been here years already!

To John and Hilary Spurling

Dehra Dun
17 February 1971

Dear John and Hilary,

This morning I went out to Ramgarh to have lunch with your uncle whom I liked very much ... [He] picked me up in a taxi, already containing a couple of his 'retainers', as he calls them. He has a rather peeling house surrounded by thick woods and lands which he farms and his rooms are exactly how one would imagine they should be: the rooms of a colonial bachelor who read Greats (Pliny in the bookshelf and volumes of P.G. Wodehouse) pictures of the Queen (sitting-room) and King George V (dining room or study). Two large and friendly dogs wander around: from time to time he orders a servant to bring a dog-biscuit which he throws to one or the other. On the walls of his bedroom (his bed neatly turned down) he has masses of framed water-colours. 'John wouldn't like all this clutter,' he said, 'look, some of them are crooked even, but I like them so I put them up!'

He was rather nervous of me at first and kept calling his bearer to bring him this or that. I think the main trouble was that he was very worried at the prospect of having a guest ... After lunch, however, he relaxed and I think quite enjoyed my visit ... We chatted for a while on the verandah and he seemed pleased when I remarked on how peaceful it was though he added 'Sometimes too peaceful'. He is very much involved with his retainers, though, and there's a lot going on. He told me there was a deadly feud between his manservant and the cook, the former having fertilized the latter's eldest daughter with twins. A plume of smoke rising from the riverside was the pyre of his driver's wife who had committed suicide the night before by setting fire to herself after a row with her husband.

He took me down to show me the farm, also very peaceful,

magnificent scenery, and on the way we passed the primary school – a score of children in a glade with blackboard and teacher. He had recently purchased two new bullocks which were eating picturesquely out of a tub: we sat and watched them under the shade of a guava tree and he pointed out two or three lychee trees and named some of the local birds for me. I was very impressed by how open-minded and un-blimp-like he is: the length of Prince Charles' hair was the only thing I noticed he found hard to accept ...

As I was leaving he asked me the name of my latest book so I said I'd send him a copy. He told me to give you his love, adding: 'I do love them very much. I don't suppose I'll see them again' ...

Love to you

Jim

Diary
Hardwar 18 February 1971

The town seems to be built up along the river ... Soon after I arrived there, an old chap dunned me for a rupee, for charity, for which he gave me a receipt. He wanted more and wasn't impressed when I told him I wasn't rich, as he had a right not to be.

On the way back to Dehra Dun in the third class, a violent argument pro and con Indira Gandhi broke out. On arrival I saw that the contestants were both white-haired men: they smiled and joked with each other at the end and departed the best of friends in spite of their hard words.

Dehra Dun 19 February 1971

From an early hour the servants hammer on my door on various pretexts since they know I am leaving and I probably represent the only chance the poor devils will have for some time of making an extra rupee. I thought of rewarding them in inverse ratio to their place in the caste system. I started off giving Rs. 5 to the sweeper (in addition to the odd rupees I've been showering on him). Rs. 3 to the dirty and dishevelled lad with an incipient moustache who trudges in with a frightful breakfast most mornings: this was ungenerous but seeing him grab the toast with his dirty hands from the serving plate to put it on mine reawakened my hygiene complexes which have been lying dormant the past few days. Shortly afterwards he reappeared with a one rupee note which was torn and which he wanted replacing. The white *sahib* in me simmering with the tension of getting my departure organized, and so I shooed the poor fellow away. When the main bearer in his black jacket started hammering on the door I indulged in a fit of pique and he returned chastened. Later in the day, back from Mussoorie to collect my chattels I relented and gave him Rs. 5. The misery of these chaps' lives can be judged by their gratitude for these microscopic sums ...

Mussoorie is an extraordinary place, built on mountain tops ... This is very much the closed season so the streets were sparsely inhabited. A lot of Tibetan-like people: I passed some splendid-looking shaven-headed monks in cherry robes, one of them spinning a brass wheel as he walked – we smiled at each other. I was sitting by the roadside by then, reading the *Hindustan Times* so that I could throw it away with a clear conscience ... I also spied an English cemetery which I went down to investigate. I hadn't much time by then so it was only a cursory inspection. The oldest graves I saw were from the late 1860s. Some of the graves had had the lead leaf of their inscriptions picked off. Many young people, girls in their twenties, no doubt young wives in sickly condition, sent up from the plains who didn't make it. Quite a few children. One thirteen-year-old boy accidentally shot. Even if I had had more time I'm not sure that I would have stayed much longer. Gravestones don't tell you nearly enough about people – only enough to depress you ...

I boarded the train in Dehra Dun noting that I had the compartment to myself until Hardwar. I just had time to finish *Nostromo*. Quite a good read but basically so unreal and fatuous. All the characters idealised out of all recognition. No doubt it is an ambitious and prophetic novel: as in *Heart of Darkness* (but more so), Conrad was trying to get to grips with colonialism and capitalism, but the characters are cardboard cut-outs: it must have been a terribly taxing book to write, for the very reason that only briefly (the passage where Nostromo and Decoud are drifting in the dark gulf) does it get off the ground ...

The platform at Hardwar was crammed with pilgrims each with baskets strung on a bamboo pole ... When we finally pulled out there were still many of them left on the platform. My companion turned out to be a very friendly and talkative man in his fifties, Mr Hira Lal Chaturvedia, the P.A. to the Home Minister of Uttar Pradesh who was in the next compartment and who had been electioneering. From time to time his bodyguard, a friendly non-English-speaking fellow with a gun and a shoulder strap studded with cartridges, came in ... This morning while Chaturvedia and I were gossiping over tea ... he sat cross-legged on the seat opposite and said his prayers, eyes closed, lips moving and hands devoutly joined. After that he gave me a cigarette.

Lucknow 20 February 1971

At the Carlton Hotel in Lucknow – a magnificent old Victorian oriental building with immensely high ceilings and long cloistered walks outside the rooms – I have a room with a million mosquitoes. I am about to spend my first night under a mosquito net. A lizard is stationed on the ceiling waiting for developments.

The little boys in Lucknow all seem to be trained to say 'Good morning, Sahib,' as I pass.

The hotel has a supply of books lent by the British Council. I have seized a splendid one by Elizabeth Bowen, *The Last September,* set in Ireland at the time of *Troubles.* [12] It's amazing, or not amazing, how quickly one comes to accept the omnipresent servants in India and to expect all sorts of minor jobs to be done for one. In the Bowen novel someone goes off to pick raspberries. I have just caught myself wondering why she didn't send the servant.

21 February 1971

... I walked around the Residency, [13] having taken a great deal of time to find it. I spotted the iron bridge first of all, over which Polehampton[14] drove on his way to the Residency. Now it is virtually disused as another bigger bridge has been built beside it carrying what looks like an arterial road. A couple of greenish yellow monkeys sat on it and at the Residency end there was a pestilential bustle, flies everywhere and evil-smelling open drains. In the graveyard of the church beside the Residency I came upon Polehampton's grave beside that of Henry Lawrence, [15] as I remember Mrs Polehampton describing it. The stone has been somewhat damaged (how?) but I could make out the inscription she chose: 'Enter thou into the Joy of the Lord'. Mention is also made of their dead infant boy ...

In the afternoon ... in the magificent garden of the Carlton Hotel ... a great number of tea-tables had been arrayed on the lawn with specially placed red chairs at the focal point. It resembled the Sunday afternoon affair I saw in Jaipur when I glimpsed the lady with four arms standing in the shrubbery. Thinking of that incident, why didn't I stop and look more closely? I think it was because I was walking with one of the bearers to collect my luggage and felt it would be a loss of dignity to moderate my pace. 'Oh mortal men, mortal men' ...

22 February 1971
This morning at breakfast the waiter standing behind my chair suddenly stepped forward to tell me he had a headache. No doubt a question-mark formed over my head. However, I recovered from my surprise and told him to come to my room for some aspirin. He did so. I gave him the tablets. He staggered away theatrically, lurching and clutching his brow. I hope at any rate that it was theatrical. I had noticed vaguely before how thin he was. His face is little more than a skull with skin and some black beard on it. I wouldn't be surprised to hear that there was more wrong than just a headache.

At lunch he came up to me, wreathed in smiles, fully recovered. I've been thinking of using this incident in 'Difficulties' [an early title for *The Siege of Krishnapur*], substituting whatever the Victorians used for headaches, *sal volatile*, perhaps, or laudanum.

24 February 1971
... One constantly sees extraordinary sights as one wanders the streets. This afternoon my feeling of unquiet stomach and general *ennui* drove me to the station: on the way there I saw a man wheeling a minuscule water-buffalo on the back of his bicycle – it was sitting in a basket on some straw. The mother, unattached, walked behind through thick traffic of bicycles, rickshaws and occasional cars and lorries. She fell behind, however, and the baby began to gaze back anxiously so she had to break into a canter to catch up again ...

All day I've been feeling defeated by India, thinking of reasons why this should be so. Being a tourist anywhere puts you in a false and useless position. No doubt it would have been better if I'd just chosen one place and gone to live there. As it is, the only way I can keep my spirits up in one servant-infested hotel after another is by moving on at regular intervals, which gives one a Flying Dutchman sensation. A more fundamental reason is my inability to get involved

J.G. Farrell, author of Troubles, *in 1971. 'I've never felt as confident about a book as this one ...' [Photo: Mark Gerson]*

A family snap of William (Bill) and Josephine (Jo) Farrell at home in Dublin. Jim was away at school in England during term time.

Jim and his older brother Robert in 1943, while staying with their Irish maternal grandparents in County Laois.

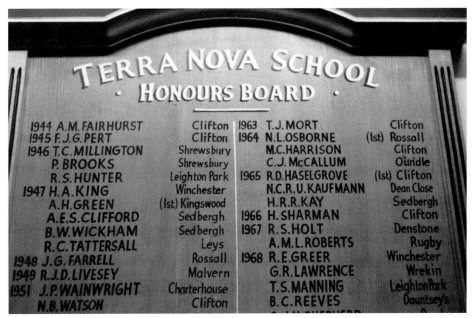

1944	A.M. FAIRHURST	Clifton	1963 T.J. MORT	Clifton
1945	F.J.G. PERT	Clifton	1964 N.L. OSBORNE	(1st) Rossall
1946	T.C. MILLINGTON	Shrewsbury	M.C. HARRISON	Clifton
	P. BROOKS	Shrewsbury	C.J. McCALLUM	Oundle
	R.S. HUNTER	Leighton Park	1965 R.D. HASELGROVE	(1st) Clifton
1947	H.A. KING	Winchester	N.C.R.U. KAUFMANN	Dean Close
	A.H. GREEN	(1st) Kingswood	H.R.R. KAY	Sedbergh
	A.E.S. CLIFFORD	Sedbergh	1966 H. SHARMAN	Clifton
	B.W. WICKHAM	Sedbergh	1967 R.S. HOLT	Denstone
	R.C. TATTERSALL	Leys	A.M.L. ROBERTS	Rugby
1948	J.G. FARRELL	Rossall	1968 R.E. GREER	Winchester
1949	R.J.D. LIVESEY	Malvern	G.R. LAWRENCE	Wrekin
1951	J.P. WAINWRIGHT	Charterhouse	T.S. MANNING	Leighton Park
	N.B. WATSON	Clifton	B.C. REEVES	Dauntsey's

The first prize – from Terra Nova to Rossall.

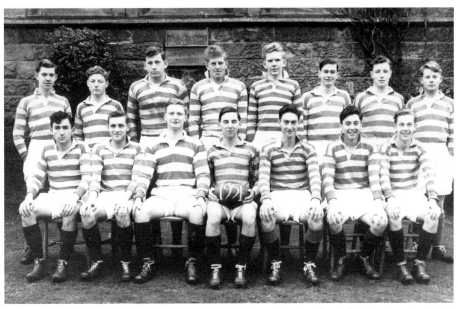

A muscular Three Quarter: Jim (front row, left) on the Rossall Rugby First XV in 1951. 'Standing by, a youth,' he noted twenty years later in India, 'superbly togged out in athletic kit ... Recollections of my own misspent youth.'

The Rossall schoolboy (centre, second row down), outwardly conforming. On seeing the 1968 film If, *Farrell wrote to an American friend: 'Although to you it will seem absurdly exaggerated, I can assure you that the school I went to was hardly different.'*

Now the suitably-clad prep-school master at Castlepark, County Dublin, setting off by ferry with a colleague to cheer on the Irish team against England in a Triple Crown rugby match, 1955.

…l companions for Farrell's Canadian Arctic labouring job at the DEW Line, Baffin Bay, included Joyce,
…y, Louis MacNeice, D.H. Lawrence and Edward Gibbon.

*Starting at Oxford all over again after polio (left), grey-haired and four stone lighter,
1958.*

Farrell self-consciously keeps on his shirt to hide his weight loss at a beach in County Kerry, despite the sun. Hilary Kirwan, once a girlfriend (right), with an English visitor – and, he suspected, rival.

Monsieur Farrell in Paris, 1963. 'I must write another book this winter, and a country which I know already is much less distracting.'

The young novelist, 1965.

'A week ago I moved into the Belvedere Hotel on West 48th Street. A sunny 'room with a view' from the 12th floor ... I have a splendid feeling of living up in the sky', 1967.

An unknown girl catches Farrell's eye in Central Park, New York.

'The desire to withdraw into the private world of another novel becomes more overpowering every day.' The first page of Troubles *was written in New York on St Patrick's day 1967.*

Farrell and Lady Faber appear momentarily ill at ease at the ceremonial prize-giving when Troubles *was awarded the Geoffrey Faber Memorial Prize in 1971. 'My hand was shaken ... by the gloved paw of Lady Faber ... There was no shortage of Praise! In fact I really gorged myself.'* [Photo: Mark Gerson]

The Ocean View Hotel in decline, Block Island, Rhode Island, USA. Photographed in 1946, before the building caught fire and its ruin became the catalyst for Troubles.

16 Egerton Gardens, London SW1. The bay window of Farrell's flat is at ground-floor level on the right.

From Mr J. G. Farrell

Sir, The building of the new British Library is surely an example of a costly "improvement" that few people, if any, actually want, least of all those who use the present incomparable reading room. Readers, I believe, willingly accept the inconveniences of the present system: if the administration doubts this they could conduct a simple survey by asking readers to mark a "Yes" or "No" on their request slips. The reading room could be kept open for longer hours in summer at an insignificant cost, particularly if there were some re-deployment of the swarms of museum guards who cool their heels in the main hall during the present (midweek) late opening. I am no less certain than Professor Thomas (March 6) that the administration simply do not realize *what will be lost*. Committees, it is well known, tend to ignore matters, such as atmosphere, which they cannot quantify. And yet where a reading room is concerned that is the very heart of the matter.

Yours sincerely,

J. G. FARRELL,
16 Egerton Gardens, SW3.
March 6.

Arguing against the new British Library in a letter to The Times.

'I'm beginning to realise that I'm going to have to give some thought to the problems of success (relative) and dangers of having one's private writing life steamrollered ...' After the Booker win for The Siege of Krishnapur *[Photo: Michael Leonard]*

J.G. Farrell in 1978. 'The years go by in a flash.' [Photo: Jane Bown for the *Observer*]

Gortfahane House, Kilcrohane, near Bantry, County Cork. 'It's extremely beautiful here, and very peaceful.' Late spring, 1979.

The rock which Farrell stood on to fish. On 11 August 1979 he was washed off by a wave and drowned.

J. G. Farrell, Saltwater House, Letter, Kilcrohane, Near Bantry, Co. Cork, Ireland. no telephone

Dear R'mary,
August 10 1979

Thanks for your note re my new book. I can't be very helpful, however, at present as I haven't finally decided on the ~~title~~ title and doubt if there's any point in announcing the book without it.

I'm running a bit behind schedule ... but I'm still confident that barring some unforeseen disaster I'll provide you with a novel of 80,000 to 100,000 words before the end of the year as agreed in my contract.

Do hope all goes well with you

Love

Jim

PS Your letter just arrived I hope to answer in a day or two.

Note the poignant date.

in things, in spite of heroic attempts. So much of the 'mystery' of India and its 'wonder' is connected with religion. I find it next to impossible to lend myself to religious enthusiasm and consequently tend only to see the misery. Aesthetically shoddiness, and hordes of people prevail. And the hygiene barrier is still not surmounted ...

Benares 1 March 1971

... Afternoon spent at the burning *ghat* ... I sat down on some steps for about an hour watching – there were about half a dozen pyres going – mostly in an advanced stage. While I was there a couple of women's corpses in coloured shrouds were brought down on green bamboo stretchers, dunked in the river and parked to wait their turn. There was no wailing or any signs of distress ... I suppose I was ten yards away from the nearest fire – some of the corpses burning were of paupers and were being burned by men who worked there, who poked away at the fires with bamboo staves, constantly stirring them up and trying to get the unconsumed parts to burn. The outside bits tended to burn least quickly, the feet and the head; a couple of feet stuck out for some time, toes rather splayed, nails paler than the dark skin (the feet of a not young man I should say) while the middle portion of the body burned, the shin-bones showed very white, the skin having burned off quickly and there being little flesh to carbonise; presently the attendant turned one of the legs over – it was when it went right over against the natural articulation of the joint that the body really stopped being a person for me and became an object ... In a narrow little alley behind the burning *ghats* holy men sat – I saw them later eating. While I was watching the fires one of the holy men came down to collect embers from some of the more thoroughly reduced fires in a shallow pan; this was to do their cooking on ... From time to time (twice anyway) I heard a dull report from one of the half-consumed bodies. Also the white ribs showed plainly for a moment ... When ... down to small pieces the attendant picked the charred lump, unrecognisable as any particular organ, up with two sticks and manoeuvred it into the river; it went in with a hiss of steam ...

There wasn't the slightest trace of ceremony about the scene (apart from the various rituals that were followed); three or four wretched crippled dogs lay about basking in the sun, peasants sat around hugging their knees; cows wandered up and down the steps

browsing on odds and ends of vegetable matter that they found –
paper, cardboard – and one of them even inspected one of the waiting
corpses (but found nothing to eat) on which sparrows played too.
One man with his son seemed a bit uncertain how to go about it
and someone standing by shouted instructions – it was all very natural and matter-of-fact.

Nobody paid any attention to me, fortunately. Boats sailed by,
including a vociferous wedding-party in a large boat being propelled
by a number of oars sprouting from odd parts – for a while this over-
loaded vessel was going round in circles on its own axis while music
played merrily. Smoke sometimes blew in our eyes and for a while it
was quite warm, particularly as the steps against which I was sitting
were in the sun ... All this, which sounded distinctly gruesome to
me yesterday when someone described it to me, now doesn't seem at
all. I think this is because a dead body being burned is so completely
an object; which is consumed so quickly (they say three to four hours
but it loses any recognisable quality very quickly) that one sees people,
bodies and so on in a completely different light. It all seems extremely
natural in some odd way.

Glimpsed in the streets of Benares ... a party of nuns with a
woman's body on a bamboo stretcher on their shoulders, jogging
through the narrow streets, broad red marks on their foreheads
chanting words to the effect that 'Rama is Truth' – they turned a
corner in front of me and vanished towards the burning *ghat* [16] ...

To Bridget O'Toole

Benares
7 March 1971

Dear Brid,

I'm writing this in the hope that the strike may come to an end
in the near future. It's hard to find any reference to it in the Indian papers but I saw a hopeful snippet yesterday. I'm preparing to
dash off to Calcutta this evening, probably just for 2 or 3 days and
mainly in order to get a visa to go to Nepal. At the moment I'm
thinking of returning April 8/9 and probably will if all goes
smoothly.

Benares is the most interesting place I've been but at the moment
I don't feel equal to the job of describing it to you. Suffice yourself

up with the information that I've taken to wearing hippy beads (they help to keep away scroungers) and haven't yet risked my wings [17] to the pudding-basin minded barbers of India ...

Love

Jim

Diary

Calcutta 9–12 March 1971

'Eating edibles brought from outside not permissable please' – a notice in the Indian coffee house.

First day spent entirely in the Salvation Army Hostel with volcanic diarrhoea, the worst I can remember. The first twinges became apparent on the train from Benares, a journey passed comfortably enough on a hard wooden three-tier sleeper in third. An hour after arrival in Calcutta I was as weak as a kitten.

To his parents

Salvation Army Hostel

Calcutta

11 March 1971

Dear Mum and Dad,

I don't know whether this was the place to stay in Calcutta in the 1920s but it certainly is now: very clean and cheap and good breakfast for Rs. 8 per night ... Everyone seemed apprehensive about riots and so forth during the polling for the election, [18] which was yesterday, but, in central Calcutta at least, it all passed off quietly. I like it here much more than I expected, one hears such dreadful things about it ... It's begun to get warmer in the last two or three days, though not yet uncomfortable – all the same, it makes the thought of a couple of weeks in Nepal seem quite pleasant. Somehow one has more energy in cooler places ...

I'm kicking myself for not making a note of your old address in Calcutta. I would have liked to go and see if the house was still there ... Yesterday, which was a holiday for the elections in West Bengal, we went to watch Shiv's [19] brother playing tennis at the Saturday Club: apparently Indians have only been admitted as members in the past four years. I'm surprised the exclusion lasted so long after Independence.

Lots of love,
Jim

Diary
Kathmandu 13 March 1971
Reading Mrs Gaskell, who is not one to miss an opportunity of putting on the sentimental screws ... This diary is running down, in concert with my touristic energies. However, I keep seeing wonders no less frequently, if not more so.

14 March 1971
This morning I rented a bicycle and cycled out to Bouddhanath to see the colossal *stupa*: a pleasant ride of seven miles or so; ... I passed two men trudging into town with a splendid dead leopard slung on a pole by its feet ... I was vaguely exploring a road leading off down a hill when two little boys seized me and made off at a gallop ... one of the little boys elected to watch my bike for 50 paise, the other to guide me. Although only eleven he was better at it than many adults I've come across – after a quick tour round he and his friend went off to the pictures which is what they wanted the money for. Memories of my own well-spent childhood ... There's another temple here with explicit painted wood carvings of erotic scenes ... all the representations of Shiva here seem to show him with erect penis. Vaginae are also carved in great detail and sometimes coloured red for emphasis. After all this cultural and athletic activity I retired to eat *buff momo* (Tibetan dumplings) at Tashi's Trek Stop where all the hippies gather when they aren't at the Pie and Chai shop ... A pile of buff horns lies on the little lane down to the Pie and Chai shop; there are a few vertebrae there too ...

Sitting in the little park beside the Maidan [20] I am approched by a Mr Ashoke Dey who gives me a grubby typewritten testimonial to read to the effect that he is quite conversant with the art of ear-cleaning. He stands by me while I read, flourishing a couple of instruments that resemble dividers – or do I mean compasses? Anyway, he grabs my ear in a most alarming manner and seems reluctant to let go ...

A bad cold has had me staggering round in a daze for the last couple of days. A pile of used tissues litters the floor of my room. I read

Mrs Gaskell's *Cranford* and *Emma*. Of the two, I enjoyed the latter more though her height of mind becomes a bit sickly if you consume too much. I couldn't make out whether she deliberately telegraphs all her dénouements fifty pages ahead or whether we're supposed to be surprised.

18 March 1971

... I went by the *stupa* at Swayambunath – where I was the other day as my cold and the rain were coming on concurrently – climbed round the back this time and sat for a while on a hillock by a monastery admiring the splendid view over the narrow strip of very green valley and the rising Himalayas. A service of some kind was going on in the Buddhist temple beside the *stupa*. Music, of a weird and ominous variety, beating of drums and blowing of great howling wind instruments with a suggestion of trumpet and chanting continually. I sat on my heels by the door and listened and watched ...

On the way home, in the village on the other side of the river I ran into the eldest of the boys from Tashi's Trek Stop. He greeted me like a long-lost friend and led me back by the hand – I bought him some chocolate pie at the Pie and Chai shop. With great tact he then bought us both a cigarette and a sweet in the bazaar on the way up. People are very sweet-natured here ...

20 March 1971

Cycled out to see the sleeping Vishnu at Budhanilkantha; a rather hard ride ... and on my way back into Kathmandu I stopped on the stout bridge, leaning myself and bicycle against the wall, to watch a buddhist funeral taking place down on the bank beside the river ... I noticed that they lit the pyre about halfway up – and as soon as the flames had begun to attack the cloth they did their best to remove it, poking it away with sticks ... In this way they uncovered a shaved head and a somewhat charred arm. They heaped straw on the body too to make it blaze better ... On the way back up I passed a group of men, I think at least a dozen, carrying an enormous dead cow upside down slung on an intricate arrangement of poles so that they could all get a shoulder under. I noticed how flies buzzed about the cow's eyes and upside down its udder sagged inwards. The men stopped to change shoulders and then went on again. No doubt they were taking it down to the river to burn it.

I forgot to record that I rattled up the twenty-two miles to Nagarkot in the back of a Land Rover in the dark: we started at about half past four, having been delayed by the non-appearance of the driver who was asleep ... then by the non-appearance of the guide who was also asleep. We finally got there, however, in time to see the sun rise from behind the High Himalayas, first lighting one peak then another and then finally appearing – a splendid sight, somewhat diminished by the touristic circumstances. We then had tea in the lodge up there (7,000 feet or so) where an oldish gentleman was playing with a baby monkey. Then rattled back via Bhadgaon, the bumps in the road were marginally less intolerable on the way back. I asked the guide if there was any religious significance in the erotic sculpture one sees in temples. He told me that one of the reasons for it (the other was to encourage procreation in a Buddhist un-sexy society at a time when the kingdom was threatened by the Gorkhas) was as a lightning conductor: the goddess of lightning conductors being a virgin goddess it was thought that this sculpture would embarrass her and keep her away ...

22 March 1971

Cycled out to the Chovar gorge where all the waters of the valley have their outlet: not very much at this time of year. With some misgivings, as massive black clouds were looming over the mountains, I cycled on three or four miles before turning back. Shortly after, while coasting down a hill at speed the back tyre burst and I was obliged to struggle back riding noisily, and to the amazement of the locals, on the rim ...

This evening I sold the blue cable [pullover] to a young Tibetan I met in the Dragon, having been pondering earlier whether it was worth taking home. I got Rs. 25 for it and a pair of socks, after some heated bargaining. I was very much inhibited in this by the fact that I didn't want him to pay much for it. I like to think of him striding about next winter looking like a Cornish fisherman in canary socks. Perhaps he will sell them, however. The pullover was somewhat too big for him, but he seemed pleased and it certainly was an improvement on his odd collection of clothes ...

To Bridget O'Toole

Kathmandu
23 March 1971

Dear Bríd,

I wonder how you are getting along during the present difficulties; even the local newspaper *The Rising Nepal* has printed a couple of news items about tension, resignations and so forth. I hope your scarlet reputation hasn't got you behind bars. Incidentally [the paper] gives me many chuckles. A letter from the Nepal Electricity Corporation began: 'Sir, the Corporation deeply regrets the unfortunate incident resulting in the electrocution of the two women which was due to a factor beyond its control.' In the same issue an editorial on medical education muses: 'There is a big question mark whether we can stand on our legs in this respect for a few years more.'

This is the most enjoyable and interesting place I've been to so far, in fact the only place I wd. actively want to return to. It's rather like one expects India to be before going there; incidentally, I've yet to meet anyone on the continent from hippies up (or down) who takes the 'India is wonderful' line that one hears in Europe. Nepal is full of refugees from the rigours of travelling round India. I return there the day after tomorrow for the last couple of weeks, by this time the hot weather has begun on the plains so I should have a taste of that before departing – necessary for my book (about which I regret to say I've virtually stopped thinking in the last 3 weeks). It was already too hot in Calcutta during the middle of the day to do anything when I was there ...

It's very easy to meet people here among the hippy, proto-hippy and senior ex beatnik (myself) population as everyone speaks to everyone without reserve. However, hippies are dull dogs, by and large, I fear – have their own ways of conforming, and limited interest in what's going on outside. They also, inevitably, I suppose, talk about money just as much as any American housewife (though in smaller amounts) ...

I've been reading for the first time *David Copperfield*, with only moderate enthusiasm – too much caricature for my taste and I find the high-mindedness becomes exhausting. I've also acquired *Hard Times* which I hope will be more grown up.

My plane leaves Bombay on the night of April 8/9 ... On the way to Bombay I plan to visit Khajurao where they have the erotic sculpture, perhaps the caves at Ajanta and Ellora too. So far no word from anyone since leaving U.K.

Lots of love,
Seamus

Diary
Benares [undated]

The journey from Kathmandu turned into an odyssey which I survived better than might be expected, given general age and decrepitude. Sat in the very front of an ancient Mercedes bus apparently designed for discomfort for the long ride down through the hills: halfbroiled by the heat of the engine, half ecstatified by the panoramas ...

In the train, a dull German and his Japanese wife: they were good company for the journey, however, as I was past doing anything more than assent to the German's travel anecdotes ... There's a half-hour steamer voyage to cross the river before reaching Patna itself. This was pleasant in the early morning ... At Patna we waited for six hours for the strike-retarded train to come. It was very hot and ... we sat around panting and eating oranges ... I chatted to a pretty Californian girl in Tibetan costume who had been in communes and in a Zen club and on macro. All this didn't make her noticeably different from any other nice, dull American college girl. Tibetans were her latest craze ... She had been corresponding with some *lamas*, she told me. I'd love to know what the *lamas* make of it all. I should think a few question marks can be seen hovering over Himalayan monasteries these days.

When the train finally came the Germans and I got into a carriage with a nice young Army officer with whom we had a simple-minded conversation about how wonderful India ... etc. At one stage while the train was standing in a station somewhere he announced grandly from an upper berth: 'These are the fetters on the Nation's economy', indicating some unfortunates who were stretching their hands through the window for alms. I was attacked by raging thirst and kept drinking from little flower-pots in the Hindu fashion ...

Aurungabad 2 April 1971

Looking in the mirror of the Pointravel Hotel, I decide that I look older and balder than when I started out on this trip, but perhaps it's only the hectic travelling of the last few days. From Benares to Satna, a long, boring and hot day in the train ... Third class from Jhansi to Jalgaon, fourteen hours, was an endurance test of another kind, particularly towards the end – the last two or three hours are always the hardest to get through ... No room to move in any direction and I'd already been sitting there for twelve hours. I did my best to read *Hard Times* by the very dim light – the one over me being *kaput.* ... In Satna and Jhansi I patronised the Railway Retiring Rooms: fortunately having one to myself on both occasions – grimly adequate, pleasant to have a shower then and there ... A departing Retiring Room-mate, aged about fifty, unsuccessfully tried to make me feel guilty about him missing his train because he had left his shirt in the bathroom and couldn't get in while I was having a shower. Having postulated all this, it then transpired that his train wasn't about to leave after all. Indeed he sat around talking for some time ...

Apart from the innumerable exquisite sculptures, the atmosphere at Khajuraho was very pleasant. I stayed in the circuit house where, in the evening especially, there was a sweet smell of flowers: jasmine, I think. The fields round about, where they were reaping the harvest with bill-hooks, made me think of scenes in medieval paintings. I trudged out into the country to see the Jain temples and then three schoolboys, companionably defecating at the side of the road, without interrupting their labours, hailed me as I was passing and directed me through the village to see the other temples. The village too had the same medieval air – narrow, winding streets and hayricks in odd corners and so forth. A man in heavily clomping shoes (no socks) of the Mickey Mouse variety that the poorer people tend to wear, shooed away the boy who was guiding me and took over. I ignored him, however, and the boy presently reappeared in a surreptitious manner.

To his parents

Bombay, Monday
5 April 1971

Dear Mum and Dad,

Many thanks for your letters, received from Thos. Cook this morning: it was nice to get word at last that all is well at home ... I also got one from Bridget saying that the *TLS* finally reviewed *Troubles*, favourably I gather. I had really given that one up. She also said that someone she knows in the English Dept. at Queens University had said it was an option on the Anglo-Irish Lit. course. This pleases me v. much; it makes some hope of a steady sale if it becomes popular with students ... [He] murmured about putting it on his course, though apparently he has been making very heavy weather of it himself and keeps asking B. what the 'moral viewpoint' is (!!!) ...

I leave Bombay on Wed. night and I gather that I'll be arriving back in the middle of Easter weekend. It was very hot in central India: I stopped off on the way back to see the famous sculptures at Khajurao [*sic*] and the cave-temples at Ajanta and Ellora. Bombay's pretty warm and humid and seems amazingly civilized after everywhere else.

Lots of love,
Jim

P.S. Here I'm staying in the Salvation Army again. 10/- per day, 3 meals plus afternoon tea <u>included</u>!

The Rogues Gallery
The Faber and Booker Prizes
1971–74

To Carol Drisko

Egerton Gardens
28 April 1971

Dear Carol,

Your ESP did not deceive you: I got back here about ten days ago and have been slowly recovering and trying to get down to work. I think I must wait until I see you to discuss India. I don't believe my feelings about the country changed significantly after Jaipur but I know that the general feeling of unavailingness increased and the depressing aspects of life there intensified ... I can no longer meld myself with another culture: I have an advanced case of spiritual hardening of the arteries and didn't even try ...

I was disappointed in the hippies too, as a matter of fact, and met only two or three who impressed me as 'real people'. However there are any number of maladjusted young Americans drifting round India, though making precious little contact, it seemed to me, with any of the Indias.

... I have a 50% definite arrangement to go with my French friends Claude and Anna to Northern Ireland, there to rendezvous with a girlfriend of mine who goes by the improbable name of Bridget O'Toole who teaches at the New Univ. of Ulster (where she's known as Red Bridie) and who has a car, in which we would then proceed South to the bogs where my uncle has his woodmill[1] in which, and this is the main point of the operation, an immense collection of books belonging to me have been mouldering for years; these I have been hoping, thanks to B.'s car, to shift back to England ... On the whole, though, since I am now in the middle of a massive and crucial effort to get into my new book I don't think I shall want to be wandering round Ireland ...

[*Troubles*] has just been awarded something called the Faber Memorial Prize[2] for 1971 (£250) which is to be handed over on May 6th. Piers [Paul] Read won it last year. Still no paperback rights sold, however, for all that.

Love
Jim

To Bridget O'Toole

Egerton Gardens
7 May 1971

Dear Brid,

The prize-giving has taken place (I say this to make up for the inexplicable failure of the national papers to headline the matter): my hand was shaken in front of a spotty young man with a camera [3] by the gloved paw of Lady Faber (I assume she kept her glove on to avoid animal contact with a member of the lower orders). It was the sort of gathering best described by the word 'function': not much drink and a lot of middle-aged men in suits – these appeared to be chairmen, directors, members of the family (I kept thinking I was at a wedding and would have to make a speech) and a sprinkling of literary odds and sods (more sods than odds by the look of them). They replaced each other shaking my hand and making a few remarks with a dizzying rapidity, one chairman melting into another so quickly that I very often found myself finishing a sentence to one that I had begun to another. There was no shortage of Praise! In fact, I really gorged myself. I also gorged myself later at the Etoile where I was taken by a v. nice young editor at Faber's called Matthew Evans. [4]

Diana's [5] dinner-party was quite pleasant, mainly because I spent the evening holding forth ... on the subject of India. The other guests after making a few attempts to change the subject sat there with glazed eyes until it was time to leave ... Things may be going a little better with mah book than when you rang (though they could hardly go worse). For £25 I'm reviewing Thor Heyerdahl [6] for *Europa* – this came via H. Tube. 1200 words.

The weather has gone terrible here again. Are there any particular weekends that wd be better for me to visit than others? I feel in any case I might have to subject the matter to the progress of my book. I hope soon to have made enough definite progress to leave with a clear conscience.

I've invited M. Evans and his wife, Janet Dawson, Jogi and Malcolm to supper on Sunday evening. I asked Diana 'back' but she said she was going [away].

Lots of love,
Jim

[*Handwritten*] P.S. There has been some talk of Radio 4 getting me to fill the ether with 'You know's. I think it would be kinder for you not to listen if it comes off!

To Carol Drisko

Egerton Gardens
12 May 1971

Dear Carol,

... I've now heard from les Simha and ... he has had hepatitis and is still convalescent; apparently it takes ages to recover from. David Caute[7] had it a year ago and has barely recovered, I gather ...

I'm in the middle of one of my more tortured attempts to get my writing off the ground, so will finish off this letter here ...

Love
Jim

To Bridget O'Toole

Egerton Gardens
28 May 1971

Dear Brid,

The lady from Radio Liberty[8] duly arrived. She said RL was based in Munich and beamed at Russia: she said she didn't know whether or not it was CIA sponsored, but said she wouldn't be surprised. It was rather alarming as, in spite of my well-known fluency, one's thoughts tend to desert one as someone sticks a microphone in front of your face with every sign of agitation (she was a virgin radiowise also, I gathered). You feel quite foolish as you sit there, your mind a complete blank across which a naked lady flits from time to time (you can never have too much of a good thing, jokewise). However, to my astonishment and gratification the playback sounded quite good: much better than I had expected. I don't think I said 'you know' at all, and although I spoke slowly I gave the impression (to myself at least) that this was because of the effort I was making to think about what I was saying. Indeed, I sounded like the sort of person that I would like to listen to on the radio myself – I await your bullying verdict on all this self-congratulation.

Actually, it scarcely matters because they only broadcast a snippet of the actual interview, translating the remainder into Russian and speaking it themselves. They aim to have literally millions of listeners throughout the Iron Curtain countries though how they know, I know not. I expect they use a system analogous to military 'body counts' in the Vietnam war; i.e. think of the most preposterous figure anyone is likely to accept. Among other Br. Writers being interviewed are such noted Commie-bashers as the appalling One Fat Novelist K. Amis, John Braineless, Cyril Connolly, and Agatha Christie, whom the Russians lap up in no uncertain fashion, it seems. Can it be that my right-wing views have seeped out? Among other things I said that I thought Solzhenitsyn must be fed up with the way capitalist countries use him for propaganda; also that I thought Fyodor, [9] with his belief in 'lerve' as a panacea for the world's ills, would have appreciated the girl from Kent State who offered a flower to a trooper the day before she was shot. [10] However, they can easily edit all this out.

I think of you pitter-pattering in and out of the bar [11] in that hotbed of lust, with everyone flashing sultries at each other in a manner un-equalled anywhere save perhaps among the '*chaud regards*' of the BM [British Museum]. I enjoyed the weekend, hectic though it was. [12]

Lots of lerve,
Jim

To Brian and Rose Knox Peebles

Egerton Gardens
1 June 1971

Dear Brian and Rose,
Thanks for your card; I've actually been back some time but have been lurking at home like a hermit while trying to get another book underway. I did call you once but an antipodean voice said you were away for the week-end. I plan to invite you to supper sometime in

the relatively distant future when I'm no longer becalmed; for the moment my social life is v. restricted. I wish my book were like *Under the Volcano*!

Love
Jim

To Carol Drisko

Egerton Gardens
2 June 1971

Dear Carol,

A last minute postscriptum to my letter the other day.

If this happens to reach you in time ...

If it is not inconvenient ...

If you have any room in your suitcase ...

perhaps you could bring me a stereo LP of Beethoven quartets, or failing that any baroque composer, Vivaldi etc. I'm about to buy myself a record playing system but am daunted by the high price of records. You'll be amply repaid! ...

Have a good flight.

Love,
Jim

To Bridget O'Toole

Egerton Gardens
8 June 1971

Dear Brid,

Somehow I have the feeling that our phone conversations are never as good as our *viva voces*, perhaps because we need a bit of physical presence to break each other's spirits. I also somehow get the feeling that you are speaking to a cranky old man who has to be humoured. However, it was very nice to be humoured the other evening anyway.

There appears to be no news except that I was co-opted by Janet Dawson [13] by virtue of my Frenchified ears to attend a screening at the French Institute of Marguerite Duras' new film. [14] On the way in we met Sonia Orwell who is a great friend of Mme Duras and who had been mainly responsible for collecting an audience for the film, rumoured to be of unparalleled boringness. Sure enough, hardly had the film begun when it became evident to me by the leaden weight of my eyelids that this was the worst (and most pretentious) film I had ever seen. It all takes place in a bare room among half a dozen or so characters who represent – as far as one could fathom – Jews taking refuge there from persecution. Before the film began Mme Duras made a pretentious but mercifully short speech to explain that whenever we heard the word Jew, we could fukk – sorry, that was a genuine mistake – we could fill in with 'negro' or some other embattled minority.

Well, the film went on and on and presently, in spite of a heavy aura of disapproval being beamed from somewhere near the back where S. Orwell was sitting, seats began to click up and narcotized individuals began to blunder about in the dark as they tried to escape. Someone not a million miles from the Smoothiechops [15] got a fit of giggles because from time to time the characters in the film would say to each other: 'This is the worst night I've ever spent in my life,' or something of that nature – which would have a few more spectators blundering towards the door.

Anyway, finally it was too much for us and we blundered out in turn but somehow made *une erreur* of direction and ended up trying to force our way into the projection box which in our desperate state we assumed to be the exit. The projectionist was not very pleased but gave us directions.

I fear my brief spell of being on S. Orwell's invitation list will not have survived this evening's entertainment. However, before the film began she introduced me to Francis Bacon who is, naturally, another of my admirers and ladled on the praise in no uncertain fashion.

I also had an encounter with a little girl from the garden one afternoon. She appeared as I was fiddling with my herbs and said she was 2 and a half and why did I keep my little gate closed. I said: 'So babies won't fall down there.' She stared at me suspiciously and said: 'I'm not a baby, am I?' Naturally, I scoffed at this idea and said: 'Good Heavens no.' At which she stared at me suspiciously again and moved off. How are your plants?

Love,
Jim

To Bridget O'Toole

Egerton Gardens
9 June 1971

Dear Brid,

Many thanks for *Crow* [16] which arrived this morning and gave me a very pleasant surprise because, by an extraordinary coincidence, I had been thinking of getting it the day before yesterday, but had made a vague decision to wait until it came out in paperback! The one or two samples I've read seem wonderful and somehow seem to accord well with my own view of things.

I've been re-reading *Un Amour de Swann* [17] – which is much better than I had remembered, so funny and just. Again, many thanks.

Love,
Jim

To Sarah Bond

Egerton Gardens
10 June 1971

Sarah dear,

Very nice to hear from you ... The prize I won was worth £250 plus a meal at the Etoile. I ate so much I almost doubled the value ... A picture of the event subsequently appeared in the *Bookseller*, myself smiling oilily like an Arab rug-seller.

One evening last week saw me bowling along the King's Rd. crammed into a car brimming with literary talent, viz., Anthony Powell, Edna O'Brien, and a nice American girl called Alison Lurie, [18] on the way to supper at Alvaros. Since then I've dropped back into my habitual anonymity, however.

Talking of literary talent, I saw Robin Cook [19] not long ago; in fact, had lunch with him. He is now married again to someone called Rose whom I haven't met, [who is] reputed to be a matron-like figure ...

See you soon.

Love,
Jim

To Robert Gottlieb (Knopf)

Egerton Gardens
16 June 1971

Dear Bob Gottlieb,

Deborah told me that you told her that you had a smashing jacket for *Troubles*. I'd love to see it if and when you have a proof. If you have an approximate date in mind for publication perhaps you could let me know as I'm thinking, though not very seriously, of paying a visit to NYC sometime this tax year.

Deborah seemed amazed at her good fortune in trusting herself to a flying machine more than once without disaster. I tell her she is becoming a skilled lady aviator.

Looking forward to meeting you one of these days.

Kind regards.
Yours truly,
Jim

To Bridget O'Toole

Egerton Gardens
30 June 1971

Dear Brid,

Thanks for your letter. I'm inclined to agree that it might be better to go abroad in September: however, I've been feeling somewhat claustrophobed here recently. I've been having an odd feeling with my writing, viz. that I'm constantly on the brink of a break-through with this book (I mean as far as getting it going goes) but after new titanic efforts still find myself on the brink. If you don't have anyone staying with you on the weekend 10-12 I might stagger across for a breather though, come to think of it, it's probably not worth the expense for a short trip and I might just declare a holiday while you're here, if you feel like it too, and we could go for London Transport walks (I fear that won't sound so enticing after the horse ate your flowers) or indeed not do anything in particular. I'm all confused at the moment with trying to get some shape into my book ...

I went to a dinner party *chez* S. Orwell the other evening. The Tubes were there, plus a nice lady called Sybil Bedford [20] and another lady, her companion; they mentioned Malcolm now and again. This turned out to be Lowry. I happened to remark on this to S. Orwell as I was leaving and she said: 'But good heavens, everybody knew everybody!' making me feel rather as if I had just alerted Jan Eccles [21] to an amazingly rare bird called a raven ...

It appeared from the conversation that Henry Tube and S. Orwell had had some great argument the other day. They were attempting to make it up. S. Orwell saying things like 'I know you're really not right wing ...' Well, it's all so boring really.

Lots of love,
Jim

To Sonia Orwell

Egerton Gardens
[undated] 1971

Dear Sonia,
Thank you very much for a delicious supper and enjoyable evening. It was all lovely, as usual. This is mainly to say that I hope you aren't counting on me for this coming week-end to meet your Irish visitor because on consulting my diary I discovered a christening I'm supposed to attend in Oxford ... (not taking a starring role, however).

Love
Jim F.

To Bridget O'Toole

Egerton Gardens
4 August 1971

Dear Brid,
I don't feel I'm the best person to cheer you up as I'm feeling somewhat low myself. However, I'm sure you'll feel much better when you get back to your Irish haunts of coot and fern, not to mention all the hot male glances in that seething seat of learning where curry is never off the menu.

I'm still being ambushed by friends who spring at me out of my past: the latest two being Dick Delaney [22] and Sarah [Bond]. Dick appeared on Sunday – we went to a play on Monday, *The Patrick Pearse Motel,* [23] which I didn't think was all that marvy, and last night we went to the Ark, [24] inviting Sarah who had rung up in the meantime. D and S got on pretty well, S pleasing D very much by telling him he had nice wrinkles round his eyes – you can judge from that the ribald, no holds barred, evening we made of it ...

Diana also appeared, to take me for a walk, and chased me round Hyde Park with her views on the literary scene, then back to my flat where even the fact that I started watching a film on tv did not immediately reduce her to silence ...

I may give you a ring in due course.

Lots of love,
Jim

[*Handwritten*] Next summer I shall retire to the country.
P.S. I like the fox called Basil.[25]

To Carol Drisko

Egerton Gardens
4 August 1971

Dear Carol,

Thanks very much for your letter, of already some time ago. I was glad to hear that the plants got through and to receive the Proust article. [26] I'm not sure what to make of Gass – the article was nicely written word-wise, but content-wise was not too satisfying for your hard core Proustophile. I hear there's a fine exhibition on in Paris until September of Proust and hope to get across there to see it, if only I can get some progress with my work.

Yes, I did attempt to wave goodbye when I heard the bus passing, but couldn't spot you and assumed that, since so much time had elapsed, you had been whisked away by an earlier bus I hadn't heard ... Delighted to hear that they still have gentlemen checking passports in Brompton Road, [27] it is, of course, part of the British tourist service that our men are trained to disbelieve lady tourists' age, and some of them, reaching the peak of their profession, actually come to disbelieve it in all sincerity.

Nothing at all new has been happening here. I've been struggling on with my work which makes slowish progress. I think I had not yet seen *Claire's Knee* [28] when I saw you. I imagine it is playing in New York. If so, go and see it if you haven't already. It's pretty good.

Back to work.

Lots of love,
Jim

To Miss Rees (Knopf) [29]

Egerton Gardens
7 August 1971

Dear Miss Rees,
Many thanks for the first copy of your edition of *Troubles*. I found
the jacket very fine indeed and the inset of the Major just as I had
imagined him. Please convey my congratulations to those responsible
... It conveys the feel of the period and the book so well.

Kind regards.
Yours,
Jim Farrell

To Russell McCormmach

Egerton Gardens
3 September 1971

Dear Russ,
It was good to get your letter as I was wondering yesterday what had
happened to you. I don't think I'll come to New York this winter
as I had hoped; to do so would merely be to shirk writing my book
for a while longer and for financial as well as various psychological
reasons I don't feel I can do that. I tend to be pessimistic about the
way the book is going so far (I've written about 100 pages) and I'm
finding it more difficult in many ways than I'd thought, even though
I'm not writing about Indians, but Englishmen in India. I've been
trying to incorporate some of the ideas of the 1850s as well as the
more superficial details of life: and this is not something I find that
I'm skilful at. Nevertheless, I'm persevering, as I fear that the book
will be monumentally dull without them ...

Depending where I am in my writing by next summer I am
thinking of looking for a cottage in the country – and you could
either come too, or use my flat if you need to be in London for
research purposes.

I had a letter from Mike Roemer a couple of weeks ago. He said
his latest film did not get a showing, as it was considered uncom-
mercial and, by some people, anti-semitic. [30]

All the best,
Jim

To Carol Drisko

Egerton Gardens
4 Oct 1971

Dear Carol,

Many thanks for your letter and the review and clipping from the *NY Times*, [31] the benevolent lack of interest was somewhat typical of the only other review I've seen, from the Briefly Noted fiction column of the *New Yorker* ... Thus the American publication seems to be an even greater non-event than the British one. Alas, no one wants novels any more ...

My present *oeuvre* is limping forward: I've been interrupted somewhat by a visit from my parents, which rendered creation impossible, and by too much research which has left me and the book in a near-hopeless muddle. I'm trying to sort it out but am tempted to strip it of all ideas and just leave the action.

I visited Paris since I last wrote – a brief three day trip to see my Fr. editor and the translator, who turned out to be a splendid fat old lady, full of vitality, who told me she had translated 22 novels by Graham Greene (you'd need to be full of vitality). She showed me some of what she'd done with *Troubles* and it seemed splendid. They're talking of perhaps bringing it out by Easter if they can get the translation done by the end of this year.

Nothing much has been happening here. I went to a launching party for Piers Read's new novel, [32] at which one or two celebrities (other than myself) were to be seen, notably Saul Bellow, wearing a jacket with two buttons on the back like a frock coat. I didn't get to exchange a word with him, however. I'm told that Read's book has had mixed reviews. I haven't been reading the papers myself.

Love,
Jim

To Robert Gottlieb (Knopf)

Egerton Gardens
8 October 1971

Dear Bob Gottlieb,

Could you let me know how sales of *Troubles* are going, if at all?

I'm assuming from the two rather miserable reviews I've seen, in the *New Yorker* and the *NYT Book Review*, that this is something of a non-event, to put it mildly.

Kind regards and best wishes,
Jim

To Bridget O'Toole

Egerton Gardens
[undated] 1971

Dear Fatty,

Here's the review, [33] I hope this time. It shd have you licking your chops in no uncertain fashion as he even has a bit of jargon there, if I do not mistake. I'll have to get you to translate it for me: it's clearly well known in the profession but has me utterly foxed.

Stephen and Yvonne [34] came to lunch. I also invited Derek Mahon and Doreen [35] and an Indian girl to whom I had [unwisely] given my address in Jaipur, a certain Roshan Lala [36] (no relation of Oh Lala!) This last was a mistaken impulse – she had just rung up 5 mins earlier – because both the Walls and Mahons seemed incapable of talking about anything but books, in spite of my attempts to change the subject to something more of interest to Roshan ... I felt somewhat guilty about not taking her sightseeing (as she had taken me out to see a Mogul fort at Amber) but, as you can imagine, this was beyond even my powers of magnanimity. She flies on to America tomorrow threatening to return in January. This evening I have organized an assembly designed to take care of all my most pressing social obligations 'at a stroke'. I have invited Roshan, the Polish translatress whose name, she handed me a card last time, seems to be Ariadna Demkowski Bohdziewicz, Claire and Shiv, [37] and I'm dreading it ...

Mahon, incidentally, said he'd been reading in Manchester the day before and that Jimmy Simmons [38] had been there too, reading his marital sonnets.

Looking forward to seeing you next week. Will you let me know if you would like something in the clothing line (such as a clothes line) for your birthday, if so, giving precise measurements; or the Habitat line, or the book line ...

It's v. rash of you to go to a *ceilidh* [39] in Derry, though brave admittedly.

Love,
Jim

To Carol Drisko

Egerton Gardens
26 October 1971

Dear Carol,

... I'm working hectically, but with deep dissatisfaction at what I'm producing. I feel I've bitten off more than I can chew this time, but have long since passed the point of no return.

I enclose a nice review of *Troubles*, in the hope that you may be able to guess at what it might be from by the type layout, [40] Knopf sent it to me with one or two others but without saying what they were from. There was also a nice one by 'Waldon R. Porterfield of The Journal Staff' ... what would that be? [41] And a peculiar one by 'the well-known novelist and critic' Jack Conroy [42] in *Showcase* whatever that is. There was a very nasty one in the *Sat. Review* I assume (it's initials were SR) by a member of the English Dept. of Colgate University [43] who ended by exhorting his readers, if they really wanted to know about Ireland in the Troubles, to go back to Yeats' poem Easter 1916, and he even had the temerity to quote the 'terrible beauty is born' bit. How simple-minded can one get? Answer, very simple-minded indeed ...

I was disgusted with Kennedy's Irish-vote-catching remarks about Ulster. [44] They really seemed to me to imply a disgraceful ignoring of the real situation. I was quite relieved to see that the *NY Times* took him to task for it and said that it raised questions about his judgment. What did people make of it in the US?

Have you received the copy of *Troubles* yet, incidentally?

Love,
Jim

To Carol Drisko

Egerton Gardens
3 December 1971

Dear Carol,

Your Chilean jaunt sounds fantastic ... With Castro's recent visit there has been a lot of Chile on the tv news here; Castro is big and fat. I hadn't realised that before: it spoiled his image a little for me. I hope Allende makes it but I'm not confident of his chances. [45] So much depends on whether Chileans have a civic disposition. I fear they don't. But who has, nowadays? ...

I met V.S. Naipaul the other evening. His (English) wife told me that while they were in NYC lately Vidya (that is 'himself') tried to meet Stokely Carmichael. [46] It seems they went to the same school in Trinidad. But Stokely failed to show.

All the best for your trip.

Love,
Jim

To Bridget O'Toole

Egerton Gardens
[Handwritten and undated 1971]

Dear B.

... Sorry I won't be seeing you before Christmas. I fear the second law of thermodynamics is at work in our relationship.

Love,
Jim

To Bridget O'Toole

Egerton Gardens
[undated] December 1971

Dear B.

... I had a drink last night with Rodney Ackland [47] and his wife: he is/was 'a famous playwright of the thirties', re-discovered and taken up by the Spurlings. He now lives in reduced circs with his wife in someone else's flat: his wife has cancer but seems to be holding her own. I'd met him once or twice at the Spurlings and like him; he's very small and dynamic, though incoherent, chain smokes and wears a bow-tie. I noticed a leaflet advertising the re-publication of one of his plays called *The Dark River* with a quote by H. Spurling of the *Spectator* calling it 'indisputably the one great play of the century' or something. His wife looked intelligent, had thick glasses, was very thin but didn't otherwise look too ill. She also smoked a lot and spoke in the same incoherent manner; they both have trouble getting going on anecdotes etc. rather like certain vilificators like M. Dean accuse me lyingly of. Among other things he said how he'd had tea with Sean O'Casey but, although he 'adored' him, could not now remember a single thing he'd said.

The S.s were also there, very subdued. I feel that their coming offspring may be weighing heavily on their future ...

Lots of love,
Jim

To Tom Maschler

Egerton Gardens
14 December 1971

Dear Tom,
Very many thanks for the handbound *Troubles*. I find it very handsome indeed; too bad about those vanishing old craftsmen.

All the best to you for Christmas and the New Year.

Yours,
Jim

To Bridget O'Toole

Egerton Gardens [48]
13 January 1972

Dear B.
... I thought the Ulster programme on tv[49] was quite boring but with certain good bits – Devlin talking to Paisley was very good indeed. Did you notice how Paisley had trouble giving his views in a normal voice? He kept having to stop ranting them. In general, I thought Devlin was v. clever. A. Sampson whom I saw next day thought Caradon was v. poor and said he had heard from some Irish senator friend that there seemed to be a good chance of the Army actually winning. A. Sampson commented warmly on how splendid you were and 'so intelligent'. I quickly sorted him out on the latter matter, with regard to politics, at any rate ...

Lots of love,
Jim

[*Handwritten*] P.S. Garry [Arnott] arrived here clutching a bottle of rum for 'Bridget's Christmas present – non-exportable, however.' I'm busy drinking it.

To Sarah Bond

Egerton Gardens
17 February 1972

Dear Sarah.

Many thanks for your Christmas card – which was the nicest I got. Indeed, I still have it and gaze at it as I eat my breakfast every day ... I went to Paris to visit Larry and Virginia Snelling and to avoid the festivities here. I was shocked to find that without the excuse of one miserable child Virginia had 'trimmed' the tree with flashing lights and God knows what. Beneath this gorgeous and festive object sat Larry in a deep gloom: his latest (and since then accepted) novel had just been rejected by the fifth publisher. This was a topic he kept bringing up over Yuletide. We ate a Christmas dinner of turkey which I personally detest, which was so massive that it had to be cooked at the boulangerie around the corner, at the house of more expatriate Americans, *Herald Trib* journalists around the corner also. One of these, an Irish American, with a few glasses of wine, became belligerent over Ulster. However, I declined to argue and pointed out soothingly that it was Christmas and that we would only get annoyed with each other. He fell into a sullen silence after that and glowered drunkenly at me as I left. (He was the host, I discovered later.)

Bridget is still working to bring about the revolution in N. Ireland and becomes enraged with my liberal equivocations. It is some weeks since we last corresponded, alas, but no doubt it is all for the best.

I'm working like a slave on my book, of which I am heartily sick. However, I should have finished by the early summer. I'm dreaming of going to take a holiday on some sunny beach. You've no idea how exhausted writing a novel makes you feel. One feels morally worn out, for some reason. It's not only me either. Other people I know feel the same ...

New York seems incredibly far away these days.

Love to you,
Jim

To Bridget O'Toole

Egerton Gardens
[undated] 1972

Dear B.

... I saw A. Sampson the day after Bernadette had slapped Maudling [50] and he remarked how the conduct of govt. resembles a series of internal family rows.

Carol Drisko in a letter mentioned that her v. right-wing Catholic housekeeper, Mrs. Maguinness, had been collecting civil rights signatures for Ulster. Carol and her friend Anna-Marie (a Communist upstairs) had been discussing whether it would be possible to use Ulster to 'raise Mrs. Mac's consciousness' and extend her sympathies to blacks, Puerto Ricans etc. I'm awaiting the outcome with interest.

Diana now treats me as if I were an Eminent Person. At her party she kept leading people up to be presented – I haven't yet fathomed whether this is respect for my literary prowess or fear of my eccentricity ...

Love,
Jim

P.S. The Cloggies [51] is good.

To Carol Drisko

Egerton Gardens
27 February 1972

Dear Carol,

... No doubt you will have read about our miners' strike, [52] as a result of which this govt. has taken a slap in the teeth (not undeserved). We're still having power cuts on rota, however, which is a bore as you can imagine. They are due to continue for another two weeks, I think.

I had lunch the other day at the Café Royal [53] with Sonia Orwell and Jean Rhys, who is a friend of hers. I seem to remember that you were enthusiastic about her books. She is incredibly old and frail and her voice is rather weak: but I liked her very much. She told me that she had fallen over six weeks earlier and broken three ribs, after drinking a bottle of white wine. I hope to be doing the same in my eighties. She's a bit helpless and Sonia had to cut up her food. In the incredibly lush turn of the century plush decor of the Café Royal she seemed like a fly in amber. It was also poignant to hear someone talking about Djuna Barnes [54] and the Joyces as acquaintances in such a setting ('Nora Joyce was very sweet'). If I see her again before she goes back to Devon in March I'll see if I can get her to autograph one of her books.

I've almost finished the first draft of my book now but I will have an awful lot of rewriting to do, I fear. I'm still hoping to get it finished by the early summer however, so I can start something new ...

Love,
Jim

To Brian and Rose Knox Peebles

Egerton Gardens
[undated] 1972

Dear Brian and Rose,
Delighted to hear that you are now in your new abode. I look forward to dropping in on you in due course. I am now on the last lap of the first draft of my book and hope to finish it in a few weeks, then take a few days off before trying to make something readable out of it. I'll try and contact you then if not before.

Love to all,
Jim

To Claude and Anna Simha

Egerton Gardens
8 May 1972

My dear Friends,
Thanks for all your news, Claude. You really deserve to have a rotten time in Las Palmas for slipping away like that with neither wife nor daughter. As for me, I have done nothing really except visit my parents in Malta for Easter, and for once I actually enjoyed myself. The weather was perfect and I came at just the right time of year to experience the countryside. For three or four months in spring the island is covered with wild flowers while for the rest of the year it is just a barren rock, too hot and swarming with two different types of moron, the worst of the two, by far, being the bourgeois British.

Anyway, with my limited knowledge I spent my time picking and classifying flowers, totally ignoring, I'm afraid, my parents' friends who occupied themselves vituperating against the socialism of Mintoff [55] ...

It seems that my novel *Troubles* (to be pronounced now *à la française* seeing that that title is to be kept) should be released in September and there is talk of bringing me over for publicity. They are intending at the same time to edit a factual account in a book by the *Sunday Times* on the Irish situation. But I shall probably come to Paris before that anyway for something of a change. At the moment, I am working day and night to finish my book on India ...

Within one month I shall be free and looking forward to seeing you all, and Elie too I hope, either here or in Paris. Oh, I forgot to mention that in two weeks time you will be able to hear the voice of your uncle Jim on the B.B.C. when he is talking about literature. [56]

See you soon,
Jim

To Deborah Rogers

Egerton Gardens
[undated] end of June 1972

Dear Deb,
I've now finished my book and shall make another attempt, accompanied by the tipstaff, to serve it on you. Either tomorrow or next week.

I feel that perhaps you may be having misgivings about agenting it and the effect on your professional reputation vis à vis your friends at Cape of my proposed infidelity [57] – not to mention my other reckless and grandiose plans. In which case do let me know. I shan't in the least hold it against you or demand the mint back.

Love
Jim

To Deborah Rogers

Egerton Gardens
15 August 1972

Dear Deborah,
... I've been thinking that probably the best idea, rather than me trying to judge the merits of the personalities involved, would be for

us simply to surrender ourselves to whichever of our suitors you judge to be making the best all-round offer; I'm sure this has been your view all along. Since Cape I've grown cautious of unspecific promises and, mind you, perhaps there's something to be said for being Hamish Hamilton's only 'star' (but of what magnitude? And what are the actual advantages?). We must confer, anyway, before making any definite moves. But, of course, there's no hurry, is there?

It's a great relief to me that it's proving popular with publishers; I was very much afraid that the book might be considered too outlandish for us to turn the headway made with *Troubles* to good account ...

Love to you,
Jim

To Russell McCormmach

16 Egerton Gardens
London SW3
23 August 1972

Dear Russ,

It was very good to hear from you [and] I feel sure that your move to Baltimore is a good idea, if only because it's a move. I feel very much in a rut myself – habits acquired over two or three years of living in the same place. I'm making pathetic attempts to change them by wearing different clothes, doing things I wouldn't normally do, and so forth. Alas, I conclude that a more fundamental change in life-style is needed.

I've now finished my India book, which is actually less about India than about the 19th century: although reaction among publishers has been favourable (publishers use a hyperbolic language in which 'excited' means 'apathetic', 'very excited' means 'faintly interested' etc.). I entertain private misgivings about its superficiality. I'm considering setting to work on another, very different, attempt to write an India book.

I have read *Enderby* [58] and know a number of real-life examples of him: the nearest personification, down to the sordid private life and dreams of grandeur, is a minor Scottish poet called Alan Riddell, [59] a middle-aged bard with a hacking cough. I loved Enderby's attempt to make Formaggio Spaghetti Surprise. Like many of Burgess' books it ran out of steam, I felt, towards the end. Burgess is a sympathetic character, however ... It's ages since I read a contemporary book that really held my interest, in spite of, or because of the fact that I've been reviewing novels for the *Listener* from time to time, a dreadful occupation that I plan soon to abandon. I quite liked *Mr Sammler's Planet* by Bellow, perhaps because I didn't have to review it. Apart from that I read Conrad's *Youth* the other day, and loved it.

By a happy coincidence I found myself having supper with one of my all-round heroes, Robert Bresson, a few weeks ago during a visit here to pick up some award from the British Film Institute. He was very friendly and open and ready to talk about making films: very much to my surprise because of the severity of his film-making style. [60] Have you seen a film of his called *Pickpocket*? I saw it for the first time the other day and was bowled over by it ...

I should very much like to come to New York to see everyone again but I don't suppose I shall, this winter, at least. It will be some consolation if you get over to Europe in the course of your year off.

All the best,
Jim

[*added in pen*] P.S. I've been reading Lord David Cecil's biography of Melbourne, whom I find a very sympathetic figure, personally if not politically. One day Queen Victoria remarked to him that there were not many good preachers about. 'There are not very many good any-thing,' replied Melbourne wearily. To a jaded novel-reviewer this seemed all too true.

One publisher, Weidenfeld & Nicolson, showed tremendous interest in the 'India book' that month; at least, the deputy chairman, Tony Godwin, did, after reading the ms. on holiday. 'I was swept away by your novel,' Godwin wrote directly to Farrell on return, bypassing Deborah Rogers, and Farrell responded, equally directly. Against his agent's wishes, the die was cast.

To Deborah Rogers

Egerton Gardens
4 December 1972

Dear Deborah,

... Do you think you could fix up my contract with Weidenfeld and get me some money soon. I've just realized that I'm running low.

Love,
Jim

To Sonia Orwell

Egerton Gardens
[undated] 1972]

Dear Sonia,

John [61] just rang up to pass on your message about the wine auction. Actually I've already had a look at the catalogue (someone else's: even the catalogue costs a quid!) and decided that it's way out of my price range. Unless something extraordinary happens there won't be anything under £3 or £4 a bottle, I fear. Besides, I doubt whether my palate is sufficiently educated or alert to appreciate this Rothschild stuff, nice though it would be to try. I've been buying *cru bourgeois* wine for around a quid to £1.30 a bottle + some Château Kirwan at £2.20 (and now I'm broke).

Hope you had a good trip.

Love
Jim

To Deborah Rogers

Egerton Gardens
[undated] early December 1972

Dear D.

If the cheque reaches you before Wednesday, which seems unlikely, give me a ring and I'll come and collect it. If not, it would be best if you held on to it until after I get back here on December 27th.

Many thanks and merry Christmas!

Jim

P.S. I can manage without it till the new year.

To a friend

Egerton Gardens
10 December 1972

Dear [anon],

I'm writing to you, [62] not just to wish you happy Christmas (though I want to do that too) but to ask you to deal more gently with [your ex-wife] who arrived yesterday at my flat very angry and distressed. She wanted me to agree that, because of your behaviour, she would be right not to [allow the children] to spend Christmas with you.

Naturally I didn't agree with this at all.

However, I want you to know what I think about this.

    1) I feel that I am the friend of both of you and the last thing I want is to get involved in an argument between you. The only reason that it matters how you treat each other is because of the children.

    2) It is quite wrong of either of you to use them as part of your personal conflict. This is why she has [now] admitted that it would be wrong not to send them [to you].

    3) Because of the circumstances of your divorce, she has the main responsibility for bringing up the children. My personal and impartial opinion from having seen [them all together] is that she is doing this extremely well. You must help her for their sake and be more understanding of the difficulties she is faced with.

    4) She believes that you have been acting badly towards her. It does not matter to me whether this is true or not, since she believes that it is true. I'm sure that you have genuine grievances against her which you equally believe to be true.

    5) I don't give a damn who is right and who is wrong. What you must do is to stop this useless quarrelling which is likely in the end to damage the only thing of importance in the whole affair – namely, the freedom of the children to love both their mother and their father without having to choose sides.

    I don't want you to reply to this letter with a list of her mistakes. At the same time I have made it plain that I am not interested in hearing about what she thinks are your mistakes. I am writing because it seems to me that she is near the end of her tether and that if you both go on the way you are going she will try to stop you seeing the children or something equally disastrous (this is my opinion). For God's sake, it does not seem much to ask that you and she should behave like adults for another four or five years until they are grown up (after that, you can fight as much as you like as far as I am concerned).

    If you think it would make any difference I'll ... talk to you about this, but I'm sure you can tell from my letter what I think ...

    Love and a merry Christmas and New Year.

Jim

To Deborah Rogers

Egerton Gardens
26 February 1973

Dear Deb

It might at some stage be worth showing *Siege* to whoever published *The French Lieutenant's Woman* [63] in the US – one or two people have remarked on the resemblance in approach ...

Love
Jim

To Lavinia Trevor [64]

Egerton Gardens
30 March? [*sic*] 1973

Dear Lavinia,

... I got the explanation of my non-hearing from Stock in the form of a letter from André Bay. (You won't recall me telling you that I called on them on Christmas Eve and was told by a young man that they were sending my book to the printer next week. Now read on.) This letter explained that the young man I dealt with had died *début janvier* (i.e. immediately after my visit) of a heart-attack; his successor is, far from sending my book to the printer, preparing to scrap it as *trop long et trop lourd*.

I was glad to hear that Christopher S.S. [65] likes me. I think the world of him. (Is he a very tall thin fellow with brushed-flat hair?)

Love,
Jim

To Lavinia Trevor

[undated handwritten note tucked inside the proofs of *Krishnapur*]
Why the devil have you only got this far in reading this wonderful book?

Signed: God

To Norman Ilett [66]

Egerton Gardens
29 June 1973

Dear Norman,

I've suggested to Weidenfeld that they send you a publicity copy of my new opus, alleging that various vague journalistic benefits may accrue and declaring that you are a colossus bestriding the Northern literary scene. Needless to say, this is merely a stratagem to get you a free copy.

Hope you and family are well,

Jim Farrell

To Francis King [67]

[Postcard Cabourg, 1884]
10 September 1973

Greetings from Balbec! [68]
And kind regards from Jim Farrell

To John and Hilary Spurling

[Postcard 'Le Jardin et le Grand Hotel, Cabourg']
[undated] September 1973

Bonjour de Balbec.

I thought of staying here but chose the cheaper solution of camping in a field outside town and riding in on my bicycle. When I woke up this morning my tent was covered in dew and spiders' webs.

Love
Jim

P.S. Much more buckets and spades here than sun-tan oil and heaving breasts.

To Rose Knox Peebles

Egerton Gardens
15 September 1973

Dear Rose,

Many thanks for your card and note which I found on my return from bicycling in France. The lady who was secretary to, I presume, Brooke-Popham, who was the C-in-C, Far East at the time sounds highly interesting. [69] What happened to her subsequently? ... At the moment, however, I'm still hopelessly at sea with all the Singapore material and still have no idea which end to pick it up. I might ask you (or your friends) for some further details, if I may ... It was nice to see you the other week. How Nina has grown!

Love,
Jim

To Francis King

Egerton Gardens
18 September 1973

Dear Francis,

Many thanks for your nice review of *Siege* [70] which I have only just seen on my return from France.

At the same time let me wish you all the best for the appearance of *Flight* [71] which I assume, perhaps wrongly, to be imminent.

Sincerely
Jim Farrell

To Norman Ilett

Egerton Gardens
28 September 1973

Dear Norman,

... [*The Siege of Krishnapur*] seems to be doing a bit better than its predecessors, incidentally. I think perhaps critics are not so different from schoolboys in liking tales of adventure, though suitably clad in intellectual pyjamas ...

Sincerely
Jim Farrell

With the next book already preoccupying him, the private, self-contained nature of Farrell's life was about to change. Weidenfeld entered The Siege of Krishnapur *for the 1973 Booker Prize, in which the judges were Karl Miller (the chairman), Mary McCarthy and Edna O'Brien.* [72] *A month before the result was announced, as was the practice at the time, he was told in confidence that he was the winner.*

To Stephen and Yvonne Wall

Egerton Gardens
[undated] October 1973

Dear Stephen & Yvonne,
You don't feel like selling me one of your many properties, do you? I'm thinking of starting a NEW LIFE outside London (!!!), and I think I see where I can lay my hands on some cash. Never mind if you don't. This is a routine enquiry.

I hope you are both well and facing up with your habitual fortitude to the prospect of winter. [73] I'll probably drop in on you one of these days but I'll give you a ring first.

Love to you,
Jim

To Francis King

Egerton Gardens
5 October 1973

Dear Francis,
I want you to know how much I'm enjoying your book … The atmosphere is splendidly evoked (forgive the reviewer's jargon).

Yours,
Jim Farrell

To Deborah Rogers

Egerton Gardens
17 October 1973

Dear Deb,
… I should like to clarify that our own relationship is on a book-by-book basis – not because I ever foresee myself approaching another agent (than which I would rather my ears dropped off) but because at some future date I shall probably want to have at least one bash at agenting myself, the result of a craving not so much for money as for self-sufficiency. Given that I am the notorious Man of a Thousand Agents, I'm sure that this is no more than you would expect. However, if you think that this would be unethical of me, do protest …

Love,
Jim

On 28 November the Booker ceremony was held at the Café Royal, where Farrell had blithely lunched with Sonia Orwell and Jean Rhys, and where the previous winner, John Berger, had publicly excoriated Booker Mc-Connell for 'sweating blacks' in the West Indies, donating half his money to the Black Panthers.

'I know the moment capitalism shows its more acceptable face is not the time to punch it on the nose,' Farrell addressed the crowded room, 'but I have to confess that I am no more enamoured of capitalism than my predecessor. Yes,' he continued, without a pause, 'I thought that would silence you.' Digs at privilege, public schools and overpaid company executives culminated in the accusation that Booker callously misused their overseas workers.

'I regret,' he added politely, before sitting down, 'that like the sea monsters in Racine's Pheadre *... every year the Booker Brothers see their prize washed up a monster more horrid than the last.' Farrell had no intention of handing back any prize-money, however; he was going to use it to research commercial exploitation for his next novel, he promised his audience.* The Bookseller *called his speech 'unmannerly'.*

To Rose Knox Peebles

Egerton Gardens
30 November 1973

Dear Rose,

Many many thanks for your letter. It was very thoughtful of you to write. I just forget the exact nature of the *Enemies of Promise* [74] but I expect they add up to something I'd have done better not to miss!

Love
Jim

To Vincent and John Banville [75]

[undated] 1973

Christmas and New Year Greetings

Dear Vincent and John,

Thanks very much indeed for your cable re the Booker. It was very kind of you to think of it. I'd have written sooner but Diana has been away and I couldn't get your address. I see from a clipping they sent me that we appeared together in a rogue's gallery in one of the

Sunday papers! Merry Christmas to you both,

Yours

Jim Farrell

To Catherine Barton

Egerton Gardens

5 December 1973

Dear Catherine,

It was very kind of you to write to me about the Prize and I was very pleased that you enjoyed the book. As you may have guessed, the characters of the two young men – or perhaps it was just their healthy youthfulness – was suggested to me by the letters you let me see. [76] But I still feel that if anything of mine survives it will be *Troubles* – though, being more readable, no doubt the *S. of K.* was a better book to win the Prize with.

Believe me, I'm ready to be spoiled by success but, alas, am not too sure how to go about it! In the meantime, while waiting for some suitably sapping ideas, I expect I shall stagger on much as usual.

Once again, many thanks for writing and kind regards to Anthony. [77]

Love,

Jim

To Mr G.S. Bishop [78]

Egerton Gardens

21 January 1974

Dear Mr. Bishop,

I should like to thank you once more, both for making possible the Booker Prize (that goes without saying!) and for last Friday's delightful lunch, an occasion which both Sarah [79] and I thoroughly enjoyed – as I'm sure was evident by our talkativeness. It was very kind of you and your colleagues to put up with us so good-naturedly!

For next year's prize perhaps I should wish you someone mild and poetic, with no interest in politics or economics!

With sincere thanks and good wishes,

Jim Farrell

To his parents

Egerton Gardens
27 January 1974

Dear Mum and Dad,

... I forget whether I mentioned in my last letter that I had lunch at Penguins last week, at their factory/warehouse in Harmondsworth beside London Airport, and then lunch the following day with the chairman and directors of Booker Bros. (I've been veritably haunting commercial establishments recently.) Both occasions went off well, particularly the Booker Bros. one which I had regarded with some misgivings. It turned out to be a very merry occasion and I got on splendidly with the Chairman, a former civil servant called G.S. Bishop, getting him to tell me about the difficulties faced by a powerful commercial enterprise in an under-developed country (I explained my interest in the Singapore/Malayan rubber crop). Marilyn Edwards, from the National Book League, who organized the Booker Prize, was also there and was very pleased at how well it went.

The chairman of Penguins, Peter Calvocoressi, is also a very nice fellow; I bumped into him again coincidentally at a dinner party two or three days ago ...

Lots of love,
Jim

To his parents

Egerton Gardens
4 February 1974

Dear Mum and Dad,

... Did you read about the mass lobbying of the House of Commons by writers last Wednesday? [80] I was at the head of a posse of doddering scribes pouring into the central lobby and demanding to see our MPs to deliver our instructions for the forthcoming vote on the Private Members Bill on 15 Feb. It proved an entertaining evening, not because of any great success with MPs but because it was nice to chat with some colleagues and exchange literary gossip. Among others, I had a long chat with Bamber Gascoigne [8] who has also written a book about India, non-fiction I think. He said he searched for ages in his atlas for Krishnapur.

When we'd finished in the Commons we moved to a nearby hall for speeches by Lord Goodman and others. Afterwards Francis King,

Olivia Manning, Frank Tuohy and I went and had supper at a restaurant in Victoria. I'd been wanting to meet Frank Tuohy for ages as he has written a novel about Poland [82] I very much admire. Olivia Manning was very eulogistic about the *S of K.* I returned the compliment by saying how much pleasure her Rumanian trilogy had given us [83] ... No more news.

> Lots of love
> Jim

To his parents

> Egerton Gardens
> 22 February 1974

Dear Mum and Dad,

... Many thanks for the address of the World Expeditionary Association. I am writing to them to find out about it.

I went to supper at Olivia Manning's flat in Maida Vale last week with Margaret Drabble, an American writer called Alison Lurie and a couple of other people. They all heaped praise on me and flourished copies to sign etc., making me feel something of a fraud. However, someone told me that Auberon Waugh had made a disparaging assessment of the book somewhere. I shall be interested to see what he has to say as, though inclined to be erratic, he often hits the nail on the head. I feel in any case that this book has had more praise than it really deserves.

I forgot to mention that we have sold the Latin American rights (Spanish). Though the advance is only $500 I gather the firm that has taken it is a good one, Argentina-based, and there is some prospect of further royalties eventually ... I see both [political] parties are now promising PLR [Public Lending Rights] in their manifestoes so perhaps things are looking up at last, in that respect at least ...

> Lots of love,
> Jim

To his parents

Egerton Gardens
3 March 1974

Dear Mum and Dad,

... The election was fun. [84] I went to an election party at the house of Paul Barker, editor of *New Society*. Though I left fairly early (2am) they were still hard at it on tv when I went to bed – and indeed still at it when I switched on the tv again the following morning ...

I contacted the World Expeditionary Soc. and they sent me their brochure. The return fare to Singapore has jumped by £50 in the last few weeks, thanks to the price of fuel, I suppose. I'm trying to decide whether to visit New York (my book comes out there on Sept 11) ... on my way to Singapore or back from, or separately from – the latter might prove less expensive ...

Pussimodo [85] is sitting on the lawn outside enjoying the Spring sunshine. I haven't seen much of him during the winter.

When you come do you think you could bring the camera [86] with you. They've taken some publicity pictures recently that I don't particularly like and I would like to shoot a reel of black and white at myself to see if I can do better. Sorry to burden you thus.

Lots of love,
Jim

To Deborah Rogers

Egerton Gardens
14 March 1974

Dear Deb,

... Weidenfeld should be sending you some money for me. I would be glad if you send it on, having made your subtraction, as soon as you can. The idea being that I want it in this tax year ...

Love,
Jim

To Deborah Rogers

Egerton Gardens
26 March 1974

Dear Deb,

I'm afraid you and Brenda [87] must by now have cast me in the role of the 'base Indian (who) threw away a pearl, richer than all his tribe'. [88] However, I do feel that what we're asking (the 25 grand, plus 2 non-negotiable options, plus two and a half per cent) is by no means exorbitant and that we should stick to it.

I should also like to suggest that we give up haggling, whether with this lot or any subsequent group. As it is they've got us on the run completely. Every time we speak to them they whittle us down some more. Let us simply state the price and if they don't want it, tell them to fuck off and leave us in peace.

This is not to say that I'm not grateful for the hard work Brenda has put in finding these people – I am.

I'm off to Paris within the hour. There's no point in giving you my address as I'll be back by the middle of next week. If, in the meantime they feel like agreeing to our terms then by all means accept them on my behalf.

Love,
Jim

To Deborah Rogers

Chez Levet
8 rue Charles Nodier
Paris
27 March 1974

Dear Deb,

Apologies for the aggressive tone I've been adopting recently – brought on partly by weariness and partly by Mr Buck's gold-plated coffee cups, which made a terrible impression on me.

I do still think I was right to insist on drawing a line on our minimum requirements, however. But if you think differently I'm prepared to listen to advice.

I'll be back doing business (or more probably not doing business) on Thursday morning. If there's anything you need to discuss in the meantime my phone number is (Paris) 606.8174 and

I'm the only person to pick it up.

> Love
> Jim

To his parents

> Egerton Gardens
> 15 May 1975

Dear Mum and Dad,

... It now seems pretty certain that I'll sell a film option for a year, re-newable for another year on the *S of K* – we're at present having the contract [89] conned by a specialist with the impressive name of Irving Teitelbaum, a solicitor who knows enough about film contracts to see that we aren't taken to the cleaners. However, as I probably mentioned before, only about 1 in 20 films are made of optioned books and perhaps less these days – though the people we're dealing with have a better record of actually making films than most, it seems ...

Must stop and go out to supper.

> Lots of love,
> Jim

To his parents

> Egerton Gardens
> Friday 7 June 1974

Dear Mum and Dad,

... There have been some promising developments on the film op-tion front: in brief [an] option arrangement with David Lean, who is reported to have read the *Siege* throughout the night in a lather of excitement (this no doubt much exaggerated on the way to my ears).

However, the point is that if D Lean did make a film of it, it would almost certainly be a blockbuster of *Dr Zhivago*-like dimensions and would put me beyond financial want for the rest of my days. I expect to sign a preliminary option agreement with him next week. All this in strictest confidence of course and please don't mention it to anyone for the moment. Apart from anything else, the actual making of the film and buying of the rights are a very long way from being assured.

Last week I also had a meeting with Fred Zinnemann, [90] an old Hollywood director/producer who had put Lean on to my book and might be associated with a possible picture. I got on with him very well. He was a very simple, straightforward and friendly sort of man. He sounded me out about writing a script for him but didn't mind when I showed reluctance.

I'm beginning to realise that I'm going to have to give some thought to the problems of success (relative) and dangers of having one's private writing life steam-rollered by lucrative sidelines. However, all that may never happen ...

Lots of love
Jim

To Russell McCormmach

Egerton Gardens
8 August 1974

Dear Russ,

Many thanks for your letter mentioning favourable comments on *Krishnapur*: they came at the right moment to cheer me up [91] as I'm badly blocked with the Singapore book at the moment. I keep writing and re-writing the first few pages, which get duller and duller. It's a bit like one of those dice games where you have to throw a double six before you can even start. But the more I cudgel my brains the fewer ideas I get. Since I saw you I sold an option on the film rights* to the most gaudy film maker in the business [92] and if he actually makes the film I may simply retire and build a shack next to yours in Washington State or Oregon.

I haven't done anything about buying myself a cottage ... in the end I couldn't quite picture myself sitting in the country in solitary splendour for more than a few weeks a year and this, combined with the feeling that I didn't want to get involved in all the boring hassle it would entail at present, convinced me that it would be a good idea to postpone it. The fact is that having lived for so long in a small room I would hardly know what to do with anywhere bigger.

I'm coming to New York on 6 Sept just for a couple of weeks (my book comes out there on the 11th) and would very much like to see you ... The point is that until I see what the situation is in New York (they might want me for some publicity reason) I can't really make any plans.

I'll look out for *Zen and the Art of Motor Cycle Maintenance* [sic][93] which I don't think can have appeared here yet ... At the moment I'm reading for the second time Stuart Hampshire's *Modern Writers and Other Essays* which seems to me to be unusually good and perceptive. In particular there are very good essays on E.M. Forster and Proust and several other people. He seems to be someone who goes to great trouble to get his thoughts straight.

I hope to see you somewhere or other ...

In the meantime, all the best.

Jim

*of *Krishnapur*

To Russell McCormmach

Egerton Gardens

13 August 1974

Dear Russ,

... I was greatly amused and amazed over the last weekend by Nixon's departure from the White House. The fact that he could go on churning out the same mock-sincere speeches about his integrity and high-flown patriotic aims struck me as utterly bizarre after all the lies he had admitted a couple of days earlier. [94]

All the best,

Jim

To Norman Ilett

Egerton Gardens

23 September 1974

Dear Norman,

Many thanks for your letter which I found waiting on my return yesterday from a hasty two-week trip to America. It was kind of you to suggest my name to the lady from Christ's Hospital but I'm afraid I really can't help. The time/effort required would be more than I can manage at the moment, though one day I shall put together a standard speech to deliver on all occasions to anyone willing to remain within earshot. A similar (though even more tempting) request filtered through from Cheltenham Ladies College not long ago. I said I'd speak to them if they paid £200 to Oxfam, with the idea of doing my bit towards a re-distribution of the world's income.

As I expected, however, and much to my relief, they failed to avail themselves of this opportunity ...

I wonder where you are in Suffolk. Friends of mine, Anthony Samson and his wife, have a cottage in a village called Walberswick where I once spent a weekend. Angus Wilson and his boy-friend live nearby. They were supposed to come to supper but couldn't at the last minute. In general the place was packed with celebrities of one kind or another. [95] I felt a little uneasy there, perhaps because of the massive tides and the unfamiliar aspect of the countryside.

It was very nice to see Bill Budge [96] at the London OR [Old Rossallian] dinner. I liked him a lot when I was at Ross and remembered him telling us how he had lodged an axe in his brother's skull (or vice versa) when he was a lad. Ever since I have assumed that this sort of thing was an accepted part of growing up in Scotland. The dinner itself, densely packed with elderly generals and clerics, justified my worst fears. One of the latter, not very nimble-witted himself, assured me that his parishioners were as thick as two bricks.

Of my contemporaries I only recognized John Phillips, who hadn't changed in the least, and [one other] who had grown fat-faced, like one of Balzac's greedy financiers. I wouldn't have thought of this except that I heard it whispered that he was a merchant banker.

I'm planning a visit to Singapore and Indonesia to begin about mid-December and lasting, if all goes well, until the Spring.

> All the best to you,
> Jim

The Singapore Grip
Singapore and London
1975–76

To his parents

[Postcard of Raffles Hotel, Singapore]
2 January 1975

Dear Mum and Dad,

I started my stay in the East in style at the Raffles but have now moved to a more modest establishment. The flight via Moscow was long but not too taxing: [1] I ate some *borscht* and *shashlik* in a restaurant of rather funereal 19th century décor at Moscow airport. Lots of Russians have gold teeth, I noticed! Singapore is almost unrecognizable from the place I've been reading about. More like Los Angeles! [2]

Love
Jim

Diary
Singapore, 4 January

While lounging at Clifford Pier and eating an orange, a young male busybody approached to make sure that I was putting the skin in a litter basket. Evidently some of Lee's [3] citizens share his views. This business of tidyness ... is perhaps psychologically useful as a reassurance to potential investors of capital in S.

Watching the Europeans bowling in the nets beside the Cricket Club, and later watching a rugby match on the *padang*,[4] I was seized by a powerful sensation of 'privilege' surviving from earlier days. How pleasant to stand there in the mild tropical evening! Of the other races watching, mainly Indians, two-thirds were clustered behind the goal-mouth. The Europeans were in the process of being overcome by a team of heavy-set, dark-skinned men. How awkward,

291

gross, ill-formed and clumsy Europeans seem beside the Chinese. The city seems to be full of beautiful young people, slim and supple: it comes as a positive shock to come across the odd European plodding along (like me) ...

The Cathedral: inside a service was going on: the congregation kneeling beneath a couple of dozen silently revolving fans that hung from wall brackets along the aisle; the shuttered sides of the building were open, as were another row beneath the timbered wooden roof; flags of brown stone on the floor; solid wooden pews with, however, rush seats and backs as a concession to the tropics. Like being underwater.

At the GW[5] the Wing Choon Yuen restaurant: the most palatial of all with an entrance yawning like a cinema; fenced in by a solid brick and pillar wall and rows of palms in brown earthenware pots decked with dragons. The name stands out in 3 red ideographs. Corrugated iron roofs with flimsy fronts to attract passersby. In the arcade run by the Wah Lian Amusement Co., a money changer, ancient and wizened, sat in a circular bamboo cage handing out change. Near the entrance (and the GW billiards saloon) a growth of bamboo fenced off in which Matthew [6] vaulting the iron fence might take refuge. The smell of the nearby river is powerful.

At the car park I eat fish balls with a taoist couple: the young man an electronics engineer. We exchanged the usual well-meant but simple-minded civilities. A large rat, out of its mind with fright, scurries by as I leave ...

6 January

In the 'Honeyland Café' by Raffles Place a small European girl, not very attractive, blonde with short hair, is sobbing to herself at one of the tables. An aloof little Chinese waiter, who has always seemed to me before full of indifference and boredom, notices the girl and an expression of profound sympathy comes over his face: it is very touching. He keeps looking at her, wants to comfort her but feels unable to invade her privacy – while I was there, anyway ...

As dusk was falling I stood on Cavanagh Br. and watched tiny powerful tugs, the shape of paper darts dragging enormously rotund lighters loaded with rubber (?) up the river: these lighters have enormous high straight sterns with meat-cleaver shaped rudders of vast size. A demi-hoop of canvas covers their midriffs. The tugs have flimsy rattan sun screens erected over them.

As you walk along you get one powerfully evocative smell after another: this morning walking along Market Street some bales were being unloaded from a van and I was enveloped in a smell of all-spice. For a blind man Singapore wd be a strong experience.

To his parents

South Asia Hotel
12 Bencoolen St
Singapore
6 January 1975

Dear Mum and Dad,

... Well, I've been finding Singapore tremendously interesting, mainly, of course, because I'm constantly on the look-out for signs of the old Singapore, now becoming progressively fewer and further between ... I'm glad I didn't leave my trip any later as many familiar buildings have a boarded-up look about them and clearly aren't likely to survive for many more weeks. Of John Little's department store on Raffles Place all that remains is a sad façade with the word 'Little' written on it and only empty air behind. No sign at all of Whiteways, and Robinsons, the most famous store of all, burned down some while ago. I went to have a look at the Great World amusement park for which I had been considering a walk-on part. It's still there but no longer functions as it used to (British Tommies whooping it up with the various local races) and is also due for renewal by the look of things ...

I find that the heat does not bother me too much, partly because, this being the rainy season, the sky has been clouded over for much of the time, which suits me fine. Apart from an occasional heavy cloudburst there hasn't been much actual rain ... By about 5pm it gets substantially cooler, though still not the ideal temperature for rugby ...

I'm becoming quite skilled with chopsticks, by the way.

Lots of love
Jim

To Claude and Anna Simha

South Asia Hotel, Singapore
6 January 1975

Dear Claude and Anna,

I intended to phone you before leaving London but had so much to do that it was too late by then; as usual I had left everything until the last moment ... Claude, I think you would be well suited to this city, despite your distaste for anywhere non-European. The food is good and for very little, in the street in the open air; each cook specialises in a particular dish, whether Chinese, Malaysian or Indian, and they can be found throughout the city. Their cooking pots can be sniffed first, as in Morocco, you are probably thinking. As I did there, I am tasting them all, the Chinese especially, but can never work out the names. Secondly, the city is absolutely teeming with cute young Chinese girls in miniskirts, and not only Chinese either, I should say, but just as beautiful. And this is the only Eastern city I've been to where everyone is well dressed, well fed and looks happy. They seem much more cheerful than the English, but that goes without saying. All this, it has to be said, is thanks to the semi-dictatorship of Lee Kuan Yew, who won't allow hippies into the country unless they cut their hair first. In the post office a notice reads: YOUNG MEN WITH LONG HAIR WILL BE SERVED LAST. Also, all the old (and rather handsome) colonial buildings are being replaced with skyscrapers.

I came through Moscow and in the airport ... watched Russian television for an hour or so, which was sickeningly boring and propagandist. All that, I'm afraid, rather turned me off the revolution ...

Best wishes,
Jim

Diary

7 January

A cloudburst this afternoon as I was coming out of the Cold Storage: the water was soon swirling ankle deep out of the Cold Storage car park and loading bay. The girl who gives parking tickets, a brown Chinese, stood there quite happily with the water swirling over her sandals: boys with umbrellas appeared and tried to earn tips by escorting people to taxis. In a few minutes a great sheet of water was sliding down Orchard Road and the deep storm drains filled in no time. Once the rain had stopped everything swiftly returned to normal once more.

The chicken that lives behind the pipes appears to have 3 toes on its feet: its chubby back legs are bent, giving the impression of a Japanese wrestler. Today while I was out it polished off a column of ants climbing the wall ...

9 January
Lunch with a young British stockbroker at the Singapore Town Club: first, the club was disappointingly not the old one with the long bar and whatnot which figured in the Fall of S. as Shenton Thomas' [7] last residence. What I saw of it was more or less what one would expect: a bar and dining-room dark-panelled and new-looking. R., approached by a fellow member called M., whispering to me that he didn't like him. He was a blue-eyed wrinkled bloke, middle-aged, a rubber-broker who had been in S. since 1946. He gave me the address of someone in Penang, corrected R. when he described Raffles' palms as 'fan' palms: they are 'travellers' palms, because if you break off a frond you find water to drink. R. gave an upper-class bark of mirth, though discomfited, and said 'Of course, you have been in S. longer than me.'

I asked R. later why he didn't like M. He said: 'Because he can be very rude.' The older members, it seemed, looked down on the younger. 'He'll be drinking at the bar now till half-past two,' said R. contemptuously, 'when he gets back to his office. Let's face it, he's a dead-beat.' R. said rather fatuously several times that he found it impossible to know 'what the Chinese were thinking', though he claims to like them OK. He himself is languishing here and looking forward to going back to London. It's so hot, he says, and there's nothing to do ... 'A man needs a good wife out here,' he declared at one point. I thought he meant for moral support, but no, he meant for business contacts ...

[His] demeanour is jolly, energetic and commanding. He wd have made (in the Army's opinion) 'good officer material', and he would, too, in mine, provided he didn't rise too high, where real intelligence was needed. He was sure of his place in the world, not apparently troubled by doubts of any sort. He was good to invite me to lunch: curry with various side dishes including pineapple and *ikanbilis* (tiny dried fish), but I didn't like him very much ... Nice fellow in some ways [but] the fact remains that he has an exquisitely suburban mental atmosphere ...

Visit to Kee Yeap ... an architect aged perhaps in mid-fifties: very agreeable and a great talker. He said he had been in Penang during the Jap bombing: the population there had assumed that it must be British planes overhead, having listened to Br. propaganda. An uncle of Kee's was killed. His father told him that a bullet-ridden man collapsed in his shop and he could scarcely believe it. He also described being taken out by the *Kempetai* [8] in the early hours of the morning while a hooded informer picked out troublemakers for the Japs: they waited for hours in pyjamas. Those taken away were never seen again.

Glimpsed from the bus on the way home from Kallang along Crawford Street: a burnt-out shophouse. Through the open window I saw a wall on which there was still a baked brown photograph of a dignified Chinese in a charred frame ...

A heavily built short-haired British matron in the Cold Storage causes me to think that in many ways there is still a lot here that would have been familiar 35 years ago. Matthew might glimpse this heavily built Br. matron being conveyed gasping by half a dozen diminutive Chinese during an air-raid ...

The house(s) in Tanglin that I hope to get photographed [9] are built about 5 feet off the ground on a series of fat square pillars, walled by wood and louvred shutters. The eaves are very wide to cope with downpours and there is a covered way leading to an out-house shed. The bigger of the two houses has, presumably for ventilation, an additional small roof crowning the roof like a hat, presumably to allow the escape of hot air; the gap between the main roof and the topmost one is louvred and left open. Sides are draped with partly unfurled split bamboo chicks ...

On Orchard Road a Chinese wake is being held: a number of wreaths with Chinese inscriptions (one 'from Jimmy') set up on easels. Screens, brightly coloured and decked with ribbons and ideographs are set up on the pavement and girls sit at two tables. Last night a number of people had gathered and were sitting around and playing *mahjong*. At the furthest end of the screens an altar has been set up with a couple of thin candles burning on each side of a portrait of the deceased, [who] seems to be a short-haired youngish man. I was somewhat inhibited and felt unable to stare too closely …

At the Hilton hotel a show for a party of tourists – suddenly, in the middle of all the fake tropical *décor*, a 'bamboo dance' that shines with a real aesthetic/cultural beauty against the dross. The fact that it emerged so suddenly, recalling a genuine cultural tradition, made it all the more shattering. Two men, *accroupis*, rhythmically slamming bamboo poles together as a man and a girl, the latter beautifully graceful and slender-legged, dance in and out of them, their steps always miraculously just saving them from being caught between the two poles …

Mang Hee Fatt Choy say the red and gold Chinese New Year signs and everywhere hang red pumpkin lanterns with red tassels; red dragons cheerfully shaking hands and log bundles of red fire-crackers.

To Carol Drisko

> South Asia Hotel, Singapore
> 12 January 1975

Dear Carol,

I'm sending you a fresco [10] instead of a waving palm tree; I'm sure you saw enough of the latter during your Haitian venture.

I'm staying in a Chinese hotel here. When I mentioned this to a young British stockbroker I was having lunch with he was overcome with astonishment and amusement and kept telling everybody he met (this was in his 'club') as if it was the most amazing thing he had ever heard. *Plus ça change*.

I'm finding this city terrifically interesting and, even, enjoyable!

> Love,
> Jim

To John and Hilary Spurling

> [Postcard of Council of War, Lord Raglan,
> Omar Pasha and General Pélissier, 1855]
> 13 January 1975

Dear John and Hilary,

… Now I understand why Lord Jim preferred knocking about in the Straits to going home to Surbiton …

> Love,
> Jim

To Brigid Allen [11]

South Asia Hotel, Singapore
25 January 1975 [12]

Dear Brigid,

Welcome to the East, assuming that you arrived on time for your flight and your dodgy Arab/Indian tickets were recognised by Aeroflot. Did you use the loo on your aircraft? If so, did it flush an alarming dark green? Perhaps this is the last word in Soviet luxury.

Things have gone well here, mainly thanks to the fact that one of the addresses/introductions I had – to a bloke in the NZ High Commission [13] – proved to be that of an admirer of m'work (that's what he says, anyway) and he has gone to great pains to produce 'interesting' Chinese and other veterans. I also got invited to the NZ High Commission to shake the hand of Sir Edmund Hillary, a man who looks like a massive, wrinkled sheep. Many New Zealanders look like sheep, I've decided: their mouths are very near their chins.

A lot of the old Singapore has been knocked down and replaced by skyscrapers but there is just about enough still left to give one an idea, at least, of what it looked like. People tend to be very vague, though, about life here in the old days, partly, I suppose because I'm not sufficiently adept at making them talk about it, partly because they don't really remember the trivial things that would interest me. I'm off to Penang tomorrow and after that may venture up to Bangkok, though everyone says it's awful, and even pay a brief visit to Saigon, provided it does not come to pieces between now and then. My itinerary and plans are too vague to establish a meeting in mid-air, I'm afraid, but if, on your flight home, there is someone continually flushing the lavatory and staring in wonder at the dark green cascade, it will probably be me ...

Love to you
Jim

Jim left Singapore on 27 January and set off up the Malayan peninsula by train, observing the countryside through the window. Kuala Lumpur was to be his first stop, followed by Penang.

Diary

27 January

Beside the river a man butchers two frail white chickens, holding their wings and then bending their throats back before cutting them with a knife and emptying out a little pool of blood; the bird feebly struggling while this is going on. His wife, crouching on the steps behind him, hands him one bird after the other. Their son, a little boy, gives a cry of alarm as the first hen is butchered, and runs away a few paces – but curiosity gets the better of him and he runs back to watch again ...

Kuala Lumpur

Having imagined heavy-set Eur. women displaying patches of red sunburn on their white skins, I saw today in the KL museum just such a sight. A woman with a pair of white diamonds in a halter across her painful-looking red shoulder-blades.

The impression given by the first sight of the steps at the Batu Caves with the hordes of worshippers pouring ceaselessly up and down was reminiscent of some grandiose shot from early Hollywood, partly because it looked so unreal; the mountain looks too steep and romantically brooding, and the ceaseless moving up and down of the crowds obscured the steps completely; a mist, or perhaps smoke from the many sacramental fires, hung over everything to complete the picture of painted scenery. Then we saw 3 *kevadi*-bearers whirling and stamping their way towards the foot of the steps, their faces in the inevitable trance, followed by a band of young men, evidently friends or helpers. We followed them up the steps, not without difficulty because of the crush, and later we saw the helpers removing the long spikes one by one and the man himself removed the silver skewer from his upper lip.

The statue of Lord Subramaniam [14] himself, placed in a small white-tiled shrine on the left wall of the vast cave, is rather small but dignified, in shape somewhat like a pear, but hard to see because of the flowers and jewels that draped him. His eyes seemed to be bulging: the impression of his pop-eyed white face being shown the gifts of coconuts, beads and even a bottle of milk, most of it in plastic carrier-bags which hawkers were selling on the way in, together with sugar cubes of incense, added a bizarre touch to a bizarre experience ... The crowds, already dense, were still growing as we left after dark ...

The Majestic [15] appears much too big for its meagre supply of guests ... [but] beneath a dozen silently revolving fans [the] food is good and cheap: a vast breakfast is available for $3 and on every table the linen napkins are folded into the shape of bishops' hats.

The jungle as a solid wall of green on which, printed like the backbone of a fish on an ammonite, one can distinguish the frond of a palm, and then gradually deciphering them, a thousand more plants of every description ...

Penang 28 January

... In the evening, after wandering round Penang looking for a suitable place to eat, an Indian restaurant presents itself. I order a *kurma* etc. which turn out to bear no resemblance to the N. Indian variety and have little to recommend them.

In the street a carpet-bagger and his assistant were haranguing the crowd in Chinese ... He had got a small boy out of the crowd to help with the act, which was the swallowing of a large steel ball-bearing ... Finally with a great to-do he got the boy to place the ball-bearing in his mouth. The boy opened his own mouth in a sympathetic swallowing gesture as the carpet-bagger was miming distress and pretending to gag on it. This went on for some time: he kept grimacing and pointing at the ball-bearing: then finally swallowed it, drank off a glass of water, lit a cigarette and prowled round the circle a few times. After more beating of drums he hawked it up again and spat it out. What he was selling I have no idea ...

I moved on to watch a travelling theatre which had set up shop nearby. Actors and actresses clad in elaborate costumes were loudly declaiming a play from a makeshift wooden stage. There were frequent changes of scene. A scarlet curtain was brought down and canvas back-cloths unrolled with ropes and pulleys: the wings looked very flimsy ... garishly painted with dragons. A scene-shifter wearing trousers and a singlet and smoking a cigarette shambled on and off ...

One could see the actors and actresses making-up back-stage because the sides and back of the theatre were only summarily covered by cloth hangings which blew about in the breeze. Elaborately rouged and pink powdered faces glared at small mirrors set up on tables, while pincers prepared a further assault on already elaborately-plucked eyebrows. [16] Several little girls sat at the corners of the stage: another, balanced precariously on a plank, gripped the edge of the wings and craned forward to peer round at what was happening on stage ...

In the Penang museum there is a photograph, unlabelled, of some function circa 1900 to judge by the dress. It shows a number of Europeans and one or two European ladies sitting in rickshaws. The padre is there, looking young and vigorous, a watch-chain visible in his black waistcoat and a white sun helmet on his head. Nearby one of the Europeans has put his hand on the straw-hat of the rickshaw coolie beside him and forced his head down so that only his hat will be visible in the photograph. [17]

There is another interesting photograph of the ladies and gentlemen of the Penang Swimming Club, circa 1910. It is very odd, somehow, to see the ladies in long dresses and wearing broad Edwardian hats loaded with silk and satin, and the men, moustached, wearing boaters ...

To his parents

Metropole Hotel
Penang
29 January 1975

Dear Mum and Dad,
... I got here yesterday evening after a pleasant day in the train from K.L. spent goggling at the jungle and *kampongs* we passed through. The train carriages still have FMS Railway and a symbol of a tiger engraved on the glass of their doors but by now are beginning to show their age ... [18]

I didn't greatly care for K.L. ... I had two strokes of luck there, though! I found a delightful old colonial hotel opposite the station called the Majestic, and my arrival coincided with Thaipusam, a Tamil festival which I had read about and wanted to see at the nearby Batu Caves ... The Majestic had some of the attributes of its fictional counterpart. Only a handful of guests seemed to be camping there in its vast collection of rooms and elderly Chinese servants doddered about forgetting what you had ordered and coming back to ask you what it was ...

Lots of love,
Jim

301

Diary

3 February

At the E and O [Eastern and Oriental] Hotel yesterday for the curry lunch. It was very good: served with *sambals*: powdered coconut, finely chopped pineapple, tiny red nail-clippings of red chili, and chopped cucumber, plus chutney. The *ikambilis* were missing. It was followed by *gula melaka* which looks like a whitish transparent frog-spawn in a fairly solid lump, the shape of a small inverted bowl: over this is poured coconut milk and a burned sugar syrup as for *crème caramel*.

By the time Farrell reached Bangkok on 4 February, the bulk of his factual research was completed. Thailand was outside the scope of his book, freeing him temporarily of the need to jot down detail, and allowing him to resume his scrutiny of human foibles. But the Vietnam War was nearing its climax, and the urge to experience an atmosphere similar to Singapore just before the fall tempted him to book a flight to Saigon.

Bangkok 4–7 February

The first impression is of the traffic and air pollution which are both atrocious; the second is of the life on the river: how complex, beautiful and self-contained it appears – and how different from the life on the noisy dust-and-smoke filled streets. This no doubt superficial impression of a sordid and degenerate city desperately trying to survive on not enough tourists was in strong contrast to the brief glimpse we had of the countryside on our trip upriver to Sena and then across country by bus to Ayudhaya ...

Daniel, [19] a French physicist returning from a conference in Kyoto, L. and I, having met by chance on the ferry, spent the rest of the day together. We ate an excellent soup, Chinese style, for 2 baht each in a stall in Sena, containing small bits of meat, noodles and spring onions in an excellent broth. Then came a somewhat hair-raising bus-ride across country in the open back of a minibus, racing all other vehicles met on the road in a completely reckless fashion in order to make them eat our dust, which was thrown up in such quantities that occasionally the vehicle in front would almost disappear. Daniel, who was pale, single-minded and slightly eccentric, though v. agreeable, showed signs of alarm. '*Incroyable mais vrai*', he kept repeating with reference to the driver's competitive spirit ...

L. has gradually revealed a tendency to use her appeal for men to help her along life's road. She spent such a long time making-up in the ladies room (her flight had been called twice) that we parted on not so cordial terms. I was anxious lest she miss the flight, which she found ridiculous and, no doubt, annoying. This extra regard for her appearance was so that she should make the strongest possible impression on any men she met on the plane ... She made a sort of declaration about having decided she wanted a permanent man and had come to the conclusion that I might suit her specifications. I was discouraging and the matter was dropped.

To his parents

[Postcard from Bangkok]
7 February 1975

Dear Mum and Dad,
... Asian taxi-drivers consider themselves dishonoured if they shift their feet from the accelerator to the brake! But the river is magnificent and full of astonishing sights ...

Love
Jim

Diary
9 February

Just before leaving Bangkok (an hour or two) I was standing by a tree in Wat Po, having just taken a look at the Reclining Buddha: he's so closely housed that it's hard to get a view of more than the soles of his feet, when two, three butterflies – kite-shaped with tails, and with pink and yellow on their wings [20] – came fluttering all around me as if they had taken a liking to the colour of my shirt and wanted to settle on me. They fluttered very beautifully, with a much slower beat of the wings than usual: a magical experience. I spent several minutes gazing at them with delight. The Thai students who were reclining in the shade of the tree no doubt thought I was mad. Just as I was leaving a third butterfly with beautifully embroidered black and white wings somewhat in the manner of a batik shirt came to lodge on the tree, too.

My first stroll in Saigon a bird dive-bombed me, scoring a hit on the front of my shirt: on the Eve of the Chinese/Vietnamese New Year, what better omen?

There was considerable chaos at Tan Son Nhut airport as crowds were returning for Tet loaded with all sorts of goods, particularly fruit and flowers. I helped an ancient Chinese or Vietnamese lady to carry a garish display of orchids. In the plane I sat next to a man I assume was the British Ambassador travelling with his secretary: he seemed to know a great deal about the VN [Vietnam] situation. From Lacy's [21] description of the Ambassador it could very well have been him. He didn't volunteer any information about himself and would probably have dreaded being unmasked by a fellow-country-man he couldn't escape from, so I refrained from interrogating him. In any case I would have preferred to sit next to his secretary.

'Novelist not journalist?' said the man at the immigration desk. I reassured him. The airport was ill-lit, whether as an economy meas-ure or as a precaution against the Viet Cong was not clear. Vast crowds clustered round the entrance waiting to greet their relatives. Unable to find anywhere to change I picked up my bags and plunged into the darkness. The first man I asked for a taxi led me to his car and, as I expected, seemed content with the prospect of being paid in dollars. His wife and two tiny boys were sitting in the front seat. On the way into Saigon she made small talk in French, saying among other things (pointing to one of the kids) *'son papa était Français'*. Her polite conversation in French was mingled with her husband's attempts in English to get me to change money advantageously at his sister's house, to hire his car on the following day, and to stay at the hotel he touted for. I declined in vague terms, not knowing quite what to expect.

But I got a room at the Continental Palace [22] without difficulty; a magnificent, high-ceilinged room with shutters looking out on to the square, a tiled floor, a vast double bed, air conditioning that labours to cool the vast area, a fine spacious writing desk, ceiling fan etcetera. In the tiled corridor I noticed a smell that reminded me of French *lycées*, perhaps it's some form of floor polish. One can have a decent French breakfast of *croissants* and coffee in an interior court-yard shaded by trees.

As I sat eating supper at one of a long row of tables open to the street [23] I was offered various commodities, including their persons, by a series of girls who always seem to be hanging about (except this morning and last night, when they had evidently gone to eat at home for Chinese New Year). Being raised 3 or so feet off the street level one feels as if one is watching a show from a balcony ...

I've seen nothing like the misery I saw in India – there are not many visible signs of the war if you leave aside the fact that most public buildings are barricaded off behind barbed wire and guarded by armed troops. Seeing a small boy, though, minus an arm, gives one a shock. I saw him on the terrace of the CP yesterday and again today, indulging in one-armed *kung fu* with another boy, the stump of his arm working in his short sleeve. Another thing, there are a number of young male beggars wearing battle-dress, some of them badly mutilated.

Returning from my walk into Pholon I sat down at a café table on the street and ordered a coca-cola. Somewhat to my alarm an elaborately dressed lady, not too young or too attractive, brought me a hot face-cloth and then sat down beside me. Fortunately there was no attempt at conversation as we did not share a language. After this I went to a Corsican restaurant on Nguyen Hué where I had a fairly good meal of *salade niçoise* and *boeuf à la corse* ...

I just gave a couple of hundred piastres (i.e. about 30 cents: big deal) to an elderly couple walking along a street off the Rue Catinat, where undoubtedly I wouldn't have given anything to them singly. The fact that they were together in their misfortune struck some sensitive or romantic chord, obviously ...

Lunch with Lacy and TA[24] at the American Embassy, the interior of which is more like a country club now, with a vast swimming pool. I shook hands with the deputy ambassador, a man in a startlingly bright suit, like a bookie ...

'*Ta on duc me*', '*Ta on thank Anton*', '*Profondes reconnaissances*' or simply '*merci*': chapels in the Basilica de N.D. [25] are plastered with small marble rectangles to this effect ... I suddenly came on a coffin draped in dusty black with an embroidered white cross set up before the altar ...

Saigon reminds me of Casa [26] ten years ago. Last night we went to a restaurant run by a Frenchman, a former mercenary: a slightly down-at-heel character. We entered by an unmarked door through the kitchen. This reminded me of going to eat with Elie [27] *chez Mme X* in Ait Ouvrir ...

13–14 February
A dinner party kindly organised by Lacy at the home of Peter Range,

the *Time* bureau chief here; he has an office on the top floor of the Continental Palace ... The food was good, served by an elderly VN [Vietnamese] with a sensitive face who seeemed strangely familiar. I saw him again this morning. He's one of the waiters at the hotel ...

To his parents

> Dai-Luc Lu-Quan
> Continental Palace
> 132 Rue Tu Do
> Saigon
> 14 February 1975

Dear Mum and Dad,

Hearing that a friend of mine (and Malcolm Dean's) was at the American Embassy here when I thought he had left, I decided to spend a few days here before returning to Malaysia, and I'm very glad I did. I've had a most interesting time, thanks largely to this friend, Lacy Wright. He speaks fluent Vietnamese and has Vietnamese friends, which meant that in a very short time I was able to get behind the scenes a bit more than one usually does.

Saigon is much more peaceful and agreeable (a pleasant French colonial town with lots of good French restaurants) than one would have supposed; apart from the troops guarding the various public buildings over Tet there are few signs of the war and the fix the country is undoubtedly in. Nobody here feels that the fall of Saigon is very imminent. President Thieu [28] has been crying 'Wolf!' a bit, I think, to get Congress to produce the cash. More about this in due course. I must pack my bags as I'm taking the plane out this afternoon.

I think on the whole I won't visit Java on this trip, but will probably head back to Europe in a couple of weeks. I find one gets dazed if one visits too many countries at a time. I'll keep you posted, however. Excuse the red ink. My other pen has given out, thanks to the copious notes I've been taking ...

> Lots of love,
> Jim

Diary
14 February
Back to Singapore by Air Vietnam; as one might expect, a rather down at heels airline. The taxi was not allowed to enter the airport gate so I sat on the back of a scooter or small m/bike clutching my bags while we rode into Tansennhut. But the supervision seemed lax. The flight was without incident and I went back to the South Asia Hotel ...

To Brigid Allen in India

South Asia Hotel, Singapore
15 February 1975

Dear Brigid,
... Wonderful though it is, and very broadening for the mind, I'm beginning to feel somewhat 'bushed' with travel ... We shall thus be reappearing in Blighty at roughly the same time, but evidently not on the same flight ...

One needs a special mental radar to find one's way through the thick fog of Aeroflot's arrangements. But my movements are: leave S'pore on Su 558 on 27 Feb at 19.40 arr. Moscow at 06.10 on the 28 Feb ... I assume they won't let you change to this flight. I could most likely subsidise your Intourist expenses, but I expect they demand payment in advance etc. I'm going to Malaya again for a week tomorrow so I won't know for sure what I'm doing until I get back here and pay another visit to the Aeroflot office ... [29]

Love,
Jim

Diary
20 February
Last Sunday a tiring rail journey to K.L. Lots of traffic because of people returning from the Chinese New Year holidays: evidently people take a week off – some do, anyway. Next morning I rent a Volkswagen and drive through K.L. to the Majestic, where we [*an assignation with L.*] had been sharing an extraordinary suite overlooking the railway station, complete with sitting-room, tv and fridge (empty of everything, even ice). We load up and drive back through

K.L. in the direction of Port Dickson, stopping for some elaborate *satay* in Kajang, supposedly the home of the good stuff. Indeed it proves to be better than that available in Singapore: the peanut sauce is not so sweet and has a more agreeable flavour.

Port Dickson is a little seaside town that straggles on along the coast from the actual port: the tide goes in and out over vast muddy sands. While it was out we paddled about until we were struck by horror at the teeming little crabs that cluster in herds at the edges of the tidal pools and gallop away like tiny pink cattle at your approach – in such numbers that its almost impossible not to tread on them. The best thing about Port Dickson is the Fairwinds Hotel where we are staying. Yet another of the crumbling, once impressive buildings that seem to dot this part of the world. Half a dozen magnificent trees stand overlooking the Straits of Malacca ... For breakfast I have sheep's kidney and bacon: delicious. The place seems to be doing little business. Just us and a couple of girls, Americans. Alas, Perkins [30] is not there when I try to telephone him. A woman gabbles at the other end. I have to summon the hotel man to interpret. He has gone to Kuantan. Where is that? On the east coast. So we set off for Malacca. It does not seem to justify its reputation as a charming little town. The main streets are noisy and full of traffic. The seafront and Portuguese settlement dull. Perhaps we have missed its special charm, whatever it it ...

To his parents

South Asia Hotel, Singapore
23 February 1975

Dear Mum and Dad,

Many thanks for your letters which I picked up yesterday on my return from Malaysia ... It's hard to imagine your icy winds [31] when basking in the tropics. On my return visit to K.L. I hired a car as this seemed the only satisfactory way of getting to Port Dickson where I hoped to visit an old retired planter whose name I had been given. Unfortunately, he was away when I got there: the only stroke of ill-luck in my plans so far. Well, since I had hired the car for a week I decided to take a more extensive look at Malaysia [and] went ... across the country to Kuantan on the east coast, then up another 40 miles to a very beautiful deserted beach called Kekaman ... There are huge breakers on many of the beaches which makes a change from the slack and sluggish waters of the Straits. I had two or three invigorating swims there. Anyway, Singapore seemed almost like home when I got here on Friday night.

I forget now how much I told you about my week in Vietnam. Did I mention that [I was] introduced to Général Trân van Dôn, who led the coup which deposed Diem [32] a few years back? He was wearing bathing trunks (when we met; not when he led the coup). This was at the old French club in Saigon, known as *le Cercle Sportif.* He's now *Vice Premier Ministre,* a very jovial fellow given to chasing women.

We also gazed at Big Minh [33] giving a party on his patio, through binoculars, from the advantageously placed patio of the *Time* correspondent, [34] who gave a dinner party for me the night before I left – thanks to Lacy, of course. There was also, believe it or not, the Papal Nuncio, a cheerful Portuguese we addressed as Monseigneur – very hot in his ecclesiastical shirt and jacket, until we persuaded him to strip it off and dine in shirt sleeves like the rest of us. He said he had trouble reassuring his Mum in Portugal that he was in no danger in Saigon. Finally there was the Reuter's correspondent and his French wife [35] with whom I had a sensible discussion about novels and to whom I recommended Olivia Manning's *Balkan Trilogy* – and a couple of very sophisticated Vietnamese girls.

I'm planning to leave this coming Thursday, 27th Feb. and will get as far as Moscow. The onward flight to London is full so I'll have to spend about 36 hours there before the next flight to London ... I'll let you know how it works out once I'm back at my typewriter ...

Lots of love
Jim

Diary
24 February

Yesterday evening I took a Port of Singapore Authority pleasure cruiser around St Johns and Kushy Islands [and] on the way back the trip suddenly became interesting. First of all great flaming sparks and pieces of fiery matter began to rain down by the rail where I was standing. Then the boat lost way – we were a few hundred yards from Clifford Pier, and the lights and loud-speaker failed (a blessing as regards the latter which had started on a tape for the second or third time). Then, after a few moments, the emergency siren began to blast repeatedly. There was something of a panic at this and a dash to put on life belts, which I didn't join, either through an elaborate anti-herd snobbism or from a just appreciation of the lack of danger – most likely a mixture of both.

After a few minutes a tug approached and lashed itself to one side and then a fire-boat to the other. There was considerable coming and going in the semi-darkness and a number of red-helmeted firemen clambered aboard with extinguishers. Then things became more tedious again as we were half towed, half nudged back to the pier. But to see the tugs steaming up with their searchlights blazing out of the tropical twilight was very impressive. The PSA man in charge of the boat, who had earlier pointed out the US aircraft carrier *Enterprise* in the outer roads (their sailors were in town shouting, swearing, drinking and vomiting in Bugis Street last night), later stopped by me – he evidently has a high regard for Westerners – to explain that it had not been a proper fire. The oil-impregnated carbon coating the funnel had caught fire; it must have crept back to the engine room somehow to stop the engines.

A well-dressed well-built young Indian also gave me his opinion. 'They panic,' he said, indicating the rest of the passengers. 'But there is no danger. They are not used to it,' he added, coming on like an old salt. I'd earlier noticed him wearing a life-belt himself, however. The result of all this was that I was an hour and a half late getting back to where L. was waiting at the Lovers' Bar. It caused me to reflect a bit, though, that in a similar situation, because of my anti-herd elitism, I might be at greater risk than more modest and realistic people.

Glimpsed at twilight on the Singapore River, an old Chinese standing to scull a tiny, frail *prau* with a lantern standing up on a stick behind him. A vast barge surges by, causing him to rock wildly in its wash.

Saigon fell to the Communists shortly after Jim's return, and his attention to the televised scenes of the American exodus would illuminate the closing scenes of The Singapore Grip. *Meanwhile, among the letters stacked up at Egerton Gardens was one from an American film producer, Robert Parrish.*

To Robert Parrish [36]

Egerton Gardens
3 March 1975

Dear Mr Parrish,
Many thanks for your kind letter about my book *The Siege of*

Krishnapur. Sorry to have taken so long to reply but I only just got back to find [it] after a couple of months travelling in the Far East, researching another book.

As regards the rights, an option was bought by David Lean a few months ago. [37] Since then nothing has been heard of him and nobody seems to know whether he means to do anything with them.

It is odd that you mention your film of *The Purple Plain.* I saw it years ago but it has stuck in my mind with great clarity which, for me, not many films do. Naturally, I'm delighted to have heard from its creator!

I see from the second address you give that we are neighbours! [38]

Sincerely,
Jim Farrell

To his parents

Egerton Gardens
6 March 1975

Dear Mum and Dad,

A brief note to let you know that I've got back here in good order. The couple of days I spent in Moscow gave me an interesting glimpse of Russian life (queues in all the shops remind one a bit of war-time) but I wasn't tempted to stay any longer ... I bought some Cuban cigars for 5 roubles on the way back ...

I enclose an ad from *The Bookseller* that Deborah had sent along. It looks promising. There was also an invitation to a party at Penguin to celebrate their 40th anniversary but ... I felt too blotted out to attend. I'm making no haste to reintegrate myself in the literary world and feel I must lead a more hermit-like existence. I also found a letter from the Society of Authors asking me to join the selection committee for their £500 travelling scholarship ... I think I'd prefer to be awarded it rather than dish it out. Also a letter from an old Hollywood film director ... I had supper with him and his wife and he told me that David Lean was a rather secretive and odd fellow. He wasn't at all surprised to hear that nothing had been heard of him since ...

Lots of love,
Jim

To his parents

Egerton Gardens
25 March 1975

Dear Mum and Dad,

Not much news since I got back. I've been hard at work and not going out much, aided by some pretty dreadful weather, cold and drizzly with odd flurries of snow ... Anyway, I'm looking forward to some good weather and have some seeds trying to germinate for when it arrives ...

I've been reading a house history of the Firestone Rubber Company, written by some unfortunate in a bland spirit of adulation but providing, nevertheless, an interesting new dimension from the manufacturing side. I'd already been interested in some govt. papers ... about a serious strike in the Firestone factory in Singapore at the beginning of the war: now I'm reading about Harvey S. Firestone's attempts to get alternative sources of supply ... So far I haven't discovered whether or not he was successful as I've just reached the Depression and they don't need much rubber anyway ...

Have a good Easter.

Lots of love
Jim

To his parents

Egerton Gardens
Good Friday 1975

Dear Mum and Dad,

This is just a P.S. to my letter the other day ... I'd love some Escudo and/or Balkan Sobranie (half and half if they have both): my pipe-smoking increases in tempo with writing, I find. Saigon and Vietnam generally seem to be in a mess now. I think I may have had a look at it in the very last relatively peaceful days ...

Lots of love,
Jim

To Deborah Rogers

Egerton Gardens
15 April 1975

Dear Deb,

... D'you remember buying me a couple of air tickets? Well, I plan to mention these under income when I finally get around to making out my tax. It seems not worth being devious for such a small sum, not to mention the risk of further aggravation. I was talking to Francis King the other day who has been persecuted for some trifling sum he forgot to mention ... If anybody owes me any money by all means get them to pay up. There may be a couple of helpings from foreign rights still to come.

Very sorry to have broken a glass at your house the other night. What an idiot I am!

Love
Jim

To his parents

Egerton Gardens
29 April 1975

Dear Mum and Dad,

... You may have seen something in the papers about another authors' demo we had – this time in Belgrave Square. Quite apart from 'the cause' [a Public Lending Rights Bill] there are usually some amusing incidents with so many writers, a good number of whom are wholly or partially dotty, present. Lord Longford, with the wind making his hair stand on end, looked particularly crazed. As it was cold we shambled round Belgrave Square a couple of times, marshalled by Miss Kay Dick, a very commanding sixty-year old spinster wearing a monocle and a cricket sweater. Francis King had brought his dog along wearing a placard which said: 'Don't let my master starve'. To give the animal some exercise he set off on his own round the square with the dog's lead in one hand and a banner in the other. Presently he reappeared saying he had been besieged by old ladies trying to press money on him, under the impression that he was something to do with cigarette-smoking experiments on beagles! I shambled round the square with Kingsley Amis who had a banner which he seemed to have made out of an old pillow-case. He had written some quite illegible slogan on it with what looked like shoe polish and held it up on two bamboo sticks. About noon I nipped off for lunch with John Guest of Longman's [39] in a nearby restaurant.

That's just about all the excitement there has been, however, as I've been keeping my head down. The weather has greatly improved, though, and my tomato plants are growing at great speed. I've planted three of them out ...

Lots of love,
Jim

To his parents

Egerton Gardens
27 May 1975

Dear Mum and Dad,

Sorry I haven't replied sooner but things have been very chaotic as I finally got round to having my place painted, which meant taking all the books off the walls and all the junk out of the kitchen and bathroom. I couldn't do any serious work while this was going on [so] while my flat was upside down I took a long weekend in the Lake District with Malcolm Dean and a couple of ladies. We stayed in a pub in Eskdale ... and one day climbed Scafell and a couple of ancillary peaks: a good twelve hours of climbing and hiking (the pub gave us sandwiches and a thermos of soup and we took a bottle of brandy for an occasional swig). I finished in good trim but ... felt stiff the next day, however.

I'm also contemplating a week in Harlech in June as Mrs Richard Hughes wrote to me again offering me the use of their cottage ... After that, though, I really must close down my social life entirely until I get my book written. The increase in celebrity attendant on the Booker Prize has meant a corresponding increase in distracting visits and invitations ...

I gather Auntie May has already written to you to say she saw me on tv – the book programme with Robert Robinson. [40] I went to watch [it] on Richard's colour set, which was perhaps a mistake as it looked like a conversation between two tomatoes. I got him to switch it to black and white for a moment and that didn't look so bad ... Anyway, the interview seemed to go off without me saying anything I felt, on second viewing, was too ridiculous. I hadn't realized how round-shouldered I'd become, though. I looked like the Hunchback of Hyde Park ...

I went to supper with [Olivia Manning] and Maggie Drabble yesterday ... I got Malcolm Dean (who is the *Guardian*'s home affairs leader-writer and has contacts in the Home Office) to take Maggie to visit a prison, as she wanted to see inside one for her latest novel. She said it was very comfortable-looking.

Lots of love
Jim

To his parents

Harlech
Friday 12 June 1975

Dear Mum and Dad,
Richard Hughes' cottage is lovely: right on the water opposite Port Meirion [*sic*] and a couple of hundred yards from his house. We walked across the estuary at low tide yesterday and visited Port Meirion and will probably go for a row today in the Hughes' boat. Both Mr and Mrs are very nice: he's a dignified looking old chap with a white beard. I've been helping him weed his asparagus bed ...

Lots of love,
Jim

To Richard and Frances Hughes [41]

Egerton Gardens
16 June 1975

Dear Mr and Mrs Hughes,
Judith [42] and I would like you to know how much we enjoyed ourselves over the past week, and what a great pleasure it was to meet you both. And the trout, we forgot to say, were delicious the other evening!

After some inner debate as to whether to bother you with it I've decided to send you, as an object of homage to the 'Old Master', one of my books which I feel has been beneficially influenced by his work (an influence freely acknowledged in public, I hasten to add). The French film-director, Robert Bresson, talking about one of his disciples who insisted on calling him *Vieux Maître*, once told me that he didn't mind being called *Maître* but felt that *Vieux* was going too far. So perhaps I should delete the adjective.

Please don't trouble to acknowledge the book but do give me a ring when in London with some time to spare so that I can invite you to some convenient restaurant.

Once again, many thanks.

Yours,
Jim

P.S. I'll keep a look-out for any re-appearance of *Le Chagrin et la Pitié* [43] and let you know in case it should coincide with one of your visits.

To his parents

Egerton Gardens
4 July 1975

Dear Mum and Dad,

... I have no news at all as I've been working away and refusing all invitations in an effort to get my book under control. This has been very hard to do [as] they've been tearing up the road in Egerton Gdns and much of the day is taken up with drilling and hammerings. But I feel I must get some progress made ...

David Lean's option of a year is up this week but nothing has been heard of him so it seems he doesn't plan to renew it. He's said to be travelling in the South Seas, which makes if difficult to get a straight answer. I don't feel strongly about this, though I could do with the money to buy a house in the country to get away from these hammerings. Richard Hughes was very funny about the film they made of *A High Wind in Jamaica*. He said some friend in the film company had shown him a letter from one Hollywood mogul to another which ended with the P.S. 'This book is a classic. Somebody better read it.' He said that at first they wanted to turn all the children into adults! ...

Well, must beetle to the letter-box.

Lots of love
Jim

To Patricia Moynagh [44]

Egerton Gardens
2 August 1975

Dear Patricia,

This may never reach you as I find I don't have either your address or the Mahons'! But undaunted – What are you doing this hot weather? Sensibly in the country, I suppose.

However, if you feel like a meal some evening would you give me a ring at 584.5137? Or some other time if you're busy at the moment. You don't seem to be in the phone book.

Yours

Jim Farrell

To his parents

Egerton Gardens

Sunday 28 September 1975

Dear Mum and Dad,

... I've been working hard since you left, having found that most of what I'd written was unsatisfactory and a new return to page one was indicated. Writing a novel has a lot in common with snakes and ladders, as I probably said before. I'm more happy about the new version.

I took some time off to give my honeysuckle a short back and sides, however, and now it looks rather bare. But I expect it will soon recover. I also picked four large red tomatoes from outside. Yesterday was Brian Pearce's birthday and he and Michelle and I went to ... the Harold Pinter play. [45] I enjoyed it but they were irritated by its ambiguities. I also went to a party at Margaret Drabble's for her new book ... Apart from that there hasn't been much to report ...

Lots of love,

Jim

To his parents

Egerton Gardens

23 October 1975

Dear Mum and Dad,

... My book is [still] uphill work. I watched with great interest the tv programme on Richard Hughes in the Born 1900 series: when asked how many drafts he did, he thought for a while and then said: 'From thirty to fifty.' This was distinctly comforting in my present circs. I forget whether I told you that I had supper with him and his wife when they were passing through London on their way to visit their children in Canada a couple of weeks ago. They were both very

317

complimentary about the *S of K* which I had sent them. The tv programme was recorded, of course.

I went to see the musical that Dad spotted in the newspaper *Happy as a Sandbag*. It was crammed with useful odds and ends of 1940s' detail and I've ordered the record for one or two of the songs that I may use snippets of ...

Now I must turn in.

Lots of love
Jim

P.S. A certain Peregrine Worsthorne, an admirer of *Troubles* and Tory columnist, is supposed to be being invited to supper to meet th'author by one of Weidenfeld's editors. Naturally I was dismayed but she claims he's really very nice despite his right-wing ramblings.

To his parents

Egerton Gardens
7 November 1975

Dear Mum and Dad,

... Hebrew translation rights of the *S of K* have been sold for a microscopic $200. I'm not sure whether this represents Israeli skill at haggling or the small size of the population it is intended for. However, as it's an advance there may be more to come if it catches on. A siege story might well appeal to Israelis.

I went to supper at the Parrishes round the corner the other day and met Irwin Shaw[46] and his son who were over for the publication of his most recent novel. He made a great fuss of me over the *S of K*, which pleased me as I used to be a fervent admirer of his in Gwanda and Balholm days,[47] though I don't think I've read anything since and doubt whether it would still be as much to my taste now. His new novel did not get very good reviews, I think. He's a very nice rather bibulous looking fellow, more like a lorry-driver in appearance than a man of letters ...

Lots of love
Jim

To his parents

Egerton Gardens
20 November 1975

Dear Mum and Dad,

... Some mysterious current in the tide of papers on my desk has caused an earlier letter of Dad's to surface in which you ask whether I know of a book by Kate Caffrey ... I saw it lying about in Tony Godwin's flat in New York: he was considering it for publication, I think. Most of these books are written from the same, rather slender sources. Curious how little was written about the fall of Singapore, given its claim to being a major historical watershed. I remarked on this to Richard Hughes when I last saw him and he said: 'If it had been a victory the bookshelves would have been crammed' ...

Work has been progressing a bit faster recently but there's still an enormous amount left to do, and I seem to be caught up in more social engagements than usual this week. I'm having supper at a friend's house this evening with Bernard Levin [48] and one or two others. I haven't met him before but enjoy his journalism in *The Times*. A curious correspondence has been going on [there] recently started by B. Levin saying he loved cats but detested dogs. Supporters of the two factions have been at each others' throats, hackles abristle, ever since. Levin threatened in his column the other day, re some union leader who had incurred his displeasure, to 'set his cat on him'! ...

Lots of love,
Jim

To Russell McCormmach

Egerton Gardens
28 November 1975

Dear Russ,

It was very good to hear from you. I'm horrified to think that it's now over a year since we last saw each other briefly in New York: I don't feel I've accomplished anything in that time, except hopelessly to complicate my Singapore novel with everything but what it really needs: viz. some believable characters and a sensible plot. Old age comes on apace.

I did read the Douglas Day biography of Lowry, [49] indeed, I reviewed it somewhere, though I can't remember where, perhaps in the *New Statesman*. I started off feeling indignant with it: I felt that to begin with Lowry's death in the style of *Under the Volcano* was in poor taste (I don't think I've changed my mind about that) and some of the writing seemed excessively journalistic and superficial. But in the end I did become gripped and amazed by it. Lowry's life really was astonishing in many ways, and it became clear to me why he had written so little that was good. What the book doesn't make clear, I think, is how he could ever have written anything as good as *Under the Volcano* and how his friends managed to put up with him. At the time it came out here one of his friends, I think it was Arthur Calder-Marshall, delivered an indignant review of it on the BBC saying that the Lowry he had known wasn't even remotely like the person portrayed in Day's biography. I suspect that though Day's picture is substantially correct there was something important about him that he missed. Well ...

I haven't read *Gravity's Rainbow*: [50] the size of it deterred me and then I haven't been reading much modern fiction recently. I did read Turgenev's *Smoke* the other day and thought it was wonderful. Have you read it? There is some hilarious satire on intellectual *emigré* Russians, and Turgenev writes very movingly about love, it seems to me. His novel *First Love* is tremendous, I think.

My fantasies of moving to the country have proved as insubstantial as most of my fantasies. My novel lies on top of me, something like a large boulder on top of a beetle, and I wonder whether I'll ever manage to roll it off and start living again. If I do, perhaps I'll visit you in the North West if you go and live there. Your moving sounds a good idea to me ...

All the best,
Jim

To his parents

Egerton Gardens
9 December 1975

Dear Mum and Dad,
... Richard and Frances Hughes are coming to supper on Thursday.

They rang up the other day to say they're spending a week in London before going back to Wales. Frances said they had a wonderful time in America. Sir George [Weidenfeld] gave a lunch party for Olivia Manning the other day to which I was invited. Olivia had just signed up with Weidenfeld, ditching Heinemann whom she found disappointing. Olivia and I were agog because Antonia Fraser and Harold Pinter, who have just 'run off' together (figuratively) were also there. They behaved with perfect decorum, however, under our four beady eyes.

... I'm going to Paris for five days for a complete change of atmosphere ...

Lots of love
Jim

To his parents

Egerton Gardens
3 January 1976

Dear Mum and Dad,
... I got back from Paris in good order, clutching a couple of dozen stuffed snails which Garry Arnott and I polished off the following day. They were delicious, particularly as Garry had got out a good bottle of wine to go with them. He believes in doing himself well over Christmas ...

A chap from Macmillan invited me to lunch at a posh restaurant during the week, called Allan Maclain [*sic*] who turned out to be (Burgess and) Maclain's [*sic*] brother. He said he had been in the Foreign Office, too, at the time but felt that his brother's defection hadn't helped his job prospects so looked for a job in publishing. He said he hadn't seen his brother since, but corresponded with him quite frequently. He was a nice fellow ...

Lots of love,
Jim

To his parents

Egerton Gardens
30 January 1976

Dear Mum and Dad,
... I paid a visit to the cottage [51] last week-end ... a good deal of it

321

tramping around the countryside armed with an Ordnance Survey map (well, two of them actually, because Lyneham is on the edge of one). [It] is all surrounded by working farms which makes a change from a lot of the villages I saw which were full of stockbrokers in Range Rovers and Volvos. I had a nice walk in Bruern Wood and peered at Bruern Abbey nearby through the bushes ... Coming back I caught the train from Kingham: the walk took me just under an hour with my suitcase (which had typewriter and ms. in it) and sleeping-bag – by no means a hard slog, indeed, v. pleasant in good weather ...

In a book I've been reading published in 1934 concerning the experiences of a journalist in China, I came across a chapter about the capture of a British coaster by pirates in 1925. The author was on it ... and it struck me immediately that it would make a good narrative novel that would be quite fun to write after my slog with Singapore. Part of its attractions would be that I could incorporate one or two of Uncle Dick's [52] salty anecdotes. D'you think he could be persuaded to provide me with technical advice? What I had in mind was perhaps getting him to get out his charts and take me over the course explaining what the Captain would have had to do ... Meanwhile, I'm soldiering on with Singapore. I find I've done almost 90 pages in January, which isn't bad going for me ...

Lots of love
Jim

To his parents

Egerton Gardens
17 February

Dear Mum and Dad,

... I went down to Lyneham last weekend to do some walking and see how the cottage had survived the cold snap; it had ... Saturday was a lovely clear, still day and I put on my hiking boots and set off to visit Stow-on-the-Wold and various other places. One can cover longish distances over bridle tracks thanks to the Ordnance Survey, though one sometimes has to ignore notices saying Private Road. By the time I limped home through Bruern Wood (with a blister) I had covered 19 miles! It's very pleasant on a clear day going up wold and down wold because you can hear sounds at a great distance. I heard the bell ringers practising at Oddington

Church from Maugersbury Hill, for example. It was very agreeable ...

> Lots of love,
> Jim

To Deborah Rogers

> Egerton Gardens
> Thursday [undated] 1976

Dear Deb,

Thanks for the cheque and details from Japan and Brazil. Is the tax deducted at source in some way recoverable or the money not liable for British tax? Presumably you think so or you wd not have judged your commission on the gross.

I wrote a few days ago asking for a copy of the agreement with David Lean. Would you mind sending me this expensive and now, alas, historic document? ...

> Love,
> Jim

To Deborah Rogers

> Egerton Gardens
> 27 February 1976

Dear Deb,

A P.S. to my other card to say: if there's any money coming my way from New York (paperback) it would be a help if I got it before April 5. I've made relatively little money this year and hope to make more next.

> Love,
> Jim F.

To his parents

> Egerton Gardens
> 5 March 1976

Dear Mum and Dad,

... Many thanks for the letter about my pirate project, Dad. It will however be a considerable time, months rather than days, before I can start on it (if I do, of course). I still have a long way to go with the present *oeuvre* ...

Must bring this to a close now.

Lots of love,
Jim

To The Times

6 March 1976

From Mr J.G. Farrell

Sir, The building of the new British Library is surely an example of a costly 'improvement' that few people, if any, actually want, least of all those who use the present incomparable reading room. Readers, I believe, willingly accept the inconveniences of the present system; if the administration doubts this they could conduct a simple survey asking readers to mark a 'Yes' or 'No' on their request slips. The reading room could be kept open for longer hours in summer at an insignificant cost, particularly if there were some redeployment of the swarms of museum guards who cool their heels in the main hall during the present (midweek) late opening. I am no less certain than Professor Thomas (March 6) that the administration simply do not realise what will be lost. Committees, it is well known, tend to ignore matters, such as atmosphere, which they cannot quantify. And yet where a reading room is concerned that is the very heart of the matter.

Yours sincerely,
J.G. FARRELL
16 Egerton Gardens,
SW3

To Robert Parrish

Egerton Gardens
10 March 1976

Dear Bob,

Your book [53] is delightful! Very funny and human. And it's very refreshing to read a book by someone who kept his wits about him at that incredible time and place. I loved the picture, blue though it is, of you and Kathy on your wedding-day. Kathy looks as if she isn't quite sure what she has let herself in for!

Many congratulations.

Jim

To his parents

Egerton Gardens
19 March 1976

Dear Mum and Dad,

... You may have seen in the paper that Tony Godwin [54] died last weekend in New York. This was a terrible shock to all of us here. He was only fifty-five. He was a very warm-hearted fellow and I was very fond of him. We're having a non-religious meeting to commemorate him on Wednesday – the idea being that we don't want anything too lugubrious. He loved parties. There was a nice obituary in *The Times* calling him the major influence in British publishing since the war and saying that his authors considered it a privilege to be edited by him ...

Uncle Dick rang me sounding enthusiastic about the pirate idea. When I asked him how he was he replied 'Very ill', with 'flu, but later conceded that he had more or less recovered. He seemed to be having an asthma attack, though, too ... I must close this now. See you next week.

Lots of love,
Jim

To Margaret Drabble

Egerton Gardens
23 July 1976

Dear Maggie,

What a magnificent supper and altogether delightful evening!

I hereby award you four rosettes plus knife and fork for distinguished gastronomical activity.

See you soon.

[drawing of rosettes and knife and fork]
Love,
Jim F.

To Deborah Rogers

Egerton Gardens
23 July 1976

Dear Deb,

I gather you are *au courant* with Brenda's letter to me exhorting me to reconsider Rosen's offer. [55] I don't feel inclined to, however. What does it amount to? A minuscule option payment which would tie the thing up for four years! At the end of which I get a minuscule lump sum which has been reducing at compound interest of at least 10% p.a. All for a film that I don't particularly want made! My only interest in a commercial venture is one that might allow me to buy a decent flat (plainly this is not the case). Otherwise it would really have to be a friend, or one of the very few film-makers I respect. I realise this must be upsetting to Brenda who is like a water-spaniel who isn't happy unless she has a duck in her mouth but really, enthusiasm for the book isn't enough ... Having said that, I've no objection to being dropped in on, assuming he's in London, by Rosen some evening for a drink between 6 and 7 on the strict understanding that he knows he's wasting his time ...

Love,
Jim

To Bridget O'Toole

Egerton Gardens
Postcard, 27 July 1976

Dear Brid,

How are you? What's new? What are you up to? Nothing much to report here except that I'm in the last lap of the <u>first</u> draft of my book which is, I'm afraid, unspeakably boring and will have to be many times re-written. Is there a drought where you are?*

Love,
Jim

*Or are whistles still wet?

To G.M. Arthursen

Egerton Gardens
25th August 1976

Dear G.M.A.

I was sorry to hear the news that Harry McNair [56] has died. I could not claim ever to have been at all close to him ... but he was certainly a significant landmark in life at the time. Altogether this has been a poor year: my New York editor, an Englishman not much older than myself to whom I was much attached, died as the result of an asthma attack in the Spring. He was followed by the novelist Richard Hughes, whom I greatly liked and respected, having been an admirer of his since the age of 9 when I picked a novel of his out of my prep school library. Hughes and his wife, both apparently in splendid form, had had supper with me a bare couple of months earlier on their way back from America to their home in Wales. It comes as a particular shock when people so alert and so animated disappear ...

It had been on my conscience for some time, actually, that I had not replied to your kind letter earlier in the year in response to some moan or groan of mine. On the whole I think I tend to be stoical about everything but my writing: I think it has something to do with the constant dislocation between my intentions and what I actually manage to get down on paper. But I'm gradually learning to plough on regardless, making less of a fuss ...

My parents are now happily settled into a little village in the Cotswolds ... I can visit them easily on a day-return from Paddington [which] suits me from the work point of view as I don't care to be away from it for more than a day at a time, particularly at the moment when the first draft of my book is nearing completion.

Once again, many thanks for writing.

Yours ever
Jim Farrell

To Brian and Rose Knox Peebles

Egerton Gardens
[undated] Autumn 1976

Dear Brian and Rose,

Delighted to hear that you are now in your new abode. I look forward to dropping in on you in due course. I ... hope to finish [*The Singapore Grip*] in a few weeks, then take a few days off before trying to make something readable out of it. I'll try and contact you then if not before.

Love to all
Jim

To Deborah Rogers

Egerton Gardens
21 September 1976

Dear Deb,

After our talk the other evening I made a few enquiries about what a, say, £10,000 mortgage would cost me per annum. The answer, around £2,000, reduces my hopes of house-owning to a heap of ashes, as I obviously couldn't persuade Sir George to produce £4,000, the minimum I'd need per year, given the speed at which I produce books. In a way I'm relieved, actually.

This suits me, too, because it allows me to postpone a decision on our business relationship as I obviously couldn't ask you to negotiate with Sir George some years into the future without committing myself at the same time to the present arrangement, which strikes me as unsatisfactory in some respects – mainly the convention which gives the agent 10% for eternity. I still boil with indignation when I remember that clause ...

In the light of the first para we may as well postpone our meeting to another time. It was good to see you looking more cheerful at M. Drabble's.

Love,
Jim

To Patricia Moynagh

[Postcard 'S. Giorgio' by Francesco Francia]
Rome
10 November 1976

Dear Patrizia,

Why do you suppose that the Romans are feigning not to understand my fluent Italian? It is most mysterious! Will the Venetians pretend to be equally baffled? I wonder. [57] Apart from that all is going smoothly so far, except that I'm eating far too much.

Love,
Jim

To Deborah Rogers

Egerton Gardens
11 November 1976

Dear Deb,

Thanks for the Spanish *Sieges* and the letter. My pleasure in seeing the former was somewhat diminished by the sight of a gross mis-translation on the first page I looked at. One or two other pages were OK but I haven't yet had time to examine it properly. Such are the trials of being a polyglot ...

Our difficulties stem, it seems to me, from the fact that the agent's duties towards his author are not clearly defined, though his rights are (10% etc). My conception of them is that the agent, in return for his percentage, finds a buyer and then either draws up his own contract or modifies the buyer's contract to suit the particular case – that part of it being strictly his business.

I can see that in some particular cases like ours the agent may find himself out of his depth through inexperience of certain types of contract and negotiations. This seems to demand sympathy etc. but to ask the author to foot the bill for it seems to me to be a bit steep – unless the agent plans to stop exercising his rights as well as his duties. Etc etc. Anyway, I shall have to call on you to discuss my financial affairs sometime so we can continue to haggle *viva voce* over this ... [58]

Love
Jim

P.S. You still haven't sent me the letter explaining why I shouldn't agent my own book!

Egerton Gardens
14 January 1977

Dear Deb,

After considerable reflection I've now decided to agent my next book myself – for better or worse. I do hope we can remain friends, though, as I have a great liking and respect for you. It's also more than likely that I shall get out of my depth or bored with handling my own affairs and ask you to deal with some future work. I feel that I really must have a bash at it, though, if only to convince myself that it's not for me. Sorry it's taken me so long to make up my mind.

Love
Jim

Battling On

London

1977–March 1979

To Bridget O'Toole

16 Egerton Gardens
London SW3
22 January 1977

Dear Bríd,

Your writing paper is v–e–e–e–e–ry nice (better than this which is just a chopped-off bit of some I made a cockup of in my typing endeavours) ... Anyway, it was very nice to see you, and in such good form ... I thought we'd got into a more brother/sister relationship than the stormy times of yesteryear, or perhaps it's old age and creeping Darby-and-Joanism.

Nothing much has happened since you left. I got an invitation from the Cambridge Eng. Soc. but have turned it down, feeling that it would take me so long to prepare something that it wouldn't be worth it. Besides, I think I feel uneasy about haranguing people with my conclusions *ex cathedra*. M. Drabble laughed at my hesitations (she was here the other night with Malcolm and another lady don – Classics, Oxon): she always addresses everyone and had indeed just come back from talking in Rugby, which brought the subject up ... Evidently M. D. bears no grudge about me reproaching her for being blotto. The matter wasn't raised, anyhow.

As for coming to visit you I don't know when I might manage it. I've been making some computations about when I might finish my book and have been dismayed by the result. Even if I manage 10 pages a day (half that is my average) it will still take me another two and a half months. However, I'm battling on and if I get exhausted I might just come anyway with what I have.* I must get it done by the summer, though.

Lots of love,
Jim

*Unlikely, though, until I've got it over with.

To Margaret Drabble

Postcard 'Henry Inlander, Woman reading'
postmarked Chelsea 21 March 1977

Dear Maggie,

Many thanks for the lovely evening. What a good cook you are! But David [1] doesn't <u>eat much</u>, does he? No wonder he's so trim.

I don't want to be interfering about your azalea but shouldn't it have more light? And it would appreciate rainwater*, too, if you could collect some. See you when you get back from America, if not before.

Love
Jim

*(no lime in it).

To Norman Ilett [2]

Egerton Gardens
[undated postcard] April 1971

Dear Norman,

Where are you? ... What are you up to? This is by way of a signal rocket. I hope you will write to me with a good excuse for not having contacted me for so long!

Love to you both
Jim Farrell

To Bridget O'Toole

Egerton Gardens
[undated] 1977

Dear Br.

Here are a few bazzy [basil] seeds. My mother has ordered some more if these don't work.

I'm finding the last furlong on my book very heavy going but I should have finished by the end of this week. I should also have finished reading *Anna Karenina*. Quite boring in places, except for the bits to do with Levin. Tolstoy was best at writing about himself.

I shall probably go to Paris at the weekend to recuperate.

Love,
Jim

To James Michie [3]

Egerton Gardens
7 May 1977

Dear James,

Many thanks for your letter and interest in my work. As you know, I plan to keep all options open until I have actually finished my book and have given myself some time to recover and get things into perspective. Most likely, though, as I think I indicated when we had lunch the other day, I shall want to decide things mainly on some sort of objective criteria rather than on personal contact.

Kind regards,
Jim FARRELL

To Bridget O'Toole

Egerton Gardens
9 June 1977

Dear Bridget,

I hope you have been enjoying the Jubilee. A couple of weeks ago Patricia Moynagh, the lady who painted the picture of trees in my bathroom ... rang up with news of a cheap flight to Venice leaving three days later; in 'a trance of efficiency' working far into the night I just managed to get my corrections finished and give the mss to a couple of people to read while I was away. (I still haven't heard what they think.) The week in Venice was v. agreeable, partly because P.M. had once lived there for 3 years and still knew lots of people and odd corners. The weather, too, was ideal and I only felt an occasional twinge of wishing I was at home. As you know, I have a tendency to feel depressed on holiday. I toyed with the idea of going to live on one of the islands in the lagoon: viz. Burano, which has a very good restaurant. We could have our writers' commune there and become known as the Hermits of Burano (can you use 'hermit' in the plural?)

When I got back it was to find, first, that my friend Alan Riddell [4] had died of a cerebral haemorrhage; next, that my father's health has been showing ominous signs of cracking up. They aren't quite sure yet what is the matter but if it turns out to be as serious as my mother fears the next few months will be very difficult. Old people are terribly defenceless and, as you know, I'm very attached to my father. So things seem very depressing all round ...

There was a big village dinner in Lyneham in the barn across the road, attended by everyone and greatly enjoyed by my parents. There was also to have been, according to my mother who may have got it wrong, 'a procession' in the field behind their cottage. I offered to make anti-monarchist speeches to it from the bedroom window but the offer was declined. My mother has since been claiming that if I had seen the Queen in colour instead of in black and white I would have been won over ...

Write and encourage me one of these days when you have time. I've been feeling cornered in the last few days.

Lots of love
Jim

P.S. I think your calligraphy is <u>splendid</u>!

To Rosemary Legge [5] (Weidenfeld)

Egerton Gardens
18 June 1977

Dear Rosemary,

I've now at long last finished another tentative version of my monsterpiece and feel that the time has come to try it out on publishers.

I came back a couple of weeks ago from a trip to Venice to recover from the strain of putting it together and have since been making some adjustments to the beginning. It may still need more revision but I think the time has come to find a publisher and get an editor's advice.

For several reasons (but mainly because I am agenting the book myself and need to get some idea of its value) I have decided to send a copy simultaneously to more than one publisher, inviting tenders. I'm aware of the difficulties of producing a book of these nineteenth-century dimensions and feel that while it might well fit into one publisher's list quite happily, it might not suit another in the least.

The advantages therefore of giving it to who[m]ever (if anyone) wants it most are clear. Other things being roughly equal, however, I'd prefer in the interests of continuity to be published by you again if at all possible.

What interests me most are

a) the number of copies in the first printing.

b) the projected price – on the assumption that you would (i) have no share in any paperback sale (ii) that you would have the same share as with *Krishnapur*.

c) and, of course, the advance in either case.

I quite understand that you might not want to consider the book under the above conditions or that, having read it, you might feel that the whole project is too ponderous to proceed with. I do sometimes feel myself that I must have been mad to have attempted a book on this scale. In any event, I trust that we'll continue to be friends.

If you are interested I should prefer to conduct negotiations by post rather than *viva voce*.

Love to you,
Jim F.

[*Handwritten*] P.S. You might give me a ring.

To James Michie

Egerton Gardens
20 June 1977

Dear James,

I've now reached the stage of inviting tenders, though no doubt the book itself will require modifications. I feel that it will stand or fall on what's there already.

My main interest would be in size of first printing, price of book, and advance – in that order – on the assumption

(i) that I would retain full paperback share;

(ii) that we would split it.

If you are still interested I shall leave in a copy to your office before the end of the week. If the book itself appeals to you (I've tried to warn you of some of its drawbacks!) I'd prefer to handle any preliminary negotiations by mail.

Yours,
Jim Farrell

To James Michie

Egerton Gardens
24 June 1977

Dear James,

Thanks for your letter. Perhaps the week ending July 23 would suit you as a closing date? I hope so.

Just in case it should be germane to your deliberations, I think a September 1978 publication would suit me better than a Spring 1978 one.

I look forward to hearing your frank opinion of the book, whether you decide to make an offer or not.

Yours,
Jim

To Bridget O'Toole

Egerton Gardens
30 June 1977

Dear Bridget,

My father went to have various tests at the neurology dept. at the Radcliffe today: they did not make it clear what conclusions they had come to, apart from saying that it was his coordination that was affected – a small part of the brain controls this, apparently. Perhaps they will let us know more in a day or two.

On the whole I think it would be easiest if you don't visit me at the moment. Perhaps we could meet somewhere in August, depending on your book and my father's condition? Now that my book is finished all sorts of projects are crowding into my overheated brain for another flight from reality!

Love,
Jim

To Bridget O'Toole

Egerton Gardens
8 July 1977

Dear Bridget,

Things are looking very bad for my father, though not all the results have come in yet ... I still feel shattered, not just by the prospect of

336

his death but by the way, if things are as they appear to be, it is likely to happen – the slow and progressive collapse of everything as his nervous system packs up. [6] However, we must do what we can to make him comfortable. According to Claude whom I spoke to on the phone the other day his condition might stabilise and continue as it is for some months ...

I received a letter from one Stephen Oliver[7] about *Troubles*: 'It is a novel which has excited and moved me greatly and I very much wish to turn it into an opera (!) ... perhaps I should mention my *Tom Jones*, commissioned by the English Music Theatre, which toured the country last year, and was broadcast from one of the Sadler's Wells' performances.' He goes on to express the hope that I might work on it with him. I have written back explaining that I am tone deaf and therefore rather lack qualifications but that I can see no objection to him making an opera of it if he wants. A noble and quixotic enterprise to be sure.

I'm also engaged, in between visits to Lyneham, in conducting a rather apathetic auction of *The Singapore Grip*. Doubtless I would get on better if I knew myself what I actually want ... Thank heaven I finished it before my father's illness became apparent. I've lost all ability to concentrate on anything for more than a minute or two at a time ...

I'll let you know if there are any developments.

Love
Jim

To James Michie

Egerton Gardens
22 July 1977

Dear James,
Thanks for your letter and offer which, however, I have to decline as it has been improved on by other publishers.

For the record, and quite incidentally, I'm shocked that you should have shown [it] to Penguin without mentioning it to me. This seems to me a decidedly slippery way to proceed.

Perhaps you would be so kind as to arrange for the script to be left at your entrance desk ...?

Yours sincerely,
Jim

John Curtis and Rosemary Legge of Weidenfeld & Nicolson were more successful, and publication of The Singapore Grip *was set for September 1978. Jim continued without an agent in London, but the US rights were now handled by Irving 'Swifty' Lazar. The legendary Hollywood agent had been introduced to him by Bob Parrish, for whom Lazar also acted.* [8]

To Mr Pantucci [9]

Egerton Gardens
9 September 1977

Dear Mr Pantucci,

Thank you for your enquiry about *The Singapore Grip*. At the moment my agent for translation rights, Irving Lazar, is on a boat somewhere off the coast of Spain and is hence uncontactable. I hope to see him, however, before he goes to Frankfurt and will let him know that you would like to see the book. Perhaps you could approach him about it at Frankfurt, if you will be there.

At the moment there are few copies of the novel and I doubt whether the chances of your taking it would warrant the expense of photo-copying it as it is extremely long. However, I will see that you get a proof copy as soon as they appear. That would be next Spring, I should think, as publication is likely to be in September.

Thank you for your interest,

Yours sincerely
J.G. Farrell

To Dr Claude Simha

Egerton Gardens
5 December 1977

Dear Claude,

Just a note to thank you for your letter and to let you know that I am still around. Since last we spoke my father's condition has got a little worse. First, they believed the symptoms were of what is called 'locomotor ataxia', which would have been frightening, and without any hope of improvement. I read some books of medicine in the library, and found it was a late effect of syphilis. That struck me as extremely odd, considering my father's cautious and not very broadminded lifestyle. But, after countless tests, they've now changed their mind and think it's more likely to be a type of arthritis in the neck. The pressure of the spinal column on the nervous system seems to be causing the paralysis of his hands and his awkward walk. I've explained all this very poorly, you know. They considered an operation for a while but decided against one, obviously because of his age (now 77). My mother was disappointed because she thought he could be put back to his old self, just like that, but I was relieved because I didn't think much of his chances of pulling through. He was already severely knocked back by the lumbar puncture to enable him to be injected with a dye for the x-rays. They now talk of putting on a surgical collar to try to lessen the pressure.

These worries were (and are) taking up much of my time, but simultaneously I'm trying to force myself into a strict regime of work. I have finally finished my Singapore novel, and at the moment am writing a screenplay for a film set in the South Pacific.[10] It's an Anglo-French joint production (French backing) and I work in collaboration with a French director, Bertrand Tavernier (of whom you may have heard), who is quite successful over there, I'm told, although I am not sure why. He is to be the producer, and one of my neighbours here, an old Hollywood exile, Robert Parrish, is to be the director. What is more likely, however, is that the film will never be made, but I will still be paid for the screenplay, so I won't care. Anyway, that is what happens to 19 screenplays out of 20.

I'm thinking of getting away from England (and England's Inland Revenue) in the next year or so, and I may come to Paris to find an apartment; my father's health permitting, of course. I am also thinking of Venice – I can now read Italian fluently and can manage to speak a little, too. Love to Anna and all the family,

Kind regards,
Jim

And how are things with you? I'm afraid I've talked about nothing but myself!

To G.M. Arthursen

Egerton Gardens
19 February 1978

Dear G.M.A.,

Many thanks indeed for your letter. I was sorry to hear that you have again had health problems to put up with ... I remember your knee difficulties at Rossall – being so healthy oneself at that age (I mean, as a schoolboy) and so quick to mend, I'm sure I was insufficiently sympathetic at the time. Oh dear, does one get wiser about such things as one gets older? Yes, one does ...

My father, fortunately, is in no great pain at present, though his right hand and arm are badly swollen. It is more a numbness and curtailment of movement. He visited the Wingfield Orthopaedic Hospital on Friday (where I spent some weary months myself as an undergraduate) and ... is to go back in three weeks for further examination. My father, incidentally, is deeply impressed by the care with which the Health Service has treated him, as am I. I think we hear too much of its shortcomings and not enough of its triumphs.

I did hear some of *Troubles* on 'A Book at Bedtime' [11] but was rather disappointed with it. In order to get through such a long book they had been obliged to perform surgery on it to the extent of removing two-thirds, of necessity leaving only such matter as kept the story going forward. Thus it seemed to me to degenerate into a steady drizzle of incident deprived of most of what made the incident significant. But the author is the worst possible judge of what effect such an abridgment might be having on someone listening to it for the first time. I thought the man read it fairly well, though he made Edward too much of a blimp and did not manage Sarah at all ... Well, maybe it got me an extra reader or two up and down the country, or gave some entertainment to those who like my father now find reading a strain. My father was immensely pleased.

My new book *The Singapore Grip* is due out on Sept 7. It already seems very distant and hardly by me at all. The publishers seem pleased with it so I'm hoping for the best.

Thank you for putting me on to Grazia Deledda. [12] I had not heard of her before and will certainly give her a try. At present I'm reading an excellent novel by Carlo Cassola, [13] the first I've read by him, called *La Ragazza di Bube*. I don't read much fiction in English these days, doubtless suffering from a surfeit of my own work, but for some reason I read it in Italian with great pleasure. Incidentally have you read Carlo Levi's *Cristo si é Eboli*, about his experiences as an exile in Calabria during Fascist times? A great, great book! I read it years ago in translation [14] and recently read it again in the original.

Well, I must get back to work. Keep well.

Yours,
Jim

To Bernard Bergonzi [15]

Egerton Gardens
24 March 1978

Dear Bernard,

A card arrived from Bridget [O'Toole] the other day saying that you had expressed an interest in seeing an early copy of *The Singapore Grip*. I have, in fact, just finished correcting the galleys. Uncorrected book proofs should be appearing in a few days, and I'll ask Weidenfeld to send you one. I don't usually change much at this stage but this time I've had to deal with one or two clumsy locutions which somehow slipped by. Old age and death of brain cells, I guess. The printer also has an annoying habit of supplying words which resemble mine, but aren't. What I mean is, in one or two places you must give me the benefit of the doubt!

I hope you are well.

Yours,
Jim F.

To Bridget O'Toole

Egerton Gardens
[undated] 1978

Dear Bridget,

Many thanks for your card. I've written to Weidenfeld asking them to send Bernard a proof copy of my book. I hope his conviction that I am the cat's whiskers survives his reading of it ...

I'm planning a trip to Cork and Kerry with my American friends the Parrishes in May: househunting for my departure at the end of the year ...

See you soon.

Love,
Jim

To Norman Ilett

Egerton Gardens
12 April 1978

Dear Norman,

It was very good to hear from you, though I was shocked and dismayed to hear that Bill Budge [16] had died. I didn't know him very well but had a high opinion of him. And he was always very decent to me when at Ross. This must have been very sad news for you, in particular.

I haven't seen GMA in some time, three or four years, I suppose ... He takes a stoical view of his physical difficulties and is generally inclined to optimism. But, good gracious! Old age is no joke. I've seen a little more of it at close quarters recently with a decline in my father's health (he's now 78 and needs constant looking after) and an old aunt [May], his sister, of whom I'm very fond, now in an old people's home in Yorkshire. All one can do is make them as comfortable as possible and hope that one can get hold of a bottle of sleeping pills when it comes to one's own turn.

I'm thinking of giving up my London life and going to live abroad, maybe in France or Ireland. I feel that life is much too comfortable here and that I've stopped experiencing things – in a rut, in short. The years go by in a flash. Also, I'm growing dissatisfied (more so, I should say) with the way I write and feel that needs shaking up, too. No doubt you will simply see this as a refusal to accept the onset of middle age, as I half do myself ...

My book, *The Singapore Grip*, comes out in September and looks like being, at least from a sales point of view, a success. As usual my own feelings about it are very mixed. I had supper with Ruth [Prawer] Jhabvala [17] last night and we agreed that it was very hard, once you had finished a book, to remember what it was you found so exciting when you were writing it. Perhaps by agreeing she was just trying to soothe me, though.

All the best to you both,

Jim F.

To Jack Kirwan [18]

Egerton Gardens
22 May 1978

Dear Jack,

Many thanks indeed for your letter ... I'm still determined to return to Ireland and still looking for a suitable place. I've more or less decided, having just spent a couple of weeks looking around in the West, that I would like to be on or near Dunmanus bay in Co. Cork. There's a ruined farmhouse around there that I might have a go at rebuilding. But house prices in Ireland have gone crazy, farmers having evidently discovered that one can make more money out of selling property than growing potatoes. While rebuilding (if this is what I decide to do) I may just rent somewhere ...

Finally, let's have a jar one of these days. I haven't been in Dublin for years but no doubt will be one of these days. Much changed, I hear.

All the best to you,
Jim Farrell

To John Curtis [19] (Weidenfeld & Nicholson)

Egerton Gardens
2 June 1978

Dear John,

Thanks for your offer [20] which I'll certainly mull over. Even before it arrived, however, some of the negative aspects of selling futures in my own work were dawning on me. My initial reaction to the offer is that I'll most likely prefer to go on backing myself to produce a winner than to play it safe and have you back me. But I'll let you know definitely in a day or two.

I enjoyed our lunch the other day.

Yours
Jim

P.S. Sorry if I've got you geared up about this unnecessarily – all I can say is that it seemed a good idea at the time. Come to think of it, that's what I'd like to have written on my gravestone – in gothick lettering: 'It seemed a good idea at the time.'

To John Curtis

Egerton Gardens
7 June 1978

Dear John,

I've now mulled over your offer for a new novel [21] and, after inspection of my thoughts, have decided I'm not remotely tempted. Temptation would not become acute, I feel, at much less than £20,000 down and £5,000 on delivery. But even then it would be a source of anxiety as to whether I could deliver on time, given that I may have to move house in the interim.

It may well be that there is no way of bridging my aspirations and your commercial prudence at this stage – and, in any case, I am sure that from your point of view there is a lot to be said for knowing exactly what you are bidding for.

Many thanks for your offer which I'm sure, given the circumstances, is a generous one.

Yours
Jim

To John Curtis

Egerton Gardens
8 June 1978

Dear John,

A brief postscript to our phone conversation earlier this morning. It has become clear to me that I would not want to give you World Rights in the next novel. The question therefore resolves itself to whether you would want to put down £20,000 next December (just possibly Feb. depending on other factors) and £5,000 on delivery for a similar contract to that of the GRIP. [22] If you do, fine, let's proceed. If you don't let's let it go – and perhaps try again at some later date.

When discussing the possible future novels there was one I forgot to mention (and which I mention now simply to keep you in the picture), which has been in my mind since *Krishnapur* and is in fact another Indian novel, this time set in a hill-station in the 1870s–80s featuring Dr McNab* as anchor-man. Hilary Spurling, to whom I described it years ago in a fit of enthusiasm, reminds me of it every time I see her. However, I don't want to typecast myself any more than I have already. As it is, whenever an Indian book comes out two or three people ring me up to ask me to review it.

Kind regards,

Yours,

Jim

* of *Krishnapur*

To David Simpson

Egerton Gardens

9 June 1978

Dear David,

... Smashing party the other evening. [23] I saw Alison [Lurie] last night and we were marvelling over how good vegetarian food could be. On the way home I sat in a deserted tube carriage and read a copy of the *Daily Mail* I found there: it said that two of my friends were splitting up from their respective lovers. London Transport provides quite a decent service when you think about it.

Yours,

Jim

To Norman Ilett

Egerton Gardens

6 July 1978

Dear Norman,

Many thanks for your letter and invitation to drop in on you this summer. Unfortunately, it looks as if this may be difficult for a variety of reasons too boring to go into at the moment ...

I quite agree with you about being a schoolmaster. It's a very hard life. I hope you have taken good care that all your kids have gone down the mines (or, well, the Treasury is just as good). You don't even get free coal, do you?

I forget whether I mentioned that among the many schemes simmering in my overheated brain is one to set up house in Paris. I made a quick dash over there last week to see the Cézanne exhibition and poke around estate agents. It's changed a lot since I last lived there but is still quite attractive in some ways. I remember once asking William Burroughs (archetypal hippie author, drug-addict and black sheep scion of Burroughs Adding Machine family) why he had come to live in London from Paris. [24] His reply was splendidly in character. 'Because the food's better.'(!)

I've asked Weidenfeld's [*sic*] to send you a review copy of my book to 1, The Cop (it's such a seductive address) ... No response is necessary but please let me know if it doesn't arrive.

All the best to your wife and self,

Jim F.

To Deborah Rogers

Egerton Gardens
24 July 1978

Dear Deborah,

This is to say that I've been obliged, *miserere mea*, to re-register for VAT as from June 25 1978 ...

I've written to Weidenfeld and to Cape to this effect so no action on your part is necessary. Hope you are well. All good wishes,

Love,
Jim

To his parents

Egerton Gardens
15 September 1978

Dear Mum, Dad, and Odd, [25]

... John Curtis rang today to say that the subscription (i.e. pre-publication) sales were 7,000 to 8,000, which he was very pleased about ...

Lots of love,
Jim

To David Simpson

Egerton Gardens
[undated] 1978

Dear David,

Many thanks indeed for your letter. I was very sorry you couldn't come and naturally we all sat around sunk in deep gloom at your absence.

The reception of *The Singapore Grip* has been pretty mediocre but I'm being fatalistic about it (I think) and sinking my teeth into another story. Maggie [Drabble] brought some freesias last night which are filling my flat with a divine scent!

> Your friend,
> Jim

By now, Farrell had made up his mind to leave London and move to Ireland, a decision influenced by advice from his accountant and his doctor. Earnings for writers in the Republic were tax-free, and both men, independently, pointed out that the financial cushion would be invaluable if – or, more likely, when – the newly discovered long-term effects of polio [26] curtailed his ability to write.

To Jack Kirwan

> Egerton Gardens
> 5 November 1978

Dear Jack,

The name of the house I'm after is Gortafane [*sic*] House (Patrick Tobin's house), Letter North, Kilcrohane, Co. Cork. I'm buying it from Mr Gerry O'Mahony and his brother and their solicitor is Frank O'Mahony, The Square, Bantry.

I assume I make out the cheque to the solicitor to hold for the brothers O'Mahony. The asking price is £22,000. I'm therefore sending a cheque for £5,500 as a deposit to send on as soon as possible. I may try and phone you tomorrow just to make sure I've thought of everything.

It was very nice to see you and the rest of the gang the other evening. Too bad about the All Blacks. I really thought Ireland would get away with a draw. [27]

> All the best,
> Jim F.

To Bridget O'Toole

> Egerton Gardens
> 5 November 1978

Dear Bridget,

... I was sorry to hear that someone made off with your typewriter and exclamation mark. But mine doesn't have one either and I seem to manage OK. Who knows? Perhaps Someone Up There is trying to tell you something!!! i.e. too many!!!!!s

I just got back from a rapid and exhausting trip to Cork and Dublin in the course of which I hope I bought a house – an old farmhouse on the very end of the peninsula between Dunmanus and Bantry Bays, on the side of a hill locally known as Letter Mountain. Ach, vot is zis? Ve haf heard of ze vine lakes and ze butter mountain, now ve are haffing a letter mountain? It's a splendid place, but very exposed, so if you need a wuthering you must come and stay. You must come and stay anyway as I'm hoping to buy a sailing dinghy and want you to give me lessons. Provided the sale goes through without a hitch I'm going to make a determined effort to settle down there. It's beyond Kilcrohane if you have a map. London already seems far away.

While in Dublin I spent an evening with my childhood friends, all of whom seem to be exactly the same as when I last saw them 20 years ago, though broods of children now cluster around them. Hilary, [28] however, one of my early amours, has become an ardent feminist and harangues people at street-corners. In the course of the drunken and enjoyable evening I spent with them, in a moment of intuition she suddenly said: 'You just couldn't bear to come back until now, could you?' We then trooped upstairs to have a look at her husband, Donald, who was lying groaning in bed with 'flu and didn't seem at all cheered up by the merry party who flooded into his room waving glasses and switching on lights ...

Love to you,
Jim

To Deborah Rogers

Egerton Gardens
20 November 1978

Dear Deb,
I received the enclosed permission request.[29] I assume it is up to someone else (Knopf?) to grant it, but I have signed the form just in case it isn't, to avoid to-ing and fro-ing ...

Also this morning there arrived an invitation to the Tony Godwin Prize [30] party. I'd love to come, and look forward to seeing you there.

Love,
Jim

To Jack Kirwan

Egerton Gardens
29 November 1978

Dear Jack,

I've been somewhat concerned recently about the prospect of the
Irish pound cutting loose from the British with attendant exchange
control problems before I've had a chance to clear my cheque to
Frank O'Mahony through an Irish bank. If there has still been no
contract from him perhaps you could pay the enclosed cheque into
an escrow account and pay the deposit from that account in due
course when he shows some sign of life.

If there <u>has</u> been some communication with him in the meantime then you could simply send him the original cheque and tear
this one up. Or if this is a bad idea for some other reason then tear
it up anyway. Naturally, one or the other should be torn up as I don't
keep enough to cover both in the account ...

All the best,
Jim

To Jack Kirwan

Egerton Gardens
20 December 1978

Dear Jack,

Re: Gortafane House

Many thanks for the contract. I return it herewith, signed and witnessed.

The earliest I could produce a cheque for the balance owing on
the property, £16,500, would be about February 16. My publishers
are committed to giving me a large slice of cash on February 9th
but it would take a little time to put it through the banks. I don't
quite know when I'm expected to pay the balance. If the British
Govt introduce exchange controls in the meantime it could take
longer to get the money into Ireland, and might even take until I
emigrate there at the end of March. However, I see that there is a
provision for paying interest at 15% p.a. on the outstanding sum.

Warm greetings for Christmas to yourself and the Kirwan clan
as a whole!

All the best,
Jim

To Piers and Emily Read

Egerton Gardens
Sunday [undated]

Dear Jay and Emily, [31]

D'you recall inviting me and Susannah [32] to spend New Year's with you in Yorks? I'm afraid we won't be able to make it then. I'd forgotten a promise to my elderly parents to spend the holidays with them: obviously the Ambassador's champagne stole away with my wits. I'd much rather visit you and will do so, even if I have to invite myself, another time. Meantime if we're both dodging tax we may well meet up in some other city. I've been thinking of wintering in Paris as an antidote to County Cork.

Love
Jim F.

To Miss Parker [33]

Egerton Gardens
18 January 1979

Dear Miss Parker,

Unfortunately I must decline your offer of a lecture tour to Belgium and Luxembourg because in February and March I am planning to move my home to Southern Ireland. Consequently I feel I shall have to remain uncommitted elsewhere in order to be able to preside over the confusion that housemoving entails.

I intend to pay a visit to India in October or November for research purposes. If I could be of any use to the British Council while there they should let me know, either at this address until the end of March or afterwards at: Letter House, Kilcrohane, Near Bantry, Co. Cork. However, I imagine that India is dealt with by a different division.

Yours sincerely
J.G. Farrell

To Bridget O'Toole

Egerton Gardens
25 January 1979

Dear Bridget,

Many thanks for your father's book [34] and the recorder, both of which arrived in good shape. I'm particularly pleased with the book which seems to be full of the sort of detail that gets left out of most history books and for which I personally have a great appetite. I shall certainly write to him to thank him.

The recorder book certainly is very simple: indeed it appears to be written for someone with irreversible brain damage: however, it may still prove too difficult for me, though I was rather encouraged by reading the first lesson. I stuck the instrument together just now and had a cautious blow – whereupon all the cats in the garden have come darting up and are standing on their black back legs trying to look in the window to see what's going on. Agreed that it is on loan, don't worry.

You've got it a bit wrong about the boats: my interest was in tramp steamers. The person on whom I was relying chiefly was a school friend of my father's from his Liverpool Collegiate days, Capt. 'Uncle Dick' Roberts. He came to visit my father, having heard that he was ill, last summer and stayed in a nearby inn, coming to chat with him. This was very decent of him. However, he had become alarmingly right-wing ... rabid indeed. Even my parents grew uncomfortable as he thundered on, only pausing to announce, looking at his watch, that it was time to put on the tv because (this was supposed to be a pleasant, social evening) the Conservative party political broadcast was just beginning.

He went back to his home in Wales after this visit, having ordered a copy of my book (he was very keen on me doing the sea story), got up one morning at 6 am, as old salts presumably will, and started writing a letter to my father, full of enthusiasm for the sea-story but adding, 'Jim has a great gift and could do it splendidly, provided he keeps his left-wing ideas out of it'. He then switched on the immersion heater, leaving the letter unfinished, made himself a cup of tea and went back to bed. When his sister went in at 9 to tell him his breakfast was ready she found that he had died in his sleep. She sent the unfinished letter on to my parents.

I found it quite moving, given the circumstances. For some reason this death reminded me a bit of Virginia Woolf's essay on Captain Marryat. [35] Sailors may be better at shoving off than us landlubbers. I'd already decided, though, even before his death, that it would be impossible to get from him the information I needed. He insisted always on taking charge. There's a miniature portrait of him at the end of *The Singapore Grip* in the character of Captain Brown. I still plan to use some of his anecdotes, though, one of these days.

I went twice to the Boat Show to decide which, if any, I should buy. The second time I went with a Canadian friend ... who has done quite a bit of sailing. We both decided that for my purposes, e.g. easy to sail, stolid rather than sporty, easy to rig (lug), usable with outboard, something called a 'scaffie' on sale there would suit me best. I was so taken with its aesthetic appearance, in particular its rust coloured sail, that I was severely tempted to buy it on the spot. However, I've decided to defer the decision until after I pay another visit to Ireland next month and have another look at the nearby slipway etc. It might be more sensible to buy one there, and cheaper. I'll see what the locals think ...

Again, many thanks for the parcel and birthday phone call.

> Love,
> Jim

To his father

> Egerton Gardens
> 26 January 1979

Dear Dad,

I hope you are comfortable in your hospital bed [36] and not too bored. If you have to cool your heels there at all you have probably chosen the best time of year since there is nothing but snow and misery going on in the outside world ...

I spent a little time in a bookshop this morning observing a middle-aged gent of saturnine appearance who was deeply engrossed in a copy of my book. I felt like going up to him and saying; 'Right now, you've had enough of a sample. Do you want it or not?' I myself hesitated for a while over the *Oxford Dictionary of Christianity* or some such title. My new book has some religious matters in it and there are a lot of technical terms ... I read the definitions without being much the wiser ...

> Lots of love
> Jimmy

To his father

Egerton Gardens
Tuesday 30 January 1979

Dear Dad,

... I woke up last night thinking of how you and Oddie and I used to play cricket with a tennis ball up against the garage door in Boscobel. [37] I don't know why. Odd and I must have been very small.

Lots of love,
Jim

To Jack Kirwan

Egerton Gardens
31 January 1979

Dear Jack,

... This might be a good time to remind you that I'm relying on you personally to charge me the going rate for the job, otherwise it will be impossible for me to ask you to act for me in future. Anyway, let me know when you want the money.

I expect to come to Dublin on about 19 Feb on a brief reconnaissance visit in order to buy a car and do a few other chores. I'll then drive down to Cork to have a look at the house where Jerry O'Mahony has been doing some work for me, and probably back to Dublin again ... I'll give you a ring once I'm established so that we can get together for a jar.

Yours,
Jim

To Deborah Rogers

[Egerton Gardens]
12 March 1979

Dear Deb,

... I am de-registering from VAT on March 24th 1979.
Hope all goes well.

Love,
Jim

To David Simpson

Egerton Gardens
14 March 1979

Dear David,

... By all means come whenever you feel like it. If you come at Easter one of us will have to sleep with an attractive Canadian girl [38] who is threatening me with a visit. But that's no problem. She can look us over and decide which. I should have explained that there are only two beds at present, that's why.

I'll try and ring you before I finally leave.

Yours,
Jim

To John Curtis

Egerton Gardens
18 March 1979

Dear John,

Many thanks for suggesting an evening. Alas, I'm pretty well booked up until I go. My furniture goes on Tuesday and I follow shortly after. And I must spend a little time with my parents before I go. Please give my love to Rosemary [39] and say I'm sorry that I shall have to put off the meal I invited her to until my next visit to London.

Yours,
Jim

To Brian and Rose Knox Peebles

Egerton Gardens
25 March 1979

Dear Brian and Rose,

... If you find yourselves in Ireland do come and see me. I meant to call and say goodbye but in all the hassle of moving time ran out.

All good wishes
Jim

To his parents

Paris, Gare du Nord
29 March 1979

Dear Mum and Dad,
All goes well so far. My friends here are in good form. I spent 3 nights
with Claude and Anna. Their children now getting big. I'm off now
to Dublin.

Lots of love,
Jim

Life is Bliss Here

Ireland

May–August 1979

To Claude and Anna Simha

Saltwater House [1]
Letter
Kilcrohane
Bantry
Co. Cork
7 May 1979

My dear friends,

I did want to write before this, but there has been a postal strike here since we last met in Paris. And it is still going on! The Irish don't give in, do they? I'm having this letter posted in England by a friend who came for the weekend to visit poor old uncle Jim in retirement.

... To make a house work in which no one has lived for twenty years takes a lot of time and can be tedious to boot ... Apart from all that, I still believe that one day it's going to be really nice and I'm not discouraged. I've even begun to plant some trees, including a comice pear ... The countryside is just beautiful. I haven't had a chance so far to go fishing, but the locals say you can catch mackerel right beside me here.

Thanks again for your hospitality during my stopover in Paris.

Love to the children.

Regards,
Jim

To Robert and Kathie Parrish

Saltwater House
8 May 1979

Dear Bob and Kathie, [2]

This is a very rapid scrawl to let you know I'm still in business – and even about to begin writing my novel in my very own study, not to mention house. However, my path has not been strewn with roses and there's still a lot to be done. Only a complete innocent could have thought, as I did, that I'd unpack my suitcase and settle down to my novel without more ado. The electricity still wasn't connected when I arrived and though Jerry [3] (who's a brick incidentally, not to say a reinforced concrete block) asserted that the ESB [4] people were about to arrive at any moment, a month passed by candlelight. Things take time here! Then there's the absence of post, [5] a petrol shortage (now over) and various other disasters ... e.g. if someone pisses in the bathroom it makes such a noise that people downstairs flinch involuntarily and run for cover. Kathie's idea for a second loo is highly necessary anyway. The worst outstanding problem is the fact that the water does not taste or smell good so I'm going to have to have a well sunk. I'm waiting philosophically for the well-borer to arrive.

However, on the plus side I'm still keen on the house which is really nice and I haven't yet felt in the least homesick for Egerton Gardens – quite the opposite, I wonder what took me so long to decide to leave (this may not last, I hasten to add). I've been digging like a fiend in the garden planting trees and vegetables. I've had Jerry Daly's brother, Michael, over here digging too. Jerry O'Mahony gave me a whole lot of cabbage seedlings so I am undoubtedly in the forefront when it comes to cabbage-owning novelists. The lettuces which I planted myself are coming up nicely though I've had to put a net over them to keep them out of the clutches of the birds and of an old grandfather hare that lives across the road. Altogether, it still seems fun.

I've seen Mrs Cronin only once. When I appeared in her shop she did a double-take that would have done credit to Laurel and Hardy in their prime. However, I won't hear a word against her. She gave me a full tank of gas at the height of the petrol strike, nodding and winking and saying she'd said nothing ...

As for Wolfie-poo, [6] he's been through a bad time. While on holiday in Portugal in January he was taken ill and collapsed at Heath Row [*sic*] with a perforated ulcer on the way back. He has spent the last few weeks in hospital and has only just reappeared on the Ahakista scene. Did you know incidentally that the beautiful house next to him belongs to Warren of the Warren Commission. Ann Colville (who has been over here for the weekend and will transport this letter) and I went to have tea with them yesterday – with Wolf and Ann, not the Warrens. He lent me *The Raspberry Reich* which I fell asleep over last night. I can hardly keep my eyes open here after 9pm incidentally ...

But where are you anyway? Are you in Black Africa? ... I'm dying to know. You're still welcome to stay here, of course, but I doubt if Kathie would be happy about the bathroom arrangements ... By the time you come Jerry may have got to work on my second loo anyway so all may be well ...

Anyway, one day I hope to see you, or at least get a letter from you if the strike ends. In the meantime love to you both,

Jim

To Alison Lurie

Saltwater House
17 May 1979

Dear Alison, [7]

Many many thanks indeed for your book which reached me the other day despite a fourteen week postal strike, kindly brought over by David Simpson (Maggie's ex-) who has been spending a week here recovering from Amnesty [8] and who will post this reply for me in London. Actually I heard you on the radio which was very nice, though no substitute for seeing you too. I still remember with great pleasure our last meal together at the Monpeliano [*sic*].[9] Despite leaks in the roof etc I like it here and so far seem to have settled in OK. There's still an awful lot to do to fix the house up, though, and the days seem too short. Also there's a petrol shortage to add to other difficulties. Please ... let us definitely meet on your next visit to Europe as it looks as if we won't on this. I'm delighted that *Only Children* [10] has been such a success and I'm greatly looking forward to it.

Love,
Jim [11]

358

To Ann Colville

Saltwater House
17 May 1979

Dear Ann, [12]

Many many thanks for your nice letter and for organising the sack of mail that David brought out with him. I could hardly believe it. It included, among other things, a good review from *Newsweek* and that was encouraging.

Contrary to expectations David has proved even less energetic than you where working in the garden is concerned ... He did wield a shovel briefly one morning but it didn't last long. His most positive contribution has been the cooking of minestrone and lentil soups. Altogether the vegetarian régime has not bothered me as much as I had expected, but then I could eat *salade niçoise* till the cows come home. We cooked my first cabbage yesterday and it was – delicious! We also walked right to the end of the peninsula, which took us all day but is a great walk with terrific views of the sea on both sides and ending in a lighthouse, sheer cliffs and dramatic waves. Great stuff. We also went down to fish ... but did not catch anything. David, being a vegetarian, baited his hook with cheese but there appeared to be no vegetarian fish around either. Later Michael Daly told us that it was hopeless fishing in that spot and that we might just as well have been fishing in the kitchen as there. He recommended another spot which we may try if the weather improves before David goes – it's grey and blustery at the moment.

I've now planted all the trees, sown the seed for night-scented stock, and have only a few seedlings left to plant. Then the really heavy work on my book can start. Actually, I did a couple of days heavy work in between your visit and David's arrival so it won't be such a shock. Jerry has installed the beam over the fire-place and it looks pretty good. The fire is still drawing O.K. but it rained very hard the day after you left and a prodigious quantity of water came down it. Also an unexplained dribble of water poured out of the ceiling just as I was falling asleep and hit me on the head! The perils of moving out of the city!

Many thanks for offering help with the curtains but I've decided to put off deciding what to do about all that until some future date, preferably after I've finished my book and seen what the carpets look like. Brick-red does sound like a good idea, though, and would give a touch of warmth to the room ...

Love to you

Jim

P.S. Could you ring [Bob Parrish] and say if it's not too much trouble could he bring me a 7 pound bag of Colombian coffee beans from the cut-rate coffee shop on Monmouth Street in Covent Garden. If they have no Colombian, Zaire or Kenyan would do. Medium roast. I'll pay him when he gets here.

Could you [also] ring Richard Farrell and say you have seen me and I'm prospering ...

To Carole Tucker [13]

Saltwater House

18 May 1979

Dear Carole,

This is by way of a signal rocket to let you know that I'm still alive, despite this never-ending postal strike and a petrol shortage ...

Well, so far things have not been going too badly and I'm beginning to feel at home here ... Minor disasters include the fact that the tractor that came to rotovate the garden which was full of brambles broke the sewage pipe to the septic tank: when I got another guy to come and rotovate a strip of land above the house (where I've decided to shift the garden to) he succeeded in cutting the pipe which carries the water supply ... No doubt it happens to everyone who is mad enough to become a householder. I remember that you were dubious when I explained that I was hoping to move in and start work on my book almost immediately. Nevertheless, I'm still enthusiastic about my builder, Jerry O'Mahony, who is a very likeable and unusual human being and the closest thing I have to a friend around here.

Anyway, things are now much more under control. I've planted some forty odd trees, including two pear trees and a crab apple, and you'd be proud of my vegetable-growing efforts ... I've also planted lettuces, onions, sweet corn, chicory, endives, celeriac, watercress, courgettes and green peppers so you see what heavy horticulture has been going on. Mainly weeds seem to be coming up so far but I expect a big vegetable glut later on in the year so you must come and help eat them ... I'd love to see you. (I could reimburse you for the flight and would very much like to do so.) ...

I'll write again when I've got my hands on enough gas to get you from and back to the airport. You'll like it here. It's very beautiful.

Love to you,
Jim

To Patricia Moynagh

Saltwater House
18 May 1979

Dear Patricia,

Many thanks indeed for your letter. How clever of you to get it to me! Naturally I was delighted to get it, having been quite cut off from everyone since leaving England. I've had six weeks of chaos and muddle but now feel quite at home here. But it's very hard work. If I'd known what I was letting myself in for I'm sure I would have quailed at the prospect. I'm only now beginning to get back to writing ...

Your pussycat picture [14] is in a commanding position in the living-room beside the fireplace and was greatly admired the other day by the four year old daughter of my builder. I meant to offer it back to you before leaving but somehow forgot in the confusion (I'm very glad to keep it, I need hardly add). Your coffee machine is marvellous and I feel guilty about taking it off you. It even came with some ground coffee wedged in it ...

Love to you,
Jim

To Bridget O'Toole

Saltwater House
19 May 1979

Dear Bridget,

This is by way of a signal rocket as the postal strike in these parts never seems like ending. A friend called David Simpson who has just spent a week here between jobs and is now going back to Blighty is going to post it for me.

A move is hard work at my advanced age but I seem to have settled in OK and so far I have not missed London. It's extremely beautiful here and very peaceful. There is still quite a lot to be done to the house in one way or another. The perils of owning things: I worry intermittently about the roof and the chimney and the water supply but with luck this will pass away presently ...

Love to you,
Jim

To Robert and Kathie Parrish

Saltwater House
19 May 1979

Dear Bob and Kathie,

Many thanks indeed for sending on the stuff. It was quite astonishing to have some contact with the outside world again and your letters were extremely welcome ... I don't know whether you noticed, by the way, that the Ayatollah is promising a place in the Islamic Heaven for whoever bumps off the Shah [15] and that now a Teheran newspaper is throwing in a package holiday to Mecca. If it goes on like this I may be tempted myself ...

When David Simpson, the kind transporter of this letter, was discussing his trip in London there was frequent mention of Black & Decker and the benefits of 'hard physical work in the open air'. However, he has spent most of his time crouching in a bush in the garden out of sight of the Management, painting a picture of the house. To some extent he has redeemed himself, though, by cooking delicious lentil and minestrone soups ... Today the sun is shining, the sea is sparkling and all seems right with Kilcrohane if not the world. I plan to start serious work on my novel again next week: that is provided I can find enough petrol to get back here after taking David to the airport. I was somewhat premature with my assertion that the petrol shortage was over.

All good wishes and love to you both,

Jim

[*handwritten*] ... P.S. My crab-apple tree has actually flowered!

To Ann Colville

Saltwater House
Kilcrohane
14 June 1979

Dear Ann,

... I'm afraid this [reply] will have to be very telegrammatic again because the Parrishes are just paying a flying visit and I still have a million letters to write.

I like the sound of Italy but it will be a while before I know what I'm doing. A number of imponderables are hanging over me, chief of which are my book, my mother, and the roof of the house, which I feel I must have replaced before winter. Also I might have to go to India in October for my book, it won't become clear for a few weeks: I'm working hard on it now. However, since I shall have to leave here while Jerry is putting on the roof etc. and doing the window and loo, it might well suit me to take a break in October. I shall try and get a letter to you once I've decided. There's also a family plan for my mother to spend a week or two here in the autumn and her time-table is not very moveable as she has to get a hospital bed laid on for my father while she is away. Therefore you must consider Italy to be a long shot (with me – why not with the Italian from upstairs? He sounds a promising development) and if any other possibilities come up do please snap them up as I really can't be counted on. I won't really feel happy leaving here or even having a visit until I've got at least a first draft of my book out of the way. That sounds inhospitable but it's better not to make any pretence about it and it goes for every-one ...

Well, I'd like to write more but I can't. Take care of yourself.

Love,
Jim

To David Simpson

Gortafane House [*sic*]
Kilcrohane
Not sure what date or day of week it is

Dear David,

... I must apologise, by the way, for giving you the impression that you were supposed to work for bed and board as opposed to heavy-handed teasing to that effect. You really weren't supposed to. Re above name of house, I'm trying to decide whether or not to go back to it as the locals can't be persuaded to call it anything else. It was an important farm in the area at one time, Jerry says (sh. for Jeremiah), that's why. I think it was just Gortafane the way *Mon Repos* is *Mon Repos* and up yours, postman.

I tried to catch your act on Radio 4, [16] the only sensible BBC programme I can get but somehow missed it. Or maybe the Irish engineers have a way of putting the BBC through a strainer so that only selected items reach us.

I'm afraid this letter has to be very telegrammatic on account of Bob and Kathie returning to Blighty almost immediately and a number of other missives to write. There are two large-scale bits of news. The first is, I found a dead rat by the fireplace this morning! One has to nerve oneself up a bit to this sort of thing if one lives in the country, I suppose. The second is: I've caught several fish! I've only actually caught one large one, which I ate (delicious): the others I threw back with the intention of catching them again next year. All pollack, by the way ...

I really enjoyed having you here. Come again immediately.

> Yours
> Jim

To Malcolm and Clare Dean

> Kilcrohane
> Thursday [undated]

Dear Malcolm and Clare,[17]
... I've settled in to my new life much better than I expected I would, mainly thanks to the blissful setting of the house ... and thanks also to one or two particularly friendly locals. People are very nice around here though I do miss my sophisticated London pals (Malcolm, in this context only, is classified as a sophisticated London pal): maybe it's just the middle classes I miss. I wish you could come here and see it: I think it would suit you. It's a nice mxture of wild and not so wild.

My book is at last making a little progress though it has a rival now – viz. fishing off the rocks. I know no one is going to believe me but I've actually been catching fish and eating them, great fun and beats writing into a cocked hat (Malcolm may need a metaphor or two now that he's back at the *Guardian*).

Thank you, Clare, for the chicken brick recipes ... I've used it several times with great success, last night with Bob and Kathie being the last.

Malcolm, I'm delighted to hear that you're going to have a son to deal with as well as the six daughters. [18] He may prove a useful ally if at any stage women's lib breaks out in your household when there's an International on the tv.

Finally, I've spent countless man-hours husbanding the gourmet seed-garden you gave me when I was leaving London ... What I have greatest hopes for is the celeriac: baby hares living in the garden keep getting under the netting and nibbling away at the lettucey stuff. Wild life here is wonderful ...

Must finish now. Take care of yourselves,

Yours

R. Crusoe (ret'd)

To Carole Tucker

Gortafane House

15 June 1979

Dear Carole,

That will teach me to boast about my vegetable garden. I went out for a walk the other day and when I came back a herd of cows was just polishing off the last of the cabbages. They'd also trampled on other stuff and nibbled at the pear trees I'd just planted. However, apart from the cabbages the rest of the damage may not be too serious. As you will see, this is the sort of cornpone drama that fills my day while you sophisticated folk have such fancy items as the Jeremy Thorpe Show! ... [19]

I can't think of any way of communicating with you except by courier. I don't know anyone around here who has a telex ... Come to India with me for a month or more this winter, or possibly Mauritius if I don't have to go to India for my book. I shall proba-bly spend Christmas in Paris so we could maybe discuss it there ...

All this sounds a bit crazy. Anyway we must meet somehow.

Love to you,

Jim

To John Curtis

Gortafane House

19 June 1979

Dear John,

... Life is bliss here, despite rabbits that eat my crops and bees that have taken up residence in the wall of my bedroom, not to mention leaks in the roof.

The book is coming along. Perhaps we could meet in Paris in October, where you could read it, make suggestions and, indeed, hand me a cheque for the outstanding £5,000 due on delivery. If the postal strike hasn't finished by early September I'll see if I can phone you.*

All good wishes

Yours

Jim

* If it <u>has</u>, let me know if this arrangement would suit you. I shall be leaving anyway in October while alterations are made to the house (before the winter storms blow in) and I may possibly be going to India, if I think it would be any use.

To Deborah Rogers

Gortafane

19 June 1979

Dear Deb, [20]

... I spend my evenings fishing off the rocks for mackerel and pollack and an old grandpa seal who looks as if he's wearing a Twenties bathing cap treads water thirty yards away and watches me with the air of someone who thinks he knows a better way of doing it.

Word has filtered through that a firm in America called Berkeley (?) or Barclay (?) [21] has bought the paperback rights of *Troubles* and my *Singapore* book. Would it be worth trying to interest them in *Krishnapur*, too? I assume Warner Bros have finished with it.

Bees have just taken up residence in one of the many cracks in my bedroom wall. If this goes on I shall soon feel qualified to drone away about Nature on some remote BBC radio programme.

Love

Jim

To Margaret Drabble

Gortfahane [*sic*] House
[undated] early July 1979

Dear Maggie,

Three months' worth of mail is pelting on my balding but grateful head, including your nice postcard from/of Turkey. Things are OK here – indeed sometimes I think that I didn't know the meaning of *douceur de vivre* until I came here (up yours, Talleyrand!). The sea (the sea, as Iris would say) [22] is very important in moving to the country as an anti-claustrophobant. I know you sometimes think of a similar move for your declining years – i.e. not yet! The locals keep coming up with different versions of what this house is really called. I'm making the above the official one. ANE is pronounced ARN in these parts. Hope your book is going well.

Love to you,
Jim

To Robert Parrish

Gortfahane House
6 July 1979

Dear Bob (not forgetting Wendy Wife),

Many thanks for the pictures of the house. One can only say: 'What a splendid residence for a gentleman!' I'm glad you didn't catch the owner pissing in the nettles with your candid camera.

I forget whether the bees had arrived in a hole in the wall over the back door when you were here – I think not. This is considered a great piece of luck hereabouts. By a coincidence Jerry had told me a couple of days earlier that he was about to purchase a swarm. It never occurred to me that he wouldn't be a bee-keeper as well as everything else. He came over and got three-quarters of them into a hive where they started a new colony but I still have the originals who have got fucking or whatever bees do and replenished themselves. I've grown fond of them and hope to buy a hive to house them in presently.

Life has been deep bliss here for the past couple of weeks. It's a sensational place to be in good weather. But there are a lot of bugs abroad in the warm evenings ... Naturally I've been spending my days fishing instead of writing. I'm slowly improving my technique and succeeded in dragging last night's supper* from the waves. It works out more expensive than buying fish at Harrod's because I keep losing bits of tackle but it's fresher ...

But the days aren't long enough. Add to that the avalanche of mail which has just descended on me delivered by a delightful postman who looks as if he might be a son of Fernandel [23] .... There was also a telegram from a certain small person in Beverly Hills [24] demanding that I ring him while he's at Claridges. My first guilty thought was that I might simply ignore it. I'm sure to be safe in Kilcrohane which isn't exactly Gstaad. Though if Schull goes on the way it's going maybe the international set will begin appearing. Anyway, it's hard enough to get hold of him with an automatic phone in the same city. If he should complain in your presence that I haven't rung him please point out that phoning out of Ireland isn't all that simple and suggest he writes me letters. I'd have thought he'd be thankful. Tell him I agree to everything. But of course he will probably have moved on before you get this.

Other news: my courgettes have suddenly decided to grow. Bob, after you left it occurred to me that I hadn't thanked you properly for the great trouble you went to on my behalf rounding up mail from friends etc. not to mention the oceans of booze, frozen chickens etc. Anyway, thanks now. Let me hear how Bert, [25] househunting etc are going.

Love to you both,

Jim

*STOP PRESS: More major fish have been caught in the meantime.

To his parents

Gortfahane House

8 July 1979

Dear Mum and Dad,

... Nothing much to report except that the weather, after a week of sunshine, has turned damp and foggy. I've taken the opportunity of making my elderflower wine today. The elderflowers outside my back door are particularly fine ... I'm keen to have bees around as there aren't that many insects about in Spring out here to pollinate my fruit trees; also there's lots of heather not far away and you remember that lovely 'eather 'oney we had in Southport ...

Well, lots of love,

Jim

To Michelle Pearce [26]

Gortfahane* House
[*Handwritten*]* This is the original name, it appears.
8 July 1979

Dear Michelle,

... I'm now paying the penalty of those blissful weeks without mail or phone (still no phone, of course) by having to deal with all sorts of dull business matters which normally don't come so concentrated. Anyway, so far things look as if they're going to be OK here. The beauty of the place is quite spectacular and I've settled in to my new life pretty well. There are still lots of things that need doing to the house, including a new roof, and there's such a vigorous growth of weeds in the garden that I shall be obliged either to buy a goat or let most of it run wild ...

The only mild pangs of nostalgia for London I've suffered have been connected with painting exhibitions I hear about on *Kaleidoscope* and can't trudge down the road to see. Both the Schiele and the Sargent [27] would have interested me. I guess they are more interesting in anticipation than in reality ...

I'm working hard on a new book, having set myself the impossible deadline of October to finish it. I certainly won't make it if the weather is as good as it's been recently. Well, have a good time in America.

Love to the boys and yourselves,

Jim

To Carole Tucker

Gorfahane House
13 July 1979

Dear Carole,

... I've been trying to write but there are so many competing interests – the prime one at the moment is fishing off the rocks. I caught one yesterday which weighed 3¼ pounds! Then a colony of bees has come ... and I'm thinking of turning them into my feudal retainers. There's lots of heather around and I have a craving for heather honey ...

I haven't been too lonely so far, though of course I miss you and my other friends, some of whom I hear on the radio occasionally, which is nice.

I've written to my editor suggesting we meet for me to hand him my book in October in Paris, but it's more likely to be November. Maybe we (you and I) could meet then, too, if you can't get over here. Write and tell me what you think.

Anyway, love to you,
Jim

To Brian, Rose and Nina Knox Peebles

Gortfahane House
13 July 1979

Dear Brian, Rose & Nina,
Many thanks for your combined letter which only arrived yesterday having spent Heaven knows how long on the way. Brian, you must certainly come and see me if you visit the *Cork Examiner*. It takes about 2 car hours from Cork.

The directions are as follows: three miles past Kilcrohane on the road from Durrus turn right at a green shop. Over brow of hill turn right at T-junction, then fork left at cattle pen. Gortfahane House is first on right (you can tell it by the weeds) ...

There is so much to do outside that I find it hard to stay at my desk. A spell of bad weather is the only hope for getting my next book out on time.

Anyway, love to you all,

Jim

To his mother

Gortfahane House
16 July 1979

Dear Mum,
Just to say thanks for your telegram and by all means come on October 6 for two weeks. I'm writing today to John Curtis to cancel or postpone the arrangement I had to meet him in Paris in October to discuss my new book. I was probably going to do this anyway as there is doubt that my book will be ready by then ... Anyway, your autumn holiday is the important thing. And you can show me how to prune my pear trees.

My carpets are now down, thank heavens, and I'm quite pleased with them. More about this and other matters when I write again in a few days. This is an interim dispatch to give you the go-ahead on the holiday.

Lots of love,
Jim

To G.M. Arthursen

Gortfahane House
18 July

Dear GMA

... Certainly moving from central London to a community deep in the country and not on the road to anywhere has not been as much of an upset as I feared that it might be. People are very friendly, helpful and interested in you, and with a great sense of fun. This afternoon I was walking back along the cliffs feeling annoyed with myself because I'd lost part of my fishing tackle (having got it snagged inaccessibly in the depths) when I was joined by an old farmer with a walking stick who laughed me out of it, and for good measure told me about some of the terrible storms he had witnessed, pointing out on the rocks how far the water had come up and adding a few fishing tips: a much more valuable catch than the unfortunate fish I'd been planning on for my supper.

When I came here in the Spring and the weather was still cold and grey a young man told me, 'Ah, just wait till the summer, it's like the Garden of Eden', and indeed it is. Things grow here with unbelievable vigour, particularly weeds.* Some onions I planted not long ago have disappeared under a green tide and I have to sift through the vegetation when I want one. However I've devoted far too little time to horticulture having given myself an impossible deadline for another novel. When in London I pictured myself out here with nothing to do but quite the opposite has turned out to be the case. Every evening I look forward to bed and a few pages of *Middlemarch* which I'm greatly enjoying but usually begin to drowse over it before I've properly picked up the threads from the previous evening ...

My move went off quite well, thanks – merely a broken plate or two and half a lamp missing – in other words, nothing at all. My father continues to hold his own, I'm happy to say, apart from falling over and grazing his elbow. Obviously one of the difficult things about getting older is the constant readjustment one has to make of the mental image one has of oneself so that it continues to correspond with reality. Sometimes I find myself that I leap for a rock which has been mentally sanctioned but find it not so easy to get there ...

    All good wishes to you,

Jim

*Maybe no *mauvaises herbes* grew in the Garden of Eden, tho'.

To Tom Gover [28]

Gortfahane House

[undated]

Dear Tom,

How are you? When are you coming to see me?

    I hear very complimentary things about your brilliant house-mastering from my pals in Dublin.

    Anyway, I hope we meet up one of these days.

Yours

Jim Farrell

To Bridget O'Toole

Gortfahane House

22 July 1979

Dear Bridget,

... I'm currently having a blitz on my novel in the hope of having it finished by the time [my mother] gets here. It's also possible that I might take a holiday in Italy or Paris or both in November, perhaps spending Xmas in Paris – but it'll depend partly on money, my novel etc. I really should get my house re-roofed before the winter storms blow in. My local friend and builder says it might be possible to do this in November although it's late in the year. He says the wind sometimes settles in the north-east for a few days: if so he could clap a roof on swiftly: otherwise I'd have to wait for Spring, dodging flying slates. It's very like the Majestic here. I even have what looks like a root growing up through the kitchen floor (Jerry claims it isn't: he says it's the legs of a table in what used to be the dairy which were set in concrete and which he had to saw off in order to get the table out) ...

I've been writing all day and I'm a bit weary. I shall now go fishing and see if I can catch my supper. Paisley really is quite bizarre. You wouldn't get away with him in a novel. I liked the exchange when he was being drummed out of the Europarliament with a Fianna Fáil [29] deputy nearby.

Paisley: 'You're a papish lout!'

FF dep.: 'And you're a bigot!'

This was reported on Radio Éireann. A papish lout, indeed! ...

Love

Jim

P.S. ... I've been too busy to make even a feeble start on the recorder. But if you bring yours it might be a good way of scaring the birds from my vegetable patch.

To Robert and Kathie Parrish

Gortfahane House

23 July 1979

Dear Bob and Kathie,

Many pieces of mail have been arriving from you in the past few days, some of them posted in April. They included your hilarious account of Lazar's visit, but who is Mary Soames? [30] (I've asked everyone in Kilcrohane and nobody seems to know.) Actually, your letter was so funny I couldn't resist reading it to Marion Wheeler [31] who was here with her boy-friend whom I quite liked, a mild, sensitive, somewhat henpecked sort of fellow. Marion is uphill all the way. I invited them, perhaps rashly, to spend the night here and when they departed after 24 hours or so they left their erstwhile host with seriously battered ears ... The one useful thing she could have done, by the way, she flunked. She could not tell me who Mary Soames is.

My other piece of news is this: my neighbours ... have arrived. As I passed by on my way back from fishing the other evening a girl in her twenties waddled out wanting to see what I'd caught (I was on the point of saying *à la* Bob Parrish: 'I'll show you mine if you show me ...' but ... I decided it was no deal). The next day a Dutchman ... in his late sixties called in to introduce himself; I said brightly: 'Oh, I think I spoke to your daughter yesterday evening.' He replied stiffly: 'She is not my daughter.' If you ever need any hints on how to get off on the right foot with your neighbours please ask. Well, despite this gaffe they keep inviting me in for drinks. They're bored stiff, I'm afraid, and Jerry is predicting that it won't be long before I'm putting up fortifications. Actually they are both quite genial but ... deeply boring. They make Jack Hedley [32] sound like Aldous Huxley.

Apart from that I'm working hard on my book. The weather has been quite cold. Fish not biting. Now I must go into Bantry to do my week's shopping.

By the way, when I had finally got through to Swifty in Claridges with 96p. worth of 5p. pieces it turned out he had nothing to say. He said: 'Can you call me back. I'm in a meeting.' I said that was quite impossible. So he improvised a few vaguely encouraging remarks about my book. Then he said: 'How did you know I was here?' 'You sent me a telegram,' I grated. 'Oh, did I?' he replied. 'Well, do keep in touch from time to time.'

All the best and love to both,

Jim

To his parents

Gortfahane House
25 July 1979

Dear Mum and Dad,

Just a quick reply to your letter of the 10th as I'm going into Bantry to buy some food and visit the library ... Some cows got in and stood glumly among my dwarf green beans near the barn but amazingly only damaged one or two. Actually I was more afraid they'd damage the young Leylandii I've planted but they managed to avoid them completely. The farmer's wife from up the road arrived just as I was showing them out, a little old lady: she was terribly upset and apologetic but I said there hadn't been much damage. It was my own fault for not having better defences in any case.

I must dash now or I'll miss the library.

Lots of love,
Jim

To Ann Colville

Gortfahane House (renamed)

26 July 1979

Dear Ann,

... I thought of writing to you yesterday but I'm glad I didn't as ... in the meantime my mother has declared her intention of coming to stay with me here from October 6th to the 20th. It has to be then because that's when the hospital will look after my father ... Then, depending on finances (I'm beginning to run short of available cash), I shall head for France or Italy, being in one or the other, probably Paris, for Christmas. It's essential that we should be in Paris at the same time sometime so that I can introduce you to Larry and Virginia. [33] What is annoying is that I have almost enough to buy a small apt in Paris but not quite – yet. Otherwise it wd be perfect for you to have while you need it. Finding a place to live is one of the biggest headaches about living in Paris unless you're a millionaire. There are one or two small signs 'no bigger than a man's hand' indeed, that I may be in a position to give the money-tree another shake quite soon – but nothing one could rely on.

I'm making rapid progress with my novel but I'm still behind schedule. People keep barging in on me the way they never did in London ...

The carpets have arrived and look OK but perhaps a little on the dark and institutional side. Things will be better when I get the more colourful curtains and bigger window. I've had neither time nor cash to do anything about that ...

Now I must go to the post in Kilcrohane before it leaves.

Love to you

Jim

[*Handwritten*] P.S. Fancy you bumping into Maureen [34] like that. I'm surprised she didn't make a pass at you.

To Robert Parrish

Gortfahane House

28 July 1979

Dear Bob,

Disaster has struck the rapidly balding head of the Laird o' Gortfahane in the shape of a demand from HM Customs and Excise for a VAT payment of £2,332.67 no less. In my innocence I <u>thought</u> I'd paid this before leaving England. However, due to some goddam strike they didn't cash my cheque and have only just tried to do so. I thought I came away with a bit more money than I expected ... alas, not for long. This means I shall have to tap my Swiss resources ...

The result of all this is that I'm working hard on my book. BBC2 are allowing their fancy to be tickled by the idea of adapting *Krishnapur* 'in 3 or 4 parts' but this has happened so often before that I can hardly raise an eyebrow, let alone count on it for hot dinners.[35] The fish have stopped biting, too, and fog has cloaked Gortfahane for the past few days. A letter from you arrived this morning saying you'd just been to Paris and Zaire seemed to be on. I thought: Great! But then I looked at the date ... April 6th.

No other news. I still haven't seen Wolfie and Curly but a man from the BBC staying in Schull is threatening me with a visit (<u>not</u> re *Krishnapur*) and I might try and invite them all over (on the other hand I might just go fishing) ...

Passing through Ahakista the other day there was a collection of huge yachts moored outside the Warrens' place and a major barbecue for wealthy people going on apace.

Love to you both,
Jim

To Carole Tucker

Gortfahane House
30 July 1979

Dear Carole,

There are no pretty women around here but there are lots of rabbits and foxes, and hares that stand up in the fields as you walk by and wonder 'What the hell – ?' And the old seal that wallows on his back watching me fish from the rocks. So you wouldn't have found a pretty housekeeper if you had come in June. However, as it has turned out it is probably all for the best, particularly if it means getting your marriage going again on a better footing.[36] One of the few virtues that I sometimes suspect myself of (if that's what it is) is a reluctance to interfere in other people's marriages and if you had come in June the weather was so good and the scenery so spectacular I'd have thrown a golden net over you, not to mention putting you to work as my gardener. I wouldn't now be in the fix I am – having to sift through the grass and bracken ...

I have been planning, optimistically, to finish my novel on October 20 so that I can give the typescript to my poor mother to dump on my brother, from whom my editor can pick it up. Your re-entry, not to say 'splash-down', into married bliss will sharpen my resolve in this respect, and I may even introduce a Daily Time Record to get myself going properly (I'm running behind schedule at the moment). Life has a remarkable way, what with postal strikes and visiting mothers, of countering all my attempts, admittedly feeble, of setting myself in domestic contentment, however fleetingly. It seems determined to keep me as a book-writing machine. Ah well, it has its compensations ...

With love,
Jim

To Claude and Anna Simha

Gortfahane House
2 August 1979

My dear friends,

... Everything here is going well, more or less, but I'm working on a new novel night and day to try to pay for this house. Whenever the sea is calm at high tide I go fishing. By a happy coincidence, it seems that the house is just beside one of the best places in the area for that! This is not to say that I can always count on fish for supper, but I'm catching some. Mostly what is called here 'pollack' (our neighbours caught mackerel the other day) which my dictionary translates as *merlan jaune* or *colin*, [37] but I am not sure that's right. The biggest up until now weighed one and a half kilos. I can only use a light rod with my one arm, so I'm waiting for you to give me a hand with the monsters! Yes, fishing is permitted here during the winter (everything is permitted here, and anyway the police rarely come to such an isolated spot as this) but people tell me that there are few fish then. The sea has to be very calm before the fish come near the rocks. I hope to learn more of the techniques and best places to fish.

At low tide yesterday I found a promising new spot which is sheltered from the weather and where the water is deep. An old seal ... spends his time with the gannets, and between them I think they eat all there is to catch here. The seal came within five metres yesterday, just below the rock from which I was fishing.

I hope to finish my novel in November, and as soon as I have I will come to Paris for a bit, maybe with a girl (there are none here). The weather is very bad here in winter, so I shall spend a few weeks either in Paris or Italy ...

I requested a telephone, and guess how long I have to wait? Two years! A new Dutch neighbour (the Dutch and even the French are buying up houses here like madmen) caused great amusement for the good people of the parish the other day when he asked at the post office in Kilcrohane for a 'phone to be installed in his house 'before Monday'!

Goodbye then, happy holidays, and see you soon,

Jim

P.S. Life is good! (for the moment)!

To Ann Colville

Gortfahane House
4 August 1979

Dear Ann,

Many thanks for your letter, which arrived this morning. It was a nice surprise, having taken a mere four days – no, three days! Can the Irish post keep this up? It verges on fanaticism ...

Despite the agreeableness of getting your letter I've become apprehensive of the postman: a couple of days ago he brought a demand from HM's Customs and Excise for a VAT payment I owe and wrongly assumed I'd paid ... Anyway, it makes the Paris flat a bit further off. On the other hand –

A BBC fellow on holiday in Schull called on me this afternoon ... He's doing a tv programme on writers (a fairly motley selection) and places and vaguely had it in mind that he might do me in Ireland. I was discouraging and said I was only interested in Simla. However, he did seem to think the BBC had decided to do a serial of *The Siege of Krishnapur* if we can agree on terms ... If it is anything reasonable I might take it instead of hanging on for a movie which keeps almost appearing but never quite does. But these deals always take such a time, not to mention actually finding a flat, transferring money etc. You'd be back in Canada before anything could be done. Just buying a place takes an age as we both know, even with the money ready and waiting.

Well, I'm pressing on with my novel at a good speed but I have serious misgivings about its quality.

Love to you,
Jim

[*Handwritten*] P.S. *Time* magazine was very rude about me, likening me to 'a windy raconteur at the bar of Raffles Hotel who you have to edge away from!' I haven't been fishing much in the past few days but I have discovered a place where there are sea-urchins, said to be delicious by Jane Grigson who has a recipe for sea-urchin omelette. How's that for sophistication!

P.P.S. Sunday evening: caught 4 major fish yesterday.

To David Simpson

Gortfahane House
5 August 1979

Dear David,

Many thanks for your letter on its most impressive stationery: as I thought, the affairs of international do-gooding organisations [38] are always attended (see similar complaint in *Singapore Grip*) by drastic luxury ... Do you still have a sheet of that paper? If so, you'll notice that at the bottom it says: *salles de conference – parcs privés pour 60 voitures*. I mis-read the last word delightfully – *parcs privés pour 60 voyeurs*! And thought, these Swiss really think of everything ...

Re your next visit to Kilcrohane, I'm working night and day on my book at the moment ... However, there may be a 'window' as we call it in the Kilcrohane Aeronautical and Space Administration for a few days in late September ... The chances are, if the only occupant when you come is the Laird o' Gortfahane himself that you would be left very much more to your own devices, which I'm sure wouldn't worry you. I'd pick you up, hand over the car to you, and get back to writing. On the other hand, I might by then be anxious for riotous entertainment (e.g. a visit to the Stella cinema in Bantry). It's impossible to tell the exact state my book will be in at that moment (in fact, we don't yet know the moment). But if I am still immersed it would be better if you brought a companion: you could even have the less damp room as I've taken to sleeping in the one that curls your pages when I have visitors: it means I can type in the morning without feeling I'm disturbing them. [*handwritten note added here:*] (the visitors, not the curled pages) ...

All the best in the meantime,

Jim

To his parents

Gortfahane House
8 August 1979

Dear Mum and Dad,
... It won't be at all inconvenient for you to come in October. I only hope the weather will be better than it has been during August ... It has been pouring all day today again. This doesn't bother me as I'm handcuffed to my typewriter but it's a nuisance for the holiday-makers ... I caught four good-sized fish the other evening – two of them were over 2 lbs, the other two were a pound each, which is a good size for me. I think I may have to take to filleting the bigger fish before putting them in the freezer if it begins to get full up. They'd also be easier to handle when using them later. Of the fish I caught the other evening I ate one, gave one to my Dutch neighbours, and put the other two in the freezer. It's a handy source of protein.

I'm going to have to get you to do some deep thinking about the most trouble-free method of horticulture here. It's clear that it will have to be some enclosed space such as a large greenhouse because apart from the weeds, the birds and rabbits are so plentiful one spends all one's time trying to rig up defences ...

I just heard on the news that Nicholas Monsarrat [39] had died in London. Pity his last book wasn't better received.

Lots of love,
Jim

[*Handwritten*] P.S. I'll make sure I have petrol!

To Robert Parrish

Gortfahane House
9 August 1979

Dear Bob,
... There's no news from here except that this time she's gone too far,

it's all finished between us. I refer, of course, to Mrs Cronin from whom I was unwise enough to try and buy some gas the other day, Bantry being bone dry (at least of gas, it was raining inside and out). Such sighings and poutings and veiled innuendoes and probings and 'Mind you I've said nothings'. If I had been trying to squeeze the petrol out of her nipples it could hardly have been any more of a performance. And all for £3 worth!

I had a letter from David Simpson the other day, saying you were just off to New York 'to see whether you might be able to live there'. No, no, I said to myself, the Parrishes could not now be thinking of yet another place in which they might be about to set up house, David must have got it wrong. A terrible suspicion has since been growing in my mind, however, that maybe you are considering such a move. Without the benefit of my advice, too! A disgraceful state of affairs. And what are you doing in Venice of all places. Has Sam Spiegel brought his yacht in there, ignoring the fact that it is inland? ...

I heard Bert T. on the radio last night being interviewed about *Deathwatch* (cheery title) and talking about the risks for movie directors of becoming voyeurs and how it was one of the central problems of the time – yawn – yawn ... Such mortal strivings seem far away out here on the Sea of Tranquillity where even a telegram from Lazar comes as the merest stirring in the trees or the faintest sighing in the chimney sort of thing.

Love to Wendy and self,

Jim

[*Handwritten*] P.S. I'm going to lunch with Wolf and Curly tomorrow. He's working on some dull-sounding tv series.

To Rosemary Legge (Weidenfeld)

Gortfahane House
10 August 1979

Dear R'mary,

Thanks for your note re my new book. I can't be very helpful, however, at present as I haven't finally decided on the title and doubt if there's any point in announcing the book without it.

I'm running a bit behind schedule – but I'm still confident that barring some unforeseen disaster I'll provide you with a novel of 80,000 to 100,000 words before the end of the year as agreed in my contract.

Do hope all goes well with you.

Love

Jim

P.S. Your letter just arrived. I hope to answer in a day or two.

Postscript

September 1979

'Barring some unforeseen disaster' he had written automatically. On the following day, 11 August 1979, Jim Farrell was drowned while fishing, after routinely writing without a break until 4pm. Rod in hand, he was washed off the 'promising' rock into Dunmanus Bay, in the treacherous early stages of a storm that ultimately took fifteen more lives in that year's Fastnet Race. His body drifted in the depths, unseen, around the long Sheep's Head Peninsula [1] and right across to the far side of Bantry Bay, near Castletownbere.

42 Elers Road
London W 13 9QD
30th September 1979

Dear Dr Simha,

I am writing to you in case you have not heard the tragic news that my brother James Farrell died on 11th August in Ireland.

It was his habit after his day's work to go fishing from some rocks near his house. How exactly it happened is not clear, but it seems that he was swept from the rocks by a large wave and was carried away before anybody could help him. His body was eventually recovered about 2 weeks ago.

As you can imagine, we are all shattered by what has happened as Jim meant so much to so many different people ...

I am very sorry to have to bring you this sad news.

Yours sincerely,
Richard Farrell

From Sonia Orwell to Hilary Spurling

100 bis rue d'Assas
75006 Paris
September 1979

My dear Hilary,

... I found a two days' old *Herald Tribune* and read about Jim. I wanted to telephone at once, I wanted to write at once, but there I was on holiday in Brittany ... unable to communicate my grief to the people I was with ... I mean the unbearable bit of death is that not only will we not see Jim again and that's just terrible, if only for his smile and giggles and sudden dogmatic outbursts and his whole general elegance which did so enhance any room he was in, but also that he won't see anything again ...

Much love
Sonia

A Disused Shed in Co. Wexford [1]

Let them not forget us, the weak souls among the asphodels.
                                                    — Seferis, *Mythistorema*

(for J.G. Farrell)

Even now there are places where a thought might grow —
Peruvian mines, worked out and abandoned
To a slow clock of condensation,
An echo trapped for ever, and a flutter
Of wild-flowers in the lift-shaft,
Indian compounds where the wind dances
And a door bangs with diminished confidence,
Lime crevices behind rippling rain-barrels,
Dog corners for bone burials;
And in a disused shed in Co. Wexford,

Deep in the grounds of a burnt-out hotel,
Among the bathtubs and the washbasins
A thousand mushrooms crowd to a keyhole.
This is the one star in their firmament
Or frames a star within a star.
What should they do there but desire?
So many days beyond the rhododendrons
With the world waltzing in its bowl of cloud,
They have learnt patience and silence
Listening to the rooks querluous in the high wood.

They have been waiting for us in a foetor
Of vegetable sweat since civil war days,
Since the gravel-crunching, interminable departure
Of the expropriated mycologist.
He never came back, and light since then
Is a keyhole rusting gently after rain.

Spiders have spun, flies dusted to mildew
And once a day, perhaps, they have heard something —
A trickle of masonry, a shout from the blue
Or a lorry changing gear at the end of the lane.

There have been deaths, the pale flesh flaking
Into the earth that nourished it;
And nightmares, born of these and the grim
Dominion of stale air and rank moisture.
Those nearest the door grow strong —
'Elbow room! Elbow room!'
The rest, dim in a twilight of crumbling
Utensils and broken pitchers, groaning
For their deliverance, have been so long
Expectant that there is left only the posture.

A half century, without visitors, in the dark —
Poor preparation for the cracking lock
And creak of hinges; magi, moonmen,
Powdery prisoners of the old regime,
Web-throated, stalked like triffids, racked by drought
And insomnia, only the ghost of a scream
At the flash-bulb firing-squad we wake them with
Shows there is life yet in their feverish forms.
Grown beyond nature now, soft food for worms,
They lift frail heads in gravity and good faith.

They are begging us, you see, in their wordless way,
To do something, to speak on their behalf
Or at least not to close the door again.
Lost people of Treblinka and Pompeii!
'Save us, save us,' they seem to say,
'Let the god not abandon us
Who have come so far in darkness and in pain.
We too had our lives to live.
You with your light meter and relaxed itinerary,
Let not our native labours have been in vain!' [2]

DEREK MAHON
(from *The Snow Party* 1975)

Chronology

1935	JGF born on 23 January, the second of three sons. The Farrell family live at 15 Hampton Court Road, West Derby, Liverpool.
1939	On the outbreak of war, with his parents and older brother, JGF goes to live in his elderly godfather's capacious house: Boscobel, 1 Preston Road, Southport. He attends kindergarten in Crofton School, nearby. A younger brother is born in 1943.
1944	JGF is sent to Terra Nova, a prep school at Jodrell Bank, near Chester.
1947	The family move to Ireland, buying The Gwanda, Shankill, County Dublin, a comfortable family house on five acres. He commutes home by train and ferry in the school holidays.
1948	By now Head Boy at Terra Nova, he wins a scholarship to Rossall, at Fleetwood, near Blackpool, where he joins Spread Eagle House.
1950	His first publication, in the school magazine; his essays are soon a regular feature. He is an all-round scholar, drawn to languages, and a fixture on the first XV rugby team, until eventual injury forces rest. In his final year he spends a term at École des Roches, a boys' school in Normandy.
1953	To his dismay, the Farrells move to a smaller bungalow nearer the sea, in Saval Park Road, Dalkey. JGF is awarded a deferred place at Oxford University, owing to the number of post-war entrants.
1954	He puts in a year as a junior master at Castlepark, a preparatory school in Dalkey, County Dublin.
1955	He travels to Canada, working initially at a clerical job in Montreal, and then taking well-paid labouring work up in the Arctic Circle at the DEW (Distant Early Warning)

Station in Baffin Bay.

1956   In the autumn JGF goes up to Brasenose College, Oxford, to read Law. His most pressing ambition is to earn a Blue for rugby, for which he trains enthusiastically. On 3 December he is rushed to the Slade Isolation Hospital (later amalgamated into the John Radcliffe), diagnosed with polio and placed in an iron lung. His parents are summoned and told that his life is in danger.

1957   In January he is transferred to the Wingfield Morris Orthopadic Hospital in Headington for rehabilitation, and on 22 February, five stone lighter and with permanent upper-body muscular damage, he is discharged. Back in Dublin, JGF undergoes intensive physiotherapy at the Central Remedial Clinic. In October he returns to Brasenose, switching to Modern Languages on the advice that Law would be too physically demanding.

1960   Gaining a Third, and determined to become a writer, he takes up a schoolteaching job in France at the Lycée d'État Chaptal in Mende, Lozère, on a one-year contract. Early attempts at a novel prove frustrating.

1961   JGF moves to Toulon to teach at the Interidant du Lycée, and succeeds in writing *A Man from Elsewhere*, under intense stress. When his contract is up he returns to London to seek a publisher.

1963   After several rejections, his book is taken up by Hutchinson. He rents a cheap basement flat at 48 Redcliffe Square, S.W.5, finds work at a nearby language school, and gets an agent, Jonathan Clowes.

1964–65   He returns to France, to teach at a Paris girls' school, using student accommodation at the Cité Université, on the outskirts. During the academic year he writes *The Lung* and sends it to his agent. He spends the following summer in Morocco, staying in the remote vilage of Ait Ouvrir, in the Atlas mountains. Attempts at a thriller, to make money, come to nothing.

1965   On return to London to oversee publication of *The Lung*, he leads a peripatetic existence, eventually settling at the Stanley House Hotel, a down-at-heel bedsit block in Notting Hill. He completes *A Girl in the Head*, and applies for a Harkness Fellowship to America, specifying a playwriting course at Yale Drama School. All three first novels are published under the name James Farrell.

1966   JGF is awarded a generous two-year fellowship, and Jonathan Cape publish his book during his absence. At Yale, he finds the course disillusioning, with the exception of the classes on writing for the cinema.

1967   He moves to New York to write in seclusion. Frustrated by his inability to find a structure for his latest, very different, book, he takes a short holiday in April on Block Island, Rhode Island. There he comes across the catalyst: the burned-out shell of the Ocean View Hotel. Under Harkness rules, he explores America by car that summer, making an unofficial detour to Mexico, impelled by Lowry's *Under the Volcano*. Returning to Manhattan, to a peppercorn-rent apartment at 203 E. 27th Street, he begins *Troubles*.

1968–70 Completing the novel on a shoestring in London proved a formidable effort. His publisher once more is Cape, but JGF finds a new agent, Deborah Rogers. After two unsettling moves of accommodation, he takes an inexpensive lease on a two-room, unfurnished groundfloor flat in Egerton Gardens, Knightsbridge, where he starts a new book, about India. *Troubles* is published in October under the shortened name, at his request, of J.G. Farrell.

1971   A £750 Arts Council grant enables him to spend January to March in India, researching *The Siege of Krishnapur*. In April he learns that *Troubles* has been awarded the Faber Prize. His circle of friends begins to widen, and although he is working at full stretch, he enjoys hosting convivial evenings in his small flat.

1972   When Tony Godwin of Weidenfeld & Nicolson offers to publish *The Siege of Krishnapur*, he agrees without consulting his agent.

1973   *The Siege of Krishnapur* is awarded the Booker Prize.

1974   A film option for it is taken out by David Lean, but not renewed. The legendary agent 'Swifty' Lazar becomes JGF's agent in America. Promotional visits to New York distract him from the concentration needed for his complex new book about the fall of Singapore.

1975 January and February are spent researching in Singapore, Malaysia, Thailand and Vietnam. 'My novel lies on top of me like a boulder on top of a beetle', he notes on his return. Writing *The Singapore Grip* proves arduous, and he increases the pressure by deciding to agent it himself when it is finished.

1977 Auctioning his book takes place under simultaneous anxiety about his father's ominous illness. With his book completed, he faces difficulties about his own dwindling health and problems over the lease of his flat. He considers living in Venice or Paris, before deciding on Ireland, attracted back by nostalgia and the tax exemption for writers.

1978 *The Singapore Grip* is published by Weidenfeld & Nicolson in September, to disappointing reviews. JGF house hunts in Ireland, and on impulse buys a remote cottage at Kilcrohane, on the coast of west Cork. It costs £22,000, and he negotiates a £20,000 advance for his next book, with an additional £5,000 on delivery of manuscript.

1979 In March he moves to Ireland, and is promptly cut off by lengthy postal and petrol strikes. He learns that a phone line will not be installed for another two years. But engrossed in gardening and transforming his house, he is content, and his health picks up. Once settled in, he begins his next, much less demanding, Indian book, and he takes up fishing, the first strenuous physical exercise since rugby at Oxford. On 11 August, after a day of writing, he is washed off rocks while fishing for pollack, within a few hundred yards of his new home. His body is recovered six weeks later, on the far side of Bantry Bay.

1981 *The Hill Station*, his unfinished ms, is published posthumously by Weidenfeld & Nicolson.

The Correspondents

Brigid Allen

Brigid Allen, a young graduate to whom Farrell was attracted in 1973, likened his behaviour with women who loved him to the tides of the sea, continually retreating and advancing. At the time she was supporting herself while completing her doctoral thesis by part-time teaching, and he constantly urged her to 'Give up and write'. She saw him less often after he won the Booker Prize, but early in 1975, when she was returning from Chandigarh, India, and he was returning from Singapore, they met at Moscow airport and spent the 36-hour stopover together. She last saw him shortly before he left for Ireland in 1979 at a farewell party in London, which she attended with her husband and baby son. Her memoir 'J.G. Farrell' appeared in the April/May 1992 edition of the *London Magazine*.

G.M. Arthursen

As Head of Modern Languages at Rossall, Arthursen had instilled in Farrell a love of French. The testy schoolmaster, whose nickname to the boys was Whiskey Joe, revealed his kind and erudite nature when he visited him in hospital during his treatment for polio, encouraged his forays to France, and kept up a regular correspondence in retirement. Farrell made a point of sending Arthursen a copy of each of his novels.

Vincent and John Banville

Vincent (b. 1940) and John (b. 1945) Banville, who are brothers, were born in County Wexford. Vincent's novel *An End to Flight* (Faber and Faber), under the pen-name Vincent Lawrence, came out in the year they were photographed with Farrell. A schoolteacher until 1988, he has written acclaimed short stories, several thrillers as well as four books for children. John Banville (who in 1998 became literary editor of *The Irish Times*) had written two novels, *Nightspawn* (1971) and *Birchwood* (1973) at the time of Farrell's Christmas card. His seventh, *The Book of Evidence*, was shortlisted for the Booker in 1989, and in 2005 he was awarded the Booker Prize for his novel *The Sea*.

Catherine Barton
Better known in publishing as Catherine Peters, she was Jim's editor at Cape for *Troubles*, and bore the brunt of his disillusion over outstanding royalty payments for *A Girl in the Head*. She took his side against her managing director, Tom Maschler, and as a result Farrell trusted her. In 1972 she lent him family papers containing the letters home of two long-dead young officers who had been trapped at Lucknow in 1857, and he acknowledged that these had influenced the characters of Fleury and Harry Dunstable in *The Siege of Krishnapur*. Catherine married the psychiatrist and author Anthony Storr in 1970.

Franz Beer
An Austrian artist, Beer was living in Paris with his first wife, Claire, in the early 1960s when Farrell got to know him, and 'a beautiful abstract painting by Franz Beer' appears in *The Lung*. In 1966, when Beer was teaching in America, he made an indirect but crucial contribution to *Troubles* by recommending that Farrell go to Block Island, site of the catalyst for the novel's structure, the burned-out Ocean View Hotel. Beer's work is now in public and private collections, including the Peggy Guggenheim in Venice and the Museum of Fine Arts in San Francisco.

Sally Bentlif
Although he considered Sally to be the most glamorous of her year at Lady Margaret Hall when he was at Oxford, Farrell's single letter to her from that period paints a more dashing picture of himself than he possessed at the time. Invited to the dance for her twenty-first birthday shortly beforehand, he had chosen to spend the evening with her step-father, far from the noise of the band, listening to his anecdotes about being a Japanese POW. When Sally was working as a literary agent with A.D. Peters, five years later, she was sent the typescript of *A Man from Elsewhere*, and the title

instantly reminded her of his personality at Brasenose. She married the writer Anthony Sampson, and both frequently saw Farrell in the years ahead.

Sarah Bond

Aged twenty-four when she met Farrell in New York, Sarah had grown up in Scotland and graduated from St Andrews in French and German, before joining a public relations firm in Fleet Street. Independent and plucky, qualities that instantly attracted him, she had just arrived in America when she burst into his life during his final weeks of the Harkness Fellowship. She was the inspiration for the character of her namesake Sarah in *Troubles*, but when they met again on his flying visit to New York in 1969 they both sensed that their love affair was over, and their letters became intermittent. On one of her annual Christmas visits to her family in England he invited her to accompany him to the Booker Prize lunch in January 1974, with the backhanded compliment that she was his only friend capable of dealing with a corporate lunch. They continued to write occasionally, but never saw each other again.

Jonathan Clowes

Clowes was Farrell's first agent in London, and a significant force at the start of his writing career. His office was in Upper Brook Street, and he acted for Farrell over the publication of *The Lung* and *A Girl in the Head*; Hutchinson had already taken *A Man from Elsewhere*. The two men were much the same age. Hardworking, original in approach, and with a growing reputation for ruthlessness in the deals he struck, Clowes was to be unpleasantly surprised, sometime after Farrell's return from America, when their business relationship was coldly ended, at second hand.

Ann Colville

Ann, who was the daughter of the Canadian painter Alex Colville and fourteen years younger than Farrell, came to know him in 1977. He attended an opening at the Fischer Fine Art Gallery, off St James, where she was the administrator, and the fact that she was renting a flat in the Chelsea house of Monika Beisner and Hans Dorflinger, two artists who were close friends of his, speeded the introduction. Farrell's relationship with Ann was lighthearted, and not exclusive on either side. Before she moved to Paris to live in 1979, she came over to Kilcrohane to spend Easter with him, but when she left, to her regret, he did not detain her. He had vague plans to join her there, however, at the time of his death.

Patsy Cumming
Patsy was the recently widowed sister-in-law of Farrell's close friend at Oxford, Bob Cumming, an American on a Marshall scholarship. Patsy's young husband, Ted, had died in 1959. (See Farrell's letter to Gabriele dated 10 March 1962.) A talented poet in her own right, she had courageously moved to Paris with her two small daughters, although still grieving, when Farrell made contact with her at Bob's suggestion. The address of her flat there appears affectionately in *A Man from Elsewhere*. After her return to America in 1962, they gradually lost touch.

John Curtis
Appointed Chief Fiction Editor at Weidenfeld & Nicolson when Tony Godwin, his predecessor and Farrell's chief friend in publishing, joined Harcourt Brace Jovanovich in New York in 1974, Curtis' calm, methodical manner soon established a good working relationship. Curtis successfully negotiated agreement for *The Singapore Grip* at long distance from Italy, where he was holidaying with his family, by bellowing out figures for the advance and print run in a noisy public phone booth. Weidenfeld had a contract for *The Hill Station* (posthumously named) at the time of Farrell's death, and Curtis was due to meet him in Paris in November 1979 for the handover of the manuscript. He learned of his death from a headline in *The Bookseller*, with disbelief.

Malcolm and Clare Dean
Farrell first met the *Guardian* journalist Malcolm Dean in New York, when both were on Harkness Fellowships in the 1966 intake, and their long friendship was based on mutual ribbing and affection. Dean was privy to the issues of the day but without pretension, and his contacts opened up Farrell's research abroad for *The Singapore Grip*. In 1978 Dean married Clare Roskill, whose commitment to social work appealed to Farrell's own ethics. After he had left for Ireland, Malcolm and Clare gave a party in London

at which everyone present was encouraged to scribble messages to be sent to Kilcrohane. 'Amazing that you should get all those ne'er-dowells to write to me,' Farrell responded as soon as the postal strike ended. 'You must have been bribing them with the birthday salmon.' There are two *Guardian* interviews by Dean: 'An Insight Job' (1 September 1973), and 'Grip of Empire', 13 September 1978. He also contributes 'A Personal Memoir' to *The Hill Station* (pp. 173–84).

Margaret Drabble

Winning the Faber Prize widened Farrell's literary friendships, though not to the extent that becoming a Booker winner would do in 1973. Margaret Drabble was introduced to him by Olivia Manning at Olivia's St. John's Wood flat, and she became a loyal colleague and confidante. At his quizzical smile, she learned to be on her guard: when he complimented her on *The Millstone* (winner of the John Llewellyn Rhys Prize in 1966), assuring her that he had almost written her a fan letter, she did not believe him, but his papers show he was sincere. They understood, and sympathised with, one another over the stresses of novel-writing, although she disapproved of his 1977 venture into screenwriting with Bob Parrish. Her essay 'Legacy of a Great Friendship' appears in *People*, edited by Susan Hill (Chatto & Windus/Hogarth Press) and she contributes, with John Spurling and Malcolm Dean, to *The Hill Station*. Stephen Cox, the hero of Drabble's 1992 novel *The Gates of Ivory*, is based on Farrell.

Carol Drisko

A dynamic American divorcée, five years older than Farrell, Carol became an unselfish emotional support from 1968 onwards, after they were no longer lovers. She was a senior editor with the educational publisher Scholastic in New York, and a vigorous correspondent. Her fondness for international travel, frequently involving flight connections through London, enabled them to re-meet fairly regularly for several years. He admired her enthusiasms and her energy, which put his own in the shade, but as the 1970s progressed, and New York faded in his thoughts, their letters gradually stopped. It was Carol who kindled his love of cooking in 1967 by introducing him to the televised programmes of Julia Child, and challenging him to cook supper on alternate evenings when he was living near her in Manhattan. She appears in *Troubles* as a guest at the Majestic Ball.

Josephine and William Farrell (Jo and Bill)

Jim's parents never tried to deter him from an insecure career in writing. They encouraged him at the beginning, and helped out with a small regular allowance in retirement, keeping their worries about his health and prospects to themselves. His extrovert mother Josephine (b. 1909) grew up in Maryborough (now Portlaoise), County Laois, where her father ran a prosperous timber business. She met Bill (b. 1901), a reflective and well-read man, at sea on a cruise, and they married in Rangoon in 1929. The couple initially set up home in Chittagong, India, where Bill was managing a United Molasses factory; he had grown up in Liverpool, the son of a prominent wine and spirit merchant, and trained as an accountant. In 1934 the combination of increasing deafness and a sharp economic downturn throughout the Empire caused by the Depression forced Bill to return. Jim, their second son, was born in Liverpool in 1935. After the war the family moved to Ireland with their three sons. In 1969 Jo and Bill retired to Malta, and subsequently Farrell's letters to them increased. Anxiety about Bill's health prompted a move back to England in 1976, and they bought a cottage in Oxfordshire, to be near hospital care, from Jim's friend Stephen Wall, whose life had similarly been changed by polio. Despite Farrell's growing worries about his father's condition, both parents outlived him. His father died in 1989, and his mother in 1999.

Gabriele

Gabriele was German, and was aged seventeen when they first met at a fancy dress party in Ireland in the summer of 1960. She was in a temporary au pair role with family friends of the Farrells in Greystones, County Wicklow, and he was enchanted by her youthfulness, pursuing her on paper when he left for France to teach. (Conversely, she had been amused by the attentions of Farrell and his contemporaries, seen by her as 'older gentlemen' in their mid-twenties.) Her motivation for choosing Ireland had been to find traces of James Joyce before going to university, and by the start of their correspondence she had returned to Germany to study for her entrance exams. When he sent her a copy of *A Man from Elsewhere*, he inscribed it: 'For Gabriela, who disliked the nihilism in this book, to remind her of Rotherfield in Angleterre. With deep affection.' His letters to her dwindled after 1963 and they lost touch, with the exception, many years later, of a chance encounter when she and her husband were staying with literary friends in London.

Robert Gottlieb

The reputation of Jim's editor at Knopf in New York was for refined and eccentric Bohemianism, and he was also a director of the New York City Ballet. Gottlieb openly admired tenacity and dedication in the performing and the writing worlds, and was renowned for having discovered and edited *Catch-22* (1961) by the then unknown Joseph Heller. A talented writer's voice, in his opinion, could be spotted within two sentences. He later became Editor in Chief of Simon and Schuster, Knopf and, from 1987 to 1992, *The New Yorker*.

Richard Hughes

Farrell had admired *A High Wind in Jamaica* since boyhood, and in 1971 he unwittingly initiated a friendship with Hughes when he wrote to congratulate him on *In Hazard*. 'It is very heartening to get a letter like that from a fellow-writer', Hughes promptly replied, 'particularly [as] I would have thought [that novel] was generally forgotten nowadays.' Their growing contact gave Farrell much pleasure, until it was suddenly cut short by Hughes' death at the age of 76 five years later.

Anne Hurst

Anne was a young Australian fellow passenger on the ferry Farrell took on return from France in the summer of 1962. She kept him at a distance by giving him her American Express address in London, and turned out to have an Australian boyfriend, Ron Robertson-Swann, whom Farrell liked as soon as they were introduced. Robertson-Swann, a sculptor and pupil of Henry Moore, married Anne that October so that, as he would subsequently claim, 'she couldn't run off with Jim'. One of Robertson-Swann's pieces, 'a beautiful sculpture in steel', appears in *A Girl in the Head*, and Farrell made a point of inscribing a copy of *The Lung*, 'For my friends Ron and Anne'.

Norman Ilett

Ilett was a likeable master at Rossall, where he also coached the rugby First XV on which young Farrell was a rising star. 'He could do it all and was dependable,' Ilett said. 'He didn't like being pushed about, and occasionally he got cross if you were rude to him. The game meant a great deal and he thought about it constantly.' In Farrell's final year a bad tackle during practice put him out of the game for the remainder of his time there, but after the ravages of polio he continued to keep in touch with Ilett, the master who had known him at his athletic best.

Francis King

The novelist Francis King was twelve years older than Farrell, and came from a family with long connections with India; he had lived there himself as a child. With a similar public school and Oxford background, King had worked for the British Council in Europe, and although his book *The Dividing Stream* had won the W. Somerset Maugham Prize in 1951, he had not resigned to write full-time until 1964. He was a Faber Prize judge in the year that *Troubles* won when they had not yet met, and when he did get to know Farrell he became a friend, and regular dinner party guest. On the eve of Farrell's departure to Ireland it was to King that he confided his last-minute doubts that he would ever complete another novel.

Jack Kirwan

Farrell's friendship with Jack Kirwan dated back to their teens and a shared love of rugby. The Kirwan family were living nearby in Dalkey Lodge when the Farrells moved to Balholm in Killiney in 1953, and during holidays from Rossall Jim gravitated to the hospitable Kirwan household. He initially fell for Jack's twin, Jill, and next for Hilary, his younger sister, but that never jeopardised their own sporting camaraderie. In adult life Jack remained in Dublin after qualifying as a solicitor, and became managing partner in the family firm. Farrell turned to him at once over the purchase of his house in Cork in the autumn of 1978.

Brian and Rose Knox Peebles

Farrell was an usher at the wedding of Rose to Brian Knox Peebles, one of his Oxford friends, in 1962, when he was briefly back from France; he was aged twenty-seven and he considered her immature at eighteen. The couple asked him to be a godfather to their oldest child, and although he had more in common with Brian, he grew to rely on their warm hospitality and gradually the age-gap with Rose dissolved. The Knox Peebles remained supportive friends, and were making arrangements to stay with Farrell in Ireland at the time of his death.

Alison Lurie

Farrell met Lurie in 1971, following his Faber win for *Troubles*, in a large group that also included Anthony Powell and Edna O'Brien. He encountered her again on a June evening in 1974 in Olivia Manning's Maida Vale flat, where, gratifyingly, she, Olivia and Margaret Drabble pressed him to sign their copies of *The Siege of Krishnapur*. Lurie had already written four novels and was teaching literature, folklore and writing at Cornell University. On her promotional visits to London, their friendship became a bantering, gossipy one. After his death she saluted him in her Pulitzer prize-winning novel *Foreign Affairs* (1984), in which Professor Vinnie Miner, the chief character, embarks on a long-distance flight: 'Then, with a sigh of relief, she returns to *The Singapore Grip* ... When the shadows of war darken over Singapore in Jim Farrell's last completed novel, the atmosphere outside the cabin window brightens.'

David Machin

David Machin, described once as 'a wry, conciliatory man of many enthusiasms and much humour', was Deputy Managing Director of Jonathan Cape, and aged thirty-six when Farrell and he were meeting socially, as well as professionally. In the small literary world he had previously been an editor with Heinemann and an agent with A.P. Watt. Machin subsequently become General Secretary at the Society of Authors, and two years after Farrell's death he joined the Bodley Head, where he was appointed Managing Director. In his own words, he 'jumped back and forth across the barrier' several times.

Oliver and Lif Marriott

Oliver Marriott was an Oxford contemporary, who had chosen a more lucrative path. He joined *The Times* as a financial journalist, and while Farrell was in New York on his Harkness Fellowship, Marriott's book *The Property Boom* was published by Hamish Hamilton and became a bestseller; this caused mixed feelings in Farrell when he found out on his return. Lif, Oliver's Swedish wife, was equally hospitable, and the couple included Farrell in their more lavish lifestyle until they moved far from London, out of reach for an impecunious novelist whose sole method of transport was a bicycle.

Tom Maschler

Tom Maschler, born in Berlin in 1933, came to England with his family in 1939, and was appointed editorial director at Jonathan Cape at the age of twenty-one. Among the many classic titles he chose to publish was one of Farrell's personal yardsticks, *Under the Volcano*. When their business relationship began in 1965, Maschler was the head of Cape, but despite his seniority Farrell's relationship with him was prickly, as these letters show. In the light of his criticisms, it should be pointed out that Maschler is now credited with being chiefly responsible for the creation of the Booker Prize, which was first awarded in 1969.

Russell McCormmach

Russell McCormmach's arrival at Christchurch, Oxford, as a Rhodes scholar, coincided with Farrell's return to Brasenose after his polio ordeal. The American trio consisting of McCormmach, Bob Cumming and Erwin Fleissner intrigued him, promising escape from the straitjacket of English convention. After Oxford Farrell kept in touch with all three, but it was the intellectually rigorous and unworldly McCormmach with whom he continued to feel most in tune. During the years they corresponded across the Atlantic, and occasionally were able to meet, McCormmach remained an academic, pursuing his conflicting twin interests of literature and science. *The Lung* is dedicated to him, and in *Troubles* he and Bob Cumming are included as guests at the Majestic Ball. Three years after Farrell's death, McCormmach's book *Night Thoughts of a Classical Physicist*, praised for being written with a physicist's precision and a poet's intensity, was published by Harvard University Press. It is a set university text.

James Michie

Michie was the senior editor of The Bodley Head when the company made an offer for *The Singapore Grip*, and it is a shame that Farrell's correspondence with him should have ended so brusquely, because they had much in common. Michie's father had once been an East India merchant, and he, too, had been to Oxford. A poet as well as a meticulous editor, two qualities Jim respected, Michie had been wooed by Graham Greene from Heinemann in 1962, and he was affectionately known as 'the Bodley Egghead'. Like Farrell, his conversational tone was sympathetically humorous and ironic.

Patricia Moynagh

Farrell was introduced to Patricia, a beautiful artist, at a dinner party in 1975, and her rebuff that evening did not deter him. Socially deft and generous, with a Roedean accent that amused and intrigued him, she had previously been a girlfriend of Bernard Levin, and she possessed a surface imperiousness that Farrell lacked. He held the power within their relationship, however, as he demonstrated when he changed it later to one of friendship. Patricia introduced him to Venice, where she had lived and worked, and designed his change-of-address cards when he moved to Ireland. In affectionate tribute, the green jumper she gave him one Christmas re-appears on the second-last page of *The Singapore Grip*.

Bridget O'Toole

In 1969, when Bridget was introduced to Farrell by his Pont Street Mews flatmate, Diana Saville, she was twenty-five and working on a literary Ph.D at Warwick University. Despite his customary scorn for academic dissection, he felt an immediate rapport: her sense of the ridiculous matched his own, and he was touched by her aura of vulnerability. Her insight, as the daughter of a 'mixed' marriage between a Liverpool Irish father and an English mother, has a bearing on *Troubles*, in which she also appears as a guest at Edward Spencer's ball. In 1970 she took up a lectureship in English and American Literature at the University of Ulster in Coleraine, Northern Ireland, but Farrell continued to turn to her and by then he had come to depend on her literary judgement. She helped him by cutting and editing *The Siege of Krishnapur* in 1972. Shortly before his death he told a friend that she was the only woman who was really important to him – so much so that he really thought he might marry her. Her memoir of him, 'Not a Crumb, Not a Wrinkle', appeared in *Irish Studies Review*, Autumn 1995.

Sonia Orwell

Jim was introduced to the widow of George Orwell (Eric Blair) by John and Hilary Spurling towards the end of 1970, and was willingly drawn into her more sociable circle. It was in her crowded and dramatically furnished London drawing room several years later that he first learned about the erotic term 'the Singapore Grip'. She was seventeen years his senior, and as he got to know her better he became sympathetically aware of the conflict with George Orwell's accountants over royalties that was steadily threatening to engulf her, and he made allowances for her mood swings. When she left London for a small bedsit in Paris, he intended to keep in touch, and the fortitude he admired in her is best expressed in Hilary Spurling's 2002 memoir, *The Girl From the Fiction Department* (Hamish Hamilton). Sonia died within a year of him, in 1980.

Robert Parrish

The American film producer Robert Parrish had exchanged Hollywood for Europe in the 1960s, ten years before he made an approach over *The Siege of Krishnapur*, only to be told of David Lean's option. He turned out to be a near-neighbour in Knightsbridge, and his career fascinated Farrell. An exuberant man with friends throughout the business, Parrish had been a child actor with Charlie Chaplin in *City Lights*, had made documentaries with John Ford during the Second World War, and had already directed eighteen films, including *Casino Royale*. In 1977 Parrish commissioned Farrell, to their mutual amusement, to write a screenplay in collaboration with Bertrand Tavernier for a Robert Louis Stevenson novel, *Beach at Falesa*. After a few companionable months the necessary financial backing fell through, but in the process Farrell grew close to Bob and his wife Kathie. They considered moving to Ireland, too, and he dedicated *The Singapore Grip* to them both. Parrish delivered the address at Farrell's memorial service at St Bride's in Fleet Street, London on 19 October 1979.

Michelle Pearce

In Farrell's first term at Brasenose College, Oxford, in the autumn of 1956, he shared digs – 14b on Staircase XV – with Brian Pearce, a congenial fellow-undergraduate. When Brian subsequently married,

Farrell took to his wife Michelle who shared Brian's enquiring, spiritual outlook. He saw them both often during his London years, and at his anxious request they stored a second copy of the typescript of *Troubles* before it went to the publishers, in case of fire. His friendship with them deepened when he began to research Victorian religious controversies for his final book, which was published posthumously as *The Hill Station*.

Piers Paul Read

Farrell met Piers and his young wife Emily during the second year of his Harkness Fellowship in New York, when Read, whose Fellowship began in 1967, inherited his Chevrolet. They came to his small apartment on E. 27th Street to collect the keys, and were given tea and home-made brown bread. Back in England they were invited to Egerton Gardens and mingled frequently at literary evenings, until they left London to live in Yorkshire. Read, too, was represented by Deborah Rogers, however, and Farrell felt a strong rivalry with him, which was exacerbated whenever their novels were reviewed on the same page. When he won the Faber Prize for *Troubles*, the knowledge that he had drawn level with Read, his predecessor, added savour to that news.

Deborah Rogers

Deborah Rogers became Farrell's second agent, in 1969. Younger than Jonathan Clowes, she had experience of working in New York with Curtis Brown, and had recently returned to London to set up her own agency, with a list based on English representation for the well-known American agent Lynn Nesbitt. Farrell liked the trans-atlantic combination, as well as Deborah's warmth of manner and optimism. She spoke of finding the best individual strategy for each writer she chose to take on, and he was impressed that Anthony Burgess was already a client. Farrell was to be her first Booker winner (she has since represented Salman Rushdie, Thomas Kenneally, Peter Carey and Ian McEwan) and, although he left her in 1977, determined to handle his own affairs from then on, she remained a loyal friend.

Claude and Anna Simha

Farrell met Claude Simha, a young Moroccan-born paediatrician working in Montparnasse, on a train to Munich, where both were heading at Christmas 1964. (Farrell was writing *The Lung*, his most autobiographical novel based on his polio experience, and living in Paris at the time.) Mutual appreciation of Proust brought the two together in conversation and back in Paris they found more in common. Claude's medical knowledge was invaluable for those aspects of *The Lung*, and his astute questioning enabled Farrell to retrieve painful emotions that he had deliberately pushed to the back of his mind. In recompense, Farrell introduced Claude to Anna, a lovely Icelandic student also lodging at his digs at the États-Unis, and was delighted when they married. The couple had two children, the eldest being his godchild, whom he privately felt he had conjured into existence. As the letters show, he made a point of keeping in touch with her, and the character of François Dupigny in *The Singapore Grip* is Farrell's mischievous take on Claude.

David Simpson

A non-smoker and vegetarian, Simpson was an intuitive man with a medical aptitude, and Margaret Drabble's partner when Farrell first got to know him in the late 1970s. Simpson ran the English branch of Amnesty, and his hobby of skilled carpentry surprised Farrell, who freely admitted to having trouble erecting a level shelf. In the spring of 1979, when Simpson was coming under fire from Bernard Levin in *The Times* for leaving Amnesty to head up ASH, he accepted Farrell's invitation to stay at Kilcrohane before taking up the post, and spent a week there in May. Each morning they set up their fishing rods on the nearby slipway to the sea, but without success. On one long walk in high winds on the lonely Sheep's Head peninsula, they were suddenly brought up short by the menacing presence of a large rock in their path, and Simpson left Ireland with a sense of foreboding.

John and Hilary Spurling

Farrell first met – and greatly liked – the Spurlings in London in 1963, and despite his frequent absences during that decade their friendship flourished. John and Hilary had been at Oxford together, and Farrell, who was so wary of marriage himself, respected their mutual commitment and integrity. John was a playwright with strong socialist principles behind his conventional public school exterior, and Hilary supported his potentially impecunious choice. She encouraged Farrell, too, and when she became Literary Editor of the *Spectator* she commissioned him to review for her in 1969. He was a kindly godfather to their son, Nat, and their mutual comradeship easily kept pace with the vagaries of his literary success. *The Times Saturday Review* on 11.4.81 carried John's valediction 'Jim Farrell – A Memoir', and he contributed a more detailed memoir, 'As Does the Bishop', to *The Hill Station*. Hilary's first biography came out in Farrell's lifetime, and twenty-six years after his death she was awarded the Whitbread (now Costa) Book of the Year Award for *Matisse the Master: The Conquest of Colour*.

Lavinia Trevor
Farrell enjoyed a teasing friendship with Lavinia, a young literary agent whom he asked to read the proofs of *The Siege of Krishnhapur*. 'For Lavinia', he inscribed a copy after publication, 'and I still don't think she's read this book.' In the feverish days before leaving London in 1979, he equipped her with his address in west Cork, but excitedly added 'Piss off!' beneath. It was, she thought, oddly juvenile and quite unlike him.

Carole Tucker
Farrell's short-lived affair with Carole, a vivacious young American lawyer working in London who had just separated from her husband, was contrary to his usual principles. He believed marriage to be a total commitment, and until then had taken care to avoid any such entanglements. Their affair was at its most intense in the emotionally charged final weeks in Egerton Gardens. In the summer of 1979 she wrote apologetically to him – 'my confusion is a chronic one' – to say that she was going to re-build her marriage, instead of coming to Kilcrohane as they had envisaged so optimistically in London. She heard of his death when she was staying with her husband in New Orleans. 'We were having people to dinner,' she described the shock, 'and I burned my hand. I sat there numb with my hand in a pan of water all evening.' A few days later Jim's understanding airmail reply caught up with her.

Stephen and Yvonne Wall
Farrell originally met Wall, a Fellow of Keble College, Oxford, under grim circumstances: both were polio victims in the Wingfield Morris

Orthopaedic Hospital in 1957 and their beds were side by side. On discharge, Wall was confined to a wheelchair, but he resumed his academic career and married his intelligent nurse, Yvonne, whom Farrell respected. Farrell often visited the couple, who lived in Oxford, and he liked to entertain them when they were in London. Wall, who refused to be defined by his wheelchair and gave no quarter in literary disputes, was editor of the influential OUP quarterly *Essays in Criticism*. It was the Walls' Oxfordshire cottage, on Farrell's recommendation, that his parents bought in 1976.

Angus Wilson

When Wilson made *Troubles* one of his three Christmas recommendations in the *Observer* in 1970 he was aged fifty-seven, and Farrell's book had been drawn to his attention by Hilary Spurling. A prolific author of fiction and non-fiction, his best-known book was the satirical *Anglo-Saxon Attitudes*, which had come out in 1956. Wilson's alertness to new writing talent was entirely in character. He lived in Suffolk with his partner, Tony Garrett, and that year founded, with Malcolm Bradbury, the Creative Writing Course at the University of East Anglia. He outlived Farrell by twelve years. Margaret Drabble's biography *Angus Wilson* was published by Secker and Warburg in 1995.

Endnotes

Threshold (pp. 5–8)

1. Sally Bentlif, in JGF's view the most glamorous of her year at Lady Margaret Hall.

2. Published 30 July 1960, under the 'Pasternak and Joyce' correspondence. Sean O'Casey had criticised Ireland's neglect of Joyce's literary reputation, citing the refusal of John Charles McQuaid, Archbishop of Dublin, to permit a Votive Mass for the 1958 Dublin Theatre Festival on the grounds that it included a dramatisation of *Ulysses*. Monk Gibbon had hotly defended McQuaid at length. Frank O'Connor's terse rejoinder was printed below JGF's letter, on the same day.

3. Isaiah Berlin (1909–97). Chichele Professor of Social and Political Theory at Oxford University during JGF's time at Brasenose. He had attended Berlin's inaugural lecture, 'Two Concepts of Liberty', on 31 October 1958, in which Berlin argued that positive liberty, used ostensibly for the public good, frequently led to the abuse of power. Negative liberty, in his view, was the freedom from interference by others, and JGF was in agreement. His distrust of communism becomes apparent in Farrell's first novel, *A Man From Elsewhere*.

4. Hugo Grotius (1583–1645) Dutch founder of natural law theories of normality.

5. Samuel von Pufendorf (1632–94) German political philosopher and statesman whose maxim was 'The will of the State is but the sum of individual wills that constitute it.'

6. Charles-Louis de Secondat, Baron de la Brede et de Montesquieu (1689–1755), luminary of the Era of Enlightenment in France, whose theory of the 'Separation of Powers' divided the administrative arm of government into three: the legislative, the executive and the judiciary. The influence of one, he warned, should not exceed the other two together. Jim was flourishing Montesquieu's name mischievously, however. His tutor at Oxford, Robert Shackleton, was the author of *Montesquieu, A Critical Biography* (Oxford 1961), and JGF despised his pedantic approach to

the Enlightenment; in his view, it overvalued the dissection of facts and undervalued the imagination.

7. Thomas Hobbes (1588–1679). English author of *Leviathan*, which established the foundation for most Western political philosophy.

8. John Locke (1632–1704), English philosopher influenced by the conclusions of Voltaire and Rousseau.

9. Jean Jacques Rousseau (1712–78) French political philosopher (though born in Geneva) and author of *The Social Contract* (1762), containing the sentence: 'Man is born free, and everywhere he is in chains.' Only submission to the authority of a 'general will', Rousseau argued, could protect individuals from exploitation.

A Man from Elsewhere (pp. 9–43)

1. Gabriele, who wishes not to be identified, was a seventeen-year-old German girl who had taken a temporary au pair role the previous summer with friends of JGF's parents in Greystones, County Wicklow. She first met him at a fancy dress party given by the Kirwans, also family friends of the Farrells, where she was amused by the attentions of JGF and his contemporaries, who were seen by her as 'older gentlemen' in their mid-twenties. Her knowledgeable interest in literature belied her job: her motivation for choosing Ireland had been to find traces of James Joyce, and she had since returned to Germany to study for her university entrance exams.

2. The correct spelling is *schwachsinnig*, meaning feeble-minded or idiotic.

3. Paul Valéry (1871–1945), French poet, essayist and philosopher who was fascinated by science, particularly the theory of light. Einstein was a friend and regular correspondent.

4. Edmund Husserl (1859–1938), the father of transcendental phenom-enology – the theory of consciousness – which led on to existentialism and had influenced JGF's hero, Jean Paul Sartre.

5. Unknown. Possibly a friend from Oxford with contacts in the book world.

6. The Lycée d'État Chaptal in Mende, Lozère.

7. JGF had spent four claustrophobic weeks in an iron lung at the Slade Isolation Hospital in Oxford in December 1956, before being transferred to a bed in the Wingfield Morris Orthopaedic Hospital of Headington for intensive physiotherapy until Easter 1957. The physiotherapy continued, on an outpatient basis, at the Central Remedial Clinic in Dublin until the late autumn of 1957.

8. John Chisholm.

9. The first draft of *A Man from Elsewhere*, subsequently destroyed.

10. Unknown. JGF has left no note about a publisher either.

11. Robert Jungk (1913–94), an Austrian writer and journalist arrested on Hitler's orders during the Second World War while working with a subversive German press agency. An English edition of Jungk's book about Hiroshima, *Children of the Ashes*, was newly published.

12. The Berlin crisis dominated the headlines: construction of the Berlin Wall had begun on 13 August, and all crossing points between East and West closed within two weeks. Khrushchev had given Kennedy an ultimatum, and that September angry public exchanges between the US and the USSR were heightening international tension.

13. The German racing driver Count Wolfgang Von Trips had been killed in the Italian Grand Prix at Monza four days earlier, on the verge of winning the World Championship. Von Trips' Ferrari had collided with Jim Clark's Lotus on the second lap and flipped over, smashing into the fence and killing fourteen race fans.

14. Patsy Cumming was the recently widowed sister-in-law of JGF's close American friend at Oxford, Bob Cumming, who attended on a Marshall scholarship. (See Jim's letter to Gabriele dated 10 March 1962.) Patsy was a talented young poet in her own right, and had moved to Paris, still grieving, with her two young daughters.

15. Gérard de Nerval (1808–55), pen-name of the romantic poet and essayist Gérard Labrunie, who believed in the significance of dreams and the spirit world. His hashish-smoking circle in Paris included Alexander Dumas père, and de Nerval supposedly had a pet lobster, which he led about on a blue ribbon. A series of nervous breakdowns culminated in suicide. Victor Hugo was an admirer; his work also influenced the Surrealists and JGF's exemplar, Marcel Proust.

16. Transl: The mistral, the cockroach and the poor; as it says in the Bible, these we shall always have with us.

17. *Nouveax francs* (new francs).

18. *La Notte* (The Night), directed by Antonioni and starring Marcello Mastroianni, Jeanne Moreau and Monica Vitti, came out that year and won the Golden Bear at the Berlin Film Festival. The young man with whom JGF identified is a successful writer, confronted simultaneously with the death of a close friend and rejection in a complex love affair.

19. At that time the daily newspaper (founded in 1904) of the French Communist Party.

20. *Toussaint* is All Saints Day, a church holiday for honouring the dead.

21. The school where JGF taught in Toulon was the Interidant du Lycée, Boulevard de Strasbourg, known familiarly as La Rode.

22. His digs at 35 Avenue Vert-Coteau were in a long road parallel to the railway tracks at the rear of the port's sprawling town. The countryside rose up behind, hence the road's original name: green hillside.

23. The satirical weekly newspaper.

24. Fleamarket.

25. A fellow teacher.

26. Directed by Francis Letterier, 1960. Also starring Reginald Kernan (with whom JGF identified), Serge Rousseau and Alexandra Stewart.

27. Aldous Huxley (1894–1963), author of *Brave New World*, whose final novel, *Island*, was published that year.

28. The central character in *A Man from Elsewhere*.

29. Two American naval ships visiting the port of Toulon. JGF was introduced to their officers at the Toulon yacht club, the Cercle Naval, and invited aboard because he spoke English.

30. Great Britain.

31. Transl: dangerous, unhealthy.

32. French colonists of Algeria. The majority were farmers or businessmen with everything to lose if made to leave; more usually referred to as *pieds noirs* (black feet).

33. Transl: in town under a downpour and without me.

34. A shy Italian fellow teacher whom initially JGF had liked (see diary entry for 2 November).

35. Both press lords. As a young journalist specialising in foreign affairs, Servan-Schreiber worked for *Le Monde*, owned by Hubert Beuve-Méry, before setting up his own magazine, *l'Express*, in 1953; contributors included Camus, Sartre, Malraux and Mauriac. Servan-Schrieber exposed French brutality in the Algerian war in a first-hand account, *Lieutenant en Algérie*.

36. A central character, a film director, in *A Man from Elsewhere*.

37. Judy Mitchell, JGF's Irish girlfriend between 1957 and 1960, whom he met in the extra-sensitive, morose aftermath of polio. Wrongly suspecting pity, he had often unleashed a destructive venom outside her experience.

38. 'All is for the best in the best of all possible worlds', the optimistic belief of young Candide's tutor, Dr Pangloss is mocked by the series of dire misfortunes that befell his pupil in Voltaire's *Candide*.

39. Carlo Levi (1902–75), journalist, artist and doctor. As a Jew and open

anti-fascist, Levi was exiled for a year by Mussolini in 1935 to the remote village of Aliano in Matera, Lucania, 'in view of the danger he represents for national security'. A fellow activist was the novelist Cesare Pavese, whom JGF also admired. Levi's bestselling autobiographical novel *Cristo si è fermato a Eboli* exposed the poverty of farmers in southern Italy. (A film adaptation, *Christ Stopped at Eboli*, appeared in 1979.) Levi was living in Rome at the time JGF visited Florence, and a year later was elected to the Italian Senate as an independent on the Communist Party ticket.

40. Lit. plastic attacks: bombs and explosions.

41. Machine gun.

42. George Whitman (b. 1913), the American proprietor of the Paris book-shop Le Mistral at 37 rue de la Bûcherie, founded in 1951. JGF had met him on a brief Paris foray two years earlier for *Oxford Opinion*, to cover a launch of *Minutes to Go* by William Burroughs and Sinclair Beiles (Two Cities, 1960). Free accommodation in the bookshop was given in ex-change for two hours' work a day, and it was modelled on Shakespeare and Company at 12 rue de l'Odéon, run by Joyce's publisher, Sylvia Beach. When Beach died in October 1962, she willed the right to that name to Whitman, and La Mistral became Shakespeare and Company in 1964.

43. Bob Cumming, who had turned to JGF for solace, and found little.

44. Harvard-educated Nelson W. Aldrich, Jr, was related to the Rockefellers, and was a scion of the 'Old Money' set of Rhode Island.

45. *The Paris Review* had been founded on a budget of $1,000 by four American graduates – George Plimpton, Harold Humes, Peter Mathiessen and John P.C. Train – in 1952. Its aim was to free literature from the straitjacket of critical jargon. Contemporary and bold, featuring self-revelatory interviews with authors, earlier editions had included work by Hemingway, Beckett and Kerouac.

46. Transl: I would perform wonders.

47. During his long convalescence at home after polio, JGF's girlfriend, twenty-year-old Judy Mitchell, had given him a Siamese kitten for distraction. He had named it Tiffany, and the kitten's 'indescribable grace' frequently brought tears to his eyes. At the time, Judy was studying at Trinity College, Dublin, where she had been elected the first female Auditor, and her aim was to hasten his recovery by lightening his introspection.

48. During the 1956–62 Algerian War, casualties are estimated to have reached 700,000. But figures vary. Thousands of Muslim civilians were killed in bombing raids and reprisals, 70,000 were killed by the FLN, 141,000 by French security forces and 12,000 in purges. French military authorities list

18,000 dead, plus 3,000 European-descended civilians.

49. On 3 January 1959, during JGF's Christmas holiday from Oxford, Judy Mitchell suffered serious head injuries in a car crash on the way to a party in County Dublin; he had changed his mind about taking her at the last minute, preferring to write. Although he had rushed to her hospital bedside and remained beside her until she regained consciousness, he had not repaid her own previous unstinting support. The permanent loss of Judy Mitchell's short-term memory put him in a moral dilemma during her protracted care, which involved re-learning how to walk and talk. In his final year at Oxford he rejected her, and guilt and self-blame influence his three early novels.

50. Jim had interviewed Burroughs and Beiles there for *Oxford Opinion* two years earlier. (See note 42.)

51. George often claimed to be the illegitimate great-grandson of Walt Whitman, but in his eighties was more hesitant. 'I like to think there might be a vague resemblance', he hinted then. 'I feel a kinship and believe the bookstore has the faults and virtues it might have if he were the proprietor.'

52. Mann wrote *Tonio Kroger* in 1901 when he was twenty-five. The novel describes the emotional journey from childhood to adulthood, and the hero and JGF have much in common: Kroger feels similar conflicting emotions towards conventional people, and is equally prepared to make personal sacrifices to become a writer. He succeeds on his own terms, achieving fame.

53. Brian and Rose Knox Peebles. JGF had been an usher at their wedding the previous year, with another Oxford friend, the writer and reviewer David Caute.

54. Rue Bouilloux-Lafont, where Patsy lived.

55. Bob Cumming was Patsy's brother-in-law; she was the widow of his late brother, Ted.

56. The first volume of the *Letters of James Joyce* edited by Stuart Gilbert (Viking, 1957). Two further volumes, edited by Richard Ellmann, would come out in 1966. 'It is certainly difficult to believe', wrote Stephen Spender, reviewing it, 'that ... there was a man of genius more centred on his work than Joyce. These letters are almost entirely devoted to operations connected with printing and publishing [his] books ... An extremely interesting self-portrayal.'

57. *A Man from Elsewhere*, his new attempt at a novel, is heavily influenced by Sartre and Camus. It portrays the moral dilemma of Sayer, a young Communist journalist assigned to blacken the reputation of a celebrated

novelist who was a fellow-traveller in his youth, to prevent bad publicity for the Party upon his death. See JGF's letter to Gabriele dated 14 September 1961, in which he says that Sinclair Regan, the novelist, is modelled on André Malraux.

58. Chatto and Windus.

59. An existential film with the theme of mortality. Cleo, played by Corinne Marchand, is a singer convinced that she has cancer, and the two hours of the title follow her through the time she has to wait for the results of a biopsy.

60. Agnès Varda (b. 1928) was a French film director, although born in Brussels to a Greek father and French mother.

61. *The Lung*, written from the perspective of a polio patient, is based on JGF's own experience.

62. A hospitable Austrian artist who was living in Rue Joanes, Paris with his wife Claire.

63. A 1954 film based on the Stendhal novel, starring Gérard Philippe and Danielle Darrieux.

64. Transl: in France we perpetrate the greatest cruelties – but without cruelty.

65. The flagrantly ambitious hero, a provincial tutor who moves to Paris and almost succeeds in marrying a nobleman's daughter.

66. Idleness.

67. He is referring to the *Kent & Essex Courier*. Brian Knox Peebles was a journalist on the staff, and had told JGF that he could get him taken on for experience.

68. *Crime et Châtiment* (1956), directed by Georges Lampin and starring Lino Ventura and Jean Gabin.

69. Transl: disproportionate pride in a cramped room.

70. An island off Lavandou, near Toulon, where the area not occupied by the army is dedicated to naturalism.

71. Laurence Durrell's *The Alexandria Quartet*, set in Egypt before and during the Second World War, was published by Faber and Faber. *Justine* had come out in 1956, *Balthazar* and *Mountolive* in 1958, and *Clea* in 1960.

72. *Albert Camus, A Study of His Work* (Hamish Hamilton, 1957).

73. Bob Cumming was then living in Thailand.

Life is Made Up of Separate Experiences (pp. 44–76)

1. A young Australian divorcée, Anne Hurst, whom JGF met on the ferry

returning to England. She kept him at a distance by giving him her American Express address in London, and would turn out to have an Australian boyfriend, Ron Robertson-Swann. JGF became friendly with both.

2. Lodovico.

3. Brian Pearce had shared digs – 14b on Staircase XV – with JGF from October to December 1956 at Brasenose College, Oxford. The arrangement came to an end when Jim was hospitalised with polio and missed the rest of that year, but they had got on very well and remained good friends. Brian had since married, and JGF approved of his thoughtful wife, Michelle. (See letter to her dated 8 July 1979.)

4. At a Berlitz school within walking distance of his flat. JGF enjoyed comparing Maigret stories in the English, French and German translations for his students.

5. Russell McCormmach, an academic physicist, was working in Philadelphia.

6. Transl: degradation.

7. Jean Ferrat (b. 1930), the French singer, poet and songwriter whose debut album *Deux Enfants du Soleil*, released the previous year, included the poetry of Lorca set to music.

8. In 1958 Jim and a band of Oxford and Cambridge friends spent part of the Long Vac at the San Fermin festival in Pamplona consciously acting out Hemingway's *The Sun Also Rises*. Jim, the polio survivor, had been cast as the impotent Jake.

9. The battle of wills between the Federal Minister of Defence and the owner and editor-in-chief of *Der Spiegel*, Germany's leading weekly political magazine, stemmed from an article disclosing that the Bundeswehr (army) was on the lowest NATO-grade of defence, and unprepared for a communist threat from the east. *Der Spiegel's* offices were raided and shut down on the grounds of treason, and the editor and senior journalists arrested, leading to protests throughout Germany.

10. JGF's grandmother, Edith Russell, who had lived in Portlaoise, County Laois. Before 1922 it was named Maryborough.

11. Transl: sexual modesty.

12. JGF was staying with his parents at home for Christmas, a season which he dreaded, considering it hypocritical in the extreme.

13. Graham C. Greene, a nephew of the novelist, worked for Secker and Warburg, and was only a little older than JGF. He had also been at Oxford (after Eton), and had worked briefly as a trainee banker in Dublin.

14. The Kirwan family lived near the Farrells in Dublin. JGF had known

them since his mid-teens, when he spent much of his school holidays at their house, Dalkey Lodge. Jack was the eldest son and a contemporary; JGF had first been attracted to Jack's twin, Jill, and a couple of years later he fell for Jack's younger sister, Hilary.

15. On Dublin bay, near the homes of both the Farrells and the Kirwans.

16. The likeable Australian sculptor Ron Robertson-Swann, by now the husband of Anne Hurst. (See note 1.)

17. Gerald and Sara Murphy, who befriended Fitzgerald and Hemingway in France in the 1920s; Gerald, heir to a fortune, had left the family business in America to become a dilettante painter, and the couple settled on the Riviera, entertaining generously at Villa America.

18. Gerald Murphy (1888–1964) exhibited his cubist oil painting *Watch* in 1925 at the Salon des Indépendants in Paris. It measured 199.39 x 200.36 cm.

19. Patsy's small Citroën 2 hp car.

20. Louis-Ferdinand Céline's nihilistic and semi-autobiographical novel (1932).

21. *The Tin Drum* (1959) by Gunter Grass deepened JGF's pessimism that bitterly cold winter.

22. A collection of short stories. Published in 1961, four years after Lowry's death.

23. The 1962 film about a doomed love affair and the domination of urban technology over the natural environment also starred Alain Delon and Francisco Rabal. The third of Antonioni's trilogy, it follows *L'Aventura* (1960) and *La Notte* (1961). JGF loved them all. (See letters dated 21 October 1961 and Easter Monday 1965.)

24. The title of his first published novel.

25. Garry Arnott, a banker whom JGF had met at Oxford; Arnott had graduated earlier, returning from the City at weekends. Witty and epicurean, Arnott made no secret of his homosexuality, and scoffed at any rumours that Jim might be homosexual too. JGF could always count on Arnott's generous hospitality without strings.

26. 'The Artist at Work' (*Jonas, ou l'artiste au travail*) from *Exile and the Kingdom* (L'Exile et le royaume), 1957.

27. Transl: you are, in the end, what you are.

28. JGF was lodging in a front basement room of a house owned by a new friend, Norma di Marco. He viewed it as a temporary arrangement at first.

29. John Profumo, Minister of Defence, had told the House of Commons in March that his relationship with a call-girl, Christine Keeler, had 'no

impropriety whatever'. On 5 June he resigned, admitting 'deep remorse' after press reports that Yevgeny Ivanov, the naval attaché at the Soviet embassy, was another of Keeler's clients. Profumo and Keeler had met through Stephen Ward, a London osteopath and socialite and Ward had been arrested and charged the day before JGF's letter with living on immoral earnings.

30. Ward took an overdose on the final day of his trial and was in a coma when the guilty verdict was brought in. He died on 9 August. Keeler was tried in a related case, and sentenced to nine months in prison for perjury.

31. 'James Farrell' by S.N. (Stephanie Netten), *Books and Bookmen*, October 1963, p. 27.

32. The address is not known, but a new friend made at this time, Dr Claude Simha, believed it was a Lycée in St. Cloud – 'certainly in that direction'.

33. Most probably *Leo Tolstoy* by E.J. Simmons (1946).

34. Heidi, whom he had taught in London. In the event, he spent more time with Claude Simha, whom he met for the first time on the train to Munich.

35. Farrell was referring to Gabriele and her friends, with whom she edited a student magazine.

36. 'Lunar Caustic' by Lowry was published in the winter-spring issue of *The Paris Review*. It appeared in expanded form as a novella that year.

37. Originally written in French, as were most of Farrell's early letters to Franz Beer.

Works in Progress (pp. 77–97)

1. *The Lung*.

2. Never published, so presumably Farrell subsequently destroyed the ms.

3. Gilles de Rais (1404–40) fought alongside Joan of Arc in 1429. A wealthy Breton baron who became a marshal of France, his career ended in a celebrated trial for Satanism, abduction and child murder: the number of his victims is put at between eighty and one hundred. Excommunicated and hanged, de Rais is linked to the tale of Bluebeard.

4. Friendship with Martin Gilbert, subsequently Churchill's official biographer, had begun in JGF's last year at Oxford, when they shared digs at 65 The High. A reference to their student days was about to appear in *The Lung*, and Gilbert's enthusiasm and questing mind moulds George Fleury in *The Siege of Krishnapur*.

5. A temporary address: see JGF's following letter to Russell McCormmach.

6. The English edition of Saul Bellow's *Herzog*, published by Weidenfeld & Nicolson.

7. Transl: behind closed doors, or in camera.

8. *Il Desierto Rosso*, released that February, starred Monica Vitti and Richard Harris.

9. It would be published as *A Girl in the Head*.

10. JGF was earning 4 guineas a script as a reader for Hutchinson.

11. The Drian Gallery, at 5-7 Porchester Place, Marble Arch, London, opened in 1957. Its director was Halima Nalecz, an artist usually described as ebullient and Junoesque, aged 46 when Jim met her. The gallery showed abstract and figurative artists, including Anthony Caro, a friend of Ron Robertson-Swann.

12. The New Vision Centre, downstairs at 4 Seymour Place, Marble Arch, was a rival gallery for young and unknown non-figurative artists. It specialised in solo shows, and the persuasive director, Denis Bowen, also a painter, was an ambassador for the avant-garde.

13. JGF made no subsequent comment about Virginia Woolf's novel (1925), indicating little interest.

14. The race riots in Watts, a residential district in Los Angeles, had erupted on 11 August 1965, initially over a minor drink-driving arrest. By the time the curfew was lifted on 17 August, 34 people had been killed, 1,032 injured, and 3,952 arrested.

15. Henry de Montherlant (1896–1972), the French writer and dramatist elected to the Académie Francaise in 1960. Camus greatly admired his work.

16. Recommended to JGF by physiotherapists at the Slade Isolation Hospital during his slow recovery from polio.

17. Coincidentally, given their first two initials as well, J.G. Ballard also lived in the Stanley House at the start of his career, in 1955. 'Today that one star hotel would be full of financial hustlers [and] celebrity hunters,' Ballard commented in his autobiography. 'Any novice writer would flee in horror. I remember [it] with affection.' (*Miracles of Life*, pp. 176–8).

18. United States Information Service.

19. Impoverished Robert Musil (1880–1942) worked on *The Man Without Qualities* for over twenty years, to the detriment of family life. He began in 1921, published the first two volumes in 1930, and died before the third was completed, leaving 1,700 pages. The novel is set in the last days of the Austro-Hungarian Empire, and believed to have many autobiographical touches. Farrell identified with the hero, Ulrich.

20. Henri-Philippe Pétain (1856–1951), a First World War hero and marshal of France, became Minister of War in 1934. As Vice-Premier in the Second World War he asked for an armistice in 1940. Germany controlled the north and west of France, including Paris, and Pétain acted as chief of state of the officially neutral – but in practice collaborationist and anti-semitic – Vichy regime. After the liberation he was brought to trial and condemned to death, commuted to solitary confinement for life by de Gaulle. In 1951 Pétain died in prison on the Île d'Yeu, off the Atlantic coast.

21. Lansing Hammond was the principle director of the Harkness Division of International Fellowships.

22. JGF applied for a playwriting course at Yale, in the Literature and Drama category specified by Harkness House. This course included writing for the cinema, his long-held ambition.

23. *The Lung* had been favourably reviewed in *The Irish Times* by Bernard Share, although JGF was rebuked for 'a gratuitous sideswipe at Dublin'. ('Respiratory Tract'. *The Irish Times,* 30 October 1965.)

24. Two books by Sergei Mikhailovich Eisenstein (1898–1948), the Russian film director of *Battleship Potempkin*, were available in translation. Familiarity with *The Film Sense* (1942) and *Film Form: Essays in Film Theory* (1949) shows that JGF took his application seriously.

25. The French film director Jean-Luc Godard (b. 1930), whose New Wave style fascinated JGF.

26. Reynir Oddsson (b. 1936) had become friendly with JGF when both were living in Paris in 1964. They met through mutual Icelandic contacts in the international Cité Université, where Jim lodged when writing *The Lung*.

27. Halldór Kiljan Laxness (1902–98) had published seventeen novels by 1955, when he was awarded the Nobel Prize for Literature. He had converted to Catholicism in 1923 and taken the surname Laxness after the rural area of his childhood, adopting his middle name after the Irish martyr, Saint Killian. In the event, JGF was never to meet him.

28. Gorley Putt, a noted expert on the novels of Henry James, was the UK Secretary of the Harkness Fellowships.

29. Mrs Widra was an administrator at Harkness House, 5th Avenue, New York.

30. The 36,000 tonnes S.S. *Nieuw Amsterdam* was a star of the Holland America line. Launched to acclaim in 1938, she had been used as troop transport during the Second World War and refitted in 1947. One of the

greatest liners on the transatlantic run, she sailed to the breakers' yard in 1974.

31. Usually JGF recoiled from giving an opinion of a manuscript, so for Rose he was – reluctantly – making an exception out of friendship.

32. Hemingway's novella, published in 1952, has only 96 pages (Scribner 1996 edition). It was awarded a Pulitzer prize and played a significant role in Hemingway's Nobel Prize for Literature in 1954.

33. An early title for *A Girl in the Head*.

34. Pen-name of the French writer and doctor Louis-Ferdinand Destouches (1894–1961). Celebrated for his innovative style (the novel Jim mentions was narrowly beaten to a Prix Goncourt in 1935), Céline's work was subsequently accused of anti-semitism. When the Vichy regime fell, he fled to Germany with Pétain and the Vichy president, Pierre Laval, whose personal physician he had been. In 1945 Celine went to Denmark, where he was imprisoned for eighteen months. Convicted of collaboration *in absentia* in France in 1950 and sentenced to a year in prison, he was granted amnesty and he returned to France in 1951.

35. Frank Tuohy (1925–99) had a similar public school and Oxbridge background as JGF; in his case, Stowe and Cambridge. He, too, had lived abroad, spending time in Poland with the British Council. *The Ice Saints* (1965) was awarded the James Tait Black Memorial Prize.

36. President Lyndon B. Johnson, President of the United States, from 22 November 1963–20 January 1969.

37. The potentially fatal enemy of plague used by Camus in his 1947 novel *La Peste* is more insidious than siege warfare, but its effect on a community is equally character-testing and divisive.

38. *The Guardian*, 12 March 2005. 'Talent Spotter' by Nicholas Wroe.

39. JGF was taking a surprisingly firm line with Maschler, who had published the inspirational *Under the Volcano* among many other seminal books.

40. Charles Raymond specialised in detailed watercolours.

41. The jacket chosen featured the line drawing of a girl in the Botticelli Venus stance, against an orange background which JGF strongly disliked.

A Craving to Write Something Good (pp. 98–125)

1. Robert Brustein (b. 1927), Dean of Yale Drama School, was a director, playwright and influential theatre critic for *The New Republic*. His subsequent awards include Fulbright and Guggenheim Fellowships.

2. Arnold Weinstein (1927–2005) had had a long-running play off

Broadway in 1961. *Dynamite Tonight*, his popular anti-war satire, had opened at the Actors Studio in 1964 with a cast that included Gene Wilder.

3. Michael Roemer and Robert Young ran the Writing for the Camera course at Yale Drama School. Their company, Roemer-Young Associates Inc, in New York, made innovative films on a shoestring. *Nothing but a Man* (1964) had just been a double prize-winner at the Venice Film Festival. Roemer (b. 1928) had a lasting influence on JGF, who described him once as his guru. Born in Berlin, Roemer had escaped Nazi Germany on *kindertransport* and been fostered in England, before reaching Harvard to study English Literature via a perilous convoy before the war's end. His bible, to JGF's delight, was the Scott-Moncrieff translation of Proust.

4. *Selected Letters of Malcolm Lowry*, edited by Lowry's widow and Harvey Breit, had been published the year before, in 1965.

5. Jonathan Clowes was Farrell's London agent, and had already acted for him over publication of *The Lung*.

6. Kenneth H. Brown (b. 1936 in Brooklyn) was an ex-Marine and Korean War veteran. His award-winning play *The Brig* (1963), based on Marine Corps punishment, had won plaudits with the Living Theatre Company off-Broadway and toured Europe, and a film of it, directed by Jonas Mekas, had won the Leone D'Oro for best documentary at the Venice Film Festival in 1965. In 2007, during the George Bush presidency, *The Brig*'s relevance to the controversial Guantánamo Bay detention camp led to a sell-out new production by the Living Theatre Company in New York and Europe.

7. Russell was then working in the Humanities Department, Case Institute of Technology in Cleveland, Ohio.

8. Released on 7 November that year, starring Donald Pleasence, Françoise Dorléac, Jack MacGowran, Marie Kean, William Franklyn and Jacqueline Bissett.

9. Subsequently Edna O'Brien was to be a Booker judge in 1973, when *The Siege of Krishnapur* won the award.

10. Bob Cumming, who had returned from the Far East and was living back home again. Dr Cumming was Bob's father.

11. Claude Simha.

12. JGF had recoiled from 'the hypocrisy' of Christmas since his teenage years.

13. He deeply resented his father's similar tactic.

14. John and Hilary Spurling, with whom JGF was firm friends by now in London.

15. The Belvedere was in decline; 'a fleabag hotel', in John Guare's view. It

had 450 rooms, to be rented by the week or by the day.

16. Boris Slattery, the main character in *A Girl in the Head*. Martin Sands' polio ordeal dominates *The Lung*.

17. JGF was researching for the still indistinct *Troubles*.

18. *The Red and the Green* (1965).

19. Where JGF, too, had stayed from the autumn of 1963 until the early summer of 1964.

20. Erwin Fleissner, a Rhodes scholar, had been a close companion at Oxford. A molecular biologist, he was now working on tumour viruses at the Sloane Kettering Cancer Research Institute in New York, and living with his wife Norma in style near Central Park, compared with JGF's lodgings. Strick's film of *Ulysses* had just come out, starring Milo O'Shea, Barbara Jefford and T.P. McKenna. JGF was unsurprised to learn that it was banned in Ireland. (The ban was not lifted until 2000.)

21. *Troubles*.

22. Trans: turnips.

23. The main character in Thomas Mann's *The Magic Mountain*, one of JGF's benchmark books. His own experience of polio found many echoes in the TB sanatorium where the novel is set.

24. A character taking shape in *Troubles*.

25. Guare (b. 1938) was a playwright, and fellow student at Yale Drama School. Subsequently he won acclaim for *A House of Blue Leaves* in 1971 and *Six Degrees of Separation* in 1990.

26. Anita Gross, Jim's agent in New York, was then working with the Lynn Nesbitt agency.

27. André Shiffrin had been a contemporary at Cambridge when Jim was at Oxford, and both had joined the Hemingwayesque jaunt to Pamplona to enact *The Sun Also Rises*. In 1967 Shiffrin was a senior editor with Pantheon, and about to become managing director. Ten years after JGF's death, high-principled Shiffrin resigned over demands by parent company Random House to cut Pantheon's list and staff by two-thirds, and in 1990 he founded New Press, a non-profit publisher. He is the author of *The Business of Books* (2000).

28. The New York literary agency handling JGF's book in the US.

29. Paul Léautaud (1872–1956), the French writer and critic whose monumental diary spanned the years from 1893 to within five days of his death. It is divided into *Journal Littéraire,* about Léautaud's literary life at Mercure de France, and *Journal Particulair,* about his turbulent relationships with women. He never married.

30. Franz Beer had moved to the US to teach and paint, with his new partner, Marlis. He lived in Providence, easily reached by JGF on the direct New York–Boston line which also served the Yale stop, New Haven.

31. A small island off Rhode Island, recommended by Franz Beer earlier for its solitude out of season. It is reached by ferry from Point Judith.

32. The ruin of the Ocean View Hotel provided the catalyst for the Majestic Hotel in *Troubles* and did give him the structure for the novel. He was on Block Island from 5–11 May.

33. An elegaic and autobiographical short novel by Giorgio Bassani about a rich, apparently secure Italian Jewish family observed in 1938; it is related in the knowledge of their deaths within five years, following deportation to Germany. The narrator, a young outsider, reminded JGF of his own emotions as a teenager when drawn to the confident, hospitable Kirwan family.

34. A teasing but deliberate exaggeration, which Carol found unsettling.

35. Sandy Ellis was an illustrator with an advertising agency in London, who drove her Mini with as much verve as she had ridden Pony Club winners in childhood. She had long blonde hair, and favoured short mini-skirts and knee-high boots. 'He liked nothing better than to take me out to an intellectual gathering,' she said once, 'and know that I was out of place.' From being warm-hearted and spontaneous, she lost confidence. He mentioned marriage once before leaving for New York, but on the icy condition that he would never live with her full-time. 'I don't think,' she mused later, 'I would have let myself marry him.'

36. On discovering that JGF was travelling with Sandy, a previous London girlfriend, Carol had given him an ultimatum: he would have to choose between them.

37. Claude Simha was Farrell's doctor friend in Paris who had helped him with medical detail for *The Lung*, and arranged the stay in Morocco in 1964. In return, Farrell had introduced him to an Icelandic student, Anna, that year, with the words 'I have a wife for you'. As Claude once commented, '*Et voilà!*'

38. Flora Knox Peebles was then aged 5.

39. 'Pan Books have made an offer of £750 which I think we should accept,' Jonathan Clowes advised on 5 April 1967, adding 'The nearest offer of £350 came from Corgi.' [Family papers]

40. The 12th Street riots in Detroit began on 23 July and lasted for 5 days, leaving 43 dead and 467 injured. Some 7,200 people were arrested and over 2,000 buildings torched. The national impact made a cover of *Time*

magazine on 4 August 1967.

41. G.M. Arthursen had taught JGF at Rossall, when Head of Modern Languages. He was one of two masters there – the other was Norman Ilett – with whom JGF kept in touch.

42. A strike by the sanitation men of New York City had begun on 3 February. It lasted for nine days, and by its end garbage was piled two feet high in places.

Beginning to Ship Water (pp. 126–164)

1. Robert Kennedy, younger brother of the assassinated US President John F. Kennedy, had been shot dead on 5 June 1968 at the Ambassador Hotel, Los Angeles, while campaigning for the Democratic Party nomination in the forthcoming presidential elections.

2. Oliver Marriott was an Oxford contemporary who had become a senior financial journalist on *The Times*. Lif, his wife, was Swedish.

3. When Sarah thought she was pregnant shortly before JGF left New York, she had suggested a hot bath and 'lots' of gin. They had put the idea into practice – unnecessarily, as it turned out.

4. JGF had left the most recent pages of the first draft of *Troubles* with Sarah, to be photocopied by her and sent on. She viewed them, half seriously, as hostages for his permanent return.

5. The Farrells had sold up in County Dublin and retired to Malta, where they had bought a flat in Bugibba. The purpose-built and rapidly expanding development on the coast was promoted as a home-from-home for the British and Irish.

6. Dr Elie Harar and his new wife Irma. JGF had spent the autumn of 1964 with Elie, whose vast practice was situated in the foothills of the Atlas Mountains in Morocco. A capacious, scantily furnished house in the re-mote village of Ait Ouvrir had come with the post.

7. See his inimitable approach to Matthew Webb's initiation into 'the acts of love' by Vera Chiang in *The Singapore Grip*, pp. 300–03.

8. Stanley Kubrick's film, *2001: A Space Odyssey*, had had a mixed recep-tion since its release on 6 April.

9. *The Property Boom* (Hamish Hamilton 1967), which had become a best-seller during JGF's absence in New York.

10. Norma di Marco.

11. His chosen method of travel in London.

12. JGF had loved Hughes' novels since discovering *A High Wind in Ja-maica* at the age of nine. Within a few years of this letter, the two men

would become friends. (See letters 16 June 1975 and 25 August 1976)

13. 'So that was what she looked like ... but to tell the truth he only half remembered her; she was half herself and half some stranger ...'

14. On 21 April 1967 Greece had been convulsed by a military coup, and Papandreou (1919–96), a deputy minister, was arrested by the colonels in charge of the new regime. He had since been released, chiefly because of a campaign outside the country – he had spent years as an academic in America. He was currently forming an anti-junta movement known as PAK (Panhellenic Liberation Movement).

15. *Le Tourbillon de la Vie* (The Whirlwind of Life) by Georges Delerue, sung by Moreau in *Jules and Jim* (directed by François Truffaut, 1962).

16. Franco Zeffirelli's film adaptation of the Shakespeare play (1967), starring Elizabeth Taylor and Richard Burton.

17. Kim Braden (b. 1949) was appearing on BBC television that year in *B & B* with her popular Canadian parents, Bernard Braden and Barbara Kelly.

18. The friendship had begun at university, when Spence (b. 1936), a Wykehamist, had been among the Cambridge contingent on *The Sun Also Rises* Pamplona trip. At Yale Spence was already being recognised as a foremost scholar of Chinese civilisation. A fellow of the American Academy of Arts and Sciences (1985), he became Sterling Professor of History at Yale in 1993. Spence's book *The Search for Modern China* is a standard text.

19. After JGF's death, Olivia Manning would dedicate her last novel, *The Sum of Things*, to him.

20. JGF's favourite Indian restaurant, situated at 21/23 Westbourne Grove, London. The Standard remained in business, little changed, until November 2007.

21. Larry, a writer, and Virginia Snelling were American expatriates, and about to move to Paris.

22. Hubert Humphrey (1911–78), Lyndon Johnson's Vice President, was now the Democratic nominee, following Johnson's withdrawal on 31 March and Robert Kennedy's assassination.

23. Bill Farrell's older sister May and her husband.

24. The anti-Vietnam riots erupted at the Democratic convention in Chicago from 26–29 August, leading to 668 arrests. Twelve thousand police were reinforced by 6,000 Illinois National Guard, and 6,000 troops were on standby. In Czechoslovakia, the invasion of the Soviet army on 21 August had ended the Prague Spring reforms of Alexander Dubcek.

25. In February 1968 Carol had spent ten strained days in Puerto Rico

with JGF, their sexual relationship effectively over. 'I wanted him to say "Come to England with me",' she revealed later, unaware at the time of his feelings for Sarah. 'And, of course, he didn't.'

26. Transl: In this house Bond was deflowered [lit].

27. The cheap restaurant in rue de la Grande Chaumière, which Claude Simha had introduced him to in 1964. It continued in business virtually as it was – except for prices – until the late 1990s.

28. Richard Farrell, who was eight years younger than Jim.

29. Dr Claude Simha.

30. On 7th Avenue and 51st Street.

31. The Major (Brendan Archer), Edward Spencer and Sarah Devlin are the principal characters in *Troubles*.

32. Sandy Ellis.

33. Zorba the Greek was a fictional free-spirited peasant. In the 1964 film of the novel of the same name by Nikos Kazantzakis, Zorba was played by Anthony Quinn.

34. Jackie Kennedy married Aristotle Onassis the following day on Skorpios, Onassis' private Greek island.

35. A medieval term to denote any remote place beyond the borders of the known world.

36. Richard Nixon had narrowly beaten Hubert Humphrey on 5 November.

37. *Hair* was playing at the Shaftesbury Theatre, London; it had opened on 27 September.

38. Spurling's play *MacRune's Guevara*, directed by Robert Stephens and Frank Dunlop, opened at the Old Vic in London on 30 May 1969.

39. JGF was researching back numbers for *Troubles*, and would splice many news items into the text.

40. Christmas cards from the Knox Peebles traditionally featured a drawing by one of their children; Fleur was a younger sister of Jim's god-daughter Flora.

41. JGF had often been to La Coupole, 102 Boulevard Montparnasse, with Claude Simha during the winter of 1963. He had jibbed at the prices, pointing out that a cup of coffee there cost as much as a (subsidised) four-course meal at the Cité Université.

42. 'The Select', dating from the 1920s had been another favourite haunt when JGF lived in Paris for a year. To reach it, he took the metro from Porte d'Orléans, opposite his digs at the Cité Université, to Vavin, which was within a stroll of Le Select at 99 Boulevarde du Montparnasse.

43. When his hair-loss while writing *A Man from Elsewhere* had worsened

in Toulon in February 1962, JGF consulted a local GP, Dr Delbos, who turned out to be a devotee of Proust. Diagnosing alopecia, Delbos had prescribed rest and handed him Guiseppe di Lampedusa's novel *The Leopard* to read; the novel had been published posthumously four years earlier.

44. General Post Office.

45. A film noir directed by Nicholas Ray in 1950. Bogart plays a potentially homicidal screenwriter who is angrily aware that his creative powers are being wiped out by working in the film industry.

46. Mailer's 1968 book *The Armies of the Night*, about the previous year's anti-Vietnam march on the Pentagon, had won the Pulitzer Prize and National Book Award. More challengingly for JGF, in that period Mailer had also covered the 1968 Democratic and Republican conventions for *Harper's Magazine*, and his book on them, *Miami and the Siege of Chicago*, was already out.

47. Norma Fleissner had energetically shown JGF around New York on his arrival in 1966. He hated being asked for his opinion on a book or ms., knowing that if he was honest it was bound to be severe, and his preferred response was to promise to read it as soon as pressures eased, and then say nothing more. But his letter to Norma did not deter her. Under her maiden name, Norma Klein, she wrote 29 books for children and young adults between 1973 and her premature death in 1989, and her publishers included Viking, Pantheon and Knopf.

48. A teasing reference for John, evoking the obsessive elderly artist MacRune in John's play at the Old Vic, *MacRune's Guevara*.

49. The review was by Martin Levin, and appeared on the date JGF wrote this letter, 23 March 1969. Presumably he had been shown it in advance.

50. Virginia Kirkus (1893–1980) was an American critic whose businesslike book review service, based on advance galleys, strongly influenced librarians, booksellers, literary editors, agents and film producers.

51. The anarchic Lindsay Anderson film starred Malcolm McDowell and had been released just after Christmas. It was about a pupil-led armed revolution at an English public school, which JGF delighted in equating with Rossall.

52. Contemporary critics acknowledge the link between *If* and the 1933 film *Zéro de Conduite,* directed by Jean Vigo, who drew on his own repressive boarding school experiences.

53. Tom Wakefield (1935–96) lived at 23 Avenell Road, London N.5. The son of a northern miner, he was headmaster of Downsview School in Hackney, and lent JGF an orthopaedic aid for his hands used by polio vic-

tims in his school. Learning that Tom yearned to become a writer, JGF advised him to be open about his homosexuality, which was still illegal. Wakefield followed his advice, and in due course literary success enabled him to take early retirement. He wrote eleven novels and a childhood autobiography, *Forties Child* (1978).

54. Carol had upheld the historic racial importance of the 1919 Chicago riots during their combative debates in New York. The exploitation of blacks after the abolition of slavery was the subject of her book *The Unfinished March* (Zenith Books, Doubleday & Company Inc, 1967).

55. His recipe can be found in *Mastering the Art of French Cooking* by Julia Child (Knopf 1961), whose televised demonstrations he had followed avidly with Carol in Manhattan. It is *Fricassée de Poulet à l'Ancienne,* pp. 258–61.

56. Richard had lost his mackintosh during the short visit to New York.

57. Segal was a senior editor with Harper & Row in New York who was said to have an eye for the *avant-garde* and to admire searing honesty – not exactly in tune with JGF.

Troubles (Aptly Named) (pp. 165–200)

1. JGF's editor at Pan had recommended Deborah Rogers as a rising star. She had set up her literary agency in London two years earlier, after gaining valuable experience of the business in New York. He did not inform Clowes of the switch of allegiance, who was to learn of it through Rogers' polite phone call.

2. JGF had known Janet Dawson at Oxford, where she read French at St Hilda's, and she helped him study for his Finals. She had fallen in love with him there, and was the model for his first published short story in *Isis*, 'Letter for Carola'.

3. His private name for the loosely envisaged story that became *The Siege of Krishnapur*.

4. *Strumpet City* was a popular historical novel about the Dublin lock-out by the Irish writer James Plunkett (1920–2003), set between 1907 and 1914.

5. V.S. Naipaul had already published ten books, including *An Area of Darkness*, a controversial view of India which intrigued JGF. In due course they would be on first-name terms, and 'Vidya' [*sic*], a Booker winner two years before him in 1971, became an occasional supper-guest.

6. *A Dance to the Music of Time*. At that date, nine of the twelve-volume series had been published; *The Military Philosophers* (1968) was the most recent.

7. The moon landing had occurred on 20 July 1969.

8. Jim's encouragement was to bear fruit posthumously, with the publication of Russell's book *Night Thoughts of a German Physicist* (Harvard University Press, 1991).

9. *A Fox in the Attic* by Richard Hughes.

10. One of the two call-girls he had got to know six years earlier. (See letter to Russell McCormmach dated 4 April 1963.) JGF modelled the character of Lucy Hughes, the fallen woman, on her personality in *The Siege of Krishnapur*. His ambivalent feelings towards her shade the emotions of the Major in *Troubles*.

11. *Dark as the Grave Wherein My Friend is Laid* (Jonathan Cape, 1969) was published after Lowry's death, co-edited by his widow. In America it had come out a year earlier, but was still being reviewed.

12. Robert Lusty (1909–91) was Managing Director of Hutchinson from 1956–73. He was knighted in 1969.

13. Anita Gross, his US agent, who was still hoping that David Segal would take *Troubles*.

14. *The Recollections of Rifleman Bowlby*, a realistic memoir of the 1944 Italian campaign in the Second World War. Officer-class Bowlby had avoided a commission in the Greenjackets, preferring to be 'accepted for what he was, rather than for what he was supposed to be'.

15. The comic novel (1932) by Stella Gibbons is a parody of the Victorian taste for melodramatic novels of rural life. Flora Poste's admirer Mr Mybug (Meyerburg) is a writer, convinced that her disinterest in him is the result of sexual repression.

16. In fact, the £20 fee was handsome enough to change JGF's mind. Earlier he had suggested a film column to Hilary and submitted examples, but she had frowned at the didactic tone.

17. Routledge had just turned down Bridget's synopsis on *Imagery* for their *Concepts of Literature* series.

18. Diana Saville, JGF's flatmate.

19. Diana's cat, rechristened Mappin by JGF in his tradition of borrowing famous shop names begun by Tiffany, his cat in Dublin. Webb became a principal character in *The Singapore Grip*.

20. The influential French New Wave film (1959) directed by Alain Resnais, about a European actress who takes a Japanese man as a lover, intercut with flashbacks to her affair with a German soldier. In January 1961 JGF wrote to Gabriele: 'On the way to Paris I drove through Nevers (have you seen *Hiroshima Mon Amour*?) and it was fascinating to see how

like it really is to the film: the same stunted trees and gabled houses.'

21. The novelist Piers Paul Read and his wife Emily. In 1967 they had inherited JGF's Chevrolet in New York at the start of Piers' own Harkness Fellowship, and called to his small apartment for tea to collect the keys. Jim still felt a strong rivalry beneath his congenial exterior, and knew that Piers, too, was represented by Deborah Rogers.

22. Where Bridget was living while attending the University of Warwick in Coventry.

23. William V. Shannon (1927–88) was on the editorial board of the *New York Times*, and his Kennedy book had come out in 1967. His path would indirectly cross Jim's again in 1979, when Shannon was the American Ambassador to Ireland.

24. JGF's great liking for congenial Peter Brown dated back to his teens in Dublin, where their parents were friends. They took up rock-climbing together at Killiney Quarry, and it was Brown, then at All Souls, Oxford, who escorted him home from hospital after polio. While JGF was still at Brasenose, Brown was shown an early version of *The Lung*. 'There were some very strong parts in the draft that I read, especially the meditations of one patient on why God had chosen him for all this. It was a chilling passage, so chilling that I remember its effect on me rather than the words themselves.' Brown's academic path led to America where *Augustine of Hippo* was written when he was 32, and established his reputation in the field of late antiquity. He later became Philip and Beulah Rollins Professor of History at Princeton.

25. Ineige, aka Inez, the precocious half-Portuguese, half-Swedish young lodger – the girl in the title – at Boris Slattery's house in *A Girl in the Head*.

26. Professor Nikolay Stepanovitch, whose self-image is dingy and unsightly. 'My neck, as Turgenev says ... is like the handle of a double bass; my chest is hollow; my shoulders narrow; ... when I smile, my whole face is covered with aged-looking, deathly wrinkles. There is nothing impressive about my pitiful figure.' (Transl. by Constance Garnett.)

27. JGF's previous agent, Jonathan Clowes, who had represented him for that book.

28. The 'hacking job' was suggested by Malcolm Dean, a senior journalist and leader writer on the *Guardian*. Practical and straightforward, Dean had become a supportive friend after getting to know JGF in New York when both were on Harkness Fellowships, and they saw a great deal of one another in London.

29. Originally written in French, as were all Jim's letters to Claude and

Anna.

30. Claude's friend Dr Elie Harar, who had been JGF's host in Morocco six years earlier.

31. Jim was bringing Bridget to meet Claude and Anna. On this visit he confided that he had proposed to her and was prepared to have children; to Claude's concern, the word 'sacrifice' was used, and Bridget was described as 'undecided'.

32. Not a new idea. On the Lowry pigrimage to Cuernavaca (renamed Quauhnahuac in *Under the Volcano*) in the summer of 1967, JGF had lingered over the ruins of Maximilian's Summer Palace.

33. See previous letter, to Carol Drisko, dated 18 December 1969. Hoping against hope for the withheld £180, JGF was to be disappointed.

34. Bernard Hollowood (1910–81) had stepped down from the editorship of *Punch* three years earlier. His energy and conflicting interests may have rankled with Powell: Hollowood was a writer, cartoonist, economist (cartoons were signed 'Mammon'), pottery expert and cricketer. His most recent book, *Cricket on the Brain* (1970), began, 'I was brought up to believe that cricket was the most important activity in men's lives.' Hollowood's predecessor at *Punch* had been Malcolm Muggeridge.

35. The sixth novel in Powell's *A Dance to the Music of Time* (1962).

36. Both by Thomas Hardy; the former published in 1886, the latter in twelve monthly instalments throughout 1878.

37. JGF's paperback editor at Pan Books.

38. With his next book in mind, the money was needed to fund the necessary research trip to India.

39. Mappin, Diana's athletic and strong-willed cat.

40. Juliet Page was a copy-editor at Jonathan Cape.

41. Major Brendan Archer's fiancée, Angela Spencer, in *Troubles*.

42. The Majestic Hotel.

43. He did not entirely get his way. The finished version reads: 'Against a background of world upheaval – race riots in Chicago, disorders throughout the Empire and the inexorable advance of the dreaded Bolshevists – events at the Majestic, both chaotic and comical, move towards the inevitable conflagration. In *Troubles*, J.G. Farrell presents the tragic-comedy of a country's struggle for independence, miniaturised and set in amber.'

44. Robina Masters was also working on *Troubles* at Jonathan Cape.

45. Jim's love of hyperbole. Rittenhouse Square is a smart area of Philadelphia.

46. The weekly rent was £3.50, and JGF described the asking price for the five years left of the twenty-one-year lease as 'very reasonable'. The lease was

signed in May, with Bridget O'Toole as his witness.

47. The apologetic tone was prompted by 'a bit of a falling-out' as Bridget later put it, owing to his offhand manner.

48. British Museum.

49. Philip Larkin (1922–85) wrote *A Girl in Winter* (Faber & Faber, 1947) when working as a librarian in Wellington, Shropshire after failing his military medical because of poor eyesight.

The Home Beautiful (pp. 201–221)

1. On the way to the World Cup in Mexico, Bobby Moore had been arrested for theft in Colombia. On release, he captained England to a thrilling 1–0 defeat to Brazil, during which he and Pele went toe-to-toe, but two years elapsed before he was cleared of the theft.

2. George Gissing (1857–1903) used to be regarded as a premier English novelist of the late Victorian era for his unsparing realism. *Born in Exile* (1892), Gissing's eleventh novel, is semi-autobiographical.

3. *The Vivisector* (1970).

4. *Mastering the Art of French Cooking* by Julia Child, Simone Beck and Louisette Bertholle (Knopf 1961). When living on East 27th Street in Manhattan, JGF had been a fan of Child's regular tv cookery demos, and he credited her with igniting his interest in cooking. The book has three fish soufflé recipes: *Soufflé de Saumon, Soufflé de Poisson, and Filets de Poisson en Soufflé* (pp. 187–92). JGF also used Child's *French Chef Cookbook* (Knopf 1968).

5. *Indian Cookery*, Mrs Balbir Singh's popular classic, was first published in 1961.

6. On 9 September 1970 JGF formally accepted the Arts Council's offer of a £750 grant. A cheque was posted to him within the week.

7. When Nigel Lawson, the editor of the *Spectator*, was sacked on losing his Eton and Slough seat in the 1970 general election, Hilary Spurling resigned in protest as literary editor.

8. Bridget O'Toole had taken up a teaching post with the New University of Ulster in Coleraine, Northern Ireland.

9. A dig at Malcolm's paternal and protective qualities, as he had taken Bridget under his wing. Usually it was grammar-school-educated Bridget and Malcolm who teased Jim – '*Poor* boy!' – for having public school hang-ups.

10. There is no trace of a 1970 interview with JGF in the *Guardian* back-numbers.

11. Catherine Barton, known professionally as Catherine Peters at Jonathan

Cape, was his ally over the shrunken royalty cheque. 'I found myself in the curious position,' she said later, 'of defending my author against my own firm.'

12. *The Times*: 'Mr Farrell is an eccentric and highly gifted writer.' *The Guardian*: 'It is this feeling of the particular reflecting the universal, a feeling so successfully pervading page after page of this clever book, that makes it a *tour de force* of considerable quality. *Troubles* is sad; tragic; it is also very funny.' *The New Statesman*: 'A most unhappy mixture of historical, political and fantastical ... hopelessly mixed up ... The construction and organisation is as flabby and redundant as in most of the products of the Gothic craze, and the essential arbitrariness of the conception in imaginative terms undermines its ... observations.'

13. This was unfortunate, because Campbell Black was a fair and regular reviewer of fiction for the *New Statesman*.

14. Irresistible, because the two Malcolms were such opposites. Malcolm X (1925–65) was the black Muslim activist assassinated while making a speech to a New York crowd, and conspiracy theories were rife during Jim and Malcolm Dean's overlapping Harkness year there in 1967.

15. The poet Bruce Williamson (1922–91) had been Literary Editor of *The Irish Times* for many years, and was senior deputy editor. His review of *Troubles*, 'House of Regrets', was published on 17 October 1970. Coincidentally, Williamson was a Shrewsbury contemporary of one of Jim's new London friends, the novelist Francis King.

16. 'Irish Airs' by Philip Norman, 18 October 1970.

17. There was an open fire in the flat directly above JGF, on which coke, a smokeless by-product of coal, was burned in winter. The large first-floor flat was occupied by the celebrated pianist Alfred Brendel, who tended to hum loudly while practising.

18. Patrick Campbell, 3rd Baron Glenavy (1913–80) wrote a popular column in the *Sunday Times* and, despite his stammer, wittily captained *Call My Bluff* on BBC tv. In JGF's youth, Campbell, a Dubliner, had been the columnist Quidnunc on *The Irish Times*.

19. Leslie Charteris (1907–93) created *The Saint* series of books which featured Simon Templar, a fore-runner to James Bond. The saint's illustration was a matchstick man complete with halo.

20. J.R. Ackerley (1896–1967) had been editor of *The Listener* from 1935 to 1959, commissioning regular contributors who included E.M. Forster, Virginia Woolf, Clive Bell, W.H. Auden, Christopher Isherwood and Stephen Spender. He was openly homosexual, despite repressive laws at the time. His memoir *My Father and Myself* (published posthumously in

1968) was described by Truman Capote as being the most original he had ever read, and Francis King told JGF that Ackerley had been one of his principal mentors.

21. Bridget believed that Labour shop-floor solidarity was the best hope for uniting the Catholic and Protestant working classes in Northern Ireland. JGF christened her Red Biddy.

22. 'Downhill All the Way', the review of *Troubles* by JGF's friend Stephen Wall, was published in the *Observer* on 11 October 1970.

23. In the mid-term Senate elections of 1970, Nixon and his Republican Vice-President, Spiro Agnew, used smear tactics to prevent the re-election of Albert Gore Senior. They accused him of being an atheist for voting against a constitutional amendment to put the government in charge of religion in state schools, and of being unpatriotic for opposing the Vietnam war.

24. JGF, a Labour voter, was depressed by the Conservatives' win in June under Edward Heath (1916–2005). His disdain for Heath's policies for unemployment, inflation and colonial unrest was usually far more outspoken.

25. Irish for Bridget O'Toole.

26. Hyde Solomon (1911–82), a member of the American Abstract Artists and a founding member in the 1940s of the Jane Street Gallery Co-operative in Greenwich Village. Another member, Nell Blaine, was a polio victim, and Solomon had helped her to restart her career from her wheelchair. Similar empathy drew him to JGF when they met in 1967 in New York.

27. 'Ireland Agonistes', *Europa* 1 (1971), pp. 58–59.

28. See the diary entry for 11 May 1967. JGF had just come across the old diary when tidying his flat.

29. Anthony Sampson (1926–2004), a pioneering editor of South Africa's *Drum* magazine, had written the influential *Anatomy of Britain* (1963); his book *The New Europeans* was newly published. Sampson was married to Sally Bentlif, whom Jim had taken a fancy to at Oxford (see his card to her in 'Threshold'), and she was now a literary agent with A.D. Peters.

30. Paul Barker, an Oxford near contemporary, edited *New Society*, which he described as being centre-left without being party-political, and non-metropolitan. Approving of both ideals, JGF contributed occasional reviews. Paul and his wife Sally lived in Kentish Town, and JGF never missed their traditional Labour-supporting election-night party, monitoring the televised results as they came in.

31. Handwritten letter to Bridget O'Toole on a page of *Krishnapur* type-

script containing two lines: '... did not so much stop the vehicle as sullenly fail to keep it going the main thing was achieved. Harry and his dog were able to alight ...' There is a handwritten note with arrow – 'part of m'piece', and elsewhere on the page another arrow to the scrawled explanation, 'tea stains'.

32. Internment without trial began on 9 August 1970, leading to the flight of 3,000 people from Belfast, and a build-up of British troops in the province to 12,500. The State of Emergency would be lifted in 1972, and reintroduced the same year.

33. David Machin was then aged 36, and Deputy Managing Director of Cape.

34. Crook (1912–2005), the *TLS* editor between 1959 and 1974, had worked his way up from being a messenger boy on *The Times* and amateur lightweight boxer. Revered by his staff and respected by publishers and contributors, including top academics, despite his lack of a formal education, he delighted in literary controversy and talent-spotting. His 'finds' included Martin Amis.

35. The novelist Angus Wilson (1913–91), whom JGF almost met subsequently when staying with Sally Bentlif and Anthony Sampson at their weekend cottage in Suffolk, near where Wilson lived. Wilson cancelled at the last minute. (See letter to Norman Ilett dated 23 September 1974.)

Two Parts White Sahib (pp. 222–52)

1. JGF's teasing nickname for the Spurlings, based on a regular *Private Eye* cartoon.

2. The well-known cigarette packet features a camel.

3. Robert Gottlieb (b. 1931) was the editor for *Troubles* at Knopf in New York.

4. Elizabeth Bowen's review, 'Ireland Agonistes', appeared in *Europa*, 1 (1971), pp. 58–59.

5. Sarah liked to spend Christmas in England with her family.

6. Ray (1921–92) was beginning his *Calcutta Trilogy* (*Pratidwandi, Seemabaddha* and *Jana Aranya*) and JGF was given the introduction to him by Shiv Chirimar, a young Indian friend from Calcutta who was studying at the London Film School.

7. Spurling's uncle, Sir Edmund Gibson, was then aged eighty and living in retirement in Dehra Dun after a distinguished career in the Indian Civil Service.

8. Lauries Hotel, Mahatma Gandhi Road, Agra.

9. JGF had taken up an introduction to the Bhagats from a friend in England.

10. Margaret Dobbs, whose name was borrowed for a character in *Troubles*: 'The gay and charming Mrs Margaret Dobbs'.

11. Another British Army battalion had been brought in on 4 February, and Northern Ireland casualties began to mount. On 6 February the first British soldier was killed, and a Catholic civilian and an IRA member were shot by the Army. On 9 February five civilians were killed by a landmine near a BBC transmitter in County Tyrone. A second soldier died on 15 February, after being shot by a sniper seven days earlier.

12. Elizabeth Bowen particularly admired *Troubles* and gave it a glowing review in *Europa*: 'a major work made deceptive as to its size by apparent involvement with what is minor'.

13. The Residency is where the real-life Siege of Lucknow had taken place, and where the action of JGF's book was set.

14. The Rev. H.S. Polehampton, whose account of the Mutiny he had studied in the British Library.

15. Lawrence (1806-57), newly-appointed provisional Governor-General, had commanded the besieged Residency and been an early casualty, when hit by a shell on 2 July 1857. 'Put on my tomb only this,' he is said to have insisted. 'Here lies Henry Lawrence who tried to do his duty.' The inscription remains.

16. JGF's full, unedited Indian Diary, in which the evidence of death – and his reaction to that – is pronounced, is published in *The Hill Station* (Phoenix paperback, an Orion imprint; originally Weidenfeld & Nicolson, 1980).

17. Bridget O'Toole referred to his hair combed back at either side of his head as 'wings'.

18. Polling for India's fifth general election was between 1 and 10 March. Indira Gandhi campaigned on the platform of 'eliminate poverty' (*garibi hatao*), and won a landslide victory. She took 351 seats out of 525, and gained a two-thirds majority in the Lok Sabha, the lower house.

19. Shiv Chirimar, who was back home on holiday and showed JGF around Calcutta.

20. Transl: open field, used to describe a town square.

The Rogues Gallery (pp. 253–90)

1. In Portlaoise, County Laois.

2. Established 1963 in tribute to Geoffrey Faber, founder of Faber and

Faber, and given in alternate years to a single volume of poetry or fiction; only Commonwealth authors under forty are eligible.

3. Mark Gerson (b. 1921) who specialised in literary portraits, preferably in writers' homes. His study of JGF is reproduced in this book, and his unique series of 161 portraits is held in the National Portrait Gallery.

4. JGF and Evans also shared a political allegiance, both voting Labour. Evans would rise swiftly through Faber and Faber to become Managing Director and then Chairman. In 2000 he was created a New Labour life peer.

5. Diana Saville, who had moved into a new flat elsewhere after Pont Street Mews.

6. The review would have been for Heyerdahl's *The RA Expedition* (1971).

7. JGF had known Caute since Oxford. He had interviewed him then at All Souls for *Isis* when Caute's first novel, *At Fever Pitch*, was shortlisted for the John Llewellyn Rhys prize, and they had both been ushers at the wedding of Brian and Rose Knox Peebles.

8. The anti-Communist Radio Liberty, set up in 1953 by the American Committee for the Liberation of the Peoples of Russia, was funded by the US Congress. Its mission statement was 'To promote democratic values and institutions by disseminating factual information and ideas'. Based in Hesse, Germany, it broadcast propaganda – sometimes jammed by the Soviet authorities – in the Russian language.

9. Fyodor Dostoevsky. JGF had caught the intimate first-name habit from Mike Roemer, his 'Writing for the Camera' teacher at Yale. Roemer venerated Proust, whom he referred to as 'Marcel'.

10. After demonstrations in response to Nixon's 30 April announcement of the American invasion of Cambodia, a State of Emergency was declared at Kent State University, Ohio. On 4 May, four students were shot dead there and nine wounded by the Ohio National Guard; some had been protesting, others merely caught up in the violence. Alison Krause, one of those killed, had been photographed on a demo the previous day putting a flower in the barrel of a Guardsman's rifle. 'Flowers are better than bullets' she was reported to have said. A poem, 'Bullets and Flowers' by Yevgeny Yevtushenko, is dedicated to her memory.

11. The university bar at Coleraine: more a figment of JGF's imagination than of everyday reality.

12. In fact, the journey to collect his books had been a miserable experience and in person he and Bridget had barely communicated. His cool politeness confirmed for her that her instinct to make a new life

independently, retaining his friendship, was correct.

13. In *Sight and Sound*, Janet's reviews appeared under the name Jan Dawson.

14. *Jaune le Soleil* (1971), from Duras' novel *Abahn, Sabana, David* (1969). Duras (1914–96), an ex-Communist, was a French writer and a director of experimental films. She had written the screenplay for *Hiroshima Mon Amour*.

15. One of Bridget's nicknames for him.

16. 'Crow', from *The Life and Songs of the Crow* by Ted Hughes (Faber and Faber, 1970).

17. Often described as a novel within a novel, from *À la Recherché du Temps Perdu* by Marcel Proust (Gallimard 1954). JGF read Proust in the original.

18. Alison Lurie (b. 1926), the American writer and academic. She had already written *Love and Friendship* (1962), *The Nowhere City* (1965), *Imaginary Friends* (1967) and *Real People* (1969), and had begun teaching at Cornell University a year earlier.

19. Cook (1931–94), a lanky Old Etonian with a taste for the underworld, had given JGF's address in New York to Sarah in 1968, with the instruction to contact him. They had met through Jonathan Clowes, when *A Crust on its Uppers* (1962) was winning Cook rave reviews; at one of his wild parties in those years JGF had met his callgirl. But by 1971 Cook was in deep financial trouble after five unsuccessful novels. Rose was his third wife, and that marriage, too, would end. His career later recovered when he embarked on a popular crime series under the pen name Derek Raymond.

20. Sybille Bedford (1911-2006) had known Thomas Mann, one of Jim's heroes, in the 1930s, and was working on a biography of Aldous Huxley, another of her friends. Her companion was probably the American novelist Eda Lord, with whom she had a twenty-year relationship.

21. A keen birdwatcher whom they both knew.

22. Dick Delaney, an easygoing Irishman, had been working on the DEW (Distant Early Warning Radar System) Line in the north Canadian arctic in 1955 when JGF took a pre-university job there. Both film fans, they had struck up a lasting rapport.

23. A bedroom farce by Hugh Leonard.

24. A popular, inexpensive restaurant at 122 Palace Gardens Terrace, Kensington, near the Notting Hill Gate end. JGF's 'greenhouse' was in the same road.

25. Basil Brush, the brisk and jolly – 'Boom boom!' – tv puppet.

26. On 11 July 1971 *The New York Times Book Review* gave its front page to novelist William H. Gass for 'Marcel Proust at 100'.

27. Checking in for flights from London airport (now Heathrow) was then done at the Cromwell Road Air Terminal, S.W.5.

28. *Claire's Knee* (1970) was the fifth in Eric Rohmer's series of *Six Moral Tales*, each a variation on the theme of a man in love with one woman who feels drawn to another, whom he in turn rejects to pursue the first.

29. Miss Rees was on the staff of Knopf in New York during the publication of the first American edition of *Troubles*.

30. Curious, because Roemer was Jewish himself, and a refugee in childhood from Nazi Germany.

31. By Martin Levin, 12 September 1971, p. 48.

32. *The Professor's Daughter* (Secker & Warburg, 1971) is set in the US, and influenced by Read's Harkness Fellowship in New York.

33. By Frederick Busch in *Saturday Review*, 25 September 1971, and deemed by JGF to be 'very nasty' (see letter to Carol Drisko dated 26 November 1971 and note 43.) The jargon he bristled at included the words 'Mr Farrell does not give us a connative experience: all is denotative.'

34. Stephen and Yvonne Wall, who lived in Oxford. By now JGF had forgiven Stephen for a 'grudging' review of *Troubles* in the *Observer*. (See letter dated 20 November 1970 to Carol Drisko.)

35. The poet Derek Mahon and his wife Doreen. He had recently read *Troubles* aloud to her at night in bed.

36. Mentioned in JGF's Indian Diary entry of 30 January 1971.

37. JGF's young Indian friend studying film, who had returned from Calcutta.

38. James Simmons (1933–2001), an Irish poet who was teaching at Coleraine with Bridget. In 1968 Simmons had founded the long-running literary magazine *The Honest Ulsterman*. His collection *Ballad of a Marriage* had come out five years earlier.

39. A session of traditional Irish music.

40. JGF's friend Larry Snelling identified it as being by James Frakes in *Book World*. Frakes (d. 2002) was a critic for the *New York Times Book Review* and professor of English Literature at Lehigh University, Bethlehem, Pennsylvania.

41. *The Milwaukee Journal* (Wisconsin), where Porterfield (1915–81) was a writer and editor.

42. Not to be confused with the worker/writer Jack Conroy (1898–1990), who wrote *The Disinherited* (1933).

43. Frederick Busch (1942–2002), only 29 at the time, which might have rankled even more, had JGF known. Busch's first novel, *I Wanted a Year without Fall*, appeared that year and at Colegate he lived on an old sheep farm where he wrote daily in a converted barn.

44. In October 1971 Edward Kennedy called for the withdrawal of British troops and the start of political dialogue for creating a United Ireland.

45. Salvador Allende, the president of Chile despite US hostility, was hosting a month-long visit by Castro, giving rise to speculation that the 'Chilean Way', Allende's democratic road to socialism, might turn into Cuban (Soviet) socialism. 'Coups do not happen in Chile,' stated General Augusto Pinochet publicly that month, but within two years JGF's fears would be justified when Pinochet assumed power after a violent military coup. At the time then it was officially said that Allende had committed suicide with a rifle given to him by Castro.

46. Carmichael (1941–98), the black activist, was born in Port of Spain, Trinidad. Naipaul was then married to Patricia (née Hale).

47. Ackland (1908–91) had written ten plays in the 1930s, his most prolific decade, and also collaborated with Hitchcock on screenplays. JGF was sufficiently taken with him to place him in *The Singapore Grip* where Matthew Webb remembers making a trip to London in 1932 'to see Gielgud's production of Rodney Ackland's magnificent play, *Strange Orchestra* at the St Martin's theatre' (p. 73). Ackland's wife, Mab Lonsdale, was the daughter of playwright Frederick Lonsdale. She died that year after this meeting.

48. In this letter JGF re-used an A4 page of the *Krishnapur* ms., torn in half, to write to Bridget on the back. The discarded words ran: '... so causes the loss of the entire fortress.' The Collector read this ~~passage in Machiavelli's treatise on the Art of War~~ passage with ~~particular~~ dismay because he had just given the order to begin ~~just~~ such a second line of defence.'

49. 'The Question of Ulster', a BBC1 debate on 5 January 1972, had already been postponed, but at last moderate Unionists had agreed to be represented. Reginald Maudling, the Conservative Home Secretary, gave a pre-recorded interview, and live contributors included Bernadette Devlin, Gerry Fitt and Ian Paisley. Afterwards panel member Lord Caradon agreed with JGF. 'We may have been dull,' he said, 'but I don't think we have been dangerous.'

50. In heated exchanges in the House of Commons following the shooting dead of thirteen marchers in Derry on Bloody Sunday that January, MP Bernadette Devlin slapped the face of the Home Secretary. Stormont

was suspended shortly afterwards, and Direct Rule was introduced in Northern Ireland.

51. Bill Tidy's regular cartoon, 'An Everyday Saga in the Life of Clog Dancing Folk', ran in *Private Eye*.

52. 'As you may have heard', JGF wrote to Sarah Bond ten days earlier, 'the "old country" has been virtually blacked out by the miners' strike which, amazingly and marvellously, 57 per cent of the population support, according to Gallup. There seems little prospect of getting rid of Heath, nonetheless.'

53. He would be there again within eighteen months as the centre of attention himself on the night of the 1973 Booker prizegiving. The Café Royal's plush décor finally vanished when it closed in 2009.

54. Djuna Barnes (1892–1982) would outlive JGF, as would Jean Rhys (1890–1979), who died three days after him. Rhys' obituary would appear beneath his, on the same page.

55. Dom Mintoff (b.1916) was re-elected the following month as Prime Minister of Malta.

56. Not known. The BBC European Service logs from 15 May–1 June give no mention, nor does the French Service programme *Lettres et Arts* which was broadcast on Mondays, the weekday when JGF wrote this letter.

57. JGF was determined that *Krishnapur* would go to the highest bidder. Without telling Deborah, who was about to begin negotiations with Gillon Aitken of Hamish Hamilton, he was to respond directly when Tony Godwin of Weidenfeld & Nicolson expressed strong interest in August. This is contrary to normal practice between author and agent.

58. Two of Anthony Burgess' Enderby Quartet, featuring the eccentric minor poet Francis Xavier Enderby, had been published: *Inside Mr Enderby* (1963) and *Enderby Outside* (1968).

59. Alan Riddell (1927–77), whom JGF had got to know in 1963 when both were lodgers at 35 Pembroke Road, Notting Hill. Riddell was born in Australia and educated in Scotland, and his peripatetic life already included spells in Greece, Spain and France. His work had appeared in *Lines, Scotland's Magazine of Poetry* (Issues 3, 19, 21 and 23), and *The Stopped Landscape* (Hutchinson) had come out in 1968; *Eclipse* was about to be published by Calder.

60. JGF had given Bresson [1901–99], a fellow-devotee of Dostoevsky, a copy of *Troubles*. 'I read English slowly and haven't finished, but I can wait no longer to tell you that I like it a lot', wrote Bresson on 13 July 1972. 'I

am touched, as I always am, when an author leads me into a new world that he has created. *Troubles* makes me wish we will meet again, so let me know when you are in Paris and I will let you know when I am in London.' On 19 February 1973 Bresson wrote again, requesting further information about the book. If a film was envisaged, however, the idea was taken no further. (Family papers.)

61. John Spurling.

62. Whenever married couples separated whom he greatly liked, JGF's sympathy was with their children. This letter to an old friend is included to demonstrate his stern conventional view of marriage and parenthood, which deterred him from such commitment himself.

63. By John Fowles (Jonathan Cape, 1969). There are obvious similarities, but *The French Lieutenant's Woman* is set in 1867, ten years later than *The Siege of Krishnapur*, and in Victorian England, not India.

64. Lavinia Trevor was a young literary agent and frequent dinner-party guest at Jim's flat in Egerton Gardens.

65. Christopher Sinclair-Stevenson, a popular editor at Hamish Hamilton.

66. Norman Ilett, a master at Rossall, had taken rugby practice for the first XV when JGF was on the team.

67. The novelist Francis King, a Faber Prize judge in the year *Troubles* won, was fast becoming a friend.

68. Cabourg, where Proust spent his summers from 1907 to 1914 at the Grand Hotel, was the inspiration for the fictional Balbec in *À la Recherche du Temps Perdu*.

69. JGF had begun research for *The Singapore Grip*.

70. King's review, 'Ritual of the Deathbed', appeared in the *Sunday Telegraph* on 16 September 1973.

71. *Flight* consisted of two novellas about emotional manipulation: *The Infection*, the first, is set around a honey-trap translator working for intelligence in Hungary, and *The Cure* is about a holiday affair between an Englishwoman and a Japanese man who exploits her trust to smuggle a bomb aboard her plane. (Hutchinson, 1973.)

72. In the Best of Booker award in 2008, between six previous winners selected from forty-one, Edna O'Brien championed JGF's cause at the Queen Elizabeth Hall in London for the public vote. (The other five finalists were Pat Barker for *The Ghost Road*, J.M. Coetzee for *Disgrace*, Nadine Gordimer for *The Conservationist*, Peter Carey for *Oscar and Lucinda*, and Salman Rushdie – the ultimate winner – for *Midnight's Children*.)

73. JGF's mention of fortitude referred to the long-term consequences of their shared experience of polio: Stephen's physical limitations were much the greater.

74. 'Whom the Gods wish to destroy, they first call promising.' Cyril Connolly's advice in *Enemies of Promise* was that writers should recognise the snares of sex and domesticity (the pram in the hall), avoid journalism and politics, and be self-disciplined. Success, he warned, was the most insidious enemy of all.

75. JGF had met the Irish brothers Vincent and John Banville at a December photo shoot for the *Sunday Times* of six literary prizewinners; the rollcall had also included Eugène Ionesco. In 2005 John Banville, too, would be awarded the Booker Prize (for his novel *The Sea*).

76. Catherine Barton (Peters), his editor at Cape, had loaned him private family letters from two young officers, Edward and Charles Metcalf Mac-Gregor, who were distant uncles on her mother's side caught up in the 1857 siege of Lucknow. Seventeen-year-old Edward had died there of cholera. In *The Siege of Krishnapur*, Fleury and Harry Dunstable are 'the two young men' JGF mentions.

77. Catherine's husband, the psychiatrist and author Anthony Storr (1920–2001).

78. Bishop presided over the celebratory Booker Prize lunch, but although JGF enjoyed his company, their paths did not cross again. (See the letter to his parents dated 27.1.74.)

79. JGF took Sarah Bond with him to the Booker lunch, because she was in England on her annual Christmas visit. 'He was disparaging of himself moving in grand circles,' she observed afterwards, 'and yet engineering it.'

80. He was involved with the Public Lending Rights Campaign, and sided with the militant Writers Guild.

81. Bamber Gascoigne (b. 1935) had much in common with JGF. Born a day earlier, on 24 January, he had been at Oxbridge and spent a year at Yale (1958-9) on a Harkness Fellowship. Cape had published his book *The Great Moghuls*, and he was a familiar face, having presented *University Challenge* on television since 1962.

82. *The Ice Saints*, awarded the James Tait Black Memorial Prize in 1965. (See JGF's letter to Russell McCormmach dated 6.4.66.)

83. He had long been an admirer of Manning's *The Balkan Trilogy*, as had his father. In 1980, after his death, Manning dedicated her last novel, *The Sum of Things*, the conclusion of her *Levant Trilogy*, to 'Jim Farrell, taken by the sea'.

84. The UK General Election, held on 28 February, had produced a hung parliament due to the abstention by Northern Ireland Unionists in protest over the Sunningdale Agreement. Failed negotiations between the incumbent Conservatives, led by Edward Heath, and the Liberals, resulted in the return of Labour under Harol Wilson, and another election held in October.

85. A neighbour's cat, known to its owners as Tibby, which so enchanted JGF that he had already written a mini-biography for children, *Pussimodo, the Hunch-backed Pussycat*, illustrated by his friend Monika Beisner. 'Mainly an excuse for Monika's beautiful drawings,' he professed to Deborah Rogers, when floating the idea to her of finding a publisher for it on 17 October 1973. Another story by him, this time about Monika's tomcat, entitled 'The Pussycat Who Fell in Love with a Suitcase', was published in *Atlantis* (6) 1973–4, pp. 6–10.

86. JGF had bought a Zeiss Contaflex camera in Canada with his first pay cheque in 1955; it had been left behind on a recent visit.

87. Brenda was Deborah Rogers' assistant.

88. Rogers had been approached by Jules Buck, of Keep Films in Belgravia, about a film option for *The Siege of Krishnapur*. JGF duly met Buck at his office, where tea was served in gold-leaf china cups, but the proposal put forward of Peter O'Toole (who co-owned the company) for the lead, and a screenplay by John Osborne, had not distracted him from the matter of money.

89. The proposed contract was with Jules Buck of Keep films. JGF did not sign, preferring David Lean's offer.

90. Zinneman (1907–97), the unassuming director, was in fact the winner of no less than four Academy Awards. His latest film, *The Day of the Jackal*, had been released the previous year.

91. Stress was increased, as the Booker award raised the bar for expectations upon publication. And there were unpredictable time-consuming consequences, too. One that brought a smile was a letter dated 8 January 1975 from Cyril Clemens, editor of the *Mark Twain Journal*. 'In recognition of your outstanding contribution to literature by your *The Siege of Krishnapur* you have been elected, in succession to the late Jean Cocteau, Honorary Member in the Mark Twain Society.' (Family papers.)

92. David Lean.

93. By Robert M. Pirsig (Bodley Head, 1974).

94. 'The speech was vintage Nixon,' wrote George Bush Senior, Chairman of the Republican Party, on 9 August 1974.

95. But JGF was adapting fast, mixing old friends and new. On 10 December 1974 Piers Paul Read noted in his diary: 'Went to dinner with Jim Farrell to meet Gabriel García Márquez.'

96. A master at Rossall in JGF's day.

The Singapore Grip (pp. 291–330)

1. JGF postponed his research trip until within sight of completing the first draft of *The Singapore Grip*, and was worn out before he began. This comment was to reassure his parents, and the small Chinese-run 'South Asia' hotel which he moved to cost a mere $3 a night.

2. He was equipped with the large-scale, out of date, street map which had hung over his desk in London, and his aim was to gather authentic period detail relating to the fall of Singapore.

3. Lee Kuan Yew (b. 1923) Prime Minister of Singapore from 1959 to 1990.

4. Transl: a lawn or field.

5. The Great World Amusement Park dated from the 1930s, when it had been a magnet for British servicemen because of its free films and boxing matches, so an important setting for his book. During the Japanese Occupation it had been used as a prison for Australian POWs and despite an expensive postwar fairground revival, it had closed in 1964, leaving only a few cinemas and restaurants in business.

6. Matthew Webb, the idealistic central character in *The Singapore Grip*, who reluctantly joins Blackett and Webb, the profitable family firm in the Far East, a few months before the Japanese attack.

7. Sir Shenton Thomas (1879–1962), Governor and Commander-in-Chief Straits Settlements and High Commissioner of the Malay States, and one of the pivotal characters of his novel. Shenton was a Japanese POW from 1942 to 1945.

8. Transl: Japanese military police.

9. By Dick Delaney (see footnote 22, 'The Rogues Gallery'), whose Singapore visit was coincidental. On Jim's behalf he took photos of several houses that were equal candidates for Walter Blackett's fictional home.

10. An Arts Council postcard in the series 'Frescoes of Florence'; JGF had taken postcards out with him.

11. Brigid Allen, a young graduate, whom he was encouraging to begin a writing career, was in Chandigarh, India, for a month, having just finished her doctoral thesis in London.

12. Two days after JGF's fortieth birthday, a milestone that went unno-

ticed in any of his letters.

13. Nick Bridge, a friend of Malcolm Dean.

14. Lord Subramaniam is the Hindu deity of youth, power and virtue, and the annual Thaipusam Festival at the Batu Caves celebrates his birthday, attracting over one million followers. In spite of his breathing problems, JGF climbed 272 steps that day (three times the wearying number inside the Residency's flagtower in Lucknow, during his research for *The Siege of Krishnapur*).

15. JGF discovered a fictional role for this Majestic Hotel. In *The Singapore Grip* Dupigny, in flight from the bombing of Penang, reaches Kuala Lumpur and is glad to find Ehrendorf in the Majestic, having a drink there by himself. [p. 313]

16. Compare p. 158 of *The Singapore Grip*: 'Matthew found himself gazing into the dressing room ... a glimpse of ... elaborately rouged and pink-powdered faces glared at mirrors while tweezers prepared a further assault on already well-plucked eyebrows.'

17. In JGF's novel, world weary, cynical Dupigny also notes this photo, described there almost word for word. 'With a sigh [he] stretched out on a comfortable rattan chair ... musing on the confident assumption of superiority embodied in that hand forcing the coolie to hide his face.' [pp. 285–6]

18. The Federated Malay States (FMS) of Selangor, Perek, Negeri Sembilan and Pahang, founded by the British in 1895, had lasted until 1946, so the emblem was the right period for his book. (The name Malaysia, incorporating the four states with the addition of the Straits Settlements and Unfederated Malay States, dates from 1963.)

19. Daniel Iagolnitzer, who subsequently became a foremost French scientist in Mathematical Physics.

20. 'One, two, three butterflies, astonishingly beautiful and of a kind [Matthew] had never seen before, with pink and yellow on their wings ...' [*The Singapore Grip*, p. 296].

21. Lacy Wright, an American diplomat met earlier in London through an introduction by Malcolm Dean when Wright had been attached to the US Embassy in Berkeley Square. He had since been posted to Saigon.

22. Saigon's most famous hotel, where André Maurois (shades of *A Man from Elsewhere*) and Graham Greene had also stayed. In *The Singapore Grip*, Dupigny looks back nostalgically to his leisurely days there. [p. 230]

23. Rue Tu Do, familiar to JGF from *The Quiet American*. US soldiers in the Vietnam War called the raised platform, where he was sitting, the Con-

tinental Shelf.

24. Thé-Anh Cao, Wright's assistant at the US Embassy in Saigon.

25. Nôtre Dame Cathedral, built between 1877 and 1880 with all the construction materials imported from France.

26. Casablanca. Jim had lived nearby at Ait Ouvrir from September to November 1964 in the aftermath of writing *The Lung*.

27. Elie Harar, the Moroccan doctor who had been JGF's host.

28. Nguyen van Thieu was President of South Vietnam from 1965 to 1975, supported by the Americans. He was to resign within two months, on 21 April 1975.

29. They did bump into each other at Moscow Airport, however. Brigid spotted him passing by, carrying his luggage and a Chinese umbrella. 'I hugged him,' she said later, 'and told Aeroflot that I had changed my mind and would take the next flight back to London with Jim.'

30. A retired tea-planter with personal experience of the Japanese occupation, recommended for JGF's research by Nick Bridge.

31. The weather in Malta, where his parents were still living, was unseasonably cold.

32. President Ngo Dinh Diem and his brother had been assassinated on 2 November 1963.

33. Général Duong van Minh, who was also said to have been responsible for Diem's assassination, but deposed by a counter-coup. His time would come – briefly – after Thieu's resignation, after which he was imprisoned indefinitely by the Communists.

34. The *Time* bureau chief, Peter Ross Range, who was a friend of Lacy Wright.

35. David and Martine Laulicht.

36. The American film producer Robert Parrish (1916–95) had been lent a copy of *The Siege of Krishnapur* by his friend Eric Ambler. 'Read this. It is an important and wonderful book,' Ambler's note had urged. 'I did and he was right. It is indeed a superb book', Parrish enthused in the letter to JGF about film rights to which this is a reply. Further financial incentive for filming an Indian story came from the legacy of Western film industry money – known as frozen rupees – which could not be transferred abroad.

37. David Lean, whose films JGF had studied at Yale, had gratifyingly taken out an option in the summer of 1974, following up Fred Zinnemann's suggestion. (See letter dated 7 June 1974.)

38. Parrish and his wife Kathie lived around the corner in Egerton Crescent.

39. John Guest (1911–97) had been literary advisor to the publisher Longman between 1949 and 1972, and had moved to Penguin.

40. *The Book Programme* on BBC2, presented by Robinson (b. 1927), ran from 1973 to 1980. Other guests included Kenneth Tynan, who during his interview had said 'Fuck' for the first time on British television, and Farrell's hero, Vladimir Nabokov.

41. Richard Hughes, the novelist, and his wife, the painter Frances Bazley. The book Jim sent was *The Siege of Krishnapur*. 'I put off answering,' seventy-five-year-old Hughes responded on 3 July, 'till I should have finished reading it. I take off my hat to you! I ought to have treated you with much greater respect ... in my ignorance I had no idea what a good writer you were.' (Family papers.)

42. Judith Wright, JGF's principal girlfriend at that time.

43. *The Sorrow and the Pity* (1971), directed by Marcel Ophuls, condensed eighty hours of documentary footage into a four-hour film about the Nazi occupation of Clermont Ferrand. Jim had taught in Mende, nearby, from 1960 to 1961 when envisaging *A Man from Elsewhere* which has a Vichy, collaborative influence.

44. Patricia Moynagh was introduced to JGF by Derek and Doreen Mahon. He followed up this approach by inviting her to dinner at the Etoile, and he took her to Paris for Christmas 1975. The green jersey that was her Christmas present to him then reappears at the end of *The Singapore Grip*.

45. *No Man's Land* at the National, starring John Gielgud and Ralph Richardson. The premier had been on 23 April.

46. Irwin Shaw (1913–84) was an American novelist and short story writer whose page-turning reputation stemmed from his first book, *The Young Lions* (1949). He and Bob Parrish had a longstanding but fiercely competitive friendship.

47. The Gwanda (Shankill) and Balholm (Dalkey) are names of the houses in Ireland where JGF lived when growing up.

48. Levin (1928–2004) had been writing a polemical column in *The Times* since 1971. A journalist who relished controversy, he was similar to JGF off-duty in being known for having many girlfriends (including, earlier, Patricia Moynagh) but not marrying, setting up compartments in his life, and – more particularly that evening – for his gourmet interest in food.

49. Douglas Day had won a National Book Award for his biography, published the previous year. A flamboyant figure, he taught at the English Department of the University of Virginia.

50. Thomas Pynchon's epic novel *Gravity's Rainbow* (Viking 1973) had been joint winner for fiction of the 1974 National Book Award. Controversy surrounded the book. The Pulitzer Prize fiction jury had unanimously chosen it for their 1974 award, but the Pulitzer board had vetoed the recommendation, saying it was unreadable.

51. JGF's parents were leaving Malta to be near English hospital care for his father, and had bought a cottage in the Cotswolds from JGF's friend Stephen Wall. He had considered buying it himself when learning in advance of the Booker win.

52. Dick Roberts, a retired seafaring friend of Bill Farrell, whom JGF wanted to consult about his pirate book idea. A chat with Roberts subsequently deterred him. (See letter 25 January 1979 to Bridget O'Toole.)

53. *Growing Up in Hollywood*, Robert Parrish's humorous memoir, was published by Harcourt Brace Jovanovich in New York in 1976.

54. He put his grief at Godwin's unexpected death from an asthma attack into *The Singapore Grip*. Walter Blackett feels 'a real pang of sorrow, that painful sense of absence, of being deserted almost, when someone whose life has been closely intertwined with your own suddenly disappears.'

55. After Lean's decision not to renew his option, lesser directors, in JGF's eyes, were unworthy of *The Siege of Krishnapur*. This American approach came to nothing.

56. McNair had been JGF's housemaster at Spread Eagle House, Rossall, and much disliked by him at the time. With maturity, he came to recognise McNair's dedication to the school.

57. JGF had taken up Italian, and helped by his fluency in Spanish and French, he was learning quickly.

58. 'With recognition,' Deborah Rogers explained in 1993, 'steel entered his soul. He could have made a good barrister, and my way was not an accurate reflection of how he would have handled [contracts] himself. He enjoyed the whole negotiation and especially loved the money side, about which he was meticulous. At the end of the day, I was having the discussions he wanted to have himself.' JGF's first choice at Oxford had been Law, a half-hearted ambition curtailed by polio.

Battling On (pp. 331–55)

1. David Simpson, Margaret Drabble's then partner, was a strict vegetarian.

2. Norman Ilett had recently retired from Rossall, and moved with his wife to Suffolk.

3. James Michie (1927–2007) was the senior editor of the Bodley Head,

and had expressed a serious interest in the auction that JGF intended to conduct for *The Singapore Grip*.

4. Alan Riddell, the raffish poet whose personality influences the character of Maurice – 'a poseur and a layabout' – in *A Girl in the Head*. (See footnote 59, in 'The Rogues Gallery'.)

5. Rosemary Legge, of Weidenfeld & Nicolson, had taken over the editing of *The Siege of Krishnapur* in mid-production, after the choice of title was agreed. In the process she had become a good friend.

6. In fact, JGF's father outlived him by ten years.

7. Stephen Oliver (1950–92) was one of the best-known young British composers of his generation. While still at Oxford, where he read music, his large-scale opera *The Duchess of Malfi* (1971) had launched his career. When the tv film series of *Troubles* came to be made, after JGF's death, Oliver wrote the score.

8. The recommendation was a *quid pro quo*. When Parrish completed *Growing up in Hollywood*, JGF had put him in touch with Tony Godwin there, as his Weidenfeld editor for *The Siege of Krishnapur* had been head-hunted by HBJ in 1974.

9. Mr Pantucci represented the Italian publishers Rizzoli Editore. The approach was not repeated.

10. The screenplay was for *Beach of Falesa*, a novella-length story by Robert Louis Stevenson for which Parrish had bought the rights some years earlier with Robert Mitchum and Richard Widmark in mind. (Coincidentally, Dylan Thomas had written a screenplay for the same story in 1959, at first called *Uma* after Stevenson's original title, and confusingly published as *Beach of Falesa* by Jonathan Cape in 1964.) JGF got on well with Bertrand Tavernier, whose subsequent interest in filming *Troubles* came to nothing – as did the necessary financial backing for their screenplay of Falesa. The script is among JGF's papers at Trinity College, Dublin.

11. Broadcast in 15 daily instalments between 23 January (JGF's birthday) and 6 February 1978. It was abridged by Jo Osborne, read by Denys Hawthorne, and produced by Maurice Leitch.

12. The Sardinian novelist Grazia Deledda (1871–1936) was awarded the Nobel Prize for Literature in 1926. A prolific author, her optimistic vision remained unaltered by incurable illness and years of pain.

13. Carlo Cassola (1917–87) was an Italian neo-realist whose detailed descriptions of the landscape and people of rural Tuscany made him a forerunner of the French *nouveau roman*. Italy's Premio Strega had been awarded to *La Ragazza di Bube* (1960) and it had been filmed in 1962,

starring Claudia Cardinale.

14. JGF had stayed in a Florence *pensione* run by Levi's ex-mistress at the end of 1961, without realising that Levi was living in Rome at the time. (See his letter to Gabriele dated 6 January 1962.)

15. Bernard Bergonzi, Bridget's supervisor at Warwick University, was writing an essay, 'Fictions of History', in which *Troubles* and *The Siege of Krishnapur* were discussed. To meet a deadline, he had asked to see proofs of *The Singapore Grip* before publication. The resulting essay appeared in a collection of studies of contemporary fiction edited by Malcolm Bradbury, and as an additional chapter in the 2nd edition (1979) of Bergonzi's book, *The Situation of the Novel*.

16. Bill Budge: see JGF letter to Norman Ilett dated 23 September 1974.

17. Ruth Prawer Jhabvala had written twelve novels by then, including the 1975 Booker Prizewinner *Heat and Dust*. She had screenwriting experience, too, having collaborated with Merchant Ivory Films since 1963. Despite Jim's chatty tone in this letter, the two found little in common.

18. Jack Kirwan was an old friend from JGF's teenage years in Dublin, when they had been drawn together by their mutual love of rugby and their similar backgrounds. They had met in the meantime, though much less often after 1964. (See JGF letter to Gabriele dated 13 January 1963.) Jack, a qualified solicitor, still lived in Dublin and was managing partner in the firm of Hickey, Beauchamp, Kirwan and O'Reilly.

19. John Curtis had stepped into Tony Godwin's shoes at Weidenfeld & Nicolson.

20. The offer was for JGF's next – unwritten – book. As his letters to Curtis within the week show, he was, however, open to negotiating a contract, and Weidenfeld quickly agreed his terms.

21. Weidenfeld & Nicolson would publish it posthumously – unfinished – as *The Hill Station* in 1981.

22. Irving ('Swifty') Lazar, of Hollywood, Los Angeles, also struck a deal between Knopf and Weidenfeld & Nicolson over *The Singapore Grip*. The money was to be sent to Jim after February 1979, via a Swiss bank account in Zurich set up by Bob Parrish, who had a home in Klosters. 'I have many friends who go back and forth at that time of the year,' wrote Lazar on 21 July 1978. 'We've got plenty of time to iron that out ... I'm pleased with everything that's going on and let's hope the book is a big smash.' (Family papers.)

23. The party given by David Simpson and Margaret Drabble was on 6 June. JGF was punctilious about sending his thanks for hospitality.

24. He had met Burrroughs while still at Oxford, but in Paris, rather than London. Wearing his *Oxford Opinion* hat, JGF had gone over by ferry and train for a launch held in Shakespeare and Company for *Minutes to Go* by Burroughs and Sinclair Beiles.

25. Robert, the eldest Farrell brother, was nicknamed 'Odd' after his early childhood pronunciation of his own name. He was on a visit from Canada, where he lived, drawn by anxiety over his father's health.

26. Now known as Post-Polio Syndrome (PPS), which affects survivors many years after their recovery, to varying degrees. PPS is mainly characterised by new weakening in muscles previously affected, but also in muscles apparently unaffected. Symptoms include progressive muscle weakness, unaccustomed fatigue, muscle atrophy and pain from joint degeneration and scoliosis. Yvonne Wall, an ex-nurse, had already observed JGF's gradual curvature of the spine.

27. In a gruelling rugby match at Lansdowne Road in Dublin the previous day, the All Blacks had beaten Ireland 10–6. This was a huge disappointment after Munster's glorious victory of 12–0 over the New Zealanders at Thomond Park, Limerick, only four days beforehand on 31 October 1978.

28. During JGF's first year in France in 1961, Hilary Kirwan, Jack's younger sister (whom he had pursued in 1955) married Donald Pratt; JGF also knew Pratt, though much less well. They still lived near Jim's familiar boyhood territory, in Ballybrack, County Dublin.

29. The request was to use a quotation from *Troubles* (pp. 28–31).

30. The annual Tony Godwin memorial prize is for outstanding American editors under the age of thirty-five. The winner travels to England to learn about British publishing.

31. Piers Paul Read (Jay was a childhood nickname) and his wife Emily were living in Yorkshire, and JGF had bumped into them at a reception given by the French Ambassador, Jacques de Beaumarchais, in the Residence in Kensington Palace Gardens, near Jim's old 'greenhouse' digs.

32. Susannah Clapp, a young writer and gifted reviewer at the start of her career, was then an editor with Jonathan Cape and wrote a radio column for the *Sunday Times*.

33. Miss Parker was writing on behalf of the Arts Council in London.

34. *The Roseland between River and Sea* by Lawrence O'Toole (Lodenek Press) was a local history about the Cornish peninsula where Bridget's family lived.

35. Frederick Marryat (1792–1848) was an English naval hero of the Napoleonic wars. On retirement in 1830 with Captain's rank, Marryat wrote popular adventure novels based on personal experience; his best-known work

is *Mr Midshipman Easy* (1836). His death, to which JGF refers, was hastened by prolonged ill-health and grief at the loss of one of his sons.

36. Bill Farrell was having treatment in the Chipping Norton Memorial Hospital, Oxfordshire.

37. The substantial Victorian house in Southport, owned by Alderman William Mawdsley JP, an elderly relation, where the Farrells lived during the war. Bill returned for a weekend every six weeks during wartime, so JGF's memory may stretch back to the age of four or five. He left Boscobel when he was ten.

38. Ann Colville, daughter of the Canadian painter Alex Colville, was the administrator at the Fischer Fine Art Gallery in London. Jim had been having a labyrinthine, occasional relationship with her since 1977.

39. Rosemary Legge.

Life is Bliss Here (pp. 356–82)

1. JGF initially called it Saltwater House, also bestowed in *The Hill Station* (p. 80) on the childhood home of Doctor MacNab's niece, Emily. He soon re-adopted the local name of Gortfahane, although not without confusion for a few weeks over the spelling.

2. Bob and Kathie Parrish, who were thinking of moving to Ireland too, had accompanied JGF on the original scouting trip when he had come across his house. As a result, they knew the area and had met all the people he mentions.

3. Jerry O'Mahony, the previous owner of Jim's house.

4. Electricity Supply Board.

5. A national postal strike in Ireland lasted from February to June 1979.

6. Wolf Mankowitz (1924–98), the English writer, playwright and screenwriter, who lived nearby with his wife Ann.

7. Alison Lurie was on a short promotional visit to London from her home in America.

8. David Simpson had recently resigned from running the English branch of Amnesty to take charge of ASH, the anti-smoking organisation, and been publicly criticised by Bernard Levin in *The Times* for doing so.

9. Montpeliano, an Italian restaurant at 13 Montpelier Street, South Kensington.

10. *Only Children* (1979), about a disastrous weekend house-party in rural New York State, set in the 1930s.

11. JGF's card to Alison Lurie was re-directed to her Ithaca, New York address, and her reply, dated 31 July, did not reach him before his death.

'I had a good time in London but missed seeing you', she wrote. 'I keep reading about how you are an eccentric living in a tower, a good image I think, and your address is great – I especially like Letter.' Mentioning that she might be in England for a weekend in October, she added, 'I don't think I'll have time to come to Kilcrohane, which also looks impossibly remote on the map. Perhaps you'll be in London, though? If not, we'll have to wait till next spring to see you ... Meanwhile how about your coming to America?' (Family papers.)

12. Ann Colville's relationship with Farrell had not been exclusive on either side, and her stay in Ireland convinced her that he was already changing, and that they were growing farther apart.

13. Carole Tucker, with whom JGF had been having an intense affair earlier that year, was an American lawyer working in London. At the time she was separated from her husband.

14. When enclosing a cheque for Patricia's painting originally, he had written, 'My conscience over the price you're asking has got the better of my mean-ness – but only slightly, as you see.' In fact, he had insisted on paying her *more* than she had asked. He had given it a fictional dimension, too. On p. 552 of *The Singapore Grip*, on the wall of the adult Kate Blackett's house, 'there is a charming painting by Patricia Moynagh of a curled-up cat'.

15. The Shah of Iran had abdicated in mid-January. Ayatollah Khomeini returned from exile in Paris on 1 February, and declared an Islamic Republic on 1 April 1979.

16. One of David Simpson's first tasks after his stay with Jim was to give a press conference for ASH about a new World Health Organisation report on tobacco and disease.

17. JGF's old friend on the *Guardian* in London, Malcolm Dean, known since the Harkness Fellowship, had married Clare Roskill in 1978.

18. Since the early 1970s the six daughters had been a teasing figment of JGF's imagination, but Clare's pregnancy had recently been identified by a scan.

19. Jeremy Thorpe, leader of the Liberal Party from 1967 until 1976 when he resigned owing to rumours of homosexuality, was on trial with three others for conspiracy to murder his alleged lover, Norman Scott. It was a major scandal of the day, and in the general election the previous month Thorpe had lost his seat. On 22 June he was found not guilty, but the case ruined his political career.

20. Deborah Rogers was now JGF's ex-agent, while continuing to act for

him over *Troubles* and *The Siege of Krishnapur*. They remained friends. He still consulted her occasionally for her professional advice, which she gave freely.

21. It was Berkeley.

22. The title of Iris Murdoch's nineteenth novel, which had won the Booker Prize the previous year.

23. Fernandel (1903–71), a popular French comic actor and singer, who was best known for starring in the *Don Camillo* films, and mentioned in Camus' novel, *L'Etranger*.

24. Their mutul Beverley Hills celebrity agent, 'Swifty' Lazar.

25. Bertrand Tavernier, their colleague on the *Beach at Falesa* screenplay.

26. Michelle Pearce, wife of Farrell's Oxford roommate Brian Pearce.

27. Egon Schiele (1890–1918) and John Singer Sargent (1856–1925). *Kaleidoscope* was a regular BBC Radio Four arts programme, aired five days a week from 1973 to 1998.

28. Tom Gover had been a contemporary at Rossall, and was now a house-master at Clifton College, Bristol. The handwritten page had the printed heading 'Notes from a Sensuous ~~Wo~~man'; Farrell crossed out the first two letters.

29. Fianna Fáil, the Republican Party, was in power in Ireland.

30. Mary Soames (b. 1922), younger daughter of Winston Churchill and his wife Clementine.

31. Marion Wheeler had got to know JGF over publication of the American edition of *The Siege of Krishnapur* in New York.

32. Jack Hedley (b. 1920) was an English actor who often played clipped, monosyllabic roles.

33. Larry and Virginia Snelling, whose wedding JGF had attended at Chelsea Registry Office in August 1968.

34. The novelist Maureen Duffy. She was a client of his first agent Jonathan Clowes (and remained so), and they had liked each other since the early 1960s. When JGF was driving down to Mexico in 1967 he had briefly lent her his apartment, complete with cockroaches.

35. An approach by Arthur Hopcraft (1932–2004) and John Irvin (b. 1940) had first been made two years earlier, based on a feature film of *The Siege of Krishnapur*. The new proposal was for television – 'We both feel confident that justice could be done' – and suggested a format of four episodes of fifty minutes. 'This would give us the opportunity to establish substantial characterisation and to tell the story fully, without diffusing its vividness.' They had recently collaborated on John Le Carré's *Tinker, Tai-*

lor, Soldier, Spy, with a cast headed by Alec Guinness, and a similar scale of production was mentioned for *The Siege of Krishnapur*. (Family papers.)

36. Carole had told JGF that though she missed him – 'I have even started reading *The Singapore Grip* for that reason' – she was not now coming to stay. She had made up her mind to re-build her marriage.

37. *Merlan jaune* is a type of whiting, and *colin* is French for hake: neither accurate, as he suspected.

38. David had used his new Amnesty stationery.

39. Monserrat's obituary would appear in the following Sunday papers on the same page as his own.

Postscript

1. Three months earlier JGF had spent a day walking the length of Sheep's Head Peninsula with David Simpson, exhilarated by the sheer cliffs and 'dramatic' waves. (See his letter to Ann Colville dated 17 May 1979.)

A Disused Shed in Co. Wexford (pp. 385–86)

1. When Seamus Heaney next met Derek Mahon after the news of Farrell's death, Heaney asked if he was going to write an elegy. 'I've already written one,' said Mahon spontaneously, surprised by his strength of feeling and the sudden realisation. 'A Disused Shed in Co. Wexford' had been published four years beforehand. In 1982 Mahon dedicated *The Hunt by Night* (Oxford University Press), a collection of thirty poems, to 'The Memory of J.G. Farrell'. In 2009, to mark the thirtieth anniversary of Farrell's death, Mahon gave a reading of the poem at the West Cork Literary Festival to a packed audience in Bantry Library, where Jim was once a member.

2. Inspiration for 'A Disused Shed in Co. Wexford', as was first pointed out in *J.G. Farrell, The Making of a Writer*, came not from *Troubles*, but from *The Lung* (p. 33). 'He remembered the door of a disused potting-shed he had once opened and the long sickly white shoots racing each other interminably across the earth floor towards the minute bead of light from the keyhole.' For a scholarly evaluation of this poem, and also of 'The World of J.G. Farrell' from *The Yellow Book* (Gallery Press), turn to *The Poetry of Derek Mahon* by Hugh Haughton (Oxford University Press, 2007) pp. 112–21 and 301–2.

Index